Canadian Inter
An Appraisal

GERARDO OTERO
ENERO, 2002
VANCOUVER
(DE NUEVO)

This book has been published with the help of grants that the following organizations have made as a contribution to public discussion of Canadian development assistance policies:

Aga Khan Foundation Canada
Canadian Bureau for International Education
Canadian Council for International Cooperation
Canadian Crossroads International
Canadian Lutheran World Relief
CARE Canada
Centre for the Study of Religion in Canada
Communications, Energy and Paper Workers Union of Canada Humanity Fund
CUSO
Horizons of Friendship/ d'Amitié
Inter Pares
Inter-Church Fund for International Development
International Centre for Human Rights and Democratic Development
Mennonite Central Committee Canada
North-South Institute
Oxfam Canada
Presbyterian Church in Canada
Save the Children – Canada
Steelworkers Humanity Fund
Unitarian Service Committee of Canada
United Church of Canada
World University Service of Canada
World Vision Canada

Publication has also been supported by the Canada Council through its block grant program.

Canadian International Development Assistance Policies: An Appraisal

Edited by

CRANFORD PRATT

McGill-Queen's University Press
Montreal & Kingston • London • Buffalo

© McGill-Queen's University Press 1994
ISBN 0-7735-1180-6 (cloth)
ISBN 0-7735-1409-0 (paper)

Legal deposit second quarter 1994
Bibliothèque nationale du Québec

Printed in Canada on acid-free paper

Second edition (paper) 1996

Canadian Cataloguing in Publication Data

Main entry under title:
   Canadian international development assistance policies: an appraisal
   Includes index.
   ISBN 0-7735-1180-6 (bound)
   ISBN 0-7735-1409-0 (pbk.)
   1. Economic assistance, Canadian. 2. Canadian International
   Development Agency. I. Pratt, Cranford, 1926–   .
   HC60.C5858 1994   338.9′171   C94-900229-1

This book was typeset by Typo Litho Composition Inc.
in 10/12 Baskerville.

Contents

Preface

Canadian development assistance has been subjected to much reappraisal and fresh assessment in recent years. There have been major parliamentary reports, extensive public hearings, detailed internal studies, an authoritative official strategy paper from the Canadian International Development Agency (CIDA), many scholarly papers, and a few brave efforts to discuss Canadian aid within a variety of broader contexts. However, no scholarly volume that offers a comprehensive overview of Canadian development assistance policies has appeared recently. Two appeared in the 1980s: Robert Carty and Virginia Smith's *Perpetuating Poverty: The Political Economy of Canadian Foreign Aid* (1982) and Monique Dupuis's *Crise mondiale et aide internationale: stratégie canadienne et développement du Tiers-Monde* (1984). The best is perhaps still the earliest, Keith Spicer's *The Samaritan State: External Aid in Canadian Foreign Policy* (1966).

This situation explains the ready and enthusiastic responses that I received from the contributors to this volume when I first invited them to participate. They recognized, as did I, that no similar work had been produced for a number of years. We hoped that the volume that we would prepare together would be useful to a wide range of academics, graduate students, undergraduates, and private scholars who are students of Canada's relations with developing countries and to the much greater number of Canadians who are concerned with Canadian aid policies as a consequence of professional or commercial interest or altruistic commitment – NGO activists and supporters, business people and consultants, public servants, and the many people who have long supported CIDA as the primary collective expression of our obligation to help alleviate global poverty.

We accepted from the start that we would focus on Canadian aid policies in recent years. The year 1977 seemed for most chapters the most appropriate year from which to begin. That year was, or so a number of us argue, a turning point in the history of CIDA: the government began a sustained and successful effort to ensure that CIDA's policies and programs reinforced and promoted other major public policies which the government valued but that were essentially extraneous to the humanitarian and development objectives that were putatively central to CIDA. As a result of this process, some ten years later the Standing Committee on External Affairs and International Trade of the House of Commons declared in the Winegard Report: "official Canadian development assistance ... is beset with confusion of purpose." Our volume thus concentrates on the making of Canadian aid policies over the period of major change, from 1977 to 1993, during which this confusion intensified.

We had no knowledge when we first discussed our collaboration that CIDA would in fact be in major turmoil 18 months later. Now, in June 1993, as the volume is being assembled for dispatch to McGill-Queen's University Press, each contributor is both hopeful and anxious that our study may prove particularly timely and helpful.

The contributors were selected on the basis of their knowledge of some particular aspect of Canadian development assistance. Some are well-established scholars, some are younger scholars who have in recent years written with particular insight on aspects of Canadian aid, and some are from the NGO community who write here on issues and events with which they have been intimately involved. The contributors share an empathetic, deep concern about global poverty and about the role that aid agencies such as CIDA can play in its alleviation. However, as readers familiar with the literature on Canadian aid will recognize, they hold a variety of views on how these agencies can best promote development and on the main determinants of Canadian aid policies.

This is not a volume with a unifying thesis. The initial letter inviting participation commented that "contributors will of course not be asked to fit their argument into any preconceived overall analysis." Contributors had an early and valued opportunity to spend a day and a half discussing early drafts or outlines of their chapters, and, as editor, I commented on each draft. However, my purpose was always to clarify the argument being made, not to change its direction or to temper its analysis. A great strength of the volume, I believe, is that no chapter has been pared down or amended so as to give the book an appearance of greater commonality of viewpoint than has been naturally the product of our shared concerns and our common quest for understanding. As a result, the two concluding chapters do not represent a consensus of the views of the contributors but are instead the responsibility of their separate authors.

Part one of our book examines in some detail the major components of Canadian development assistance. Chapter one provides an overview of the main activities of CIDA's country-to-country, bilateral programs and of those parts of Canada's development assistance that are not part of those programs. The next three chapters, by David Protheroe, by Mark Charlton, and by Tim Brodhead and me, examine respectively Canadian multilateral aid, Canadian food aid, and CIDA-supported activities of the Canadian NGOs – the three most important components of Canada's aid activities additional to the bilateral programs.

Part two consists of seven chapters, each on a major policy issue or set of issues with which CIDA and the Canadian government have had to deal. This part includes David Morrison (chapter 5) on the factors and influences that have determined Canada's choice of the countries that have been the main recipients of Canadian aid; Phillip Rawkins (chapter 6) on some central issues of organizational strategy and management and program delivery; David Gillies (chapter 7) on the place of export promotion in Canadian development assistance; Marcia Burdette (chapter 8) on CIDA's growing emphasis during the years 1988–92 on using its aid to influence the macroeconomic policies of recipient governments; and Terence Keenleyside (chapter 9) on the hesitant and erratic use of Canadian aid to promote improved human rights. This second part concludes with two chapters on two policy initiatives that started with a regional focus but had wide potential implications. Katharine Pearson and Tim Draimin examine in chapter 10 the less successful and more hesitant attempts to expand Canadian NGOs' involvement in a dialogue on Canadian aid policies in Central America, and Martin Rudner discusses in chapter 11 the successful strategic use of Canadian aid to create long-term linkages between important sectors of the economies and societies of the more rapidly developing countries of Asia and their counterparts in Canada.

Part three consists of two chapters. In chapter 12, Jean-Philippe Thérien analyses the influence on Canadian policies of the practices and development ideas of the other major OECD aid donors and places the Canadian record in a comparative perspective. In the chapter 13, I consider why humane internationalist values seem to have had so little influence on CIDA since 1950 and more particularly since 1977, and I suggest what appear to me to have been instead the major determinants of Canadian development assistance policies.

Our volume is missing several pieces that, in the best of worlds, we would have been able to include. I would have liked, in particular, to have had essays on aid and the environment and on emergency humanitarian aid. We decided, I think wisely, not to delay publication in order to find people who might write them. We acknowledge and regret these lacunae; the first (missing) chapter would have told a complex tale of imaginative leadership, institutional ambition, intra-bureaucratic rivalries, and intrusive special interests, and the second, a story of government-NGO cooperation that was sometimes strained but was in the final analysis a significant success.

The goodwill and support of many individuals and organizations greatly aided preparation of this volume. The Canadian Council of International Cooperation, under the executive directorship first of Tim Brodhead and then of Betty Plewes, was constantly and imaginatively helpful. It stands out as a model of energy, focused commitment, and goodwill. Maureen O'Neil, executive director of the North-South Institute, and her colleagues with responsibilities for aid issues, Andrew Clark, Clyde Sanger, and Ann Weston, were always encouraging and generous towards this project. Relations among academics, NGO staff persons, and independent research institutes are not always smooth and unruffled, but when they are, as has been true in this case, they can be of great value to the university scholars and, I hope, to the NGO activists and the independent researchers as well.

We are pleased to acknowledge the valuable conference grant that we received from the Social Sciences and Humanities Research Council of Canada. This permitted us a day-and-a-half-long meeting in Ottawa and a very helpful session with Arthur Wright, a vice-president of CIDA. I also wish to thank the SSHRC for a grant supporting the research on which chapters 1, 4, and 13 are based.

A further expression of appreciation and gratitude remains to be expressed. As preparation of this volume was nearing completion, I encountered a problem that I had not adequately anticipated, although I should surely have done so. The market for scholarly books in Canada is such that a subsidy is often required before a publisher is able seriously to consider a manuscript on even major issues of Canadian public policy. The Canadian Institute for International Peace and Security (CIIPS) had assisted with the publication costs of *Human Rights and Canadian Foreign Policy*, which Robert Matthews and I had edited a few years earlier, and I had rather assumed either that this present volume would also be helped by CIIPS or that we would be able to attract a publication subsidy from the Social Science Federation of Canada (SSFC). However, by the time the manuscript was ready to be considered, CIIPS had been abolished, and I learned that edited volumes were not eligible for a publication subsidy from the SSFC. I also then quickly discovered that CIDA was uninterested in helping us.

After consultation with Tim Brodhead, whose interest in the project was greatly appreciated, I wrote to some 30 NGOs that were actively engaged in development work and humanitarian assistance overseas. They therefore had an interest in Canada's development assistance policies and might be willing to help us with publishing this study as a contribution to public discussion of these policies. I also wrote to the International Centre for Human Rights and Democratic Development, appealing to the close connection that exists between successful economic development and improved human rights and strengthened democracy. Although none of these organizations had been consulted at all about the volume and therefore had had no say in its planning or in the selection of contributors, no less than twenty-three of them agreed to contribute to the required subsidy. These bodies are listed on page ii, above. The contributors and I recognize that in almost all instances these decisions to assist this project fell outside the normal activities of these organizations and were exceptional. We are therefore all the more grateful for this aid and for the implicit confirmation that our book has a good chance of making a valuable contribution to the continuing public dialogue and debate about Canada's international responsibilities and opportunities vis-à-vis global poverty.

In a further gesture of support to our combined efforts, the contributors have waived all royalty rights in order that the final product can be as accessible as possible.

I would like to express my appreciation to Philip Cercone, Joan McGilvray, and Peter Blaney of McGill-Queen's University Press, who have always been encouraging and helpful, and to John Parry, whose careful and meticulous final editing has been much valued by me and by all the contributors.

Finally, a deeply felt personal acknowledgment. The University of Toronto, the students here who have studied with me over the years, and my colleagues in the Department of Political Science and at University College have constituted a highly congenial, supportive, and intellectually challenging community to which I have been greatly indebted for over 30 years.

Toronto, December 1993   Cranford Pratt

As this book went to press, the Canadian development community learned of the unexpected and tragically premature death of Ian Filewod. He was a delight to work with – warm, spontaneous, and deeply sincere. The energy, sympathy, intelligence, and commitment that Ian brought to his work remain a model for all of us. We mourn his loss.

PART ONE
Major Components of Canadian Aid

1 Canadian Development Assistance: A Profile

CRANFORD PRATT

This volume concentrates by deliberate design on the evolution of Canadian development assistance policies since 1977. The logic behind this decision will become clear in the concluding chapter, where an effort is made to identify the several major stages through which Canadian aid policies have passed since 1950. The argument, briefly put, is that the appointment of Michel Dupuy as president of the Canadian International Development Agency (CIDA) in 1977 marked the intensification of Ottawa's continuing and effective effort to ensure that CIDA's policies reflected Canadian foreign policy objectives and long-term economic interests. For a brief period before that date, it had been an open question whether CIDA would be able to make a reality of the rhetoric that claimed that the primary objective of Canadian aid was to help the poorest peoples and countries to develop. From 1977 on, it became increasingly clear that this objective must share primacy with and, indeed, often yield to foreign policy and commercial objectives.

The argument is not that everything suddenly changed in that year, with humanitarian considerations dominating before that date and self-interested national concerns afterwards. It is clear from much in this volume that foreign policy and commercial objectives were very influential, particularly in the period 1951–68, and that humanitarian and development considerations remained after 1977. Nevertheless, 1977 does mark an important disjuncture in the history of CIDA. From 1968 to 1976, it seemed at least possible that CIDA would be given the space within government to pursue its humanitarian and development objectives without major intrusions from other departments wishing to bend its policies to suit their own objectives. In contrast, from 1977 on, CIDA's policies were increasingly integrated into overall Canadian foreign policy and into the government's economic and commercial strategies.[1]

This chapter is introductory to the detailed, substantive chapters that follow. It provides a profile of Canadian aid so that readers can more readily see these chapters in the overall context of the broad range of policies being pursued and of their shifting comparative importance.

DIMENSIONS AND MAIN COMPONENTS OF CANADIAN AID

Canadian development assistance to Third World countries has been substantial since the late 1960s. As a proportion of gross national product (GNP), it has ranged since then between a low of 0.41 per cent, in both 1970 and 1982, to a high of 0.50 per cent in 1975–76, 1978–79, and 1988 (see Table 1).

Canadian governments have repeatedly made commitments to reach the internationally endorsed target of 0.7 per cent of GNP. The first such promise was made in 1970, and the most recent, in CIDA's estimates for 1993–94.[2] Nevertheless, since 1975 there has been no consistent and sustained movement towards that target, and the date by which it is supposed to be reached has repeatedly been pushed farther into the future. There have been several large cuts to the aid budget in recent years, so that, since 1988, aid as a proportion of GNP has been considerably lower than the 0.5 per cent achieved in that year. That this downward shift is to continue was confirmed in December 1992, when it was announced that the aid budget was to be reduced by a further 10 per cent in each of the next two years, and in April 1993, when further cuts were foreseen when the estimates were presented. The North-South Institute has predicted that Canadian official development assistance (ODA) could fall to 0.39 per cent by 1994–95.[3] In May 1993, CIDA's president, Jocelyne Bourgon, predicted to CIDA personnel that this proportion would drop to between 0.37 per cent and 0.36 per cent in 1997–98.[4]

Although aid expenditures now constitute less than 2 per cent of the total expenditures of the federal government, the sums involved are substantial. In 1990–91, for example, Canadian ODA totalled $3,021.42 million. This compared with federal government expenditures of $11,222 million on national defence, $13,265 million on unemployment insurance benefits, and $4,854 million on hospital care.[5] Some 75 per cent of this Canadian ODA is administered by CIDA. The major ODA items that are budgeted separately and administered by

Table 1
Canadian development assistance as a percentage of GNP, selected years,
1960–61 to 1991

Year	1960–61	1965–66	1970–71	1975–76	1981–82	1984	1988	1991
% of GNP	0.16	0.19	0.41	0.50	0.42	0.42	0.50	0.45

Sources: *Twenty-five Years of Development Cooperation, 1985 Report* (Paris: OECD, 1985), 93 and 295, and *Development Cooperation, 1992 Report* (Paris: OECD, 1992), A-76.

other departments or agencies are the funds for the several structures within the World Bank (which are channelled through the Department of Finance), the modest development aid expenditures by a few provincial governments, and the activities of several development-oriented crown corporations (including, in particular, the International Development Research Centre, or IDRC).[6]

Table 2 subdivides Canadian development assistance into a number of major categories in order to demonstrate both the comparative significance of these categories and shifts in their importance over time. The three major categories of Canadian aid since 1975 have been government-to-government (bilateral) aid, multilateral aid, and food aid.

Prior to 1975, the balance among these three major forms of aid was less consistent from year to year. Multilateral aid, especially before 1970, tended to make up a smaller proportion of Canadian aid than it did later. In the early years, the role of food aid fluctuated markedly, although from 1960 on it has tended to constitute approximately 25 per cent of bilateral aid.[7]

A few other programs have become more significant in recent years, as Table 2 indicates. The expansion in "special programs" is explained by CIDA's greater use of each of the two main components of this category – that is, non-governmental organizations (NGOs) and non-governmental institutions (which include, in particular, educational institutions and cooperatives). Public corporations created especially for specific aid purposes also became much more prominent. The growth of "business cooperation" reflected CIDA's increasing effort to involve the business community in its activities and to ensure that it derives real benefits from the aid program. The growing objective need over these years for humanitarian assistance explains the greater-than – twenty-five – fold increase in CIDA's annual expenditures on such assistance between 1975–76 and 1990–91.

Several major features of Canadian development assistance need to be highlighted in this overview. The first cluster of these relates primarily to government-to-government assistance.

Table 2
Commitments of ODA ($million) by type of program (CIDA funds plus other Canadian government sources)

Type of program*	1975–76	1985–86	1990–91
Government-to-government	404.66 *44.8*	665.35 *30.6*	925.00 *30.6*
Multilateral	213.87 *23.7*	711.84 *32.7*	792.50 *26.2*
Voluntary sector	30.40 *3.36*	155.40 *7.15*	251.34 *8.3*
Humanitarian assistance	4.93 *0.5*	41.40 *1.9*	111.09 *3.7*
Business cooperation	0.11 *0.01*	27.83 *1.3*	62.31 *2.01*
Food aid	222.54 *24.60%*	347.81 *16*	382.28 *12.7*
Public corporations	27.00 *3.0*	137.41 *6.3*	168.44 *5.6*
Administrative costs	–	98.99 *4.6*	180.05 *6.0*
Other	–	-11.94 *0.5*	143.40 *4.7*
Total	903.51	2,174.09	3,021.42

Sources: Calculated from CIDA Annual Report, 1976–77, 1985–86, and 1990–91.
* "Government-to-government" consists largely of CIDA's geographic bilateral programs; includes scholarships but excludes food aid. "Multilateral" includes resource transfers made to or notes unconditionally encashable by the international financial institutions and grants to UN, Commonwealth, and other multilateral technical cooperation agencies and to international NGOs; it excludes food aid. "Voluntary sector" consists of major programs with Canadian NGOs and non-governmental institutions and two smaller programs, Management for Change and Public Participation Programs. "Humanitarian assistance" is bilateral and multilateral aid for emergencies and refugee relief, but excluding food aid. "Business cooperation" involves assistance to companies in Canada and in developing countries to facilitate long-term business cooperation; since 1984, it has been administered by a separate Business Cooperation Branch in CIDA. "Food aid" is channelled through bilateral and multilateral channels and, in recent years, through Canadian NGOs as well; in the early 1980s, an average of 27 per cent of this aid was for refugee and famine relief, but by 1990–91 this proportion had risen to 40 per cent (CIDA, Annual Report 1990–91, 54). In "Public corporations," CIDA or government makes grants to the International Development Research Centre (IDRC), Petro-Canada International Assistance Corp. (PCIAC), the International Centre for Ocean Development (ICOD), and the International Centre for Human Rights and Democratic Development (ICHRDD). "Administrative costs" of all the programs, by CIDA and others, have been counted as ODA only since 1982. "Other" includes imputed cost of most LDC students in Canada ($92.94 million in 1990–91), an imputed ODA element of Export Development Corp. loans ($62.26 million in 1990–91), provincial ODA ($33.19 million in 1990–91), and loan repayments, as a negative (-$60.42 in 1990–91) (CIDA, Annual Report 1990–91, S 5).

GOVERNMENT-TO-GOVERNMENT
ASSISTANCE

Aid to individual countries for specific development projects and programs – that is, bilateral aid – is the primary form of Canada's official development assistance (ODA). Although this aid is the subject of separate aide-mémoires to recipient governments, CIDA, as donor, determines the total for each country and, after consultations, decides on projects and programs. Thus CIDA's bilateral aid reflects both the importance that Canada attaches to each recipient country and CIDA's judgment on how these funds should be spent.

Choice of recipients. By 1976, it was clear that Canada had determined upon widespread dispersal of its development assistance; 33 countries received Canadian bilateral aid in 1961, 84 in 1976, and 119 in 1989–90.[8] Nevertheless, a measure of concentration had long been pursued. By the mid-1970s, it was well-established practice to focus on some 30 countries. The list of recipients changed over the years, but concentration continued. With each such country, Canada has had a sustained aid relationship based on an annually renewed, five-year Canadian projection of the expected total bilateral program with that nation. These countries have been the major recipients of Canadian aid. The many other recipients of bilateral aid received smaller amounts on a project-by-project basis only.

Although the proposal was frequently recommended, and often officially endorsed, that Canadian aid should go to few countries, this was never accomplished, at least until the major turn of policy in 1993, which is discussed in the concluding section of this chapter. Until then, powerful factors worked for wide dispersal of aid. They had indeed become even more influential recently. To illustrate, the proportion of total Canadian ODA that went to the top ten recipients was 53.2 per cent in 1970–71, 25.6 per cent in 1980–81, and 21.2 per cent in 1990–91.[9] As a consequence, in 1975, Canadian aid as a portion of the total aid received was greater than 10 per cent in only 18 countries – ten of them small Caribbean states that received only 3 per cent of Canadian bilateral aid.[10] By 1981, excluding the Caribbean states, Canadian aid constituted more than 10 per cent of the total ODA received in only four states – Cameroon, Guyana, Pakistan, and Sri Lanka.[11] In 1989, this was true of Botswana, Cameroons, Colombia, Ghana, Guyana, Jamaica, and Swaziland, but in each of Colombia, Guyana, and Swaziland, Canada's aid totalled under $11 million.[12] Finally, in only two of the 15 countries that got the most Canadian aid in 1990–91 did that amount exceed 10 per cent of the total aid received. If Canada is unlikely to be able to exert much leverage on the domestic policies of aid recipients if its aid to that country is but a small percentage of the total aid obtained, then Canada had not acquired – nor probably had it sought – significant policy leverage through its development assistance.[13]

A major study by the Economic Council of Canada published in 1978 concluded that the share of bilateral funds allocated to each of the many countries receiving Canadian aid seemed not to have been influenced significantly by either the relative poverty of the country nor by the extent of Canadian exports to it – two factors that might have been expected to have been influential.[14] David Morrison, in chapter 5 of this volume, examines the considerations that have in fact determined Canada's selection of countries to receive development assistance and the distribution of that aid as between the many recipient countries. He concludes with a discussion of the dramatic evidence early in 1993 that the Department of External Affairs and CIDA are resolved to cut severely the number of recipient countries.[15]

Terms and conditions.   The financial terms of Canadian aid have long been generous. In the earliest years, all Canadian aid was in the form of grants. From 1964 to 1986, a portion was extended as loans, although since 1977 all aid to the least-developed countries has been as grants. For a few years, in the late 1960s and early 1970s, loans constituted an important portion of Canadian bilateral aid.[16] However, the terms of these loans made their "grant equivalency"[17] very high. The grant element of Canadian aid – the portion of the total program made up of grants, plus the grant equivalent of the loans – was 93.8 per cent in 1970–71 and 98.9 per cent in 1983–84. This last figure contrasts with a grant equivalency of 90.7 per cent for the total aid commitments of all members of the Development Assistance Committee of OECD in the same year.[18]

The terms attached to Canadian aid have nevertheless long been criticized. At its inception, Canadian aid was tied wholly to the purchase of Canadian goods and services. This condition was relaxed only slowly and hesitantly. From 1970 to 1987, 80 per cent of Canadian bilateral aid and almost all Canadian food aid were tied in this way. By the mid-1980s, these arrangements were more constraining than the tying requirements imposed by any other OECD country except Austria.[19] Since 1988, there has been some relaxation of these stipulations.[20] Nevertheless, the tying of aid continues to reveal CIDA's sensitivity to the interests of Canadian exporters.

The details, determinants, and consequences of CIDA's tying requirements are discussed by David Gillies in chapter 7 as one of several major examples of the significance that Ottawa has always attached to promotion of Canadian commercial interests.

Sectoral distribution.   The distribution of Canadian bilateral aid by economic sector is summarized in Tables 3 and 4.

The shifting emphases reflected changes in CIDA's view of how development could best be assisted. Thus large infrastructural projects

Table 3
Allocation of bilateral aid in 1968 by field of economic activity ($million)

Field*	South and Southeast Asia	Anglophone Africa	Francophone Africa	Caribbean	Total
Agriculture	0.20	0.07	–	0.35	0.62
Commodities	17.21	–	–	–	17.21
Education	0.38	0.19	0.14	0.46	1.17
Energy	6.26	–	–	–	6.26
Food	60.93	2.00	2.50	–	65.43
Health and social services	1.03	0.04	0.004	0.14	1.21
Industry	0.45	0.18	–	0.37	1.00
Natural resources	0.49	1.33	–	0.99	1.81
Communications	0.01	0.94	0.002	–	0.95
Transportation	9.38	0.06	0.19	1.25	9.88
Public utilities	3.07	1.77	–	1.27	6.11
Technical assistance	6.13	8.05	5.72	3.34	24.24
Total	105.55	14.64	8.39	8.17	136.75

Source: CIDA, Annual Review 1967–68, 36–8.
* The categories in this table are not the exact equivalent of the categories in Table 4 below. In Table 4, the large technical assistance component does not appear separately but is distributed throughout the sectors.

were favoured in the 1950s and early 1960s, and education in the 1960s. In the 1970s, there was greater interest in social services, reflecting a new concern to reach and to help the poorest. In the late 1970s and the 1980s, emphasis shifted to human resources development and to economic and financial assistance.

However, responsiveness to CIDA's evolving views on Third World needs was never the sole nor perhaps even the major factor. Because aid was tied significantly to Canadian goods and services, what CIDA chose to do was influenced heavily by what could actually be done with those goods and services, as well as which sectors of the Canadian economy CIDA and Ottawa wished to favour.

Thus while CIDA's changing sense of how best to help development affected sectoral distribution of bilateral aid, response to that influence was often slow and sluggish. Only rarely, as with the post-1985 emphasis on human resources development and on economic and financial assistance, has it been relatively swift and major. However, consistent failure to focus on agriculture (despite Ottawa's recurrent claim to the contrary), the steady and substantial aid to energy and transportation

Table 4
Sectoral distribution of bilateral aid

Sector	1975 (%)	1978 (%)	1989–90 Amount	1989–90 %
Agriculture*	7.0	17.9	156.82	11.16
Human resource development†	5.7	7.2	182.38	12.98
Energy	0.8	13.6	106.19	7.56
Health and population	11.8	2.8	74.03	5.27
Mining, metallurgy and survey,			8.65	0.62
and industry	4.1	0.8	61.26	4.36
Communication	6.6	–	23.98	1.71
Transportation	7.8	24.1	53.07	3.78
Economic and financial‡	36.4	18.3	333.25	23.71
Multi-sector unallocatable	20.0	15.8	405.79	28.87

Sources: Calculated from CIDA, *Annual Report 1989–90*, 114–15, and "Canada in a Changing World,"
Part II, 3A:192.
* Includes fisheries and forests.
† Includes education, human resource development, and institutional support in 1989–90. In 1975
and 1978, it is the total of education and planning and public administration.
‡ Balance of payment support through food aid and lines of credit.

sectors, and the persistent importance of food aid all illustrate the pervasive influence of tying and of the interests of Canadian exporters.

Forms of aid. Canadian bilateral development assistance has always taken one of four forms – project aid, commodity aid, lines of credit, and technical assistance. What is meant by each of these is perhaps self-evident. Project aid is the provision of specific development-related projects. Commodity aid is the provision of specified quantities of named Canadian commodities; food aid has always been the largest element in commodity aid. Lines of credit are authorizations to purchase Canadian commodities up to stated values; these are sometimes tied to specific sectors or purposes.

Over the years, there has been marked movement away from project aid to both commodity aid and lines of credit. Many factors explain this. Project aid for CIDA is administratively intensive. Moreover, it typically generates staffing and foreign-exchange needs in recipient countries that often cannot be met, especially in times of sustained economic crisis. In contrast, lines of credit and commodity aid are easily administered and readily restricted to Canadian products. They directly ease a recipient's foreign-exchange crisis and are therefore particularly welcomed by hard-pressed countries.

Technical assistance includes provision of Canadian experts and training of Third World nationals (see Tables 5, 6, and 7).

Table 5
Publicly financed Canadian technical assistance personnel

Year	1966	1970	1976	1983	1990
Total	1,714	3,080	2,289	3,454	4,517

Sources: DAC (OECD), Annual Report, 1969, 1978, 1985, and 1992.
Note: These figures include several CIDA-assisted volunteer programs and Canada World Youth, whose purposes are educational and political rather than directly developmental.

Table 6
Fully or partly financed Canadian technical assistance by sector and number of personnel*

Sector	1968†	1972†	1976†	1983‡	1986‡	1990‡
Education	918	1,155	704	102	1,664	1,572
Human resource development	–	–	–	–	–	103
Economic and financial		86	44	29	94	38
Public administration		79	50	15	–	–
Institutional support and management		3	35	–	397	653
Power, transportation, and communication		95	289	170	449	728
Industry, mining, and geo. surveys	370	38	183	27	272	601
Health and nutrition		71	26	4	321	507
Population settlements					206	139
Water and sanitation					237	227
Agriculture, including food and fisheries		66	270	233	760	1,154
Women in development						63
Other					9	146
Total	1,288	1,600	1,605	593	4,309	6,129

Sources: CIDA, Annual Report, 1969, 1972–73, 1976–77, 1982–83, 1985–86, and 1989–90.
* This information was presented in greater detail in the later annual reports than in the earlier ones. As well, the terms used for various sectors were occasionally changed. I have tried to organize these figures so as to make them as comparable as possible.
† Total number within each category that were overseas during the year.
‡ Number actually overseas on a specified date in the year in question. As many assignments are for less than a year, these figures are lower than the total number on assignment during the year. In 1976, the one year when figures are available for both estimates, there were 694 assignments on 1 January and 1,605 on assignment at some time during 1976.

Table 7
Students and trainees supported by Canadian ODA

Year	1962	1965	1970	1979	1983	1986	1989
Total	682	2,274	2,757	1,762	1,705	7,941	12,052

Sources: DAC (OECD), *Annual Report*, 1969, 1985, and 1991.

Table 6 demonstrates that Canadian technical assistance personnel have worked in a wide range of economic sectors, though with revealing shifts in emphasis. Some sectors – in particular, power, transport, communication, and renewable resources – were always significant. Others have either fluctuated notably or only recently been emphasized. Provision of educators, for example, declined substantially in the late 1970s and early 1980s but then increased. Similarly, provision of experts in health and nutrition fell severely between 1976 and 1985 but then grew dramatically. Canadian technical assistance has always been tied rigidly. CIDA has rarely financed training outside the recipient country except in Canada, and it has not paid for non-Canadian technical assistance experts. These activities have long been major components of Canadian aid. In 1988–89, for example, they constituted 11.2 per cent of Canadian official bilateral assistance.[21]

Privatization of aid implementation. Canadian businesses and consultants have been increasingly involved in implementation of bilateral aid. Almost all projects but the smallest are done by Canadian contractors after a contract competition.[22] Since 1971, recruitment of technical assistance personnel has been done not directly by CIDA but by non-governmental institutions (NGIs), consultants, or private corporations under contract. Typically as well, private contractors, rather than government agencies, supply commodities financed through lines of credit or commodity aid. CIDA has also made extensive use of the private sector for a large and widening set of responsibilities previously carried out within the agency. These include preproject investigations, preparation and evaluation of proposals, mid-term reviews of projects, and evaluation of projects.

In the absence of this extensive privatization of the aid process, CIDA's bureaucracy could have become gargantuan and much less responsive to newly perceived needs. However, other factors have also affected this process: a political need, as seen by CIDA, to increase the numbers of private-sector firms with a stake in the aid program; an ideological preference within the government for relying on the private sector rather than the public sector; and politically motivated ceil-

Table 8
Canadian multilateral aid: disbursements – CIDA funds and others ($million)

	1970–71	1975–76	1982–83	1990–91
International financial				
institutions (IFIs)	36.39	158.83	325.18	559.92
UNDP and UNICEF	16.47	28.0	68.20	83.25
Commonwealth and				
La Francophonie programs	0.22	4.64	14.82	22.31
Population and health programs	1.73	8.82	11.70	16.75
Renewed natural ressources				
programs	0.57	5.78	12.68	31.13
Refugee and relief programs	1.78	2.93	13.17	18.98
World Food Programme (WFP)	16.31	99.34	117.55	182.10
Grants through External Affairs				
and others[†]			26.71	38.68
Other programs	1.67	10.22	4.51	19.16
Total	74.44	318.56	690.84	912.47

Sources: CIDA, Annual Report, 1975–76, 1984–85, and 1990–91.

* Some consolidation of figures in some tables has been done for comparability.

[†] It was not until the 1980s that grants or portions thereof made by the Department of External Affairs (DEA) or by other departments to a large number of international institutions were treated as ODA. In 1990–91, payments to 20 organizations were so treated. These included portions of DEA grants to the World Intellectual Property Organizations, UNESCO, and the Universal Postal Union and the total grants paid to the Pan American Institute of Geography and History and the UN Fund Drug Abuse Control. The concept of development assistance has clearly become extremely elastic.

ings imposed on the number of CIDA's permanent staff, fixed at 1,161 in 1985 and at 1,120 in 1986–87.

These constraints led CIDA to contract out as much work as possible and made it reluctant to engage in staff-intensive activities. Extensive privatization has meant that CIDA itself has become less and less a repository of knowledge about development gained from direct, close engagement with aid projects and programs by its own staff.

MULTILATERAL AID

As can be calculated from Table 2, multilateral aid constituted 24.0 per cent of total ODA commitment in 1975–76, 32.7 per cent in 1985–86, and 22.9 per cent in 1990–91. Although it was somewhat less in earlier years 17.3 per cent, for example, in 1970–71,[23] – it has clearly always been a very significant component of Canadian ODA.

Table 8 shows the types of multilateral programs that have been supported by the Canadian government and are treated as ODA. Canada's involvement in multilateral activities has been wide-ranging, though dominated by disbursements to international financial institutions. Note the number of separate institutions being supported. Thus, for example, in 1990–91 Canada was a full participant in each of the member units of the World Bank and in each of the regional development banks, while CIDA assisted eight francophone programs and the integrated Commonwealth Fund for Technical Cooperation, fifteen separate international renewable natural resources programs, and eighteen other programs, in addition to its contributions to the World Food Program and to the major international relief and rehabilitation agencies.

David Protheroe provides a detailed analysis of Canada's multilateral aid in chapter 2. It is a record of international activity that, though perhaps spreading CIDA's activities rather thinly at times, is nevertheless impressive, revealing the ability of CIDA's bureaucracy to continue to ensure that development considerations substantially influence the detailed administration of many components of the aid program.

FOOD AID

Food commodities have always been a large component of Canadian aid to the Third World. Table 9 shows that food aid constituted between 16 and 28 per cent of total Canadian aid between 1967 and 1991. Bilateral and multilateral channels have always been used. The number of countries receiving bilateral food aid reached 24 in 1987–88.[24] Canadian food aid via the World Food Program, by far the largest multilateral channel, was also in the same year sent to 54 countries, many of them also receiving Canadian bilateral food aid.[25]

Food aid might well seem a desirable, uncontroversial, and convenient form of assistance. Famines and natural disasters occur frequently, so that food aid as emergency relief will always have high priority. Many poor countries are not self-sufficient in food and must spend scarce foreign exchange on food imports. In such cases, food aid frees foreign exchange for the purchase of other essential imports. For the Canadian government in turn, there are obvious factors that make the giving of food aid attractive. Its Canadian content is extremely high, it can be easily and swiftly cut or increased, it does not demand scarce administrative resources, and it is welcome in any recipient country that faces a genuine food shortage. Moreover, Canada recurrently produces substantial surpluses in a wide range of food products, thus making food aid an attractive way to dispose of a portion of these surpluses. Finally, provision of food aid establishes links that may later

Table 9
Canadian food aid ($million)

Channel	1967–68	1970–71	1975–76	1982–83	1987–88	1990–91
Bilateral		86.40	119.32	141.45	237.80	176.78
Multilateral	8.3	19.32	103.22	122.04	172.77	182.10
NGO	–	–	–	9.71	26.10	23.40
Total	68.2	92.75	222.54	273.21	436.67	382.28
As % of ODA	23.4%	17.8%	28.4%	16.5%	16.6%	12.6%

Sources: CIDA, Annual Report, 1969, 1972–73, 1984–85, 1989–90, and 1990–91.

facilitate market demands in these countries for Canadian produce. As a result, food aid has often seemed natural for Canada, serving high-priority needs in recipient countries, helping Canadian domestic economic interests, and being administratively simple and convenient.

However, this coincidence of interests is often more apparent than actual. In years of global food shortages, the interests of poor countries and Canada's immediate economic interest will tend to work in opposite directions, with the poor countries needing more food aid while Canadians seek to expand sales. Thus, for example, Canadian food aid fell in total quantity in 1974 and in 1980, years of more-than-average global scarcity. Food aid can also harm food production in recipient countries. It can generate consumer tastes for new grains that cannot be produced locally, and it can depress food prices, decreasing local growers' incentives to increase output.

Domestic interest groups in Canada, and, perhaps even more, the Department of Agriculture, the Wheat Marketing Board, and other government agencies responsible for marketing of specific agricultural products, from the start helped determine both the total value of food aid and its distribution among commodities. Gradually Canadian food aid policies became less parochial. A major international effort, culminating in the World Food Conference in Rome in 1974, secured more responsible and more coordinated international action in the face of the recurring global food crisis. In response, CIDA developed greater expertise regarding food aid and sought to make Canadian policies more responsive to the long-term development needs of recipient countries.

Mark Charlton, in chapter 3, examines the interplay of commercial, political, bureaucratic, developmental, and humanitarian influences that has shaped Canadian food aid policies. The 1970s saw some rather delicate three-way fencing among CIDA, which was seeking to improve the developmental impact of Canadian food aid; the Department of External Affairs, regarding it primarily as a facilitator of cordial diplomatic relationships; and the Ministry of Agriculture and others, seeking to promote the interests of Canadian producers. Few components of Canadian development assistance are more revealing of the complex dynamics of aid policy making.

CIDA, NGOS, AND NGIS

The External Aid Office first assisted the overseas development work of a Canadian non-governmental organization (NGO) in 1965 when it made a sizeable grant, of $500,000, to Canadian University Service Overseas (CUSO). In 1968, soon after CIDA was created, an NGO division was established. From the start, its objective was to assist the wide range of Canadian voluntary organizations engaged in development work in the Third World. In 1969, almost $4 million was distributed to 42 organizations.[26]

Most of these grants were to assist ongoing activities such as building of a community centre and furnishing of a school in Cameroon, by the Société des Saints-Apôtres; manufacture of drill rigs and training of well diggers by a local development society in India, which was being assisted by the United Church of Canada; and recruitment of young volunteers by CUSO. By 1985, CIDA was able to report that the Special Programs Branch had disbursed $155.4 million to 4,984 projects and programs (Table 10).[27]

Matching grants have been the funding mechanism most frequently used by the NGO Division. This has involved CIDA in matching, usually on a 3:1 basis, the financial commitment of the sponsoring NGO for any project that CIDA wished to support. The division has thus responded to development needs as they have been identified and presented by Canadian NGOs and is therefore frequently and aptly called the "responsive" program.

This partnership of CIDA and Canadian NGOs expanded swiftly. Introduction of the responsive program coincided with and was no doubt stimulated by a great expansion in voluntary Canadian development work overseas. There were some 20 Canadian NGOs so engaged in 1963. Ten years later there were over 120 of them.[28] There were forceful reasons for CIDA greatly to increase its responsive program with these NGOs. They had, far more than CIDA, the capacity to identify and to assist small, local projects that directly aided poor people to increase their productivity and to improve their welfare. Moreover, as CIDA itself commented in 1980, their development work was "flexible,

Table 10
CIDA support to NGOs and NGIs, exclusive of food aid ($million)

	1968–69	1970–71	1973–74	1978–79	1984–85	1987–88	1990–91
Canadian NGOs*	3.97	8.50	20.77	55.60	74.92	132.8	141.69
Canadian NGIs†					62.50	111.4	109.65
International NGOs				5.45	18.00	24.75	26.17
Total	3.97	8.50	20.77	60.51	155.42	269.0	277.17

Sources: CIDA, Annual Report, 1969, 1972–73, 1978–79, 1984–85, 1987–88, and 1990–91.

* In the late 1970s, CIDA began to extend food aid to NGOs for their overseas work. In 1978–79, the value of this assistance was $1.70 million. By 1990–91, it totalled $23.40 million.

† Non-governmental institutions (NGIs) became in 1979 a new category of NGO. Before that date, they were labelled NGOs. They include not-for-profit development agencies such as CUSO and WUSC and institutions such as credit unions, cooperatives, colleges, and universities.

fast, low-cost and 'grass-roots.'"[29] There were political advantages as well to be gained from a vigorous responsive program. It linked CIDA with the large numbers of Canadians who were volunteers, workers, and supporters of these NGOs, thus increasing the likelihood that they would be part of CIDA's constituency of domestic support. As well, the NGO projects supported by CIDA often fitted closely the popular perception of what development aid should be about. As a result, CIDA's NGO Division grew rapidly (see Table 10).

Gradually, as is discussed in detail in chapter 4, NGOs' involvement with CIDA became more substantial and more complicated. In the 1970s, the Special Programs Branch also turned to credit unions and cooperatives, universities and colleges, and professional associations such as the Canadian Teachers' Federation as substantial reservoirs of skills and experience appropriate for development work. In 1979, a separate division, Institutional Cooperation and Development Services, was created within CIDA to administer a grant program appropriate for these non-governmental institutions (NGIs). To their number were also added a few organizations previously dealt with as NGOs, particularly CUSO and the World University Service Canada (WUSC), whose role as recruitment and placement agencies CIDA especially valued and which in consequence received grants vastly in excess of any funding that they could themselves raise. In 1984–85, $62.5 million was distributed through this division to finance 669 projects and programs, with 49 NGIs each receiving grants of $200,000 or more.[30] By 1990–91,

$109.65 million exclusive of food aid was disbursed to Canadian NGIs, with 59 each receiving at least $200,000.[31]

In a further development, CIDA's bilateral programs began in the 1980s, through country-focus programs, to engage a limited number of NGOs and NGIs in activities that CIDA was anxious to have undertaken. In addition, a few NGOs and NGIs were invited to submit tenders for some regular bilateral contracts. These new forms of funding quickly became an important part of the CIDA/NGO/NGI relationship. In 1984–85, for example, $35.3 million was made available to a small number of Canadian NGOs and NGIs through the bilateral division's country-focus programs, in contrast to $137.42 million through Special Programs.[32] By 1990–91, the respective figures were $181.6 million and $251.34 million.[33]

A further unit within Special Programs had also been created in 1975 to handle grants to international NGOs (INGOs), which were offering "a framework, facility and capability for coordinated or specialized development action that cannot be readily undertaken by Canadian NGOs."[34] In its first full year of operation, this division gave $1.4 million to 31 INGOs.[35] By 1984–85, grants totalled $18 million, and by 1990–91, $26.17 million.[36]

Although CIDA and the government have long presented CIDA's work through the NGOs as one of its most successful operations, the relationship between CIDA and the NGOs has become not only more complicated, as is obvious from the above, but also much more stressful and occasionally conflictual. Chapter 4 considers in some detail both the increasing complexity of this relationship and the disagreements and difficulties that have emerged within it.

CIDA AND CANADIAN COMMERCIAL AND INVESTMENT INTERESTS

Given the intimate access of Canadian business lobbies to government decision-makers and the responsiveness in general of Canadian public policy to the interests of the corporate sector, it is hardly surprising that as CIDA's budget grew, Canadian exporters and investors were quick to urge that CIDA promote their interests through the aid program.

Much illustrates that CIDA has long been responsive to this lobbying. Canadian policy on tied aid, already briefly discussed, is one example. CIDA has long reserved part of its bilateral program for richer developing countries of special interest to Canadian businesses. This portion, first fixed at 10 per cent in 1975, was increased to 20 per cent in 1978 and to 25 per cent in 1988. As well, CIDA successfully pursued joint financing of some major capital projects with the Arab Development Fund, to the distinct advantage of Canadian capital exporters.

In the mid-1980s, CIDA began to link its aid to expansion of Canadian capital exports to recipient countries. The purpose was to secure for Canadian corporations contracts for major capital projects which they would otherwise not get, either because they were not price-competitive or because another government had offered a similar aid-financed inducement. Activities of this sort have become a major component of the bilateral program. To illustrate, from 1978 to 1986, CIDA and the Export Development Corporation (EDC) jointly financed 22 projects with a total value of $1.5 billion, with CIDA's participation therein being in excess of $500 million.

The persistent special responsiveness of CIDA to the interests of Canadian exporters and the consequences of this for the quality of Canadian aid are discussed in detail by David Gillies in chapter 7.

One further and important illustration of CIDA's responsiveness to business interests is provided by its efforts to cater to the business community. A Business and Industry Program was introduced in 1971, was expanded and retitled in 1978, and in 1984 became the Business Cooperation Branch.[37] This branch has worked hard to interest Canadian businesses in extending their operations to developing countries.[38] Though initially preoccupied with promoting joint ventures of one sort or another between firms in Canada and those in less developed countries (LDCs), it has broadened its services to Canadian businesses in a number of ways. Its Canadian Project Preparation Facility, for example, coaches businesses on how to compete successfully for contracts with the World Bank and other international financial institutions (IFIs). In 1991, in response to frequent business complaints that CIDA was biased towards NGOs, a special fund was created to respond to development proposals from Canadian businesses for initiatives in selected countries of special interest to those firms.[39]

This emergence of programs catering to business was not easily accomplished. Many people in CIDA were clearly suspicious of it.[40] A 1991 report commented on the dominant attitudes in CIDA in these terms: "Historically consideration for Canadian economic interests abroad and the use of profits or benefits to motivate firms or individuals are looked at with suspicion if not contempt."[41] This internal resistance was overcome only gradually. As Table 11 indicates, spending on the promotion of Canadian business involvement in developing countries remained very low until the mid-1980s. However, from then on, constraining attitudes became less influential. This change coincided with and was intimately related to the greater scepticism towards state intervention in the economy that had become powerful within government even before the Conservatives came to power in 1984. This scepticism served to blunt and indeed to overwhelm the earlier inclination within CIDA to suspect that Canadian commercial self-interest

Table 11
Growth of industrial cooperation expenditures by CIDA ($million)

Year	1971–72	1976–77	1979–80	1985–86	1990–91
Total	0.06	0.20	3.95	27.83	62.31

Sources: CIDA, Annual Report, various years.

is likely to be of little positive relevance to poverty-oriented development. Instead, in the new ideological climate, the full and free operation of market forces and expanding foreign investment were accepted
as central to development. Thus the self-interest of Canadian business,
the political concern of CIDA to win friends in both government and
the private sector, and the new development ideology within CIDA all
contributed to much greater emphasis on the catalytic role of both indigenous and foreign businesses in the developing countries.

AN END OF AN ERA?

Much that was happening in the latter months of 1992 and the first few
months of 1993, as this volume was being considered for publication,
suggests that an era of Canadian aid policies is rather painfully and cha-
otically coming to an end. There have been in these few months

- announcement of further major cuts to CIDA's budget; rejection by
  cabinet of a major reorganization of CIDA that had severely divided
  CIDA but to which its president and senior vice-president were
  deeply committed;
- preparation by an assistant deputy minister in External Affairs of an
  "International Assistance Policy Update" (January 1993), strongly
  endorsed by the new secretary of state, which would establish the
  clear subordination of CIDA to External Affairs and which proposed
  to shift significant resources from development assistance to aid to
  the countries of eastern Europe and the former Soviet Union and to
  promotion of Canadian trade opportunities in the richer and more
  rapidly developing Third World countries;
- the leaking of this policy update to the press and to the NGO community;
- a major and sucessful effort by that community to abort this effort to
  effect these dramatic changes without public discussion and just
  months before a federal election;
- the rapid transfer of Marcel Massé from the presidency of CIDA and
  then his swift resignation from the public service and the resignation also of Douglas Lindores, the senior vice-president; and

- the sudden and controversial abandonment of virtually the whole of CIDA's bilateral programs in six African countries, including two, Tanzania and Ethiopia, which are among the poorest on the continent.

As this is being written (May 1993), most observes and many officials, including Jocelyne Bourgon, who became president of CIDA in March 1993, think that there is bound to be a major review of Canadian aid policies, either as a separate exercise or as part of a wider review following the federal election.[42] This volume does not and could not hope to examine the many options that are likely to be considered as part of that major review. However, chapter by chapter, it does provide careful appraisals of many of the major components of Canadian aid up until the crisis of December 1992 to March 1993. As some of the actions in these last months seem to have been taken with little sensitivity to, and perhaps in some ignorance of, Canada's decades of involvement in international development assistance, it seems to the contributors at least possible that a major policy review in 1994 may make their chapters more useful than they had dared to hope they might be.

NOTES

1 The importance of the new policy directions that came with Dupuy's appointment in 1977 was first identified by Robert Carty and Virginia Smith in *Perpetuating Poverty: The Political Economy of Canadian Aid* (Toronto: Between the Lines 1981) 94–5.

2 Canadian International Development Agency (CIDA), *1993–94 Estimates, Part III, Expenditure Plan* (Ottawa: Supply and Services 1993), 5. This reference to Canada's commitment to this target was made probably because the prime minister had reaffirmed it in no uncertain terms at the United Nations Conference on the Environment and Development (UNCED) in Rio de Janeiro in 1992. There is, however, no indication that this commitment has any relevance to public policy. The reference in the estimates is expressed in as minimal a fashion as possible – "Canada remains committed to eventually achieving the ODA/GNP ratio target of 0.07 %." The External Affairs internal memorandum "International Assistance Policy Update" (January 1993), prepared by an assistant deputy minister for submission to cabinet but leaked to the press in early February 1993, comments that the commitment is "increasingly irrelevant."

3 Andrew Clark, "Secret Paper Steers Aid Policy Changes," *Review: A Newsletter of the North-South Institute* (spring 1993), 1.

4 This forecast was included in a set of documents distributed within CIDA in April 1993.

5 *Canada Year Book, 1992* (Ottawa: Statistics Canada 1992), 236–7.

6 The closing of two of these, Petro-Canada International Assistance Corp. and the International Centre for Ocean Development, was announced in December 1992.

7 For a discussion of Canadian multilateral aid and food aid in the early years of the aid program, see Keith Spicer, *A Samaritan State: External Aid in Canadian Foreign Policy* (Toronto: University of Toronto Press 1966), especially 178–87 and 196–207.

8 Economic Council of Canada (ECC), *For a Common Future: A Study of Canada's Relations with Developing Countries* (Hull: Supply and Services 1978), 91, and Groupe Secor, *Strategic Management Review Working Document* (9 October 1991), 13/1.

9 *Development Cooperation, 1992 Report* (Paris: OECD 1992), A-56.

10 ECC, *For a Common Future*, 99.

11 CIDA, *Canadians in the Third World: CIDA's Year in Review, 1982–83* (Ottawa: Supply and Services 1983), 117–19.

12 CIDA, *Annual Report 1990–91* (Ottawa: Supply and Services 1992), S60–S61.

13 A recent report to CIDA uses as a guide to CIDA's policy leverage the percentage of the countries receiving Canadian bilateral aid in which that aid constitutes 10 per cent or more of the total bilateral aid received. Groupe Secor, Strategic Management Review Working Document (9 October 1991), 92.1–95.1.

14 ECC, *For a Common Future*, 98–103.

15 External Affairs internal memorandum "International Assistance Policy Update" revealed these departments' ambitions, and the decision virtually to eliminate bilateral aid to six African countries, announced in February 1993, shows a similar commitment in CIDA.

16 From 1971 to 1974, grants constituted just less than 50 per cent of Canadian bilateral aid. William Donahue, "Canadian Foreign Aid Policy, 1965–1974," MA thesis, University of Alberta, 1976, p. 70.

17 The major donors use a common formula to estimate the value to the recipient of the special interest rates, maturity provisions, and trace periods that are a feature of ODA loans. Loans must have at least a 25 per cent grant equivalency if they are to be regarded as ODA. For more detail, see OECD, *Twenty-five Years of Development Cooperation, 1985 Report* (Paris: OECD 1985), 172.

18 *Ibid.*, 106.

19 OECD, *Twenty-five Years*, 218.

20 Fifty per cent of Canadian bilateral aid to Africa and to the least developed countries elsewhere may now be used to meet local costs of Canadian-assisted projects, as may also 33.3 per cent of bilateral aid to other aid recipients; CIDA, *Sharing Our Future: Canada's International*

Development Assistance (Hull: Supply and Services 1987), 51–2. Food aid, however, continues to be very significantly tied; only 5 per cent of bilateral food aid and 20 per cent of multilateral aid may be untied.

21 OECD, *Development Cooperation 1991* (Paris: OECD 1991), 182.

22 For any contract of greater value than $100,000, CIDA submits to the minister for external relations a list of up to 10 possible firms. The minister selects three to five of these, who are then invited to submit proposals. The minister, after receiving CIDA's advice on these submissions, decides which firm will be offered the contract. CIDA, *A Briefing Book for Parliamentarians* (n.d., but 1986), 117.

23 CIDA, *Annual Review 1972–73* (Ottawa: Information Canada 1973), 63.

24 These included 15 African states, five Caribbean and Latin American Nations, and four Asian Countries. The largest recipient by far was Bangladesh, which received food aid to the value of $67.53 million. The next largest were Egypt ($20 million) and Mozambique ($19.50 million). CIDA, *Annual Report 1989–90* (Ottawa: Supply and Services 1990), 98–9.

25 These included 23 states in Africa, 19 in the Caribbean and Latin America, and 12 in Asia. The largest quantity of this food aid went to China ($55.22 million), followed by Bangladesh ($11.0 million) and Malawi ($8.03 million). *Ibid.*, 99–100.

26 CIDA, *Annual Report 1969* (Ottawa: Supply and Services 1969), 33.

27 CIDA, *Annual Report 1984–85* (Ottawa: Supply and Services 1985) 37. These figures include grants to non-governmental institutions (NGIs) as well as NGOs – a distinction explained below.

28 CIDA, *Annual Review 1972–73* (Ottawa: Information Canada 1973), 51.

29 CIDA, *Canadian and Development Cooperation Annual Report 1979–80* (Ottawa: Supply and Services 1980), 20.

30 CIDA, *Annual Report 1984–85*, 39 and 69–70. In that year, the three largest NGI recipients were CUSO ($17.14 million), Jeunesse Canada Monde ($9.22 million), and WUSC ($3.94 million).

31 CIDA, *Annual Report 1990–91*, Table F, p. S27.

32 CIDA, *Annual Report 1984–85*, 37 and 69–71. The figure of $137.42 million is exclusive of food aid given to Canadian NGOs for their overseas work, which totalled $21.49 million in that year.

33 CIDA, *Annual Report 1990–91*, 527–30.

34 CIDA, *Annual Report 1975–76*, 79.

35 CIDA, *Annual Report 1976–77*, 32.

36 CIDA, *Annual Report 1984–85*, 71, and *1990–91*, S30. By far the largest recipient over the years has been the International Planned Parenthood Association. A number of the grants are to international organizations that are but tangentially related to development. For example, in 1990–91, the Global Committee for Parliamentarians, the Third

World Academy of Science, the International Federation of Families, and International Communication Management each received grants ranging between $280,000 to $400,000.

37 More recently still, the two branches, Business Cooperation and NGO, have been integrated into a single Canadian Partnership Branch, further augmenting their importance.

38 These include analysis and dissemination of information related to possible investment opportunities, financing of investigative missions by Canadian business people to developing countries, "get-acquainted" missions to Canada by business persons from developing countries, starter studies and feasibility studies by Canadian companies considering specific business cooperation, and grants to cover "some of the risks which they would not encounter if the project were undertaken in Canada." CIDA, *The Industrial Cooperation Program: Investment* (Hull: Supply and Services 1991), 2.

39 CIDA, *Invitation Calls for Proposals on Private Sector Development Initiatives Fund (PSO Fund) for Colombia, Morocco, Pakistan and Zimbabwe* (Hull: Supply and Services 1991), 2. "When in full operation this Fund is expected to cover 20 countries and to represent at least 10 % of the bilateral budget for each participating country," 2.

40 CIDA spending on these programs was submerged within an undifferentiated category of "miscellaneous programs" in CIDA's *Annual Report* until as late as 1984–85.

41 Groupe Secor, Strategic Management Review, 16/2.

42 At the April 1993 CCIC/CIDA Liaison Committee, Bourgon is reported as favouring a post-election public foreign policy review; CCIC, *The Political Scene* (April 1993), 2. Two months later, at a meeting during the annual conference of the Canadian Association for the Study of International Development, she expressed the view that such a review was inevitable because of the public support that had been generated for it in the preceding few months.

2 Canada's Multilateral Aid and Diplomacy

DAVID R. PROTHEROE

This chapter reviews the recent history, concentrating on the 1980s, of Canada's multilateral aid policies and the political, economic, and other factors that lay behind them. It points out many accomplishments of Canada's diplomacy and spending patterns in this field but also identifies several constraints and failures of will that have diluted the ideal of policy-making predominantly driven by development considerations. For 30 years, this country has directed much-above-average portions of its official development assistance (ODA) through multilateral channels. This came to 32 per cent of total aid in 1990/91,[1] which shines in comparison with the 1989–91 three-year average of 21 per cent for the countries of the Development Assistance Committee (DAC).[2] In the 1980s and so far in the 1990s, Canada has for most years been the fourth- or fifth-largest multilateral donor,[3] providing 7.4 per cent of all DAC multilateral aid in 1991, which also compares well with what would be an indicator of normal burden-sharing – Canada's 3.4 per cent of DAC GNP. These considerations invite a closer look at the multilateral channel in Canada's aid strategy and overall foreign policy.

The world's multilateral aid system consists of some 35 major agencies, which may be grouped into three categories. First, there are the technical assistance and relief-giving United Nations funds and programs, among which the largest are the UN Development Programme (UNDP), the World Food Programme (WFP), the UN Children's Fund (UNICEF), the Office of the UN High Commissioner for Refugees (UNHCR), and the UN Relief and Works Agency (UNRWA).

Second, there are the specialized agencies, in particular the World Health Organization (WHO), the Food and Agriculture Organization (FAO), the UN Educational, Scientific, and Cultural Organization (UNESCO), and the International Labour Organisation (ILO). Since their informational and regulatory functions benefit all countries, only a portion of their expenditures counts as ODA.

Third, there are the loan-making multilateral development banks (MDBs): the International Bank for Reconstruction and Development (IBRD), or World Bank; its affiliate for "soft," or low-interest loans, the International Development Association (IDA); and the regional development banks (RDBs) – the African, Asian, Inter-American, and Caribbean development banks (AfDB, ASDB, IDB, and CDB, respectively), which also have soft-loan windows called funds (AfDF, ASDF, the IDB's Fund for Special Operations, and the CDB's Special Development Fund). Sometimes these banks are called international financial institutions (IFIs), a term that also covers the International Monetary Fund (IMF) and the International Fund for Agricultural Development (IFAD).

In the 1980s, Canada's multilateral program was split roughly 60–40 between the IFIs and the UN system (funds and programs plus Specialized Agencies).

In 1990, multilateral ODA (excluding the European Development Fund) totalled $10.9 billion; while the banks lent another $9.9 billion in non-ODA (or non-concessional) funds from borrowings on private capital markets. Beyond this sizeable amount, multilateral assistance has been held to have some special developmental advantages. These include: procurement of goods and services by these agencies untied to sourcing in any one country; pooling of money and expertise that global membership permits; the multiplier effect that small government outlays in the banks have by serving as security for raising much larger amounts of private capital; and the fact that only multilateral organizations can handle such inherently international problems as environmental damage and infectious diseases and deal with diplomatically sensitive tasks such as refugee relief. Moreover, participation by developing countries themselves in decision-making by multilateral agencies makes recipients generally favour this form of aid; as well, the UN agencies and the banks have concentrated their programs more than have bilateral agencies in the poorest countries and classes.

For donor countries, multilateral aid has special advantages as a mechanism for quick and easy disbursement of aid funds; for providing platforms and funding opportunities to advertise a government's commitment to the solution of much-publicized world problems; and sometimes for side-stepping the domestic political sensitivities that bilateral programs in such fields as population control could entail. Another bonus is the IBRD's role as the world's repository of expertise and data on economic and social trends in developing countries. But perhaps donors' biggest interest in multilateral aid lies in the role played by the World Bank in influencing the economic policies of recipient governments to accord with Western preferences, thereby buttressing the world trade and financial order. (The IMF of course plays a similar role, but its loans are directed to shorter-term balance-of-payments stabilization, not development, and thus do not qualify as ODA – although this traditional distinction between the World Bank and the IMF is becoming less clear-cut these days.)

Despite these advantages for donors, support for multilateral aid tends to be more fragile than is the grounding for bilateral or nongovernmental aid. Even the IBRD's crucial policy-advice role is of a longer-term nature and in any case favours only that agency and to some degree the regional banks. In the competition for aid funds, multilateral aid's bilateral and other competitors also enjoy more immediate advantages – assured procurement returns, direct control over planning of projects, and ability to target aid to countries of highest political or commercial priority. To boot, donors have generally regarded the UN system as poorly administered, imperfectly coordinated, and susceptible to politicization of functional mandates. The delicacy of the grounding for multilateral assistance is also underscored by its connection with the philosophy of "burden-sharing," or generosity on condition of reciprocity by other donors and in rough proportion to national wealth. Burden-sharing norms have characterized multilateral aid far more than they have bilateral aid, because donors have specific national interests propelling them to be more independently generous in their bilateral programs. It is also a double-edged sword: in relatively good times, this reciprocity tends to undergird the multilaterals, but in constricted budgetary circumstances, it can entail an unravelling of support.

The 1980s gave many examples of the fragility of an aid channel that depends on donors maintaining a longer-term conception of their interests. Probably the clearest illustration was the belligerent attitude of the US Reagan administration in the early 1980s towards agencies critical of the United States or limited in their Cold War uses. This led the United States to prefer bilateral aid for its strategic utility and to cut or eliminate American funding and even withdraw from several multilateral agencies. Another illustration was that in almost all donor countries multilateral aid was comparatively vulnerable in the harder budgetary context brought on first by the 1981–82 recession and then by continuing deficits even when prosperity returned at mid-decade.

When DAC ODA levels began to decline in 1978, DAC multilateral aid (excluding EDF) fell even faster (from 32 per cent of DAC ODA in 1978, its all-time high, to 21 per cent in 1985). After 1986, both bilateral aid and multilateral aid rebounded, but the multilateral component still underperformed, rising to about 25 per cent in the late 1980s. Since then, there has again been a weakening of the position of multilateral aid, to a three-year (1989–91) average of 21 per cent of DAC ODA.

Yet multilateral aid escaped complete collapse by virtue of its value to donors in promoting market-sensitive recipient policies via the banks' structural adjustment lending, its uses in debt-management schemes, its indispensable role in refugee and famine crises, and increasingly the appreciation that economic sustainability and structural adjustment require new investments in human resources (technical assistance being a specialty of the UN system). It is even conceivable that multilateral aid may ultimately grow faster than bilateral aid in the 1990s: certainly the need is there for stronger multilateral action in such areas as environmental protection, combatting AIDS, and dealing with refugee proliferation and the social consequences of structural adjustment. While at this time of writing in 1993 the outlook for ODA in general seems discouraging in view of ubiquitous budgetary constraints, the fact that so many of the world's problems that cannot be ignored for ever are multilateral in nature may give multilateral aid a boost later in the decade.

Let us turn now to the story of Canada's recent role in the multilateral aid system.

CANADA'S MULTILATERAL AID POLICIES IN THE 1980S

Prologue

To appreciate Canada's role in the troubled affairs of the multilateral aid system in the 1980s, a brief look at the previous period would be useful. From the appointment of Robert McNamara as president of the World Bank in 1968 to the beginnings of acute deficit-consciousness in most Western countries about 1978, there unfolded a highly innovative era for the multilateral aid network. The multilateral agencies, most of which were created in the 1940s to 1960s, were finally rewarded by healthy funding, and this raised multilateral aid to 32 per cent of DAC ODA in 1978. More important, the multilateral system became the ODA policy-leader, with McNamara's strategy of attacking poverty directly rather than merely trusting in infrastructure-led economic growth to end it eventually and by virtue of the higher concentration of the MDBs and (somewhat less convincingly) the UN system in the poorest countries.

Simultaneously, this era 1968–78 was one of mostly sterling achievement for Canadian diplomacy in the multilateral domain. Canada's leadership roles were many. It's official target of 35 per cent of ODA (minus food aid) for multilateral aid, announced in CIDA's *Strategy for International Development Cooperation, 1975–1980* (1975),[5] surpassed the international norm of 20 per cent expressed in the Commission on International Development's Pearson Report of 1969.[6] (The real target was about 30 per cent of total ODA, since the better-known 35 per cent figure was calculated on the basis of ODA minus food aid.) Either way, targets were exceeded in practice, peaking at 44 per cent in 1976–77, though in large part for the accidental reason of under-disbursement of bilateral targets caused by planning problems. Canada was an early advocate of McNamara's new strategy at the World Bank and of extending it to other multilateral agencies;[7] consequently, Canadians helped define new eligibility criteria favouring the poorest countries in the UNDP, ASDB, and IDB.[8] When some replenishments encountered obstacles from disputes in the negotiations or the failure of the US Congress to approve funds in time, Canada offered supplementary funds or early release of contributions to IDA (on three occasions[9]) and doubled its share of the ASDF in 1976 to help rescue the endangered first replenishment.[10] Perhaps Canada's biggest achievement was its promotion of more concessional multilateral lending via the soft-loan special funds of the regional development banks (RDBs), especially the African Development Fund (AfDF), which Canada sponsored vigorously as its leading advocate among DAC countries.[11] In addition, Canadians played the leading role in creating three smaller multilateral programs[12] – the Caribbean Development Bank (CDB) (1969), the Commonwealth Fund for Technical Cooperation (1971), and the Programme spécial de développement of la Francophonie (1975). Canada has since been the largest donor to each.

To be sure, a few blemishes appeared on this record in the 1970s. These included slowness in untying contributions to the ASDB and IDB;[13] failure to increase spending sufficiently to maintain tonnage contributions to the World Food Programme (WFP) during the food crisis of the early 1970s (but Canada did show remorse by later becoming the first donor to make a tonnage rather than dollar commitment to the WFP);[14] and partial responsibility, by reason of reluctance to increase funding until some other donors did the same, for program cuts in the UNDP in 1976.[15] But overall, the period 1968–78 was a near-golden age in Canada's multilateral aid diplomacy, a worthy companion to the better-known pinnacle of Canadian foreign policy in the

1940s and 1950s, which culminated in Lester Pearson's Nobel Peace Prize (1957). Not before or since has this country lived up so thoroughly and ubiquitously to the middle-power ideal – that of a financially supportive, initiative-taking, mediating actor with a moderately progressive development philosophy in the multilateral system.

No doubt such influence was facilitated by some transitory factors, such as the fast-growing CIDA budget and the shrinking funding predominance of the United States in multilateral institutions (from 40 per cent to 30 per cent in the 1970s and then to 20 per cent in the 1980s), creating a somewhat more equal footing among donors. But Canada's accomplishments in the 1970s were nonetheless genuine.

The 1980s

The 1980s were to present a less congenial setting for multilateral aid in general and for Canadian leadership, because of budgetary constraints in almost all donor countries. Two policy issues dominated the multilateral scene over the decade: management reform, which donors demanded as a prerequisite for maintaining or increasing funding, and ongoing debate about the degree to which policy reform in recipient countries and consequent aid conditionality should be the highest priority for the multilaterals, especially MDBs.

As Table 1 shows, Canada was among the minority of countries that did not decrease their multilateral share of ODA significantly in the 1980s, and because of this it became the fourth- or fifth-largest multilateral donor in most years. The Canadian multilateral share in most years remained between 35 per cent and 40 per cent of ODA and never slipped below 30 per cent. This accomplishment was somewhat unexpected. In the aid climate of the late 1970s, cabinet had instructed CIDA to lower the multilateral share of ODA to below 30 per cent, primarily because economic returns from bilateral programs were more certain.[16] There was also some pressure from business lobbies and their allies in government, with one report having radically proposed that multilateral aid be cut by half.[17] Moreover, government officials believed that Canada's stakes in the MDBs had become too high as a result of back-sliding on burden-sharing by several other donors[18] and that the improved organization of the bilateral channel obviated the need for multilateral disbursements above their official target. But the upshot was that these intentions did not in fact come to pass in the actual recorded disbursements of the 1980s.

Several factors explain the unexpected resilience of the multilateral channel in the 1980s after the decision in 1979 to pare the program. One was the wish to maintain Canadian funding to UN agencies when

Table 1
Canada's multilateral aid ($million), selected years, 1970–71 to 1990–91

Recipient	1970–71	1976–77	1980–81	1982–83	1984–85	1986–87	1988–89	1990–91
UN Agencies*								
UNDP	15.3	29.4	41.3	56.8	60.5	65.7	76.4	73.3
UNFPA	1.0	5.0	7.0	9.5	10.6	14.9	13.8	13.2
UNICEF	1.2	6.4	9.0	12.5	13.6	17.1	17.2	17.3
WFP	16.3	83.9	97.8	117.5	146.0	166.4	188.4	182.1
Multilateral IHA†	1.8	6.6	8.4	13.2	12.8	15.0	17.5	18.9
Specialized Agencies‡	2.1	6.8	9.3	15.4	16.7	18.3	26.2	25.7
Total (UN Agencies)	38.1	140.5	180.3	229.2	265.8	304.6	346.9	341.5
Commonwealth	0.3	5.5	11.4	13.4	15.9	18.4	21.5	21.1
La Francophonie	0.1	3.2	6.9	6.8	6.6	7.5	9.7	7.9
Research Institutes	0.6	5.7	8.3	12.9	13.9	16.2	18.9	18.9
IFIs								
WORLD BANK GROUP								
IBRD and IFC subscriptions	–	–	4.2	29.0	40.0	17.6	23.7	18.2
IDA	24.9	140.4	177.1	164.4	167.7	266.3	232.4	276.1
ESAF (IMF)§	–	–	–	–	–	–	16.0	25.8
REGIONAL BANKS								
AfDB	–	19.2	30.1	45.9	46.1	130.2	130.6	129.1
ASDB	2.8	77.2	51.3	57.2	92.0	139.6	118.4	84.7
CDB	0.7	5.6	6.9	1.1	6.9	11.3	0.3	5.9
IDB	–	27.5	25.9	27.6	23.5	24.3	2.7	14.5
IFAD#	–	–	–	–	–	7.1	–	13.2
Total (IFIs)	28.9	270.3	295.5	325.2	376.1	596.3	526.0	559.9
Total multilateral ODA	68.2	427.3	506.4	592.5	684.5	978.6	928.8	972.2
Multilateral ODA as percentage of total ODA	19.24	44.35	38.76	35.25	32.64	38.81	31.52	32.17

Sources: CIDA, Annual Report, various years.

* "UN Agencies" does not include the IBRD or IFAD, which in legal terms are UN Specialized Agencies but are completely independent in practice; see "IFIs" below.

† "Multilateral International Humanitarian Assistance UNHCR," as calculated officially by CIDA, includes contributions to UNDRO, UNRWA, and, before 1986–87, UNETPSA and UNFN; it excludes UNICEF and the emergency work of the WFP/IEFR.

‡ "Specialized Agencies" includes a percentage of the assessed contributions to regular budgets that DAC permits to be counted as ODA and the voluntary, extra-budgetary contributions to trust funds. The main organizations included are FAO, ILO, UNESCO, and WHO, but not the IFIs.

§ The IMF's Enhanced Structural Adjustment Facility (ESAF) was made ODA-qualifiable in 1988.

Most IFAD payments have been in alternate years, which were not those selected for this table.

it turned out that the United States and other donors were cutting their own contributions. Other reasons included Canada's response to famines in Africa in the mid-1980s, which made for a surge in WFP contributions; the political attractiveness of some UN sectoral programs and the Commonwealth and la Francophonie; and after 1986 the resumed growth of some IFI replenishments, beginning with IDA-8. There always seemed to be some element of the multilateral program that the government wished to expand, which largely compensated for those components under pressure. Moreover, the program habitually gets a boost from unplanned, end-of-fiscal-year transfers: because it is so easily disbursed, this channel functions as a safety-valve to meet aid targets when disbursement bottlenecks occur in bilateral and other programs.

The prognosis for the multilateral share of ODA for the rest of the 1990s is not easy to foresee. On the one hand, prospects for the UN system appear better than they did in the 1980s, given the renewed prestige of the UN and the evident global needs in the environmental, health, and refugee areas. The foreign policy and domestic interests served by multilateral aid (discussed below) and the measure of protection from cuts afforded by multi-year IFI commitments also remain intact. But the deciding factor will probably be whether, at some point in a cycle of aid cuts that began in Canada's April 1989 federal budget and that appear at this writing not yet finished, multilateral aid is pared more than proportionately. So far, this has not really happened. For example, the multilateral program took one-third of the April 1989 federal budget cuts as they applied to ODA ($385 million for 1989–90), which is what one would expect on the basis of recent multilateral shares of ODA (32 per cent in 1990–91).

However, as a new round of bank replenishments was being negotiated in 1991 and 1992, Canada's difficult financial position and the paring of ODA forced Canadian negotiators to seek lower shares in the replenishments. Since most of the replenishments involved substantial increases and therefore no drops in Canada's dollar outlays, one reason for the renegotiation of shares was to avoid a surge in the multilateral share of ODA in the wake of large cuts in the bilateral program. While all of this is unfortunate on grounds of development and national image, Canada did not cut any already-agreed-to IFI or UN commitments; rather, it reduced its share of future replenishments and lowered some pledges to UN programs from previous years. There was also some delaying of encashments to IFIs in 1992, but this is tolerated, if not desired, by the banks. Of course, this modest praise applies only to maintenance so far of the traditional multilateral share of Canada's ODA and to its formal keeping of agreements – it will not be good news if that share of ODA is maintained, while the total ODA and multilateral budgets both shrink.

In the early 1980s, two new strands were added to the policy framework of Canada's multilateral program. In addition to the 35 per cent – of-ODA target, in 1982 a formal target was set for the IFI share of ODA at 18–20 per cent, which was a decrease from the 1970s. It was also decided to reserve 2 per cent of ODA for international humanitarian assistance (IHA), most of which is multilateral.

But as things turned out, at decade's end the new aid strategy, *Sharing Our Future* (released in March 1988),[19] cancelled all previous multilateral targets, replacing them with the sole target of one-half of ODA each for the National Initiatives and Partnership programs. The Partnership Program includes Multilateral (minus IHA multilateral, which is now under National Initiatives), as well as the voluntary sector and a few others. By itself, this change should have little effect on the future multilateral share of ODA, since the absorptive capacity of the NGO program is insufficient to crowd out the multilateral channel.

As for Canada's multilateral diplomacy in the 1980s and early 1990s, it continued the tradition of an active, ideologically moderate, and friendly participant in the system. But now there was added a more hard-nosed and unsentimental edge to this participation, especially in relation to burden-sharing norms, issues of organizational management, and Canada's general concurrence with the conditionality of MDB lending on policy change in less developed countries (LDCs). If indeed it ever was, Canada was no longer a soft touch. But all the same, this country was (until 1991–92, at least) a consistent if not fast-growing financial contributor, it was not among the most cold-blooded in its embrace of structural adjustment, and its emphasis on management change was constructive rather than punitive.

Here were the highlights of Canada's involvement in the major multilateral agencies in the 1980s and early 1990s.[20]

CANADA AND THE MULTILATERAL AGENCIES

Canada and the IFIs

IBRD (World Bank) and IDA

The multilateral development banks (MDBs) have two kinds of funds. Regular, or non-concessional resources come from borrowings on private capital markets, and, except for the smallish, paid-in portion of donors' capital subscriptions, they do not count as ODA. The ODA-qualifying concessional windows – the International Development Association (IDA) and the soft-loan funds of the regional development banks (RDBs) – derive from direct outlays by governments. Policies differ in some ways between these regular and concessional windows – for example, with regard to eligibility of countries for loans and the proportions of policy-based lending.

Canada supported but, as a modest-sized member, was not especially influential over the IBRD's General Capital Increase of 1979 ($40 billion) and that of 1988 ($75 billion). These large increases were saleable to donor countries probably only because of the simultaneous reorientation of IBRD lending towards structural adjustment, or "programme" loans. Such loans were intended to give material backing and time for implementing politically difficult policy changes (such as removing food-price subsidies and trimming public sectors) in order to increase the market-sensitivity, agricultural productivity, and international competitiveness of the economies of borrowing countries. By contrast, traditional "project" lending is geared to specific infrastructure, industrial and agricultural, and social services projects and, as such, is more investment-oriented than is program lending in support of policy changes. But the donor community saw such changes as developmental prerequisites if borrowing countries were to make the most of future investment projects, stimulate growth, and reduce debt loads. The theory was that without appropriate policies, particularly market-determined prices, development would in the long run be frustrated by the waste of resources that price distortions imply.

Canada endorsed fully this new IBRD strategy when it was initiated in the early 1980s. But Canada was also an early convert to a softening and elongating of structural adjustment in response to warnings in the mid-1980s about the injurious effects of IBRD-and IMF-induced austerity on social services and in view of the potential for environmental damage to forests and lands from all-out export offensives.[21] Gradually a Canadian position emerged that was, in the OECD context of the 1980s, pragmatic and ideologically middle-of-the-road: structural adjustment was seen as a prerequisite for development, but other forms of lending remained necessary to maintain essential social services, to continue productive project investments, and to recognize the RDBs' lesser capacity, because of their mainly technical rather than macroeconomic expertise, to plan adjustment loans effectively. In these stances, Canada sided with the majority of donors, disagreeing with the American tendency to support only lending for policy change. The majority view generally prevailed, as structural-adjustment lending came to settle at about 25–30 per cent of total lending in the World Bank and IDA and 15–25 per cent in the RDBs – the latter, moreover, limited to policy lending in specific sectors.

On the World Bank's concessional side, in the negotiations leading to IDA-6 (1981–83, $12 billion), Canada requested (for the first time) and got a lower IDA share (down from 5.83 per cent in IDA-5 to 4.30

per cent in IDA-6). But implementation of IDA-6 proved troublesome. In 1981, the new, conservative US Congress unilaterally stretched American IDA-6 payments over four years rather than the previously agreed-to three and also back-end-loaded them. The result was that a cut in IDA lending was needed in 1981, after most donors, including Canada, retaliated against the United States by making pro rata cuts in their own IDA-6 contributions. Some countries soon repented and joined in a $500-million rescue package of voluntary contributions for 1982, but Canada did not, because of limited budgetary leeway.

These reversals of Canada's several past "saviour" roles in IDA were mitigated only slightly by a Canadian proposal that ended the bickering over IDA-6 but in a way involved some costs to IDA. Canada proposed in 1982 that IDA-6 be formally extended to four years, to recognize the de facto situation imposed by the US Congress, and that only non-US donors would contribute to that fourth year. But to avoid unfairness to the non-US donors, there would also be a Parallel Fund with procurement restricted to contributing countries. Canada and six other governments joined this. Most others preferred to avoid such aid-tying in a multilateral institution and thus created an untied Fiscal Year 1984 Account.

For IDA-7 (1985–87), Canada preferred a slightly increased replenishment, having resumed ODA growth momentarily. But American insistence forced IDA-7 to $9 billion, the first-ever drop from one IDA replenishment to the next. Canada accepted a somewhat higher share, 4.50 per cent, and also participated in the same proportion in a supplementary funding mechanism, the Special Facility for Sub-Saharan Africa. IDA-8 (1988–90) saw an increase to $11.5 billion, in which Canada raised its share to 5.0 per cent. There were also supplementary contributions of $900 million, but Canada did not join in these because its 5.0 per cent of the basic agreement already included a one-time extra 0.25 per cent to help compensate for declines by the United States and others. In IDA-9 (1991–93), approved in December 1989 at $15.1 billion, Canada reverted to its basic share of 4.75 per cent.

The IDA-10 accord (1994–96, $18 billion) was approved in the fall of 1992. Canada's approach to the negotiations was shaped by the increasing pressures on its aid budget from previous or impending ODA cuts. The result was the lowest-ever Canadian share of an IDA replenishment – 4.0 per cent. The lower share of a higher replenishment will entail a dollar outlay by Canada almost identical to that for IDA-9. This level is hardly inspiring, but Canada at least did manage to conserve its seventh place ranking in IDA.

Throughout the IDA replenishments of the 1980s, Canada's policy preferences were among the more developmentally enlightened – for instance, its strong support for a geographical shift in favour of Africa on the grounds of need, its opposition to American proposals to attach interest rates to IDA loans and shorten maturities, and its advocacy of a relatively modest proportion of policy-based lending in IDA. In sum, except for its rather legalistic approach to IDA-6, Canada's activity in IDA in the 1980s was fairly credible developmentally. But it did evince tougher adherence to burden-sharing reciprocity than in the past, and its lower participation in IDA-10 does not constitute a promising beginning for the 1990s.

Regional Development Banks (RDBs)

The main common issue in the RDBs in the 1980s was to define their role in relation to structural adjustment, given that their staff expertise lay in project lending and technical fields rather than in macroeconomic analysis. The United States pressed for the largest use of policy-based lending, while most other donors, including Canada, wanted to preserve project activities as the dominant focus of operations. Compromises gradually established policy lending at about 15–25 per cent of total lending, with the emphasis on structural adjustment in certain economic sectors. Replenishment efforts were most successful in the ASDB and the AFDB, which were less resistant to donors' preferences on adjustment lending than was the IDB. The non-US donors' more moderate positions on these matters essentially prevailed – perhaps not surprising in view of declining American contributions.

African Development Bank.   The biggest trend of the 1980s regarding the RDBs was the elevation of the AFDB to a size similar to the ASDB and the IDB. During the 1980s, Canada exercised considerable influence as fourth-largest shareholder in the AFDB proper (4.9 per cent of regular resources) and third largest in the fund (10.5 per cent of these concessional resources in AFDF-5). Aside from its stake in the small Caribbean bank, these investments have been Canada's highest in any of the RDBs or their concessional funds. In the 1970s, Canada had been the largest AFDF contributor. While in many ways critical of the AFDB's management, especially of its attempt to incorporate 25 per cent policy-based lending into the loan portfolio without sufficient expertise in macroeconomic analysis, Canada did favour the large capital increases and fund replenishments of the 1980s.

The AFDB's status as African-run and bilingual (English and French), as well as the evident needs of the region, have predisposed Canada to support it strongly and to look past some of its administrative weaknesses. In negotiations for AFDF-5 (1988–90), Canada helped resolve issues by promoting a large replenishment increase, by itself taking on a full 1 per cent share increase to compensate for an American decline, and by proposing to balance the resource increase with tough conditionality in the form of a mid-term review of performance. AfDF-6 (1991–93) involved a significant increase in resources, to $3.2 billion from $2.8 billion in AfDF-5. However, both budgetary pressures and some decline in CIDA's confidence in the bank led Canada to reduce its share to 8.25 per cent, dropping Canada to sixth rank among donors. But this remains Canada's largest position in any of the three major regional banks.

Asian Development Bank. The ASDB was unusual in actually having an excess of ordinary capital resources in the 1980s, which permitted the last general capital increase (GCI 1983–87) to be extended through to at least 1993 because of falling loan demand from traditional borrowers. For balance-of-payments reasons, several borrowing countries cut back investments in large capital projects – the traditional stock-in-trade of the ASDB. Meanwhile, thanks mostly to the meteoric growth of Japan's aid program, the bank's concessional fund also saw healthy, real-growth replenishments in the 1980s and in ASDF-6 (1992–95). Canada has been and remains the fourth-largest contributor. However, in ASDF-6, the Canadian share was negotiated down to 7.3 per cent from the traditional 8.5-odd per cent, for the familiar budgetary reasons.

The issue arose as to whether and to what extent the ASDB should move into policy-based program lending and greater emphasis on the private sector, so as to take up the slack from dwindling public-sector infrastructure projects. The United States pressed for the policy-based option, while Japan and most others, including Canada, wished to preserve the bank's focus on projects. Decisions taken in 1989 favoured the Japanese by placing a 15 per cent cap on policy lending and by beginning to shift project lending from physical infrastructure to social infrastructure and services – direct alleviation of poverty, which the ASDB had not emphasized in the past. These and other developmentally advanced positions were pursued by Canada and its Nordic co-constituents and included support for women-in-development projects (with not fully satisfactory results so far), for environmental analysis and programming (with more success), and for conditionality to promote good governance in recipient countries.

Inter-American Development Bank. The IDB was the hapless cousin among the RDBs in the 1980s, losing much of its previous importance in hemispheric development. Especially sharp conflicts between the

United States and Latin countries over the appropriate balance be-tween structural adjustment and project lending delayed negotiation of the seventh general increase in resources (GIR) until 1989, thus stretching the previous GIR resources over almost double their in-tended period. Management failings of the bank and planning con-straints in borrowing countries led to under-identification of projects and thus to a two-thirds drop in annual lending between 1984 and 1988. The policy debate was also embittered, and replenishments were further delayed, by American attempts to acquire a veto power over regular IDB loans similar to that which it already had over loans from the concessional Fund for Special Operations (FSO). The final compro-mise on the Seventh GIR in 1989 involved a healthy capital-base en-largement (but not a large FSO increase), a loan-referral mechanism to give the United States the power at least to delay loans, and a 25 per cent target for policy-based lending.

Canada's view on most of these issues fell between those of the United States and the Latin American members and reflected a desire to be a bridge-builder. For example, Canada favoured only moderate levels of structural-adjustment lending and more focus on reducing poverty directly. It also wanted more donor control over loan approv-als, but by donors as a group, not simply by the United States. However, on management reform, Canadians pressed just as vigorously as the Americans. Although Canada is the second-largest industrial member of the IDB, its influence has not been as great as in the other RDBs. This results from Canada's more modest share in the IDB (4.39 per cent in the Seventh GIR), the funding predominance of the United States, and the tendency for decisions to be made de facto between the United States and the larger Latin countries.

Women and the Environment.   In all the RDBs in this period, Canada was among the leaders in advocating environmental action and the definite leader in promoting women-in-development (WID) programming.

Canada and IFAD

The International Fund for Agricultural Development (IFAD) is a uni-versally vaunted loans program for small farmers. But it suffered badly in the past decade from disputes over burden-sharing between DAC donors and those of the Organization of Petroleum Exporting Countries (OPEC). Since the early 1980s, OPEC members, which had originated IFAD in 1976, have repeatedly claimed hardship caused by declining oil prices, and Western countries demurred at taking on ever-larger shares of the original 50–50 split in contributions between the two groups. Subsequent compromises enlarged the DAC share to 66 per cent in the latest replenishment, but at the cost of declining resources in successive replenishments. Originally pegged at $1 billion for IFAD-1 (1978–80), funding fell to $565 million for IFAD-3 (1990–92). As of mid-1993, a new replenishment has been delayed again over the same issues of size and shares, although operations continue with leftover moneys.

Canada, while preferring larger replenishments, also adopted DAC members' general reluctance to see OPEC contributions fall, at least without adjustments in the currently equal voting status of the DAC, OPEC, and borrowers groups. Canada's refusal to contribute at all to IFAD's 1986 Special Program for Sub-Saharan Africa – it was one of only two countries to do so – was as much intended to pressure OPEC in the negotiations on the core-program replenishment as it was derived from the stated reason of protecting the core program from dilution into special-purpose funds. But this country did increase its share in IFAD-3 substantially, to 4.0 per cent (from 3.2 per cent in the previous round), albeit of a smaller replenishment. Canada remains sympathetic to the mandate of IFAD but questions whether it should continue as a separate entity if lower OPEC funding makes tripartite voting obsolete. Administrative savings might also be an advantage of amalgamation with IDA or the FAO.

Summary

To recapitulate, Canada's roles in the IFIs in the 1980s made up a mixed picture. There was a noticeable shift towards firmer insistence on reciprocal burden-sharing by others as a condition of Canadian generosity: this was evident in Canada's pro rata retaliation cuts to IDA in 1981, its failure to participate in the $500-million rescue plan for 1982, its sponsorship of the procurement-restricted IDA Parallel Fund for 1984, and its somewhat punctilious approach to the 1986 IFAD Special Program for Sub-Saharan Africa. But Canadian traditions were only modified, not overthrown. Most of these lapses took place in the financially difficult and testy political atmosphere of the early 1980s. Prior to the renegotiation of Canadian shares in most of the MDBs in the early 1990s, Canada did generally support the higher replenishment options in the World Bank and RDBs and made several generous gestures, such as the 0.25 per cent special share increase in IDA-8 and the big increase in its share of AfDF-5 refunding. The tradition of enlightened positions on programming emphases, including a moderate stance on structural-adjustment lending by IDA and the RDBs, and of mediating gestures (especially in AfDF-5 and the solution to the IDA-6 impasse) was also by and large continued.

An area where enlightenment and political moderation may clash is that of aid to countries abusing human rights. This issue became quite controversial in the 1970s and 1980s in relation to the lending practices of the MDBs. Canada supported adherence to the constitutions of the banks, which confine lending criteria to economic and technical considerations. It has been argued that this orthodox position is mistaken, because economic welfare is itself impeded under conditions of severe abuses, and that in any case Canada has never been fully consistent as among its stances at the banks, at the UN, and in its bilateral aid programs.[22] A competing view is that preserving fragile multilateral institutions from possible breakdown over such divisive issues is a moral value too. It seems likely that the human rights policies of the banks will be revisited in the 1990s as a less polarized world appears to make aid conditionality on these grounds more realistic than in the Cold War era.

Canada and the UN Agencies

In the UN aid system, the biggest issues of the 1980s were the frequent financial crises of the first half of the decade (particularly those arising from American funding cuts); the growing tendency of donors to make direct, extra-budgetary contributions (above and beyond regular dues) to the Specialized Agencies, thus undermining the UNDP's intended role as the priority-setter and coordinator for UN technical assistance; and the problems of "politicization" and regular budget increases imposed by the Third World majority in the Specialized Agencies. However, this picture brightened considerably in the late 1980s as the Cold War waned and North-South relations became more pragmatic.

In these events, Canada was responsibly supportive of a system under strain, at least maintaining and sometimes increasing its funding, and on a few occasions directly coming to the rescue of agencies in dire financial straits. This support, coupled with simultaneous UN-bashing by the United States and some others, caused Canada's share of total UN funding (voluntary and assessed), which has always been well above Canada's share of DAC GNP (about 3.4 per cent), to rise from 6.8 per cent in 1980 to 9.1 per cent in 1988. (It slipped back to 7.7 per cent in 1991, after the 1989 budget cuts.)

Canada by and large maintained its funding to the UN Development

Programme and refrained from undermining the UNDP's "central funding" role by itself avoiding substantial extra-budgetary contributions to Specialized Agencies (giving less than 2 per cent of the total of such contributions). This "central funding" policy has been a long-standing preference of CIDA's Multilateral Branch, which has resisted, mostly with success, innumerable suggestions by other departments that CIDA contribute more to the many special funds or activities of their counterpart Specialized Agencies. Canada's adherence to the UN's own preferences in this regard contrasts to some extent with the Nordic countries, which, while comparatively more generous, have made many more direct contributions to the Specialized Agencies. Donor governments are easily tempted to expand these (often valid but uncoordinated) extra-budgetary contributions because earmarked programs such as the WHO's AIDS fund have more political appeal than do contributions to the anonymous UNDP pool. (However, Canada's merit is somewhat diminished by the fact that it, unlike the Nordics, has alternative outlets for such political purposes in the Commonwealth and la Francophonie.) In 1983, Canada chaired a committee that attempted, though unsuccessfully, to solve the UNDP's perennial financial problems by exchanging multi-year funding commitments for increased donor influence over UNDP country programs (which are at present drawn up principally by recipients themselves). Canada also made supplementary contributions to help make up for a cash shortfall in that year, and in 1985 it was instrumental in bringing about the "Canadian compromise" of an 8 per cent growth target for the Fourth UNDP Programming Cycle.

In the UN Fund for Population Activities, Canada was among the donor countries that rescued this agency from collapse by compensating fully for the US cutting off of contributions in 1986 after accusing the UN-FPA of supporting abortion and involuntary sterilization in China. Canada was also very active in international humanitarian agencies. The 1980s saw worsening refugee and emergency situations in the Third World.

While the donor community responded admirably in the case of the Office of the UN High Commissioner for Refugees (UNHCR) until 1984, after that a measure of "compassion fatigue" began to plague UNHCR as much as its more congenitally troubled cousin the UN Relief and Works Agency for Palestinian Refugees in the Near East (UNRWA). Canada's record, however, was among the most forthcoming – it earmarked in 1982 some 2 per cent of ODA for humanitarian assistance;

it maintained funding to UNHCR; it became in 1982 the first donor to guarantee its contributions to UNRWA in cash (rather than tied commodities); and it made a particular issue in priority-setting meetings of the plight of female refugees.

Canada's contributions to both the UN Children's Fund (UNICEF) and the World Food Programme (WFP) were on an upward track in the 1980s. Of all UN agencies, UNICEF has been the most financially fortunate, by reason of its obvious political appeal to donors. With regard to the WFP, Canada has been the second-biggest contributor (20 per cent of total contributions) and channels twice as much of its food aid through the multilateral route as does the United States (about 45 per cent versus 20 per cent). But Canada continues to trail some other major donors in meeting the cash-to-commodities ratio of one-third cash desired by WFP management. (As tied aid, in effect, deliveries to the WFP are a rare example of excellent procurement returns for Canada in the multilateral system; a higher cash contribution would trim these side-benefits while Canadian farmers are hurting from the US-European grain subsidies war.)

In the UN Specialized Agencies, Canada broadly supported the efforts of the Geneva Group of Western donors throughout the 1980s to encourage spending restraint (or "zero real growth") in regular budgets. Under the one-country, one-vote system operating in these agencies, budget levels can be imposed by the Third World majority. Attempts to hold the line, some successful, required some threatening of non-payment by the Geneva Group. But Canada was not among the hardest-liners – for example, rejecting the US call for weighted voting and preferring to interpret "zero real growth" such that some deserving agencies could have increases. Canada joined other DAC countries in condemning "politicization" of the agendas of Specialized Agencies by the Southern majority. Resolutions censuring Israel and impractical declarations on the world economy produced the main complaints – but, like most middle powers, Canada was less frenzied in its irritation than were the larger Western powers.

After the United States and the United Kingdom withdrew from the UN Educational, Scientific, and Cultural Organization (UNESCO) in 1984 and 1985, respectively, over the proposed "new world information order" and poor financial accountability, External Affairs did briefly consider Canada's withdrawal but then decided to maintain its traditional policy of reform from within.

At the Food and Agriculture Organization (FAO), the same issues – politicization, chaotic management, and personal empire-building by the director-general – surfaced. Uncharacteristically, Canada campaigned openly for ouster of the director-general, and when the West's favoured candidate in the election of 1987 lost to the incumbent, it unprecedentedly delayed payment of its annual assessment and again considered withdrawal. Indications are that since 1988 more serious efforts at reform have been made at the FAO under the influence of such pressure by Canada and other donors.

Canada and Other Multilateral Agencies

Canada has probably been the most vigorous member in relation to the aid activities of both the Commonwealth and la Francophonie. It has certainly been the largest donor to their aid funds, though not to the umbrella organizations. Canada has also been a modest but enthusiastic player and above-average donor in the Consultative Group on International Agricultural Research (CGIAR). With regard to the UN Environment Programme (UNEP) and generally the rise to prominence of environmental action in the programs of many other multilateral agencies, Canada's interest fluctuated. After having been a leading advocate of international approaches to environmental needs in the 1970s, Canada did not figure among those most far-sighted countries during the growth-obsessed early 1980s. However, when the political profile of environmental issues rose again in the mid-to-late 1980s, especially as a result of the Brundtland Report (1987) and the publicity about damage to the ozone layer, Canada did resume a role of environmental activist in the multilateral system, particularly in its urging of environmental assessments of all multilateral bank projects.

Conclusion

It can be concluded about Canada's multilateral performance in the 1980s that this country typified donors' new concern about the effectiveness of multilateral agencies and some of their policy directions but happily was unusual (so far) in never permitting its multilateral assistance to slip significantly as a percentage of ODA. Having become the fourth-or fifth-largest multilateral donor, Canada understandably displayed a new toughness. And that did reverse some of its more idealistic "middlepowermanship" and flexibility on burden-sharing of the 1970s. But Canada's traditions – of above-average financial support and extraordinary financial help in a pinch, of constructive criticism of management failings, of reasonably enlightened policy stances, and of helpful mediation – did not fundamentally alter.

DETERMINANTS OF CANADA'S
MULTILATERAL AID

It remains to consider what influences, constraints, and opportunities lay behind Canada's multilateral aid policies in the recent past. What has determined the volume of Canada's multilateral aid, the size of major allocations to agencies, and the main objectives and standing policies of the Multilateral Program? This reseach identified 14 factors at play in multilateral policy.[23] They cannot be discussed here at length, but their variety may be illustrated by simply listing them according to their "positive," "neutral" (i.e. variable), or "negative" relation to the ideal of basing decisions primarily on developmental considerations.

"Positive" factors are

• analysis and assessment of developmental or humanitarian needs and priorities;
• ratings of the relative efficiency and effectiveness of the various multilateral agencies.

"Negative" factors are

• pursuit of procurement advantages insofar as that undercuts developmental priorities;
• acquiescence to particularist domestic pressures;
• contributions or decisions made primarily to enhance Canada's image;
• (perhaps) those unplanned multilateral disbursements that result from under-disbursement in other aid channels.

"Neutral" factors that, depending on the situation, may either enhance or undermine developmental goals are

• burden-sharing expectations of other countries vis-à-vis Canada;
• long term Canadian political ties and associations;
• national or at least broadly based economic interests in Third World regions and specific multilateral institutions;
• the budgetary situation of the Canadian government;

- Canada's areas of sectoral expertise;
- bureaucratic or intragovernmental bargaining;
- Canada's desire to maintain its status or voting strenght in the MDBs where voting power is based on member countries' contributions;
- the role of key individuals in Ottawa and in Canadian delegations.

Examples can be found of the operation of any of these factors in particular decisions and allocations. Their number points out the complexity of the process and the fact that non-developmental considerations do affect a field that touches on broader foreign policy and economic goals. In what follows, I attempt to assess which among them have been the most important.

Factors Shaping Multilateral Aid

The budget for Canada's multilateral assistance includes Department of Finance funds for IBRD capital subscriptions and IDA payments; that portion of External Affairs's financing of the regular budgets of UN Specialized Agencies, the Commonwealth and Francophonie umbrella organizations, and a few other agencies that DAC calculates to qualify as ODA; and, of course, the outlays of CIDA's Multilateral Branch (principally, funding of the RDBs, UN technical assistance and humanitarian funds, and multilateral food aid via the WFP). This budget, or the multilateral share of ODA, has resulted broadly from the interplay of three factors: the dollar implications of a pre-established target expressed as a percentage of ODA; the implications for Canada of the financial plans of multilateral agencies and the traditional contribution shares of donors; and any changes suggested by continuing assessment of Canada's development priorities, budgetary realities, and foreign policy and other interests in various organizations. Although the long-standing official target for the multilateral share of ODA (35 per cent of ODA) was abolished in 1988, internal government planning still assumes a de facto target in that vicinity, and therefore the principles described below still apply informally since *Sharing Our Future*.

Why has Canada's multilateral assistance been around 30–40 per cent of ODA – why not 10 per cent or 50 per cent? The chief factors discouraging multilateral aid are its untied nature and the consequent assuredness of economic returns to Canada from tied bilateral and other channels, the lack of direct Canadian control over the end-uses of multilateral expenditures, and the public relations drawback that multilateral projects are not identified with any one donor country.

Counterbalancing these negative factors are the encouraging factors, which have overcome these disadvantages to make multilateral aid a significant portion of Canada's aid for 30 years now, both exceeding the DAC average and leading the largest Group of Seven (G-7) donors in terms of the share of multilateral aid in total aid. There are eight factors that appear to create a congenial setting for multilateral aid in Canadian foreign policy.

The first three factors relate to some clear Canadian interests. First there is a perception of a special Canadian stake in maintaining strong multilateral institutions, in both their developmental and their non-developmental functions. This is more than the cliché that it normally sounds like. There are genuine interests of middle and smaller powers in the multilateral mode of decision-making on international problems, which avoids complete dominance by a few great powers. Probably the most important concrete interest, however, lies in the fact that the major multilateral aid agencies happen to have links to other bodies in which crucial international political and economic matters are decided. This applies to the UN Security Council, election to which would be difficult for smaller Western countries not pulling their weight in the UN development system. It bears even more strongly on participation in the Group of Seven and its annual economic summits, which is related to membership in good standing in the World Bank and IMF. Canada's membership in this elite club did not occur automatically, and an above-average presence in the aid system was a help to Canada's claim to participation.

Second, there is the value of individual multilaterals in serving domestic regional or provincial priorities and special concerns. Examples would be the Asian Development Bank for British Columbia and Canada's Pacific interest generally, the World Food Programme for the prairie provinces and the agricultural sector, the Commonwealth and perhaps the Caribbean Development Bank for English Canada, la Francophonie for French Canada, and the African Development Bank as symbolic of the bilingual nature of Canada. These informal links have been the result not so much of specific lobbying by provinces or regional industries as of traditional anticipatory accommodation of regional interests by foreign policy-makers. These are not the kinds of considerations that would be up-front in annual or medium-term decisions on Canada's funding levels or policy priorities. But they are there in the background to Canada's membership and are examples of choices by a country whose fragile internal structure has made foreign policy highly derivative of sub-national concerns. The large number of these domestically defined "natural ties" with the developing world also helps explain the lack of institutional concentration of Canada's multilateral program – unlike, for example, Australia's marked priority to the Asian Development Bank. In this respect, multilateral assistance parallels the very dispersed pattern of Canada's bilateral aid.

Third and similarly, multilateral institutions have been useful in solidifying Canada's profile and identity in the world. Unlike many other middle powers, and perhaps rather like Sweden, Canada has sought significant influence over the affairs of almost all multilateral organizations. This generalized ambition is in part the result of a somewhat self-congratulatory self-image as an enlightened middle power with ideas to contribute and the qualifications to build bridges in these agencies – and, while this attitude is sometimes exaggerated by spokespeople, it is not totally false. Probably it is also related to a need to remind the world that Canada's views and interests are not necessarily those of the United States and to a need to project a positive image to the world diplomatic class – an image that by now has become quite solid and distinctive.

These self-interested motives probably do not have any severe anti-developmental consequences, although they surely do not lead to the most developmentally optimal mix of supported agencies possible. A very few ineffective multilateral agencies have been dropped by Canada, and almost all of the institutions that are supported happen to be seen as reasonably useful developmentally.

Fourth, another fundamental factor behind Canada's high multilateral share of ODA is the essential confidence of CIDA and others in the developmental effectiveness of the multilateral aid system: belief that the comparative size of agencies roughly matches Canada's own ranking of developmental priorities, that most are reasonably well-managed, and that the role of the MDBs especially in encouraging liberal (i.e. market-oriented) economic policies in recipient countries is a developmentally necessary one. Despite making criticisms of some agencies, Canada did not lose its basic confidence in the system in the 1980s, as some other countries did. Besides the above interests that make Canada favourably disposed, substantive reasons for this confidence do exist in multilaterals' tendency to focus spending on the poorest countries and classes more than do bilateral agencies and in the inherently international nature of some important development problems.

There are a few other determining factors at play. Fifth, Canada has fully accepted responsibility for burden-sharing at least in proportion to national wealth, which not all donor countries have done. Canada is to be found frequently above and rarely below what its share of contributions would be on the basis of wealth (some 3.4 per cent of DAC GNP). This acceptance deserves some praise, given the limited control over replenishment levels possessed by mid-sized donors. Sixth, certain disbursement conveniences help in building up multilateral aid's share of ODA. These include its usefulness as a safety-valve to disburse funds quickly, its ability to provide some assistance to countries not eligible for Canadian bilateral operations, and its value in conserving scarce CIDA person-years by channelling most technical assistance through UN agencies. Moreover, the bank portion of such aid improves Canada's performance against the politically important ODA:GNP ratio target. DAC rules permit donors to count their bank contributions as ODA at the time they are promised (the promissory "note deposit" stage) rather than at the time they are actually paid (the "encashment" stage). Aid agencies thus take ODA credit sooner rather than later, to help in the achievement of targets.

Seventh, multilateral aid, especially to the sectoral UN agencies, has proven useful to politicans concerned that Canada should be seen to be doing something about well-publicized world problems. This partially cosmetic function tends to surface at Commonwealth and Francophonie summits and is also present in contributions to "UN Years" and to the UN Environment Fund and the WHO fund to combat AIDS. (These are generally useful funds, but small in relation to the problems.) Eighth, Canada has always treated annual UN pledges and multi-year IFI replenishment agreements as strong moral commitments. This has insulated, if not completely spared, multilateral aid from budget cuts, since when an aid cut comes along some multilateral items have been locked in for a few years ahead.

Some other occasional factors do not seem to influence inordinately the size and make-up of the multilateral program. The first concerns direct lobbying by specific businesses and interest groups. Such salesmanship is less prevalent than in the bilateral program, largely because Canada does not control the expenditures of international organizations. Lobbying has been strongest in food aid, but even there the pressures have concerned the product composition of food aid in general more than the specifically multilateral aspect of it. More surprising perhaps, interest groups have also been relatively silent about the overall level of multilateral aid and have pressed little for specific initiatives. The Winegard Committee of the House of Commons reported in 1987 that it "received very little testimony on multilateral programs as such."[24] To be sure, the corporate sector's views are not irrelevant: the business community generally prefers tied bilateral aid, and this attitude no doubt bears on the possible upper limits of the multilateral share of ODA. While the recommendation of the business-oriented Hatch Committee in 1979 to cut multilateral aid by half was not accepted by the government, it probably did influence the decision of cabinet the same year to shrink the multilateral channel modestly (which we have seen did not come to pass in practice). But, by and large, business has quietly accepted the fact of a strong multilateral share.

Much the same applies to groups more or less sympathetic to multilateral aid or particular agencies. With the exception of UNICEF-Canada, none has been very active on behalf of its favourites. For example, most private associations in fields covered by UN Specialized Agencies have left any special pleading to the Canadian government departments concerned. The voluntary, or NGO community broadly supports multilateralism but dislikes the structural-adjustment and human rights policies of the banks; the net result is essentially inattention. Among the most dependable underpinnings for the multilateral program are probably general public opinion and the political parties, which have been well-disposed towards the UN, and (unintentionally) the media, which keep world problems in the public eye and force governments to respond. But these vague kinds of support have not added up to vigorous intervention on behalf of the multilateral channel.

Hence the general picture in interest-group activity is one of a bureaucracy left with a free hand on multilateral policy, within some understood (but quite generous) limits on the growth of the multilateral share of ODA. The government and CIDA thus have probably anticipated the principal interests of key groups (or regions) and incorporated them into the multilateral program (the purest example being the very big Canadian presence in the WFP), without these groups or regions needing to lobby vociferously.

What of procurement considerations in multilateral policy-making, especially in relation to the MDBs, in which governments have invested particularly large amounts of money? Canada's procurement records are generally very poor, although they improved somewhat in the 1980s and some equipment/construction and consulting firms have always done well. Certainly the government attempts to improve Canadian performance through information services to businesses and consultation with the Canadian Export Association and others.

It is doubtful that Ottawa decides on relative Canadian shares in the banks and funds significantly on the basis of better or poorer Canadian procurement records. These records are quite variable from year to year, which would make it hard to know which ones to reward, and the banks would frown on such instability. To be sure, economic or commercial motivation affects Canada's shares in each bank, but it relates more to general, longer-term regional trade potentials or benefits of G-7 participation than to immediate gains for specific Canadian interests. (But even such longer-term economic motives may be less important than political ties and foreign policy and developmental goals. Canada's highest stake in an RDB is in the AfDB, whose region has the least commercial potential at present.)

Procurement considerations do enter into Canada's multilateral pol-

icies as a general constraint on upward movement of the multilateral
share of ODA and at the level of encouraging the banks to extend loans
in sectors where Canadian expertise and competitive advantages exist.
It is difficult to know by how much this last factor might undercut developmental priorities, but it did not, for example, prevent Canada
from supporting reorientations of the MDBs away from infrastructure-
led growth in the 1970s.

Weighing the eight factors named above that encourage a high multilateral share of Canada's ODA against the discouraging factors of a
poor Canadian procurement record and the public-relations and
donor-control disadvantages of multilateral aid, it seems plausible that
all these considerations would converge to establish a normal multilateral share of Canadian ODA in the vicinity of 30 per cent. Since
1972–73 this share has fallen below 30 per cent only once (1973–74).
It has fluctuated above that level since then, with an all-time high of
44 per cent in 1976–77 and a post-1980 peak of almost 40 per cent in
1985–86. The average for the period from publication of CIDA's
Strategy in 1975–76 to 1990–91 was 36.4 per cent, and for the 1980s,
35.4 per cent. The latest three years available (1988–89 through
1990–91) averaged a lesser share (31.9 per cent), primarily because of
replenishment delays in the RDBs.

Distribution of Multilateral Aid

In 1975, Secretary of State for External Affairs Allan MacEachen gave
an account of the basis for the distribution of the multilateral budget
among agencies: "The choice of which multilateral institutions receive
Canadian assistance is ... chiefly historical and political ... There is ...
also the additional element of effectiveness, since our policy is to concentrate relatively limited Canadian funds on those agencies with the
greatest developmental potential."[25] The present research broadly cor-
roborates that statement. It is not the custom to reconsider from
scratch each year the appropriate levels of support for each multilateral
agency. Allocations are to quite a large degree historically embedded
(but not totally rigid). At various points in the past, case-by-case decisions were made to join each agency and take on a certain share of the
financing, based on developmental, foreign policy, and economic considerations. Given Canada's respect of burden-sharing and the strong
wish of the agencies for stability in their donors' funding, considerable
inertia thus characterizes distribution of the multilateral budget in the
short term, helped also by the multi-year nature of commitments to the
IFI group and the WFP. Some modest room remains for reallocations
among the banks and a bit more for UN agencies, and over a lengthy

period such incremental shifts can add up to big changes, but there are certainly constraints on quick and radical shifts in funding.

In broad terms, distribution of the multilateral budget among banks and agencies seems to be based about equally on three factors – Canadian officials' confidence that the relative sizes of the major multilateral agencies correspond essentially to their developmental worth and therefore that this should be mirrored roughly in Canada's own allocations; perceptions of Canada's political – that is, historical, regional, and foreign policy – interests in specific agencies; and views of Canada's longer-term economic objectives, such as regional trade aspirations and the IBRD-IDA link to the G-7. Although this way of putting it emphasizes the more static aspects of the make-up of the multilateral budget, changes in relative levels of support do occur when new agencies are created, in cases of institutions in severe crisis, in reallocations imposed by budget cuts, in responses to new development priorities such as the recent environmental thrust, and in a more limited way in the fine-tuning of annual budget-setting. But the weight of the big foreign policy interests, in conjunction with Ottawa's faith in the effectiveness of most agencies, does tend to militate against wholesale change in the short or medium term.

Conclusion

Let us conclude by returning to the question of departures from the ideal of determining the size and make-up of the multilateral program primarily on the basis of developmental needs. The two main potential dangers would be any distortions of development priorities from business and similar lobbying and any improper supremacy of foreign policy and long-run economic goals. Interest-group pressures have set limits on the growth of the multilateral share of ODA, which situation is perhaps acceptable in that multilateral assistance is not the only legitimate aid channel. Such pressures have not, however, prevented Canada from having one of the highest multilateral shares among DAC countries.

Certainly, lobbying (or anticipation of potential lobbying) has sometimes distorted developmental priorities. Examples include Canada's failure to meet the WFP's cash-commodities ratio; the over-representation in Canada's WFP deliveries (relative to product demand in the Third World and world prices) of secondary products such as oils, flour, and fish, whose producers in 1983 persuaded cabinet that non-cereals should receive 25 per cent of the value of Canada's food aid basket (no longer an official target, but still reflected in practice); some politically inspired grants to Commonwealth and Francophonie programs of a primarily cultural nature; and some extra-budgetary grants to the International Atomic Energy Agency (IAEA), which largely serve as seed-money for the pursuit of commercial sales in this area. The multilateral program would be improved if these distortions were eliminated. But on balance such pressures do not appear to have subverted the goals of the program in any fundamental way.

With regard to the possibility of an undue ascendancy of Canada's foreign policy and long-term economic interests, the presence of these interests does not seem to have damaged the overall developmental credibility of the multilateral program. But occasionally it is a problem. For example, but for political considerations, Canada might well have a smaller stake in the AfDB on grounds of limited organizational effectiveness, and but for long-term economic interests in some RDBs, support of IFAD might be somewhat higher for its developmental merits. Perhaps the promise of *Sharing Our Future* to fix developmental considerations as the first priority among competing aid objectives will help in this regard.

One should not expect radical or rapid reallocations: the traditions of the multilateral agencies themselves discourage abrupt changes in donors' financial commitments, as do multi-year bank replenishments and the limited absorptive capacities of some agencies. Nor does the strong role of foreign policy and long-term economic interests seem to undercut developmental priorities significantly: in contrast to motives of immediate gain for Canadian interest groups, which have not been a major factor in the multilateral program, these longer-term aspirations are generally consistent with developmental needs and sometimes reinforce politically more fragile developmental values. In the few cases where departures from development priorities have resulted from the play of these big interests, funding adjustments should be considered.

At the time of writing, there are some clouds on the horizon that could reduce the place of the multilateral element in Canada's aid program. In the past, when cuts have been imposed on ODA, multilateral has not suffered more than proportionately, for reasons given above. Strong forces still underlie a solid multilateral share of ODA. What, however, if there were to be more catastrophic aid cuts, say of 25 to 50 per cent, which no longer seems so unthinkable in view of the various fiscal and debt crises facing all Canadian governments in 1993? Perhaps at some point in a cycle of cutting, the 30 per cent floor that has been the base of multilateral aid for 20 years would no longer be politically tenable in view of the limited economic returns of this program. In that case, the analysis above might have to be regarded as something less than the immutable laws of Canadian aid policy-making and rather as the workings of the system within a given (moderate) level of turbulence in its environment.

The limitations of its past performance and the possible clouds in the forecast pointed out here cannot take away the generally admirable multilateral performance of Canada and the accomplishments of Canadian diplomacy over three decades. Although Canada's previous middle power idealism was muted in the 1980s, a sympathetic realism towards the multilateral network did carry forward. At least this much, it is to be hoped, will endure.

NOTES

1 Expressions of the form "1989–90" relate to the government of Canada's fiscal year or to events that occurred within the period of these two calendar years, while those of the form "1988" refer to a calendar year.

2 The DAC average given excludes contributions of European countries to the very large European Development Fund (EDF). Some sources count the EDF as multilateral aid, which would then raise the DAC average to about 25 per cent. In my view, this latter practice is misleading, because the EDF should not be considered a genuine "multilateral" agency, in view of its restricted membership and the non-membership of developing countries. There are problems in defining a multilateral agency, but the essence is probably that membership should be wide and should include both industrial and developing countries. Moreover, to consider the EDF as multilateral aid is unfair to non-European DAC members, which can count only their contributions to the UN system and the MDBs. A better term for such organizations (the Arab funds are similar) might be "multi-national" agencies, which are really combined bilateral agencies.

3 If we count the EDF as multilateral aid, Canada would have usually been seventh or eighth.

4 Dollar figures are Canadian dollars for expenditures of the Canadian government and US dollars for expenditures of other governments and international organizations or for comparisons between Canada and other governments.

5 Canada, CIDA, *Strategy for International Development Cooperation, 1975–1980* (Ottawa: CIDA 1975).

6 Commission on International Development, *Partners in Development* (Pearson Report) (New York: Praeger 1969).

7 Author's confidential interviews.

8 Author's confidential interview regarding the UNDP. On the ASDB, see Robert Wihtol, *The Asian Development Bank and Rural Development* (New

York: St Martin's Press 1988), 192. Regarding the IDB, see CIDA, *Annual Review 1970–71* (Ottawa: Information Canada 1971), 54.

9 Paul Gérin-Lajoie, *Journey to Justice* (Ottawa: CIDA 1971), 11.

10 Dick Wilson, *A Bank for Half the World: The Story of the Asian Development Bank, 1966–1986* (Manila: ASDB 1987), 84.

11 Robert Gardiner and James Pickett, *The African Development Bank, 1964–1984* (Abidjan: AfDB 1984), 58.

12 Author's confidential interviews.

13 CIDA, *Annual Aid Review 1975: Memorandum of Canada to the DAC* (Ottawa: CIDA 1976).

14 *Montreal Gazette*, 20 November 1974.

15 Author's confidential interviews.

16 *Ibid.*

17 Canada, Export Promotion Review Committee (Hatch Committee), *Strengthening Canada Abroad* (Ottawa: Industry, Trade and Commerce 1979), 11.

18 Author's confidential interviews.

19 CIDA, *Sharing Our Future: Canada's International Development Assistance* (Ottawa: Supply and Services 1987).

20 Most of the information in the remainder of this chapter comes from confidential sources. To conserve space, not every piece of information will be cited as such, only where there is a special reason to do so.

21 See especially Giovanni Cornia, R. Jolly, and F. Stewart, eds., *Structural Adjustment with a Human Face: Protecting the Vulnerable and Promoting Growth* (London: Oxford University Press 1987).

22 Renate Pratt, "International Financial Institutions," in Robert O. Matthews and Cranford Pratt, eds., *Human Rights in Canadian Foreign Policy* (Montreal and Kingston: McGill-Queen's University Press 1988), 159–84.

23 David R. Protheroe, *Canada and Multilateral Aid: Working Paper* (Ottawa: North-South Institute 1991).

24 Canada, House of Commons, Standing Committee on External Affairs and International Trade (SCEAIT), *For Whose Benefit? Report of the Standing Committee on External Affairs and International Trade on Canada's Official Development Assistance Policies and Programs* (Winegard Report) (Ottawa: Supply and Services, May 1987), 58.

25 CIDA, *International Development Cooperation: Statements by the Honourable Allan J. MacEachen, Secretary of State for External Affairs* (Ottawa: Information Canada, September 1975).

3 Continuity and Change in Canadian Food Aid

MARK W. CHARLTON

From its modest beginnings in 1951, the Canadian food aid program has evolved into a large and complex part of Canada's overseas development assistance. During the past four decades, over four billion dollars, or fully one-fifth of all Canadian foreign aid, has been offered in the form of food commodities. Although Canada's relations with developing countries have become more complex in light of such issues as trade and monetary reform, food aid remains one of the largest single components of Canada's development assistance.

No other form of Canadian assistance can inspire as powerful a public emotional response as food aid. For many Canadians, food aid evokes images of bags of wheat bearing the Canadian maple leaf being unloaded in a dusty feeding camp in remote corners of Ethiopia and Somalia, or the skeletal figure of a starving child clutching a cup of milk.

Despite its powerful symbolic and emotive appeal, the Canadian food aid program remains controversial. Even CIDA officials have at times expressed widely divergent views of the role that food aid can and should play in Canada's relations with the Third World.[1] The debate over food aid as a form of assistance reflects more generally disagreements over the objectives of Canadian development assistance and the proper strategy for its allocation. Thus an examination of the evolution of the program and the way in which it is administered can provide some useful insights into the overall priorities and objectives of Canadian foreign policy in the Third World.

The Canadian food aid program has experienced a series of significant changes and reforms during the past two decades. Until the early

1970s, it was little more than a loosely connected collection of disparate programs designed to meet a plethora of sometimes conflicting objectives. In the absence of a comprehensive policy framework, minimal effort was made to coordinate its elements, or even to assess their impact. However, Canadian food aid policies and programs underwent substantial change in the wake of the world food crisis of 1972–74. For the first time, the Canadian government carried out an extensive review and assessment of its program. New policy initiatives changed both the substance and the administration of food aid. After this watershed, consolidation and restructuring took place, as many of the policy themes introduced after the world food crisis were elaborated and refined in the 1980s and early 1990s. CIDA policy statements since publication in May 1987 of *For Whose Benefit?* (Winegard Report) have, for the most part, reiterated themes already evident in policy of the early 1980s.[2]

This chapter shows at least three areas of change in the program during the past two decades. First, major organizational changes in administration have institutionalized the program. Second, there has been a significant evolution in the policy rationale for the program, with food aid having been declared a useful "developmental" resource which can be used to promote agriculture and food production and to assist recipient countries in reforming domestic agricultural policies and undertaking structural adjustment. Third, there have been changes in the programs themselves, involving shifts in the balance among delivery channels, geographical distribution patterns, and the make-up of the Canadian food aid commodity basket. These changes, in both thematic and substantive focus, reflect a number of forces shaping Canadian food aid policy.

INSTITUTIONALIZATION

Although food aid has always been a single item in CIDA's budget, prior to 1978 Canadian food aid "program" was essentially a misnomer. What existed was a conglomeration of disparate programs, established at different times for diverse reasons. Responsibility for each program remained with those departments or branches that initiated them. Thus country-to-country food aid transfers were the responsibility of desk officers within CIDA's bilateral branch. Agriculture Canada took the lead in both program and policy decisions regarding the World Food Programme (WFP). External Affairs determined Canada's food aid contribution to the United Nations Relief and Works Agency (UNRWA), while CIDA's NGO division dealt with allocations of food aid, primarily skim milk powder, to NGOs. Once food aid projects were approved, the CIDA's Materiel Management Division and the Department of Supply and Services handled procurement and delivery. No real effort was made to coordinate programs or to fit them into a broader policy framework for food aid.

The 1972–74 world food crisis revealed that this bureaucratic fragmentation, which necessitated extensive intra-agency discussions before any decision could be made, undermined CIDA's ability to respond to rapidly changing circumstances. Following a highly critical report by Canada's auditor general, CIDA created the Food Aid Coordination and Evaluation Centre (FACE) in 1978. Although detailed planning and implementation of specific food aid allocations remain the responsibility of the respective branches, FACE coordinates all aspects of Canadian food aid policy. Until its creation, CIDA had no specialized personnel of its own for dealing full-time specifically with food aid.

Creation of FACE benefited the food aid program in several ways. For the first time, CIDA was able to generate a database regarding food aid needs and uses and to provide that information to desk officers, who did not ordinarily have access to, nor the time to evaluate, such information. By coordinating the budget process, CIDA, through FACE, could now attempt to ensure that particular program and allocation decisions fitted within a broader set of policy criteria. This arrangement reduced the incentive for desk officers to see food aid as simply a "throw item" which enabled them to transfer resources to a recipient relatively easily, while meeting disbursement targets.[3]

In addition, FACE became the focal point for defining policy and ensuring that policy discussions took into account evolving norms and principles as articulated in such a forum as the Committee on Food Aid Policies and Programmes (CFA).[4] CIDA could thus be more proactive on food aid issues, both within CIDA and in interdepartmental discussions.

Finally, FACE became the primary contact point with domestic suppliers who wished to see their commodities included in the food aid program. While domestic economic priorities still influence food aid decisions, the presence of a full-time commodity officer has helped produce a more proactive stance towards external pressures, weeding out of some of the more inappropriate commodities, and defence of CIDA's decisions to outside actors.

THE EVOLVING RATIONALE

When food aid was first provided by the Canadian government, there was little understanding of its potential developmental role in an aid program. As a result, food aid came to serve a wide variety of sometimes conflicting aims and objectives as programs were established in response to particular situations. Domestic economic considerations have played a prominent role, especially the desire to dispose of Canadian agricultural surpluses, thereby saving the government the cost of storing and handling excess stocks; to generate value-added benefits by using excess milling capacity to process food aid commodities within Canada; and to develop and maintain markets for Canadian agricultural products. In addition, the highly visible nature of food aid has made it an attractive instrument for expressing diplomatic support for new governments or for friendly governments facing political and economic crises; providing an "opener," or "diplomatic calling card," when Canada wants to signal its intention of strengthening relations; enhancing Canada's image and influence in multilateral forums; and occasionally "punishing" countries by withholding allocations of food aid. In addition, Canadian policy-makers have long felt that the highly visible nature of Canadian food aid shipments helped build a domestic constituency for Canadian aid more generally.[5]

Because Canadian aid officials felt that responsibility for food aid had been imposed on them for domestic economic reasons with little developmental justification, they saw food aid merely as an "add-on" to the "real" work of developmental assistance. As a result, by permitting recipients to sell food commodities locally, food aid transfers became a useful way for them to generate local budgetary revenues and ease balance-of-payments constraints, with minimal administrative burden.[6]

However, the food crisis of the early 1970s and the resulting focus on food aid in such international forums as the World Food Council and the Committee on Food Aid Policies led Ottawa to assess its food aid policies so as to develop a comprehensive policy framework. A confidential CIDA-Treasury Board report (1977), the first serious evaluation of the impact of Canadian food aid, found that, in the five countries examined, accounting for 75 per cent of Canada bilateral food aid, "food aid appears to accommodate policies discouraging domestic production in both the short and long term."[7] Moreover, on the whole, it "does not reach the poorest segments of the populations of recipient countries."[8] Because the report raised so many questions, an interdepartmental working group was struck to develop a more coherent policy framework following expiration of the Rome pledge.

The resulting "Food Aid Policy Recommendations" (1978) observed that food aid should be conceived as a transitional measure, complementary to the recipient's own agricultural development. More important, it posited humanitarian concerns as the "main rationale," noting that "food aid should be provided primarily to address the nutritional needs of the poorer segments of recipient-country populations" while also being "complementary to the recipient's agricultural strategy."[9] But, reflecting bureaucratic compromises, the report also noted that food aid should benefit Canada by including surplus disposal and adding value to agricultural commodities and should be consistent with Canada's foreign policy.[10]

Nevertheless, in emphasizing the humanitarian rationale, the report committed Canada to distributive rather than macro-economic objectives.[11] The Report of the Task Force on North-South Relations (1980) recommended that food aid be used "only as a transitional measure ... [as] part of a detailed and well-integrated food production plan in which food aid would gradually decline and assistance for food production would increase."[12]

Although "Food Aid Policy Recommendations" became the framework for Canadian allocations, subsequent CIDA policy statements have backed away from humanitarian or distributive objectives. Beginning in 1983, an even more comprehensive corporate review of the program was undertaken. This study found growing consensus in the academic literature and in the donor community concerning the central role of the policy environment provided by the recipient government. Even the best-managed food aid will fail to have a positive impact if the government is not committed to promoting its agricultural sector, lacks a food strategy, and pursues urban-biased food policies. From this perspective, the corporate review identified two primary rationales for Canadian food aid. First, food aid should support balanced economic growth by providing additional resources to recipient governments "setting sound economic policies and promoting sectorally equitable growth."[13] In this case, Canadian food aid "can free scarce foreign exchange for additional investment in agriculture, reduce upward pressure on domestic food prices, and smooth adjustments in the agricultural sector."[14] Second, in cases where such "balanced growth" policies are not being followed, the review recommended that "policy dialogue to bring about key structural reforms in the recipient is an indispensable proviso to any food aid assistance."[15]

These two rationales have been repeated and elaborated upon in virtually every CIDA statement of food aid policy since 1983. CIDA's *Strategic Plan for Food Aid* (1984), as approved by the President's Committee, noted "increasing the quantities of food aid available in food deficit countries" and "accelerating the pace of development by freeing foreign exchange and generating domestic resources for investment" as the program's two primary objectives. "Providing supplementary food to nutritionally vulnerable groups" and "offering basic subsistence during emergency relief and rehabilitation situations" were identified as secondary objectives.[16] The emphasis on broader "developmental" or stabilization objectives can be seen in CIDA's most recent aid strategy paper, *Sharing Our Future* (1987): future allocations "will be used especially to help the recipient country reform its agricultural policy and/or carry out structural adjustments."[17]

As we see below, the shift in emphasis from distributive to broader macro-economic objectives has affected the program in important ways.

SUBSTANTIVE CHANGES IN THE PROGRAM

The Scale of Canadian Food Aid Flows

Since 1951, the Canadian government has spent more than $4.3 billion on food aid. Canadian officials have frequently stressed the importance of this aid by noting that Canada is the largest per-capita donor of food aid in the world. Nevertheless, on a global scale, Canadian food aid remains relatively small in comparison with the average annual amount of $2.5 billion that the United States provided throughout the 1980s. During this period, the European Community (EC) greatly expanded its programs, displacing Canada as the second-largest donor. Thus, by 1988, Canada accounted for 10 per cent of global cereal food aid, while the EC accounted for 12 per cent and the United States for 57 per cent.[18]

Although the physical volume of Canadian food aid increased in the 1980s, reaching an all-time high in 1987–88, its actual share of total Canadian ODA expenditure declined in the 1980s. Throughout most of the 1970s, food aid accounted, on average, for nearly one quarter of total Canadian overseas development assistance (ODA). But beginning with budget cuts in 1979, food aid declined to an average share of 15 per cent of ODA, except for the years of African famine in the mid-1980s, when it reached about 18 per cent again.

The gradual decline of food aid as a component of Canadian aid programs has been welcomed by those who are sceptical of its value in promoting development. In 1987, the Winegard Report devoted at mere page and a half of its 140 pages to the topic of food aid. It recommended that, because of the "mixed record of food aid," a ceiling of 10 per cent of total ODA be placed on food aid, with the exception of emergency shipments.[19] However, the Conservative government rejected the proposed ceiling and announced instead that it was planning to continue increasing food aid by 5 per cent annually, noting that "it considers the use of food aid an effective and flexible instrument for helping developing countries face emergency situations or major balance of payments deficits."[20]

Table 1
Canadian food aid disbursements, 1970–71 to 1989–90

Fiscal year	Volume Q(MTN)	Value ($million)	Food aid as % of total ODA
1970–71	1,163.5	104.2	29.8
1971–72	941.1	79.8	20.0
1972–73	801.4	112.4	21.1
1973–74	712.0	115.7	19.4
1974–75	665.2	174.5	23.3
1975–76	1,033.1	222.6	24.5
1976–77	1,102.8	240.1	26.3
1977–78	971.5	230.4	21.9
1978–79	711.8	191.2	16.4
1979–80	558.4	187.7	15.0
1980–81	521.5	183.4	14.0
1981–82	568.2	235.7	15.1
1982–83	777.6	273.2	16.4
1983–84	900.0	332.5	18.0
1984–85	948.8	385.5	18.4
1985–86	850.4	347.8	15.9
1986–87	1,334.8	402.7	15.9
1987–88	1,533.3	436.7	16.6
1988–89	1,055.4	431.5	14.7
1989–90	865.2	371.6	13.1
1990–91	1,049.4	382.3	12.3

Sources: CIDA, Food Aid Centre, "Bilateral Food Aid Program as of 30 June 1978,"
"1990/91: Food Aid Program Annual Report," and CIDA, Annual Report, various years.

Despite this commitment, food aid soon faced cuts, but not because of the Winegard Committee's call for a ceiling. Following the 1988 election, the Mulroney government turned its attention to fiscal management and deficit reduction. In April 1989, it announced a 12 per cent cut in CIDA's budget for 1989–90, with a total of $1.8 billion to be dropped from the aid budget over the following five years; $66 million of the $360 million to be cut from the aid budget in the first year would come from the food aid program. As in the austerity cuts of a decade earlier, food aid was seen as an easy area to target.[21] Thus, by the 1990–91 budget, food aid had slipped to only 12.3 per cent of total ODA, the lowest share of Canadian ODA since 1963. Despite this slippage, food aid still plays a larger part in Canadian development assistance than is the case with other donors, except for the United States. On a global level, food aid accounts for less than 7 per cent of total ODA spending in recent years.

Table 1 indicates the annual value and volume of Canadian food products shipped during this period. Major year-to-year fluctuations can be attributed partly to the fact that the program is budgeted in terms of financial totals, not physical volume. Thus changes in commodity prices can substantially affect the actual physical scale of the program. In the early 1970s, the budget grew by 97.5 per cent from 1971–72 to 1974–75, but volume was 30.3 per cent less. Levels recovered following the Rome commitment to provide one million tonnes of grain per year. But they fell again as a result of food aid being targeted in budget cuts imposed in the late 1970s.

Because of the uncertainties that such fluctuations can cause for recipients, efforts have been made to hedge in the food aid program. The Food Aid Convention (FAC), established in 1967 as part of the International Grains Agreement, cites a specified volume of grain that each member is obligated to provide annually. The agreement set Canada's floor level at 475,000 tons annually. This was increased to 600,000 when the convention was renegotiated in 1980, but Canada's actual share of the total FAC pledge actually fell from 11 per cent to 8 per cent.

Canada's reluctance to maintain its share of the FAC as the convention was increased resulted from concern that Canada may be forced into a position "where an international commitment has eliminated almost all choice of level for our aid program, and we could be committed to deliver food aid even when it is not appropriate."[22] However, since 1982 Canada has consistently provided significantly more cereal aid than called for in the agreement. By the mid-1980s, as CIDA moved to respond to growing food needs in Africa, Canada provided 1.2 million tons of cereals, or twice its pledged level, accounting for 10 per cent of total FAC cereal aid. Although volume has slipped in recent years, shipments of cereals remain well above Canada's minimum commitment of 600,000 tons annually.

Multi-year agreements with bilateral recipients have also helped in dealing with sharp fluctuations in the food aid program. Canada's multilateral contributions to the WFP are determined as part of a biennial pledging conference at which each nation agrees to provide a specified level of commodity and cash donations during the following two years. But bilateral food aid has been shipped only on a year-to-year basis, with new agreements being negotiated with each recipient every year. In years of budget reductions, bilateral food aid has frequently been a favoured target for reductions, since, unlike many other forms of development assistance, it is committed only for one year and can be easily terminated. To address this situation, CIDA as early as 1975 began promoting multi-year agreements with at least the most important recipients.[23] This initiative encountered strong initial resistance from departments such as the Treasury Board and Finance, which were reluctant to diminish their budgetary control by allowing financial commitments beyond one year. However, in 1981 CIDA received authority to negotiate a three-year agreement with Bangladesh. Since that date, CIDA has been given authority to enter into similar agreements with at least six other recipients. In *Sharing Our Future*, CIDA committed itself to providing at least 75 per cent of total Canadian food aid under multi-year agreements.[24] The aim of this policy is to give recipients greater stability and continuity in food aid flows, while CIDA retains sufficient flexibility to reallocate some resources as needs shift.

Choice of Delivery Channels

Canadian food aid is delivered through three "channels," or organizational vehicles – bilateral, or government-to-government arrangements; multilateral institutions; and non-government organizations (NGOs). Food aid transfers take three forms – program, project, and emergency. Each channel is designed to accomplish different objectives and places different administrative demands on the donor agency. Thus selection of a particular combination of delivery mechanisms reflects the priorities that policy-makers wish to attach to certain objectives.

In theory, project and program food aid can be delivered through either bilateral or multilateral channels. But in practice, Canadian officials have preferred to specialize by providing all of Canada's program food aid through bilateral channels, while using multilateral channels to deliver project food aid. In addition, a relatively modest NGO program has been undertaken as a more recent alternative.

First, bilateral food aid consists of direct, government-to-government transfers of food commodities. These transactions consist of bulk shipments of food aid commodities in relatively sizeable volumes directly to the recipient government. Once the shipments arrive at the designated port of entry, the commodities are turned over to the recipient government, which assumes full responsibility for their disposition. In many cases, the food is sold on the domestic market and thus generates revenues for the recipient government.[25] Because it is quickly disbursed and less intensive administratively, program food aid is particularly suited to addressing broad macro-economic objectives such as provision of balance-of-payments support, generation of local budgetary revenues, and ensuring domestic price stability.

Second, Canadian food aid is delivered also through multilateral aid organizations such as the WFP, the International Emergency Food Reserve (IEFR) operated by the WFP, the United Nations Relief and Works Agency for Palestinian Refugees, the United Nations Chilren's

Fund (UNICEF), and the International Committee of the Red Cross. However, more than 95 per cent of Canada's multilateral food aid is provided through the WFP. Canada has consistently ranked as the second-largest donor to the WFP, accounting for about 20 per cent of its total resources. All Canadian contributions to the WFP take the form of project food aid, which addresses primarily distributive objectives and is used as a component of vulnerable groups' feeding programs or as an input to "food-for-work" schemes, where food is used to pay for wages of workers on development projects such as road building or construction of irrigation systems. In recent years, a growing share of multilateral food aid has been distributed free in emergency situations.[26]

Third, since 1976, CIDA has distributed small amounts of food aid to non-governmental organizations (NGOs) under the rubric of "special programs." The first such effort was the NGO–Skim Milk Program, where CIDA provided skim milk powder to NGOs that were willing to cover the cost of transportation and distribution. This milk is used mostly in mother-and-child health projects and in vulnerable-group feeding projects. More recently, CIDA has provided funding to the Canadian Foodgrains Bank, a consortium of church and voluntary development agencies, which gathers principally food commodity donations, primarily grains, directly from Canadian farmers for distribution overseas, especially in response to food emergencies. At the very most, special programs have accounted for only 9 per cent of Canadian food aid, and that was during the Ethiopian famine; the program is very small in comparison to the 30 per cent of American food aid that is supplied through private voluntary organizations.[27]

Each channel offers distinct advantages. Bilateral food aid can provide greater visibility to Canada, especially in responding to emergencies or in demonstrating political support for a regime. Canadian policy-makers directly decide which countries are to be allocated bilateral food aid and under what terms. Because program food aid relies on large shipments of bulk commodities, it permits shipments of larger quantities of such surplus commodities as grains and canola oil than project aid would permit. Developing new markets and gaining value-added benefits from the disbursement of canola oil is largely dependent on use of bilateral program food aid.

The WFP facilitates much broader geographical coverage, especially in reaching countries that may not be eligible for bilateral assistance.[28] At times, the WFP has served as an outlet for surplus commodities that the bilateral program could not accommodate.[29] Because the WFP administers Canada's contribution, the burden placed on CIDA is reduced.[30] As well, contributions to the WFP have been seen as

Table 2
Channels for Canadian food aid ($million), 1970–71 to 1990–91

Year	Total food aid value	Multilateral		Bilateral		NGOs	
		Value	% of total	Value	% of total	Value	% of total
1970–71	104.2	17.0	16.3	87.1	83.4	–	–
1971–72	79.8	15.6	19.5	64.2	80.8	–	–
1972–73	112.4	16.4	14.5	96.0	85.4	–	–
1973–74	115.7	20.9	18.0	94.8	81.9	–	–
1974–75	174.5	16.1	9.2	158.4	90.7	–	–
1975–76	222.6	105.5	47.4	117.1	52.6	–	–
1976–77	240.1	89.1	37.1	151.0	62.9	–	–
1977–78	230.4	91.3	39.6	139.1	60.4	2.1	0.9
1978–79	194.5	98.0	50.5	93.1	47.9	3.3	1.7
1979–80	187.7	97.8	52.1	85.7	45.7	4.1	2.2
1980–81	183.4	106.8	58.2	73.1	39.9	3.5	1.9
1981–82	235.7	113.4	48.1	118.3	50.2	4.0	1.7
1982–83	273.2	122.0	44.4	141.4	51.8	9.7	3.6
1983–84	332.5	146.3	43.9	175.8	52.9	10.3	3.2
1984–85	385.5	149.6	38.8	214.4	55.6	21.4	5.6
1985–86	347.8	150.3	43.2	163.1	46.9	34.3	9.9
1986–87	402.7	166.3	41.2	210.9	52.3	25.4	6.3
1987–88	436.6	172.7	39.5	237.8	54.4	26.1	5.9
1988–89	431.5	188.4	43.6	217.9	50.4	23.9	5.5
1989–90	371.6	173.6	46.7	174.5	47.0	23.5	6.3
1990–91	382.3	182.1	47.6	176.8	46.2	23.4	6.1

Sources: CIDA, *Annual Report*, various years.

enhancing Canada's image with Third World countries, which have tended to be very supportive of the WFP.

Because of the range of objectives facilitated by each channel, Canadian policy-makers have been slow in defining the proper balance among the various channels. As Table 2 shows, bilateral food aid was the predominant delivery channel until the mid-1970s. In 1975–76, however, when Canada moved towards fulfilling its pledge in Rome, multilateral food aid increased from 9.2 to 47.4 per cent of the food aid program in one year. Although this figure decreased somewhat during the next two years, it grew again, reaching fully 58.2 per cent in 1980–81.

The dramatic shift towards multilateral channels reflected a growing perception that multilateral food aid was more effective and better targeted than bilateral food aid. Criticisms in the 1970s – that Canadian food aid was mismanaged, was diverted by corrupt recipient governments, and discouraged local food production – were all direct attacks on program food aid. The 1977 CIDA-Treasury Board study, while giving a generally positive review of WFP aid, found that in many cases Canadian bilateral program food aid had not been an effective balance-of-payments support and had in fact accommodated policies that provided a disincentive for increased local food production. When confronted with their critics, CIDA officials were forced to admit that bilateral food aid was biased largely in favour of urban populations and failed to reach the poorest population groups.[32] At the same time, support for greater use of multilateral channels was clearly growing among the Canadian public, the NGO community, academics, and members of Parliament, largely because this form of aid was widely perceived as being more effective in achieving distributive food aid objectives. The 1980 report of the Parliamentary Task Force on North-South Relations recommended much greater use of the WFP for Canadian food aid.[33] Despite this recommendation, and the growing domestic support that it represented, CIDA officials began to question the widely held assumption that multilateral channels provided a superior channel for such assistance. Several factors help to explain this change in thinking.

First, as shown above, the emerging rationale for the 1980s stressed "developmental" food aid, with its themes of structural adjustment and linkage to policy reform. Thus it was increasingly argued within CIDA that, if food aid is to be used as leverage to encourage policy reform, then only a fairly substantial flow of program food aid would provide a level of resources sufficient to convince governments to undertake reforms.

Second, the deteriorating economic environment within many recipient countries in the 1980s made project food aid less attractive. Falling commodity prices, stagnating exports, and heavy debt-repayment loads seriously reduced the amount of foreign exchange available for commercial food imports. As the focus of greatest need shifted to Africa, with its mounting economic crisis, this region provided a much less suitable environment for absorbing large amounts of project food aid. As a result, CIDA officials began to play down the benefits of project food aid, while looking for faster-disbursing forms of aid in order to respond to the economic situation. Thus one CIDA document points out that project food aid because of its administrative intensiveness places a high demand on technical and managerial skills that are often in short supply; requires additional inputs of services and equipment, funding for which is not readily available; and involves recurring costs that recipient governments have difficulty funding.[34]

Third, there was growing concern that the WFP had reached its capacity for handling project food aid effectively. Since 1983, relations between the WFPs secretariat and its parent body, the Food and

Agricultural Organization (FAO), had become so acrimonious as to impair the efficiency of the organization. Canada joined other donors in pressing for reforms within the WFP and even at one point delayed announcing its pledge to the WFP as a means of increasing pressure for reform.[35]

In reflecting this change in thinking, the 1984 Strategic Review suggested that any future expansion of non-emergency food aid take place through bilateral channels.[36] Since then, a practice has emerged in CIDA of channelling approximately 55–60 per cent of Canada's food aid through bilateral channels. As Table 2 shows, slightly greater emphasis has been placed on bilateral food aid since the early 1980s and continues into the 1990s. Although Canada still transfers a much greater share of its food aid through multilateral channels than other donors, continued focus on program food aid runs against the recommendation of the Winegard Report in 1987, that bilateral food aid "should be handled with greater care and used more sparingly than in the past."[37]

Despite this general trend in favour of greater bilateral food aid, CIDA has increasingly emphasized use of multilateral and NGO channels for delivery of emergency food aid. Because CIDA has traditionally not identified emergency food aid as a separate category, it is difficult to measure exactly what role such shipments have played. The best guess of CIDA officials in the 1970s was that only about 10 per cent of Canada's bilateral food aid was emergency assistance, in the sense of being distributed free for direct human consumption.[38] As CIDA has redirected more of its food aid towards Africa, recent official statements identify 37 per cent of total Canadian food aid as being in the form of emergency assistance in 1990–91.[39]

With emergency food aid shipments, how can the donor be assured of effective delivery to target groups? In contrast to regular program food aid, which enters the country's normal commercial channels, emergency supplies require some specific institutional mechanism in place in order that food be distributed directly to the affected persons. In some cases, such institutional channels may not exist or do so only in rudimentary form. In other cases, government control makes these channels susceptible to manipulation. Since most recipient governments are obviously unwilling to relinquish control to external agencies of something as politically important as domestic food distribution channels, the problem of ensuring that all target groups are reached is a vexing one for donors, especially when the glare of media attention raises demands for greater public accountability. It poses an even greater dilemma for donor agencies such as CIDA, which have only limited field staff and monitoring capability.[40]

CIDA addressed this problem in 1984. It decided that, in countries where it neither has a strong aid presence already nor has confidence in the recipient government's distribution channels, it would direct more of its emergency food aid through alternative channels, such as the WFP or NGOs, which have a stronger presence in the field.[41] This strategy was particularly evident in the Canadian response to the famine in Ethiopia in the mid-1980s. The ability to reach the neediest groups was severely complicated by the fact that the Ethiopian government was fighting insurgency movements in Eritrea and Tigre, two of the areas most seriously affected by the drought. Frequent charges were made that the Ethiopian Relief and Rehabilitation Commission, the government agency that controlled distribution of food aid, was preventing aid from reaching many in the northern provinces, resulting in large movement of refugees into Sudan. As a result, CIDA chose to deliver a larger share of its food aid to Ethiopia through NGOs and international agencies. In 1985–86, fully 54 per cent of Canadian food aid to Ethiopia was channelled through NGOs, representing the largest use of NGOs as a channel to one country in the history of the program. Since then, CIDA has made increased use of the WFP as a channel for emergency food aid in this region of Africa. For example, in 1989–90, 54 per cent of Canada's food aid to Ethiopia and 58 per cent of its food aid to Sudan were channelled through the WFP.

However, use of alternative channels for emergency food aid has not been without its problems. This became evident, before the fall of the Mengistu regime, when the Ethiopian government expelled the Red Cross and other NGOs from northern areas. It was no longer possible for donors such as Canada to rely on these agencies to monitor distribution of food aid. Some NGOs, such as Oxfam Canada, argued that the Canadian government should make more resources available to finance "transborder shipments" of food aid into the north. NGOs operating in Sudan could channel food supplies to the Eritrea and Tigrean relief societies, which would then distribute them in areas under rebel control. Oxfam maintained that expulsion of voluntary workers from the north was only further indication that the Ethiopian government was intent on controlling all food aid distribution and using food as a weapon in the prosecution of its campaign against the insurgents. Only use of back-door channels could prevent more extensive starvation.[42]

Despite this plea, CIDA initially opposed use of Canadian government monies to fund increased transborder shipments, citing two foreign policy reasons. First, it argued that relations between Sudan and Ethiopia have been delicate and that the Sudanese government had expressed to donors its opposition to transborder shipments through

Sudan as a violation of national sovereignty. Second, CIDA argued that since the Ethiopian government saw the conflict as solely an internal matter, it could use transborder shipments as an excuse to "ban all Canadian NGOs from functioning in Ethiopia."[43] Underlying these arguments was Ottawa's strong reluctance to take any actions that would appear to undermine the sovereignty of the Ethiopian government and to give de facto recognition to the opposition forces.

Nevertheless, following a parliamentary report that recommended increased support for transborder shipments, CIDA did make more food aid available for such shipments. However, determination of the exact level of such funding continued to be a sensitive issue. When Canadian food aid to Ethiopia declined in 1989, some members of the Canadian NGO community expressed concern that the government had seriously underestimated emergency food needs in areas of the country outside government control. According to one NGO estimate, 67 per cent of Canadian food aid was targeted to civilians in government-controlled areas, while 80 per cent of the most seriously affected population lived in areas outside government control. At issue was how emergency needs are determined. Since CIDA was reluctant to disclose how these estimates were arrived at, some NGOs believed that Ottawa had relied too extensively on estimates by the WFP and the Ethiopian government, which were biased in favour of the interests of the central government. NGOs argued that there needed to be more systematic, independent assessment of needs outside government-controlled areas in order to ensure that the needs of the most seriously affected were actually being met.

This situation and the Canadian response to it demonstrate the basic dilemma with emergency aid situations.[44] In cases where it does not fully trust the recipient government's capacity or will to distribute its food supplies in a fair and equitable manner, the donor must rely on alternative channels for monitoring or distribution. But these organizations work within the country only with the permission of the recipient government. As an intergovernmental organization, the WFP is committed to recognizing the sovereignty of all governments and is therefore prohibited from supporting such activities as unofficial transborder shipments.[45] In addition, it must often rely on the official estimate of need put forward by the recipient government. NGOs continue to operate within a country only with the approval of the host government, and many that have ongoing development projects are reluctant to take actions that might threaten their presence in the future. Thus, while a donor may wish to circumvent direct government control by using such channels, the recipient government still ultimately controls the situation. As a CIDA vice-president noted, "It is the whole problem of trying not to get yourself into a situation where the only arms that you have to use are cut off. Where does that leave you?"[46]

Geographical Distribution

A crucial question in any aid program, of course, is which countries actually receive assistance. The answer frequently tells much about the economic, foreign policy, and developmental priorities of the donor government.

Since the food aid program began, more than 52 countries have received bilateral food aid from Canada. Despite this large number, Canada has tended to concentrate on a few recipients in any given year, with the maximum number receiving such assistance in a year reaching only 25. Initially, the program provided large shipments of grains to a few Asian countries under the auspices of the Colombo Plan. From the 1950s through the 1970s, four Asian countries – Bangladesh, India, Pakistan, and Sri Lanka – accounted for fully 75 per cent of the $1.6 billion worth of aid. Beginning in the mid-1960s, as the size of the program dramatically increased and Canadian foreign policy interests broadened, shipments were directed towards both francophone and anglophone Africa. Even larger amounts began to be directed to Africa during the Sahelian drought in the early 1970s. But these shipments tended to be small in comparison with those sent to Asia. Thus, even during the Sahelian drought, Africa still accounted for less than 20 per cent of the total bilateral program. In contrast, since its independence in 1971, Bangladesh alone has accounted for 30 per cent or more of bilateral food aid each year.[47]

Since 1980–81, there has been a significant shift towards Africa. In that fiscal year, for the first time, Asia received less than half of Canadian bilateral food shipments. Despite fluctuations because of changing conditions, by 1989–90, Africa received 51.4 per cent of Canadian bilateral food aid. This mirrors a global trend by both bilateral and multilateral donors to assist Africa in response to growing needs there. Canadian food aid to Africa tends to be more widely disbursed than that to Asia. For example, 13 African countries got food aid in 1989–90, with the largest recipient, Mozambique, receiving only about half the amount of Bangladesh. Even during the height of the African famine in 1984–85, four non-African countries (Bangladesh, India, Jamaica, and Sri Lanka) received more bilateral food aid than Ethiopia. Nevertheless, Table 3 shows a shift in geographical priorities as more African countries become top recipients of Canadian food aid.

Table 3
Distribution of Canadian food aid, by region, 1975–76 to 1990–91

	Percentage share of total bilateral food aid		
Year	Asia	Africa	Americas
1975–76	85.1	13.0	1.8
1976–77	78.8	19.3	1.8
1977–78	66.3	18.9	9.2
1978–79	72.9	15.4	13.7
1979–80	75.6	17.4	8.3
1980–81	39.8	38.4	3.4
1981–82	42.0	42.8	15.0
1982–83	67.4	32.5	–
1983–84	59.0	26.7	14.0
1984–85	47.5	44.4	7.9
1985–86	51.5	37.8	10.2
1986–87	57.0	30.0	12.7
1987–88	44.3	47.8	9.1
1988–89	39.5	46.8	13.5
1989–90	36.1	51.4	12.0
1990–91	33.9	50.3	15.7

Sources: CIDA, Annual Report, various years.

Recent bilateral food aid allocations reveal two trends. First, in response to domestic demands that food aid be more "hunger responsive," more is being directed towards countries experiencing serious food shortages, especially where this has been exacerbated by domestic conflict. Thus, during the past seven years, increased amounts have gone to countries such as Ethiopia, Mozambique, and Sudan. In the mid-1980s, 80 per cent of Canada's food aid was going to the thirty or so major recipients of Canadian aid – the so-called core countries – but by 1989–90, fully 38 per cent of bilateral food aid was being sent to "non-core" countries.

Second, increased amounts of food aid are being earmarked for countries facing severe economic crises or that are undertaking structural adjustment, where food aid is extended as a means to increase the flow of resources to these countries. This factor explains inclusion of nations that have not regularly received Canadian food aid (Bolivia, Egypt, Ghana, Peru, and Zambia) or have not received it for some time (Morocco and Tunisia). In each case, Canada intends food aid to assist policy dialogue with the recipient government in the context of structural adjustment. In 1989–90, 23.5 per cent of Canada's bilateral food aid went to "middle-income" countries. Some, such as Jamaica, Peru,

Table 4
Major recipients of Canadian bilateral food aid (%), selected years, 1975–76 to 1990–91

1975–76		1979–80		1985–86		1990–91	
India	51.5	Bangladesh	39.95	Bangladesh	49.67	Bangladesh	45.7
Bangladesh	27.9	India	19.94	Jamaica	16.78	Mozambique	17.7
Pakistan	17.5	Sri Lanka	3.98	Pakistan	13.93	Ethiopia	16.8
Tanzania	5.8	Zambia	3.49	India	13.13	Jamaica	14.7
Sri Lanka	3.9	Tanzania	3.42	Ethiopia	12.45	Pakistan	13.9
Ghana	3.7	Zaïre	3.23	Sudan	11.95	Sudan	10.9
Mali	2.9	Portugal	3.0	Sri Lanka	7.80	Ghana	6.9
Niger	2.7	Jamaica	1.94	Ghana	5.05	Angola	5.9
Vietnam	2.5	Senegal	1.93	Mauritania	4.78	Peru	5.9
Haiti	0.9	Sudan	0.09	Niger	4.39	Rwanda	5.1
Percentage of total	98.6 %		83.7 %		85.7 %		81.7 %
Total no. of recipients	12		13		21		22

Sources: CIDA, *Annual Report*, various years.

and Tunisia, are not even classified as having food deficits by the United Nations. Thus Canada is allocating more food aid to assist stabilization, help in coping with broader economic crises, or as support for structural adjustment (Table 4).

Donor-Recipient Relations

Canadian officials have tended to see the food aid program as a responsive one, in which CIDA acts primarily in response to requests from recipient countries. As a result, CIDA has traditionally made little effort to influence use of food aid within the recipient country. As a middle-power donor, without the political baggage of a former colonial power, Canada has seen such aid more as a relationship and image-builder than as a source for coercive leverage. Officials were content if generous food aid, with minimal strings attached, helped to create a friendlier environment while providing support to a recipient's economy. Other Canadian federal departments, such as External Affairs and Agriculture Canada, with an interest in the foreign policy and commercial aspects of food aid, were reluctant to see sensitive issues raised that might disrupt the overall relationship with recipients. Even when CIDA officials admitted that food was not reaching the poorest people continued aid was often justified on the grounds that it helped maintain domestic political stability.[48]

As a result, little effort was made to develop administrative mechanisms for controlling use of food aid. The main "control" instrument has been the requirement that recipients establish a counterpart fund. Revenues generated from the sale of Canadian food aid would be placed in the fund, and Canadian and recipient officials would jointly agree on development projects to be supported out of these monies. In theory, at least, this mechanism would give Canada some control over the use of the monies arising from the sale of food aid and assurances that it was not simply freeing up funds for expenditures on other items such as military hardware. But in practice, Canadian officials took a "hands-off" approach, seeing counterpart funds primarily as a burdensome bookkeeping exercise that could upset donor-recipient relations. As a result, recipient governments could do pretty much what they wanted to with these funds, leaving Canadian officials unable to explain the ultimate impact of food transfers.[49]

This approach came under increased challenge in the early 1980s from two quarters. There was growing concern that, in order to maintain domestic support for the aid program, there be clearer demonstration of the effectiveness of aid disbursements. As CIDA President Catley-Carlson noted before the WFP's Committee on Food Aid Policies and Programmes in 1985, unless donors could prove that food aid was well managed and assisted development, they "will not be able to maintain public and parliamentary support for a substantial Canadian food aid programme."[50] However, CIDA's evaluations of its own programs and reviews of the academic literature suggested that the policy environment of the recipient country was the principal determinant of the effectiveness of food aid. Hence the rationale that transfers should be linked more closely with policy reforms within the recipient country, especially in agricultural policy.[51]

As CIDA sought to identify means to ensure that food aid promoted policy reform, severe limits to CIDA's capacity to exercise influence became clear. The level of food aid provided by Canada to any given recipient is usually too small to encourage recipients to attempt reforms. Moreover, linkage of food aid to political dialogue and structural adjustment assumed an analytical competence on macro-economic issues traditionally lacking in CIDA's project administration–oriented staff.

In order to compensate for these limitations, CIDA has pursued two strategies. First, as CIDA noted in Sharing Our Future (1987), "Food aid will be provided when the recipient country has, or is willing to adopt, a sound agricultural policy."[52] This strategy is essentially one of "positive conditionality," which one official defined as "being supportive of a government when it is taking a policy direction that we can support."[53] In this case, CIDA agrees to provide food aid to countries that it believes are already pursuing constructive economic and agricultural policies but that need additional financial support to maintain reform. Canadian food aid may not be directly linked to structural support but may encourage continuance of reform. According to a policy adopted by CIDA in the mid-1980s, CIDA is no longer required to establish a counterpart fund in such cases.

Second, in nations where CIDA does not have confidence in agricultural policies, it has indicated that "food aid will be provided to countries with which CIDA, alone or with other bilateral and multilateral donors, has the capacity to engage in a dialogue on agricultural policies and to ensure an adequate follow-up."[54] In order to compensate for its own limited influence in such situations, CIDA has advocated trilateral co-operation, among itself, other bilateral and multilateral donors, and the recipient government, in promoting policy dialogue. Thus CIDA has concentrated on relating food aid to policy reform in recipient countries where a consortium of donors or a consultative group is already in place. Linkage of food aid to agricultural policy reform there is but part of a much larger effort to negotiate structural adjustment with the recipient government. An example of this has been provision of Canadian food aid to Mali as part of the multi-donor Cereals Marketing Restructuring Project, which aims to end the monopoly held by the state cereals marketing board and to increase producers' prices for grains to stimulate production. This project is an element in a broader effort led by the international Monetary Fund (IMF), the World Bank, and the United States to make future assistance to Mali conditional on reform of public finances and enterprises and on greater emphasis on private-sector activities. Letting other donors, particularly the IMF and the World Bank, set policy while Canada supplies additional resources through food aid appears to be a trend endorsed by CIDA in President Marcel Massé's recent statement that "a lot of our actions in development in the future will have to be *planned from the centre,* which means, in my view, that the World Bank will have to take on a much greater influence as the planner for the multilateral and the bilateral agencies (e.g. CIDA)."[55]

In situations where encouragement of policy reform is a primary aim, CIDA has shown renewed interest, especially in Africa, in using counterpart funds to ensure that monies freed up by sale of food aid are directed to suitable agricultural projects. A joint management committee is usually created to decide about use of these funds for development. Counterpart funds may be used to help pool the resources of donors. For example, in Mali, money from the sale of Canadian and other food aid is deposited in a common counterpart fund managed by the WFP. Usage of these funds is thus negotiated by the donors as a collective group, rather than individually.

As part of its effort to stress policy reform, CIDA has advocated supplying food aid to selected recipients under multi-year agreements, instead of the usual single-year arrangement. The argument for the former is based on two assumptions. First, Canada must supply enough resources to encourage recipient governments to take policy reform seriously. Second, as a donor, Canada must ensure continuity in supplies to politically risky reforms. Thus far, CIDA has entered into multi-year agreements with Ghana, India, Mali, Peru, Senegal, and Sri Lanka, all in the context of discussions of broader structural adjustment.[56]

As linking food aid to policy reform has become a more central priority, CIDA has become more willing to terminate food aid when it feels that recipient governments have not taken sufficient action to reform domestic agriculture. In the mid-1980s, CIDA terminated food aid shipments to Tanzania because it had failed to reform agricultural policy as proposed by donors.[57] More recently, it stopped food aid to Sri Lanka because of its poor performance in structural adjustment.[58]

The Canadian Food Aid Basket

One of the most important decisions affecting the quality of Canadian food aid is selection of the food commodities to be sent. Because these commodities vary so much, so too may their impact on the recipient. Since the 1960s, more than 20 food products have been included in Canada's food aid basket at some time. Nevertheless, wheat and wheat flour have consistently accounted for the largest share from the beginning. During the 1950s and 1960s, they made up fully 90 per cent of the total, and since the early 1970s, about 75 per cent.

The traditional role of wheat reflects the fact that food aid began as a mechanism to deal with the large surpluses of Canadian grain that accumulated in the 1950s and 1960s. Nevertheless, there are good reasons why cereals have remained predominant. Compared with other food commodities, grain provides a high level of protein and calories at low cost. It is easily and relatively cheaply transported in large volumes and is generally widely acceptable to local tastes. Furthermore, it offers the only type of assistance for which donors have committed themselves to providing at least a minimum amount.

Despite these advantages, the 1970s witnessed diversification of the aid basket, as more expensive, processed foods made their way into the program. Some products such as canned beef and powdered eggs entered as "one-shot" efforts. Others, such as skim milk powder and canola, have played a growing role primarily because of continuing lobbying by domestic agricultural and food processing interests, such as the Canadian Dairy Commission and the Canadian Millers Association.

In the case of skim milk powder, the program has been an important outlet for surplus stocks, in some years accounting for over 25 per cent of exports. Canola oil is used deliberately to create a market for this new Canadian product. Moreover, early shipments of unprocessed canola seed have been replaced by processed oil, giving direct support to the canola processing industry, in keeping with guidelines established in 1978 that emphasize "commodities with a value-added content."[59]

Inclusion of a growing range of products, many in response to domestic surpluses, has raised concerns regarding selection of Canadian food aid. High-value, processed commodities tend to be directed to middle and higher-income developing countries that can absorb them. Because of their higher price, such products provide less calories and protein per dollar and are generally more acceptable to urban populations than to the rural poor. CIDA has increasingly employed developmental criteria in selection of food commodities. Recent policy statements,[60] while not mentioning commercial policy objectives, have set three fundamental criteria: need, as determined by acceptability for local diets and adequate nutritional balance; program effectiveness – adequate transportation and distribution facilities for the commodity; and cost-effectiveness – maximum nutritional impact in relation to financial resources, as measured in part by the ratio of proteins and calories to dollar spent. See Table 5.[61]

Cereals and pulses provide the most protein and nutritional value per dollar, and fish the least. Non-cereals are more expensive and create additional problems. Skim milk powder demands careful control of distribution and monitoring systems and in many areas cannot be consumed because of lactose intolerance. In many countries, fish and skim milk powder are considered luxury items; distribution of them to poorer populations increases administrative overhead expenses for the recipient government.

CIDA has had problems in getting the best value for the dollar out of its procurement. For example, according to Treasury Board guidelines, food aid products must be purchased at world prices. But the auditor general found that the Canadian Dairy Commission had in fact charged CIDA $4.9 million over world prices for skim milk powder between 1979 and 1982. He also discovered that CIDA was paying $150 per tonne for fortifying milk powder with vitamins, when the normal commercial price was $20 per tonne, representing an overpayment of $3.6 million between 1980 and 1984.[62] Such pricing policies thus

Table 5
Commodity composition of Canadian food aid ($million), 1972–73 to 1990–91

Fiscal year	Wheat	Wheat flour	Dried skim milk	Fish	Oil	Other
1972–73	57.0	10.3	8.2	1.9	2.4	3.0
1973–74	82.8	9.1	5.7	0.7	9.3	5.1
1974–75	97.2	12.1	12.9	0.6	14.9	11.5
1975–76	150.5	24.8	10.5	3.2	24.4	8.8
1976–77	114.0	49.7	14.0	1.0	31.9	2.8
1977–78	93.0	43.6	18.6	2.7	36.6	3.9
1978–79	84.0	55.7	13.1	7.5	15.0	5.9
1979–80	96.7	34.0	8.7	6.0	25.6	4.1
1980–81	97.6	31.6	10.1	5.8	10.3	13.5
1981–82	122.5	35.5	12.7	17.3	14.0	6.7
1982–83	157.6	38.6	16.6	9.6	24.1	7.1
1983–84	171.8	49.1	19.1	20.8	33.2	38.2
1984–85	156.9	51.1	17.4	30.2	33.7	21.8
1985–86	127.9	57.2	18.3	29.3	35.0	14.6
1986–87	162.6	46.8	20.0	27.4	62.0	10.5
1987–88	199.5	48.1	11.3	33.2	33.0	26.2
1988–89	182.5	45.5	13.1	37.0	35.9	26.6
1989–90	162.8	33.3	17.9	29.2	21.3	22.4
1990–91	162.5	32.1	18.2	30.2	19.0	24.6

Source: CIDA, Food Aid Centre.

transfered some $8.5 million of the Canadian food aid budget to Canadian producers and processors without increasing the volume of food aid.

Despite adoption of developmentally oriented criteria, pressures from domestic lobby groups and other departments continue to affect the make-up of the Canadian commodity basket. The new importance of wheat flour may be attributed partly to a shift of focus to Africa, where milling facilities are sometimes lacking, but the Canadian Millers Association has been aggressive in lobbying for an increase in flour aid, particularly in light of lost export markets. In 1980–81, Canada exported 694,000 tonnes of wheat flour, nearly half of this to Cuba. But in the mid-1980s Canada lost its market position in Cuba and Canadian flour exports sank to a low of 164,000 tonnes in 1989–90. To counter this trend, CIDA sustained fairly high levels of flour aid throughout the 1980s, accounting in some years for more than half of Canada's flour exports.

The clearest example of the impact of domestic pressures is the decision by the cabinet in 1983 requiring that the food aid basket be composed of at least 25 per cent non-cereal commodities and subsequent expansion of fish aid in the 1980s. This decision was rooted in an escalating interdepartmental dispute over the nature of the commodity basket in the early 1980s, when CIDA was subjected to increased pressures to include larger amounts of fish in the program.

From CIDA's standpoint, fish aid contradicted its selection criteria. Fish is generally much more costly than other traditional Canadian food aid products in relation to the nutrient and protein value provided. In some countries, it is regarded as a luxury item and may not be a priority or may not be acceptable, particularly in landlocked countries where fish is not a regular part of the local diet. In addition, cans of fish are more difficult and costly to transport and distribute than bulk shipments of grain.[63]

Nevertheless, because of persistent interdepartmental pressures, the issue was eventually referred to cabinet, which decided that at least 25 per cent of the food aid budget should be spent on non-cereal products. Although non-cereals had already been at or above 25 per cent for some time, the decision opened the door to rapid expansion of the fish component of the program. Fish aid increased from $5.8 million (3.25 per cent of the budget) in 1980–81 to $37.0 million (or 8.6 per cent) in 1988–89, from which peak level it dropped to $30 million in 1990–91.[64]

As Table 6 shows, diversification of food aid into non-cereals has enabled CIDA to balance food aid purchases regionally by using products from non–wheat-growing regions of Canada. With expansion of skim milk powder in the 1970s and fish aid in the 1980s, every province now supplies some food aid. Without these products, Quebec, British Columbia, and the Maritimes would play no role. Thus concerns about regional balance appear to be more important than has generally been acknowledged.

Recent economic studies have shown that the Canadian commodity basket is generally less influenced today by surplus availabilities.[65] Nevertheless, rapid expansion of fish aid demonstrates that domestic interest groups, working in conjunction with other government departments, especially for a commodity such as fish that has strong regional political significance, can still expand the role of a particular commodity, despite CIDA's developmental concerns. However, CIDA officials believe that developmental criteria for commodity selection have assisted them in defending particular country-level decisions. They point to suspension of the $5-million fish aid program to Zaïre, despite the strong pro-fish lobby, because of concerns that the aid was benefiting primarily urban elites and that the government had not shown serious commitment to agricultural development.[66]

Table 6
Food aid purchases by province (in tonnes), 1986–87

Province	Wheat	Flour	Vegetable oil	Skim milk powder	Fish	Pulses	Maize
British Columbia	–	2,395	–	–	–	435	–
Alberta	191,385	34,806	64,646	1,501	–	2,219	–
Saskatchewan	512,958	21,685	9,011	1,876	–	1,188	–
Manitoba	156,587	7,010	37,847	1,877	–	3,989	–
Ontario	120,588	35,106	8,637	1,876	–	3,438	11,761
Quebec	–	63,914	1,224	11,259	860	–	–
New Brunswick	–	–	–	188	4,915	–	–
Prince Edward Island	–	–	–	–	240	–	–
Nova Scotia	–	5,288	–	188	1,788	–	–
Newfoundland	–	–	–	–	1,477	–	–

Source: CIDA: *Sharing Our Future: Canada's International Development Assistance* (Hull: Supply and Services 1987), 56.

As a partial solution to such problems, it has frequently been suggested that CIDA "untie" more of its food aid budget to allows purchase of food commodities in one Third World country for shipment to another. Such triangular exchanges would not only expand the range of commodities provided by Canada but would enable speedier delivery of more appropriate products, particularly in emergencies. The supplying country would expand its agricultural exports, thus multiplying the impact of Canadian aid. Triangular food aid has been strongly promoted by the secretariat of the WFP, recipient countries, and many NGOs as encouraging development-oriented food aid. In 1980, Canada's Parliamentary Task Force on North-South Relations suggested that "every effort be made to supply food-deficit developing countries with food aid purchased by Canada from neighbouring food surplus developing countries."[67] Nevertheless, the Treasury Board issued directions in 1984 that established CIDA's untying authority at only 5 per cent, and then only "under emergency and other special circumstances."[68] The President's Committee of CIDA went even further in 1985 by allowing untying only in emergencies where appropriate foods were not available for speedy transportation, as a "one-time"–only situation and not part of an ongoing arrangement, and only as part of a first phase, limited response to an emergency. Even then, "it may be appropriate to seek the approval of the Minister for specific untying proposals."[69] Given Treasury Board restrictions and the desire of CIDA officials to "maintain interdepartmental support for an untying provision," a CIDA manual suggests that untying "will be used in a limited and careful manner."[70]

The issue of untying food aid was again raised by the Winegard Committee. It proposed that CIDA ease restrictions in cases where food aid can be purchased in neighbouring, developing countries that have exportable surpluses.[71] In response, the government stated that it would not modify its policy of untying only 5 per cent of Canadian food aid.[72] CIDA has not made use of even this limited authority. According to one study, triangular exchanges and third-country purchases made up only 1.8 per cent of Canadian food aid purchases between 1983 and 1988, in comparison with a global average of 7 per cent. For the European Community, such exchanges accounted for 11.3 per cent of its food aid purchases.[73] As a result, CIDA's involvement in triangular exchanges, along with that of the United States (0.2 per cent), lags far behind that of most other donors.

CONCLUSIONS

During the past decade and a half, the Canadian food aid program has gone through restructuring and consolidation. Canadian food aid has become much more internationalist in character, as it responds to the resolutions issued by the World Food Conference and the Committee on Food Aid Policies and Programme. Multi-year programming, greater emphasis on multilateral channels, and policy statements emphasizing integration of food aid transfers into the food strategies and development plans of recipient countries bring Canadian policies and programs in this field much more closely in line with the emerging concepts and norms of a developmental food aid regime.[74] However, tensions between various objectives underlying the program still exist. Tying requirements have been tightened rather than relaxed. Greater use of fish and other processed items suggests that disposal of surpluses can still override developmental considerations. Despite rhetorical commitment to triangular food aid, Canadian practice lags far behind that of most other donors.

In spite of the many problems raised by food aid, there has generally been strong domestic support. This stems in part from that strand of domestic political culture that Ronald Manzer calls "ethical liberalism" and whose application to foreign policy Cranford Pratt labels "humane internationalism."[75] Food aid can, as no other form of development assistance is able to, fulfil that basic humanitarian instinct of ethical liberalism that seeks to assist in the "alleviation of hardships due to circumstances beyond one's control."[76] Nevertheless, evolution of Canada's strategy during the past decade has been influenced more heavily by policy paradigms rooted in the other strand of Canadian public philosophy – economic liberalism. While distributive objectives still play an important role, broader objectives – such as balance-of-payments relief, generation of local revenues, and stabilization of domestic supplies and prices – have increasingly shaped food aid.[77] To this extent, the program mirrors recent ideological shifts in Canadian aid more generally and in the international donor community at large.[78] Linking of food aid to structural adjustment appears generally more acceptable, especially to finance officials, than direct economic support. To such officials, particularly those who fear the potential disincentive effects of food aid, linking of such assistance to structural adjustment and to policy dialogue legitimizes large shipments of "stabilization" food aid. However, attention is withdrawn from earlier and still legitimate concerns about whether food aid actually reaches the poorest people.

Following the crisis of confidence that overtook the program in the 1970s, Canadian officials succeeded in making food aid a more respectable part of the development assistance program again. But political support will be maintained only if they can demonstrate that the benefits of "developmental" food aid go not just to resource-hungry *governments*. Unless it can be demonstrated clearly that benefits reach the neediest *people*, the many improvements made in administration of food aid will be overshadowed by renewed cynicism concerning the "real" motives of food aid.

NOTES

1 See, for example, the comments of a CIDA official that "There are only a few circumstances in the world where food aid makes good sense," in Canada, Parliament, House of Commons, *Minutes of Proceedings and Evidence of the Special Committee on North-South Relations*, 1st sess., 32nd Parl., Issue No. 11 (2 October 1980), 11:47.

2 House of Commons, Standing Committee on External Affairs and International Trade, *For Whose Benefit? Report of the Standing Committee on External Affairs and International Trade on Canada's Official Development Assistance Policies and Programs* (Winegard Report) (Ottawa: Supply and Services, May 1987).

3 For a fuller discussion of the creation of FACE and its impact on bilateral programming, see Mark Charlton, "The Management of Canada's Bilateral Food Aid: An Organizational Perspective," *Canadian Journal of Development Studies* 7 no. 1 (1986), 7–19.

4 The CFA was originally the WFP's Governing Council. Following the World Food Conference in 1974, the title of the committee was changed and its mandate expanded to include examination of the general principles underlying food aid policy. Canada has been a member since its founding.

5 The objectives pursued in the Canadian food aid program are discussed in Mark Charlton, *The Making of Canadian Food Aid Policy* (Montreal: McGill-Queen's University Press 1992).

6 Cf. Charlton, "Management."

7 CIDA–Treasury Board, "Evaluation of the Canadian Food Aid Programme," May 1977, 15.

8 Ibid., 16.

9 Interdepartmental Working Group on Food Aid Policy, "Food Aid Policy Recommendations," (mimeo Ottawa, 26 June 1978), 24.

10 Ibid.

11 Some CIDA officials interviewed claimed that humanitarian objectives were placed first largely in response to public perceptions of food aid, while broader macro-economic developmental objectives continued to receive priority from desk officers in programming decisions. Cf. Charlton, *Making*, chap. 2.

12 House of Commons, Parliamentary Task Force on North-South Relations, *Report to the House of Commons on the Relations between Developed and Developing Countries* (Ottawa: Supply and Services 1980), 49.

13 CIDA, Program Evaluation Division, Policy Branch, "Summary Report on the Evaluation of Canada's Food Aid Program," mimeo (Hull, n.d.), 17.

14 Ibid., 17.

15 Ibid.

16 CIDA, "Strategic Plan for Food Aid," mimeo (Hull, 1984), 2.

17 CIDA, *Sharing Our Future: Canada's International Development Assistance* (Hull: Supply and Services 1987), 54. The distinction between distributive and stabilization objectives is analysed in Charlton, *Making*, chap. 7.

18 World Food Programme (WFP), *Food Aid: Flows – Directions – Uses* (Rome: WFP, May 1989), 15.

19 Winegard Report, 58.

20 Canada, *Canadian International Development Assistance: To Benefit a Better World, Response of the Government of Canada to the Report of the Standing Committee on External Affairs and International Trade* (Ottawa: Supply and Services 1987), 70.

21 *Globe and Mail*, 28 April 1989, A13, and 29 April 1989, A8.

22 Interdepartmental Working Group, "Food Aid Policy Recommendations," 9.

23 CIDA, Task Force on Food Aid and Renewable Resources Policies for CIDA, *Report to the President's Committee* (Hull, April 1985), app. IV, 30.

24 CIDA, *Sharing Our Future*, 54.

25 In contrast to the United States, Canada provides bilateral food aid almost entirely in grant form, rather than as loans. The only exception has been for recent food aid shipments to Jamaica.

26 Emergency food aid as a share of the WFP's total allocations has increased from 9.3 per cent for 1963–72 to 24.3 per cent for 1970–88. WFP/CFA: 27/P/7, 3.

27 There are several reasons why the Canadian NGO program has remained so small. Canadian NGOs generally have much smaller absorptive capacity than their much larger American and international counterparts. More important, they have preferred to keep more of an arm's-length relationship with CIDA for fear of generating the negative image of some large American agencies which are frequently seen as essentially an arm of the US government. Further, many fear that too much focus on relief may undermine their longer-term developmental thrust.

28 For example, both China and Cuba have been recent recipients of Canadian multilateral food aid. In fact, in 1986–87, China's $75.44 million made it the largest single recipient of Canadian food aid, surpassing even Bangladesh, which received $61.48 million.

29 In 1983–84, CIDA was able to place fish aid with only three bilateral recipients, whereas the WFP shipped Canadian fish products to 22 countries.

30 According to one CIDA estimate, Canadian bilateral food aid required 16–18 person-years to plan and implement, whereas Canadian multilateral food air required only 4 person-years. In contrast, the WFP devoted about 150 person-years to administration of Canada's contribution. CIDA, "Notes on Project and Programme Food Aid," mimeo, n.d., 3.

31 CIDA–Treasury Board, "Evaluation," 15.

32 See, for example, the exchange in House of Commons, *Minutes of the Special Committee on North-South Relations* (2 October 1980), 38–39.

33 Parliamentary Task Force, *Report to the House of Commons*, 50.

34 CIDA, "Notes on Project."

35 For a detailed discussion of FAO-WFP relations, see Mark Charlton, "Innovation and Inter-organizational Politics: The Case of the World Food Programme," *International Journal* 47 no. 3 (summer 1992), 630–65. The WFP is required by its constitution to engage only in project aid. Recently, the WFP's secretariat has sought ways to increase its absorptive capacity by "monetizing," or selling some of its food aid. Canada has joined other donors, such as the United States, in resisting such a move, seeing it as a means for the WFP to become involved in program food aid. Canadian officials argue that the WFP should stick with what it is most efficient at – project food aid.

36 CIDA, "Strategic Plan."

37 Winegard Report, 58.

38 Author's interview, Multilateral Branch, CIDA, June 1979.

39 CIDA, Food Aid Centre, *1990/91 Food Aid Program Annual Report* (Hull, 30 July 1991).

40 Even decentralization such as that proposed in the Winegard Report would not improve the situation in regard to emergency food aid, since plans such are directed primarily towards CIDA's core recipients, which generally do not get large amounts of emergency food aid.

41 CIDA, "Strategic Plan."

42 Author's interview, Oxfam Canada, Ottawa, February 1990.

43 House of Commons, *Minutes of Proceedings and Evidence of the Standing Committee on External Affairs and International Trade*, 2nd sess., 33rd Parl., Issue no. 73 (28 April 1988), 73:15.

44 For more discussion of the human rights dimensions of supplying food aid to Ethiopia, see Jason Clay, "Ethiopian Famine and the Relief Agencies," in Bruce Nichols and Gil Loescher, *The Moral Nation: Humanitarian and U.S. Foreign Policy Today* (Notre Dame, Ill.: University of Notre Dame Press 1989).

45 For a critique of the WFP's role in emergency feeding, see Rachel Garst and Tom Barry, *Feeding the Crisis: U.S. Food Aid and Farm Policy in Central America* (Lincoln: University of Nebraska Press 1990), chap. 5.

46 House of Commons, *Minutes of the Standing Committee on External Affairs and International Trade* (28 April 1988), 73:19.

47 For a useful study of Canadian aid to Bangladesh which gives significant attention to the role of food aid, see Roger Ehrhardt, *Canadian Development Assistance to Bangladesh* (Ottawa: North-South Institute 1983).

48 CIDA, "Food Aid and Food Policies in Bangladesh," mimeo (Hull, 1980).

49 House of Commons, *Minutes of the Special Committee on North-South Relations* (2 October 1980), 11:39.

50 "Notes for Remarks by Margaret Catley-Carlson to the Committee on Food Aid Policies and Programme, 20th Session of the WFP, Rome, October 1985."

51 Cf. CIDA, "Summary Report."

52 CIDA, *Sharing Our Future*, 56.

53 Author's interview with CIDA official.

54 CIDA, *Sharing Our Future*, 56.

55 Cited in Inter-Church Fund for International Development and Canadian Council of Churches' Committee on International Affairs, *Diminishing Our Future: CIDA Four Years after Winegard* (October 1991), 18.

56 The Treasury Board has approved a multi-year agreement for Egypt as well, but for administrative reasons Canadian food aid is currently being provided under single-year agreements.

57 CIDA, "Summary Report," 35.

58 CIDA officials note that because of nutritional needs they would have continued shipments of humanitarian food aid but that they were unable

to identify channels able to target food aid reliably to specific groups. Author's interview with CIDA officials.

59 Interdepartmental Working Group, "Food Aid Policy Recommendations," 24.

60 See, in particular, CIDA, "Food Aid: A Programming Manual," mimeo (Hull, March 1986), D10-D11.

61 Ibid.

62 Parliament, *Report of the Auditor General to the House of Commons, 1984* (Ottawa: Supply and Services 1984), 9–15.

63 Author's interview, Multilateral Branch, CIDA, May 1990.

64 The formal cabinet requirement of 25 per cent non-cereals was only for three years. Nevertheless, CIDA planners know that, if the percentage of non-cereals were to drop significantly, the composition of the food aid basket would once again become a cabinet issue. Thus the requirement still functions as an informal rule of thumb. Ibid.

65 S. Shapouri and M. Missiaen, *Food Aid: Motivation and Criteria*, Economic Research Service, U.S. Department of Agriculture, Foreign Agricultural Economic Report No. 240.

66 Author's interview, Multilateral Branch, CIDA, May 1990. Until suspension of the program, Zaïre was the largest bilateral recipient of Canadian fish aid.

67 Parliamentary Task Force, *Report*, 49.

68 Treasury Board, "Terms and Conditions of Country-to-Country Food Aid" TB 793024, 29 March 1984, 2. In 1975, Ottawa committed itself to untying up to 20 per cent of the food aid budget for purchases in developing countries in response to emergencies. However, this untying authority apparently was never formally authorized by the Treasury Board. Cf. CIDA, *Strategy for International Development Cooperation 1975–1980* (Ottawa: CIDA 1975).

69 CIDA, Food Aid Centre, "Food Aid: A Programming Manual," mimeo (Hull, March 1986), B:10.

70 Ibid.

71 Winegard Report, 39.

72 Cf. Canada, *To Benefit a Better World*, 58.

73 Edward Clay and Charlotte Benson, "Aid for Food: Acquisition of Commodities in Developing Countries for Food Aid in the 1980s," *Food Policy* 15 no. 1 (February 1990), 37.

74 On the concept of a developmental food aid regime, see Raymond F. Hopkins, "The Evolution of Food Aid: Toward a Development-First Regime," in J. Price Gittinger et al., eds., *Food Policy* (Baltimore: Johns Hopkins University Press 1978).

75 Ronald Manzer, *Public Policies and Political Development in Canada* (Toronto: University of Toronto Press 1985). See also Cranford Pratt, "Canada: An Eroding and Limited Internationalism," in Cranford Pratt, ed.,

Internationalism under Strain: The North-South Policies of Canada, The Netherlands, Norway, and Sweden (Toronto: University of Toronto Press 1989).

76 Pratt, "Canada," 49.

77 On the impact of these two strands of Canadian political culture on food aid, borrowing from the insights of Pratt and Manzer, see Charlton, *Making*, chap. 6.

78 Cf. Robert Clarke, "Overseas Development Assistance: The Neo-Conservative Challenge," in Maureen Appel Molot and Fen Osler Hampson, eds., *Canada among Nations, 1989: The Challenge of Change* (Ottawa: Carleton University Press 1990).

4 Paying the Piper: CIDA and Canadian NGOs

TIM BRODHEAD AND CRANFORD PRATT

This chapter provides an overview of the role that Canadian non-governmental organizations (NGOs) have played within Canada's official development assistance (ODA) program and of the evolving relationship between the NGOs and the Canadian International Development Agency (CIDA). After a period from the late 1960s to the mid-1980s, during which CIDA and the NGOs seemed to draw closer together, the pattern has become far more complex. A number of factors have led CIDA to "use" NGOs for a far wider range of responsibilities while also developing major new programs within which it, rather than the NGOs, identifies projects to be supported. As well, CIDA has become more selective about the NGOs that it supports and more cautious towards NGOs' aspirations to greater policy influence. At the same time, NGOs' financial dependence on government has been increasing while some within the NGO community have become more outspoken on policy issues generally. All of this was occurring at a time when CIDA faced severe cuts to its expected revenues, some NGOs experienced declining public support, and many NGOs questioned long-accepted priorities in their operations. The conclusion seems unavoidable: CIDA-NGO relations in the next few years will be marked by uncertainty and redefinition, CIDA will increasingly assert closer policy control over the NGOs that it assists, and a common NGO approach to CIDA and to the government may become impossible to sustain.

SETTING THE STAGE: CANADIAN NGOS
TO THE MID-1980S

In Canada, as in every democratic society, public responsiveness towards the needs and aspirations of disadvantaged sectors of society has long generated a host of citizen organizations concerned to meet these needs and aspirations and to lobby the government in their regard. These voluntary organizations have always included some whose concerns extended beyond Canadian borders. This international dimension of Canadian humanitarianism became much more substantial after the Second World War. In the years after 1945, and more especially from the early 1960s, there was a major upsurge of Canadian NGOs that concentrated their work primarily in Third World countries. Some were involved in emergency relief, some in providing charitable assistance; more and more, however, were engaged in assisting development.[1] A major study of Canadian NGOs working in the Third World estimated that their number had grown from 25 in 1960 to some 220 by 1987.[2] Each year, hundreds of thousands of Canadians contributed to these organizations. By 1984–85, their total annual contributions were an estimated $280 million. In addition, over 30,000 volunteers worked for them and some 500 Canadians were overseas on development assignments under their aegis.[3] All of this activity represented and gave active voice to a humane internationalist strand of the Canadian political culture that was particularly robust from 1960 to the mid-1980s.

The term "non-governmental" covers many types of organizations. For our purposes, it is helpful to categorize them by their mode of operation. This produced four subsets of NGOs in Canada.

Fund-raising branches of international agencies. Some of the largest NGOs in Canada are or originally were branches of international agencies. Thus, for example, Oxfam (Canada) and CARE Canada were initially fund-raising branches, raising monies that were then disbursed by their parent agencies. Each of them is now an autonomous Canadian agency, Oxfam being fully so while CARE is in what can fairly be described as a federal relationship with the head office and with other CARE national offices. Other major NGOs in Canada continue to act very substantially as fund raisers for international agencies, most of which are based in the United States. These include World Vision Canada and Foster Parents Plan, the largest fund raisers among the NGOs, with World Vision raising $69.6 million from the Canadian public in 1992.

Canadian development and humanitarian fund-raising agencies. Many of these bodies exist entirely on their own without any institutional links with either an international agency or with another, larger Canadian institution. They were launched by groups of private citizens to meet specific needs and to provide opportunities for Canadians to contribute to development in quite specific ways. This substantial group includes Canadian Organization for Development through Education (CODE), Fondation Léger, Inter-Pares, Match International, Tools for Peace, and Unitarian Service Committee Canada (USC Canada). This sub-category of NGOs also includes agencies and operations that are directly part of other, larger Canadian organizations with activities far wider than this development work and with international links that have generated an interest in development. Thus there are, for example, major church development agencies such as the Canadian Catholic Organization for Development and Peace, the Christian Reformed World Relief Committee of Canada, and the Primate's Fund for World Development. As well, the YMCA/YWCA and a growing number of trade unions and professional associations have overseas development programs.

Non-profit development agencies. These are agencies that raise very little money from the Canadian public, often have no particular Canadian base or constituency, and instead rely on CIDA funding for most of their finances. Such organizations (also called public-service contractors) have sometimes started as popularly based but have gradually become dependent primarily on CIDA grants. This reflected CIDA's recognition of the importance of the development needs that they sought to meet, as in their sending of Canadian cooperants to work in Third World countries. CIDA therefore began to extend very substantial grants to these organizations. The scale of their operations increased greatly, and they became heavily reliant on government funding. This, for example, was the path followed by the Canadian University Service Overseas (CUSO) and World University Service of Canada (WUSC).[4] WUSC and CUSO still have their constituencies on Canadian campuses, engaged in development education work, and have broadly based governing councils. Nevertheless, their dependence on CIDA has become very great. In 1991, each of these agencies received a total of just over $25 million from its various government sources of funding.[5] Public-service contractors continue to be created as individual Canadians close to government respond to clear indications from government that it would support, or at least wished to see created, an NGO to meet needs that it had perceived. The South

African Education Trust Fund and the Mandela Fund are recent examples.[6]

Development education organizations. These agencies concentrate on public education and on awareness-heightening and occasional lobbying in Canada. Only rarely are they involved directly in projects in the Third World. They include several organizations that are national in their reach, such as the Latin American Working Group and Ten Days for World Development, both of which are coalitions of Canadian churches. Most development education agencies, however, are community-based, the product of local initiatives and each limited to a specific locale. Such education centres exist in many of the larger Canadian cities.

The broad categories of overseas programs engaged in by the first three of these four categories of NGOs are well known. They include emergency work among peoples devastated by drought or uprooted by civil strife; personal charitable activities such as child-sponsorship schemes; welfare projects that bring specific benefits such as clean water or rural dispensaries to Third World communities; development projects and programs that seek to improve productive capabilities by providing such services as irrigation and training; and support for Third World NGOs that engage in development work. Initially, this support frequently involved sending of volunteers or cooperants for extended periods. Indeed, this was the primary activity of CUSO and a major part also of much church development work. More recently, as Third World nations are more and more producing their own educated and skilled people, the number of cooperants has diminished[7] and Third World recipients hope to secure more specialized skills through them.

Canadian NGOs have organized themselves in various, quite different ways as they pursue their objectives. A few operate through their own field offices or those of international agencies to which they are linked directly. These agencies run their overseas operations without involving any mediating Third World organization. In emergency relief operations, ability to mount major projects quickly and efficiently and knowledge of local needs, capabilities, and politics are often very great assets.

Almost all other NGO projects, in contrast, entail financial and/or personnel assistance to Third World organizations. Some of the larger NGOs such as CUSO and Oxfam (Canada) have overseas offices, with obvious advantages for selection and monitoring of projects. Most, however, have to rely on recurrent but infrequent visits from representatives of their Canadian headquarters. Numbers of them, such as the church development agencies and the YMCA and YWCA, have close links with partner institutions in the Third World and with global structures such as the World Council of Churches. In these cases, much of their assistance either is channelled through these institutions or goes to projects recommended by them.

NGOs that are part of or related to international organizations, such as UNICEF Canada and the Aga Khan Foundation Canada, depend heavily on these bodies in identifying appropriate projects. A few, such as World Vision, still transfer funds to their international centres and leave project selection and implementation entirely to them. A 1985 CIDA survey indicated that 54 per cent of the NGO projects surveyed had originated in a direct or indirect request from indigenous NGOs, 24 per cent from an international parent or affiliate of the Canadian agency, 8 per cent from another Canadian agency, and 8 per cent from the overseas staff of the funding agency.[8]

The popular perception that NGO assistance is more likely than official aid to reach and to help the poorest peoples is not without foundation. The motivation for their assistance is primarily humanitarian and is largely unsullied by geopolitical or economic ambitions. Selection of projects and programs is guided by this motivation, and institutional linkages reinforce it. Yet the NGO rhetoric of "people to people" and "reaching the grass roots" rests on links that are often thin, indirect, and short-lived. As shall be shown, in recent years CIDA has become less persuaded by such rhetoric and is now actively reassessing its relationship with Canadian NGOs. As well, the NGO community itself is redefining its role.

SETTING THE STAGE: CIDA-NGO
RELATIONS TO THE MID-1980S

Although the motives underlying Ottawa's development assistance were mixed, they were in part an expression of the humane internationalist component of Canadian values. Not surprising, therefore, CIDA created in 1968 an NGO division, which channelled CIDA funds to NGO projects that it felt merited support. From the beginning, CIDA matched funding provided by the NGO, usually on a 3:1 ratio, but sometimes at more advantageous ratios.[19] No doubt, there was some tailoring of project proposals to what NGOs felt would be of interest to CIDA. Nevertheless, projects were proposed to the division by the NGOs and, if funded by CIDA, were then administered by the NGOs. The work of CIDA's NGO division was therefore appropriately labelled the responsive program.

The NGO division quickly grew in importance. The alliance of CIDA and the NGOs was widely seen to assist the Canadian aid effort. CIDA accepted that the NGOs had relationships with Third World institutions and communities that were more intimate and closer to the grass roots than could ever be achieved by an official aid agency. NGOs could therefore produce projects that would reflect felt community needs and would typically reach poor communities and help to meet their needs. It was also recognized that the cost of some types of development assistance, particularly of recruiting and sending volunteers overseas, was much less when undertaken by NGOs than when done directly by government or by "for profit" firms. Commercial and diplomatic advantages were anticipated from expanding links between Canadians and Third World peoples resulting from greater NGO activities. Domestic political advantages were also expected to flow from this developing relationship between CIDA and a rapidly expanding network of Canadian NGOs.

For these same reasons, as well as in search of skills that could be enlisted for development work overseas, CIDA soon began to extend grants to Canadian non-governmental institutions (NGIs), especially cooperatives and universities and community colleges, for projects that would involve them in such endeavious. In 1981, CIDA created the Institutional Cooperation and Development Services (ICDS) to administer these grants.

The budgets of the NGO and the ICDS divisions, quickly became substantial. Their disbursements to Canadian organizations increased more than five-fold from 1976–77 to 1985–86, rising from $37.6 million to $133.8 million.[10] In 1989–90, this total had risen further to $220.1 million, with a further $20.3 million going to international NGOs.[11] Although private giving to the NGOs rose steadily during these years, it did not keep pace with the growth in government support. The proportion of NGO revenues that came from CIDA therefore rose steadily; for the years 1987–89, it was estimated to be 40 per cent.[12] This proportion varied markedly from one NGO to another. In 1991, 16 of the 18 agencies whose executive directors then belonged to the International Development Executives Association reported that 67 per cent of their total revenues came from government sources.[13] Canadian development education agencies were also major recipients of CIDA funding. Indeed, they were more dependent on CIDA on average than were humanitarian and development agencies.[14] The non-profit development agencies, the so-called public-sector contractors, of course continued to depend almost entirely on government funding.

Despite increasing financial reliance on CIDA, some Canadian NGOs have engaged in lobbying to influence policies relevant to international development and Third World issues. The strength of such activity has reflected the depth of public interest in particular questions. The Nigeria/Biafra war in the late 1960s, for example, mobilized the energies of a great many people, as did the debate over a new international economic order in the late 1970s and the struggles against oppression in southern Africa and Central America in the 1980s. NGOs that were vocal critics of government – Oxfam, for example, or CUSO – did not find their CIDA grants threatened.

The organizations most actively engaged in such advocacy tended to be those involved primarily in development education and those with close links to partner organizations in the southern hemisphere. In contrast, "branch" NGOs and public-service contractors were constrained by their greater sensitivity to the need to raise funds from government or the public. Umbrella organizations such as the Canadian Council for International Cooperation (CCIC) and l'Association québécoise des Organismes de coopération internationale (AQOCI) were also mandated to articulate members' interests and policy positions, and a network of church-supported bodies (including Ten Days for World Development, the Inter-Church Committee for Human Rights in Latin America, and the Taskforce on Churches and Corporate Responsibility) emerged to take on education and advocacy roles.

The majority of Canadian NGOs are members of the CCIC, which was formed in 1968 as a result of the Centennial International Development Year program. From the beginning, the CCIC was financed substantially by CIDA, which valued the existence of a single body of NGOs to which it could relate. Building a constituency in Canada of those favouring Canadian development assistance was an early objective. In 1970, the CCIC, with CIDA's support, launched the Development Education Animateur Program (DEAP), which was the incubator of much of the regionalized development education work that grew up across the country.

Although the CCIC undertook advocacy from its first days, it was constrained by the diversity of its membership; some organizations withdrew because of disagreements over particular policy positions, while others, such as UNICEF and the Red Cross, either refused to join or left quickly, because they did not wish to take positions on any issue of public policy. When, in the 1970s, the CCIC pronounced on subjects that were "domestic," such as the Berger commission of inquiry into the Mackenzie Valley pipeline, the tolerance of some member agencies was stretched almost to breaking point. Rarely was there sufficient consensus to enable the CCIC to express forcefully an NGO viewpoint on any controversial issue without risking the disaffection of some of its members. Its comparative acquiescence on public policy issues was the result far more of this absence of consensus than of any real or anticipated pressure from CIDA. The NGO community tended to regard all policy discussion as a distraction from the practical task of meeting human needs and to see any analysis as narrowly ideological. Laws governing charitable bodies in Canada, like those in Britain, also restrict "political" activity, although in recent years this has been interpreted to permit limited, non-partisan work in support of an organization's charitable purposes.

Underlying and perhaps causing the lack of consensus on aid policy have been significant ideological differences among the NGOs. Most NGOs fall into one of three broad types of internationalism – mainstream liberal, reform, and solidarist, or radical. The first has always been by far the most prevalent. Such NGOs are a manifestation internationally of the humanitarian values of the dominant Canadian political culture.[15] These values enjoin caring towards the poor, but within a context set by the powerful presence of liberal economic values. Such NGOs do not challenge, so much as express, the international dimension of Canadian values. The reformist and solidarist strands, in contrast, are outside the dominant ideology, with the former seeing the need for major international intervention to promote more equitable international political and economic relationships, and the latter seeking fundamental transformation of Western values and societies as a prerequisite to real development in the South.

Mainstream NGOs have been hobbled by their lack of any explicit theory of change to guide their programming and priorities, while most reformist and solidarist NGOs lack strong constituencies that understand and support their approaches. The experience of being fully engaged in development work often radicalizes political consciousness, so that staff members of NGOs have often been more sympathetic to reformist or solidarist positions and more inclined to public advocacy than have been most of their supporters. This, in our view, has been true in particular of the church agencies and of Oxfam and CUSO.

The guiding philosophy of CIDA's funding meanwhile also evolved. Initially it was "responsive," intended to encourage and facilitate people-to-people participation of Canadians in international development by supporting projects proposed by Canadian NGOs. Nevertheless, initiative was not left entirely to the NGOs. CIDA inducements and incentives affected the choice of programs developed by NGOs; for example, a special fund was created for child immunization projects. CIDA also influenced the selection of countries in which NGOs chose to work. It made bilateral funds available and offered more advantageous matching ratios for projects in nations or regions of special interest to Ottawa. It also prohibited use of its funds – as, for example, in Cuba in the late 1970s or more recently for non-relief activity in Eritrea – for activities that seemed to run counter to Canadian foreign policy. Generous incentives brought a large number of new actors into development work, many of them heavily dependent on continuing government support – educational institutions, professional groups, and inter-agency coalitions collaborating in common programs such as the South Asia Partnership or the relief-oriented Africa Emergency Aid, later to be succeeded by Partnership Africa Canada (PAC).

The most dramatic change in the early 1980s was the increase in government funding for NGOs following introduction of "country focus" programming by Marcel Massé during his first term as CIDA's president. The approach was originally designed to permit greater flexibility for CIDA in choosing appropriate channels for aid delivery; specifically, it permitted large-scale "use" of NGOs to implement bilaterally funded projects. Some in the NGO community initially resisted this initiative, foreseeing growing dependence on CIDA funding and possible relegation of NGOs to the limited role of project implementors within a closely defined CIDA framework. Although the latter was indeed the initial intention,[16] in its early implementation the country focus programs did not prove threatening. Most of the projects that received such funding were in fact identified and designed by NGOs, not CIDA, and access to bilateral funding permitted a number of organizations to support substantially larger projects than they could have done with just their own resources. In addition, a few NGOs and NGIs began to get bilateral program funding through regular contracts offered to them by CIDA without competition from either other NGOs or the private sector. Table 1 shows the pattern of funding from the responsive program and from bilateral country-focus projects and contracts.

By the mid-1980s, there was thus not only widening cooperation between CIDA and the NGOs but also a fair measure of common accord between them about NGOs' role within Canada's aid program. CIDA's responsive program, viewed as one of the most progressive among OECD countries, averaged about 8–10 per cent of CIDA's budget. Although many Western aid agencies had by then introduced similar programs, CIDA was devoting proportionately more of its funds to this than was almost any other Western government's aid agency.

As further evidence of widening cooperation between CIDA and the NGOs, support for well-established agencies was increasingly taking the form of fewer but larger grants for more broadly defined programs, rather than a larger number of smaller grants for a series of separate projects. This arrangement increased the autonomy of Canadian NGOs and permitted them to engage in longer-range planning and to respond with greater speed and flexibility to Third World needs.

Table 1
CIDA funding of NGOs ($million), 1985–86

	Special Program Branch	Country Focus	Active contracts*
NGOs and volunteer sending agencies	164	23.2	20
Educational institutions			75.2

Source: Corporate Memory (1992), CIDA's "statistical data bank."
* Total value of outstanding contracts, many of which cover several years.

Although the movement of staff between government and the non-profit sector had largely stopped because of limitations on government hiring, there remained a free trade in ideas. For example, the importance in development of gender issues, of human rights, and of institution-building, and the continued priority of Africa's needs, were advocated initially among NGOs and then taken up by CIDA. Coalitions of NGOs, created usually under the aegis of the CCIC, pressed government to initiate or increase aid to particular countries, such as Mozambique and Cambodia, and in turn were delegated major responsibilities for allocation of funds. Finally, the work of NGOs provided a public face to Canada's aid program, eliciting political support and offering an avenue for Canadians' involvement. Public lobbying by some NGOs on Third World issues was accepted as legitimate, and in any case most NGOs were located solidly within the mainstream of Canadian society and reflected its political norms. The alliance of CIDA and the NGOs seemed secure, rooted in shared objectives and common interests.

INCREASING COMPLEXITY AND GREATER
TENSIONS: CIDA-NGO RELATIONS SINCE
THE MID-1980S

Many of the characteristics of the relationship of CIDA and the NGOs discussed above have continued to the present day – most notably, the greater trust extended towards the NGO community by the NGO division. Until the early 1980s, the division primarily considered applications for contributions to help finance specific projects from the full range of NGOs with which it dealt. Successful applicants then received regular, accountable advances, with each fresh advance being dependent on CIDA's receipt of a satisfactory report on how the previous advance had been spent. The NGOs were thus on a fairly short "leash," with a fair measure of CIDA supervision and control.

By the mid-1980s, the NGO division at any given time was involved with some 150 NGOs and was contributing to several thousand projects. It became apparent that the division could not provide effective service to nor sustain an informed overview of so many NGOs and projects. Common sense, reinforced by the ethos of the division, suggested greater delegation of responsibility to at least some NGOs.

In the early 1980s, the division began to accept requests for program rather than project support from NGOs with a record of satisfactory projects and good administration, accounting, and long-term planning.[17] Each such NGO submits proposals outlining in general terms the countries in which it would work, the sectors on which it would concentrate, and the people and organizations that would be its partners overseas. Program support is given usually for a period of three years. CIDA clearly has much less control under this mode of support. It can be selective about the activities supported by its funds, and of course any serious misuse of its funds will jeopardize the chances of renewal. Nevertheless, CIDA was giving up much of the more detailed overseeing that was possible with project contributions.

NGOs were allowed to seek program support only after an institutional evaluation had confirmed that their management was sound and that they had a good record of accountability and of coherent, long-term, and strategic projects. By 1989, some 22 NGOs were on program support. At that point, the division decided to move NGOs onto this mode as quickly as they were competent to manage it. By the end of 1992, 46 organizations were getting program support, and 44, project support. The intention is that by 1994 the division will deal directly with NGOs only in the program format. It is expected that the division will then be dealing with 64 NGOs.

CIDA did not want to cease helping the many smaller NGOs for which these delegations of responsibility seemed inappropriate. In 1989, it decided to create four regional funds, each administered by an NGI, a consulting firm, or a provincial council of NGOs. The last of these four funds became operational in April 1992. Under these arrangements, NGOs obtaining less than $250,000 apply to their decentralized fund, where decisions are taken on the basis of peer review and funding is almost always by accountable advances. As of January 1993, 110 NGOs received funds in this manner, and a further 90 still got project support from the NGO division.

In parallel to the move from project to program assistance and as a separate exercise, CIDA began in 1989 to support a few NGOs – four in that year – with three-year, non-accountable grants. By the beginning of 1993, 28 NGOs were being funded on this new basis. Before moving to grant funding for any organization, CIDA undertakes an institutional evaluation more demanding than that preceding a move from project to program support, to ensure that the NGO is fully accountable. These evaluations are carried out by private consulting firms, guided by a steering committee set up by the division and the NGO concerned. Evaluations so far have concentrated on management systems, financial aspects, and administration.

Thus grant funding has recently devolved responsibility to at least the most competent of the major NGOs. These NGOs can use the grants largely as they wish on projects, programs, and core administration. CIDA's main control has rested in the initial evaluation and in the fact that any serious misuse of a grant would jeopardize its renewal.

CIDA has also delegated more responsibility for allocation of its funds to coalitions of Canadian NGOs. Some of these, such as Partnership Africa Canada and the Reconstruction and Rehabilitation Fund, allocate substantial sums. They are thus a further example of the cooperation that has emerged between NGOs and the NGO division.[18]

By 1991, both the evolution from project to program funding and the encouraging of smaller NGOs through the four decentralized funds were far advanced. As of July 1991, 17 per cent of the NGO division's responsive funding was for projects, 78 per cent for programs and institutional grants, and 5 per cent for grants from the decentralized funds.[19]

There was clearly substantial trust between CIDA's NGO division and the NGO community. For as long as the evaluations that determined an NGO's promotion from project contribution to program support to institutional grants has focused on NGOs' financial and managerial competence, the partnership between CIDA and the NGOs grew closer and closer. However, as shall be seen, in 1992 the leadership of CIDA determined to use these evaluations and additional controls to ensure greater ideological cohesion among the activities that it was supporting. Changes in CIDA and the government and the NGO community were generating complications and tensions in their relations.

Changes within CIDA and the government

CIDA began in the mid-1980s to emphasize macro-economic policy reforms in Third World countries. By 1988, it saw this initiative as essential for the growth and development of those nations' economies.[20] More recently, its focus widened to include changes in political, sociocultural, governmental, and environmental policy that it judges necessary for "sustainable development," although macro-economic policies remained crucial.

Belief in macro-economic policy reform reflected the new confidence of the World Bank and the IMF in the structural adjustment that they were requiring of Third World governments as a prerequisite for assistance. When Marcel Massé returned from his five years as an executive director of the IMF and again became president of CIDA, he quickly concentrated the bilateral program on encouragement and underwriting of structural adjustment, in close cooperation with the IMF and the World Bank.[21]

This shift brought CIDA into line with the neo-conservative policies of the Conservative government elected in 1984. However, it created a gap between the new development ideology at CIDA and the values and development thinking of much of the NGO community. Many NGOs favoured a quite different approach – helping poor communities to meet their basic needs, a development strategy close to that advocated by the Winegard Report. As well, CIDA's greater concern for a coherent policy framework undermined the pragmatic pluralism implicit in the idea of a responsive NGO program. The NGO division and its program were not yet directly under threat, but they did appear more anomalous than ever.

In October 1991, CIDA published the Secor Report,[22] prepared by a consulting firm working closely with the leadership, which recommended reorganization of CIDA. The document proposed far greater integration of all CIDA-financed activities in any country around CIDA's strategic plan for that nation. This strategic plan would be the responsibility of the "corporate office," a new, high-powered, macro-economic unit in the office of the president and senior vice-president. The report offered mechanisms to ensure that area branches and country programs – which it several times referred to critically as "fiefdoms" – know and accept the corporate office's strategic analysis for their region and country.

The report, reflecting no doubt the views of the leadership, sought also to ensure that the agencies that executed CIDA's policies understood and accepted CIDA's strategic analysis. Senior members of appropriate NGOs and private-sector firms were to receive special support and instruction so that they could implement CIDA's policies. These NGOs would need to be "registered, pre-qualified and certified by the Agency."[23] Only these NGOs, along with similarly certified NGIs, consultants, and businesses, would be eligible to implement bilateral programs.

Although the announced intention had been to have a series of consultations with the NGO community, in December 1992 CIDA presented to cabinet, without that consultation, a set of recommendations based on the Secor Report. A leaked aide-mémoire shows categorically that CIDA wanted much greater policy control over NGO activities that

Table 2
CIDA funding of Canadian NGOs and NGIs ($million), 1990–91*

	Partnership Branch	Country focus (integrated country programs)	Active contracts[†]
NGOs	115.2	60.3	159.6
NGIs	109.4	80.0	235.0

Source: CIDA, Corporate Memory, 1992.
* These figures do not include food aid distributed through NGOs.
† Total value of multi-year contracts awarded in 1990–91.

it was supporting – a full retreat from its long-standing ideal of responsiveness. There would be a major role for selected NGOs, but it would still be as implementors of policies.

These recommendations had already been anticipated within CIDA. Massé, on his return in 1989, revived the country focus program that he had initiated eight years earlier. This time it was called integrated country programming, but it too sought greater coherence among CIDA's activities in each country. A few agencies, particularly those with limited fund-raising potential, could qualify for an increasing number of bilateral contracts. This pattern clearly reflected the same concern to enforce policy coherence that underlies the Secor recommendations. CIDA was already providing extensive support, through country-focus bilateral funding and regular bilateral contracts, to some favoured NGOs and NGIs. By 1990–91, this arrangement was producing more funds for these favoured organizations than the whole responsive program was providing to all NGOs and NGIs (Table 2).

The general neo-conservatism of government policy and its responsiveness to corporate lobbying, however, led to reversal in 1991 of this recent, rapid expansion in the funding of NGOs through bilateral programs. Ottawa was becoming sensitive to the private sector's concerns that it was being excluded from a significant portion of bilateral contracts because of this expansion of "sole-sourcing" of contracts to selected NGOs and NGIs and because such NGOs and NGIs could compete with profit-making firms for bilateral contracts. Informal estimates indicated that by 1990–91, over 50 per cent of all new bilateral contracts were being offered to selected NGOs and NGIs. In 1991, the minister responded to the lobbying and created a Private Sector Development Initiative Fund as a responsive program, available only to the business sector, and severely cut NGOs' and NGIs' access to both country-focus and bilateral bidding channels. As the minister as well can decide who should receive the larger bilateral contracts and must approve each decision to offer an NGO or an NGI a bilateral contract, the expanding agency role that had been conceded to selected NGOs and NGIs was substantially curtailed.[24]

CIDA began as well to define its role, especially in Southeast Asia, more in political than in either developmental or economic terms. The countries of the region are geopolitically important. Canada had little presence or influence there, and the earlier preoccupation with helping Canadian exporters of capital goods to penetrate these markets had collapsed. CIDA sought increasingly to use its development assistance, which was marginal everywhere except in Bangladesh, to develop links with powerful sectors of these societies that would outlast the aid program and would give Canada significant influence, despite its being a small player. As one official expressed it, CIDA was shaping a noncommercial foreign policy for Canada in the region.[25]

In Thailand, CIDA was not inhibited in the pursuit of this objective by the absence there of Canadian NGOs that might have assisted in developing links with Thai organizations. CIDA's Thailand-based officers directly funded Thai NGOs. However, for much of Southeast and South Asia, CIDA saw Canadian NGOs as essential to this process and offered major inducements to draw them in. For example, when the South Asia Partnership began in 1981 as a program to strengthen small NGOs in Bangladesh, India, and Sri Lanka, CIDA offered to match the contributions of Canadian NGOs on a 4:1 ratio rather than the normal 3:1. A few years later, CIDA offered a 9:1 ratio for NGOs willing to undertake projects in Sri Lanka. Similarly, in the early years of the Philippine Development Assistance Programme (PDAP), CIDA used a 9:1 ratio to attract Canadian NGOs to that nation. The whole process in effect turned on its head the traditional rationale for CIDA's support to Canadian NGOs. The Canadian NGOs were not providing local knowledge and grass-roots contacts that CIDA lacked but, rather, CIDA had identified the "need," which had a significant diplomatic and political purpose, and then induced Canadian NGOs which often had little knowledge of the country, to become involved.

In its pursuit of lasting links between these countries and Canada, CIDA also encouraged creation of new Canadian voluntary organizations, such as the Asia Pacific and the Thai-Canada foundations. In another context, relating to aid to southern Africa, CIDA secured creation of the South African Education Trust Fund because it did not think the strong NGOs already active vis-à-vis South Africa sufficiently sensitive to Canadian foreign policy concerns and considered that those NGOs could not obtain the involvement and financial contributions of Canadian educational institutions.

It became clear in some countries that CIDA had less need than it had realized for Canadian NGOs to be its intermediary with local NGOs. In the Philippines, local NGOs were well organized and every bit as competent and responsible as Canadian ones. CIDA officials working there grew more self-confident in their judgment of local needs. By the mid-1980s, CIDA officials in a number of Asian countries had instigated creation of coalitions of local NGOs with which CIDA then dealt directly.[27] Often coalitions of local NGOs, such as PDAP in the Philippines, were delegated responsibility for allocation to local NGOs of substantial CIDA funds. For example, in the three-year period beginning 1988–89, the South Asia Partnership was to receive over $10 million from CIDA. During phase 2, PDAP will get almost $15 million for a six-year period. Many of these coalitions provide for participation by Canadian NGOs, but it is clearly secondary and will probably diminish over time.

One final twist in this complex tale remains. As CIDA has grown more assured about its analyses, so also has it reacted defensively to policy differences with NGOs that have been particularly active in the countries involved. This happened in the disputes over allocation of food aid in the Horn of Africa, over aid to the African National Congress in southern Africa, and over projects and programs with the corrupt and repressive regimes in Guatemala and Guyana. In the dispute in the Horn, CIDA's senior vice-president went beyond questioning the content of the NGOs' concerns to dismiss the notion that CIDA could have anything to learn from them; any criticism, he seemed to imply, was in bad faith.

Few generalizations will hold across such a wide variety of practices. However, in recent years CIDA has become far more ready to be proactive in its relations with Canadian NGOs, using the undoubted power of its funding to shape NGOs' involvement in ways desired by Canadian foreign policy–makers. Indeed, CIDA's recommendations that followed the Secor Report reveal its desire for much greater policy control over NGOs' CIDA-financed activities. Dealing with CIDA clearly has become progressively more complex for Canadian NGOs since the early days of the responsive program.

Changes within the NGO Community

Four related changes within the NGO community coincided with the developments within CIDA just described and increased the strains in CIDA-NGO relations. These were differing responses to new opportunities for CIDA funding, the increasing importance of coalitions of NGOs, the emergence of articulate and competent Third World NGOs, and growing uncertainty and disagreement over what NGOs should be doing.

Differing Responses to the New Opportunities for CIDA Funding

It is not the case, although it have been might expected, that the politically more conservative organizations easily entered into the new funding opportunities proposed by CIDA, while the more politicized ones did not. For example, the Canadian Catholic Organization for Development and Peace (CCODP), Inter Pares, and Oxfam Canada – each a strong public critic of many government policies – have nevertheless sought and received contracts for country-focus projects and participated in CIDA-funded coalitions. Some major conservative NGOs, such as Foster Parents Plan, confident of their programs and having their own sources of finances, have not entered these new relationships.

The large public-sector development agencies have taken advantage of these new opportunities to expand their activities. Access to contracts attracts mainly public-service contractors, while coalition funding requires a contingent contribution which not all of these agencies are in a position to make. Thus WUSC and CECI have sought only the former, CARE and CHF have gone for both, and others, such as Save the Children, have in the main pursued the latter. Most NGOs have not been involved in country-focus funding or tried to get regular bilateral contracts.

It has thus been many of the larger public-sector contractors, as well as a few more entrepreneurial-minded development NGOs, that have looked for funding in these new ways. Differences between NGOs that are public-service contractors and those that have their own constituency and a significant capacity to raise funds have thus intensified. Inevitably, many of the former have become even less sympathetic to any public policy advocacy that would complicate their relationship with CIDA.[28]

This intensification of differences contributed to the CCIC's continued difficulty in engaging these major NGOs actively in its advocacy. The CCIC had made itself nearly indispensable by its lobbying for NGO interests and by helping in the creation and administration of NGO coalitions. Public-service contractors are therefore not much inclined to break openly with the CCIC. However, they and the larger, more conservative NGOs have tended to regard much that it does as irrelevant. The executive heads of 22 of the largest NGOs, including all the major public-service contractors, value instead their own informal group – the

International Development Executives Association (IDEA) – which they had already set up as a forum and meeting place.

It is therefore no easier now than in earlier years to win strong and near unanimous NGO support for any advocacy work on public policy issues. For example, many of the larger NGOs were unhappy when the CCIC produced in 1991 a "report card" on CIDA that compared its performance unfavourably with the objectives set out in *Sharing Our Future* (1987).

Any advocacy stronger than that has been unlikely to be accepted. An attempt a few years ago to organize a boycott of a particular CIDA policy collapsed ignominiously, even though that policy had been strongly contested. The board of directors of the CCIC, after extensive discussion, resolved that no Canadian NGO should agree to manage the counterpart funds that would be generated by resumption of Canadian aid to El Salvador. CIDA, for its own reasons, was determined to provide some $27 million worth of Canadian phosphate fertilizer to El Salvador. It had no difficulty, despite the CCIC's resolution, in signing a contract with Canadian Hunger Foundation to manage distribution in El Salvador of the resulting counterpart funds.

However, when CIDA tried too transparently in early 1993 to exploit potential divisions between the IDEA group and the CCIC in order to win the former's support for, or at least acquiesence in, proposed major changes in Canadian aid policies, it failed. The major NGOs in the IDEA group retained a sufficient sense of solidarity with the CCIC and were suspicious enough of the government's intentions that they rejected its efforts to meet separately with them. Instead, they joined the common front of NGOs opposing the major changes which External Affairs, with little to no public discussion, was seeking to effect.

The Increasing Importance of NGO Coalitions

Several substantial coalitions of NGOs emerged in the early 1980s, mainly in Asia and at CIDA's instigation. In Africa, however, coalitions instigated by the NGOs or involving them as equal and committed partners from the start provoked staff resistance in CIDA. The potential of coalitions is illustrated most dramatically by African Emergency Aid (AEA).[29] In late 1983 and into 1984, there were increasingly ominous and authoritative international warnings that a massive famine was imminent in several areas of Africa. In October 1984, dramatic media coverage of the disaster in Ethiopia generated a major expression of compassion and generosity in Canada, which Canadian NGOs in turn sought to mobilize and to direct. In the next two years, they raised an unprecedented $60 million for African relief work.[30]

At the same time, Ottawa decided that in many African countries it must substantially supplement government-to-government aid with large grants to international humanitarian organizations and to Canadian NGOs able to work in the distressed areas. NGOs and their international equivalents alone had links to local structures that could get aid to the neediest people, often located in areas beyond the reach of the recognized government. CIDA therefore needed their help.

A consortium, Africa Emergency Aid (AEA), was formed of Canadian NGOs active in African emergency relief, or anxious to become so. Forty-nine NGOs finally participated. In less than two years AEA handled project selection and administration of over $56.6 million, almost all of it CIDA funds or food aid allocated to it. A total of 254 projects were assisted in 22 countries, with over 50 per cent of funds going to activities in Ethiopia and just under 25 per cent to Sudan.[31] All this was not to be accomplished without serious disagreements. Opinion was divided on such painful issues as whether to assist communities that had been forcibly moved by the Ethiopian regime and were still its responsibility, and whether and how to provide emergency relief within rebel-held areas in Ethiopia and in Sudan. However, the NGOs were powerful and essential partners in African emergency relief; they were not easily ignored or bypassed. The whole AEA operation of 1985–86 was, by any criterion, a major achievement.

Similar structures were put together for more specific activities, usually involving both CIDA and the CCIC in their instigation. Solidarité Canada Sahel (1985) brought together 30 NGOs. CIDA gave it a $1.5 million, three-year grant, renewed in 1989, to urge Canadian NGOs to participate in Sahelian development.[32] The Cross Border Consortium, which spent $4 million in each of 1988 and 1989, wanted to ensure that people in Eritrea and Tigre got assistance proportional to that going to Ethiopia. CIDA grants covered 90 per cent of its total budget.[33]

The success of this AEA funding mechanism led directly to Partnership Africa Canada; PAC, set up in 1986, now constitutes a body of over 150 NGOs. For CIDA, it allocated $75 million for 1987–92 and is responsible for a further $75 million for 1992–97. Although all of these coalitions and consortia usually act under the umbrella of the CCIC, each has tended to become substantially autonomous. Indeed, in 1993 PAC became fully independent of CCIC. By and large, they have not been used to promote NGOs' views on broader policy issues. Instead, they have concentrated on administration. CIDA seems to regard them as largely cooperative and non-threatening.

Another small cluster of coalitions evolved from working groups within the CCIC that had been formed to mobilize pressure on CIDA and the government over Canadian policies in southern Africa. Leaders came from solidarity groups such as the Toronto Committee for Liberation in Southern Africa and from the few politically radical NGOs such as Oxfam (Canada) and CUSO, which had long been active in southern Africa. When nationalist governments finally gained power in these countries, Ottawa, which had been reluctant to extend even non-military aid to African liberation movements, scrambled to improve its political image. These Canadian NGOs had long had good relations with the new governments and suddenly became a diplomatic asset.

Although at first reluctant, CIDA finally did not seek to dissuade PAC from supporting the coalitions of Canadian NGOs that quickly emerged for Angola and Mozambique. Cooperation Canada Mozambique (COCAMO) in 1988–91 administered a $7.3 million, three-year program, of which $6.3 million came from CIDA. Program Angola has had a total budget for its first three and a quarter years of just over $9 million; $6.9 million of this amount has been CIDA funds, provided through PAC.[34]

COCAMO and Program Angola represent a marriage of convenience. CIDA and the Canadian government benefited politically in the region from the activities that CIDA was supporting. The NGOs in turn have had more resources not only for their African work but also for popular education in Canada – an unexpected bonus for the solidarist groups that receive them. One key to these arrangements is that these coalitions operate in countries not of major interest to Ottawa.

A quite different pattern emerged in regard to both Zimbabwe and South Africa. During the long years of their liberation struggle, a number of NGOs, particularly CUSO and Oxfam, had developed close relations with the major liberation movements and were in genuine solidarity with them. Ottawa refused direct assistance to these movements, even after Pierre Trudeau had endorsed the legitimacy of their struggle at the 1973 Commonwealth prime Ministers' Conference and after Brian Mulroney's tough stance in 1985–86 on sanctions against South Africa. It denied even non-military aid extended indirectly, through the NGOs. The NGOs, in contrast, believed that political liberation was essential to any true development. They continued to assist the African National Congress (ANC) with non-military aid but got very little in matching funds from CIDA for these projects.

After the dramatic events in South Africa in 1989, Ottawa scrambled to improve its relations with the ANC. However, in South Africa, as earlier in Zimbabwe, it did not turn to existing NGOs. No one in government suggested that an NGO-dominated structure like those hurriedly devised for Angola and Mozambique should be the main Canadian

channel for aid to South Africa. There, External Affairs and CIDA made
it clear that they would stay more thoroughly in control.[35]

The same pattern was repeated in 1989, when the NGOs already active in Central America sought CIDA's support for an NGO-controlled
Central American Peace and Development Fund. Much energy was devoted to negotiating this proposal, but the CCIC and CIDA finally failed
to reach agreement. The region, unlike Angola and Mozambique but
very much like Zimbabwe and South Africa, was politically too important for CIDA to accept any real delegation of power to NGOs, especially
when they included many that were strongly critical of US policy in the
area.[36] A Central American monitoring agency set up by the NGOs took
on an exclusively policy focus but received no CIDA funding.

The Emergence of Third World NGOs

Support for fledgling NGOs overseas has, of course, been a central emphasis for many Canadian NGOs. Canadian NGOs therefore welcomed
the coming into prominence of indigenous NGOs, which did, however,
complicate their work. In nations that have a strong contingent of CIDA
officials serving, as well as developed coalitions of local NGOs, local
CIDA officials and local NGOs have been ambivalent about their need
for much involvement by Canadian NGOs. Most continue to be involved
but, unless their roles change, are likely to become less important.

Third World NGOs have begun to articulate demands that challenge
both CIDA and Canadian NGOs. They call on Canadian NGOs to be
much more political on their behalf. They want their Canadian counterparts to address issues of Canadian public policy that affect the development prospects of the Third World. They also want greater
delegation of power to Third World decision-making structures, and
they are anxious to develop links with citizens' groups in Canada that
are engaged in activities similar to their own.[37]

These demands were easily predictable but have proven difficult
to respond to. Some links developed between overseas NGOs and
Canadian groups engaged in similar issues. However, the call for
greater political engagement by Canadian NGOs ran up against the
engrained hesitancy of many Canadian NGOs to engage in policy
advocacy. These NGOs are expressions of Canadian compassion, not
of an ideological, anti-capitalist Canadian solidarity with the world's
oppressed.

Even the call for a greater sharing of decision making has produced
only token gestures. PAC brought into its board four Third World members, selected by the Africa umbrella body Forum of African Voluntary
Development Organizations (FAVDO). Five people from overseas

churches now join some 70 Canadian participants at the large annual policy meeting of the World Outreach Division of the United Church of Canada. Similar reforms occurred in the Inter-Church Fund for International Development (ICFID). The hesitancy of these measures may suggest reluctance to share power. It was a result also of anxiety about a possible adverse impact on fundraising if the Canadian organizations appeared to lose control of aid allocation. More intriguing still, solidarist considerations are easily drawn upon to oppose any major delegation to substantial NGO structures in most Third World countries, with the argument being made that these structures will themselves not represent the poor. The blend of considerations differed from NGO to NGO, but less decision-making has evolved to Third World structures than might have been expected.

The conclusion is unavoidable. Many Canadian NGOs have neither grappled sufficiently with the call from their Third World partners for a fuller, more genuinely equal partnership nor taken up their challenge to become more forthright critics, on their behalf, of CIDA and government policies.

Uncertainty and Disagreement over What NGOs Should Be Doing

There is widespread anxiety among Canadian NGOs that Canadian commitment to their work is declining. The first and continuing reaction to this has been redoubling of effort. Yet the misgivings increase. There is talk of aid fatigue, growing preoccupation with more immediate and often personal issues, a declining sense of national purpose, and a shift of public interest from development to environmental issues. Sharing these anxieties, the CCIC in 1989 commissioned a major study, *Mobilizing Support for International Development*,[38] which also took seriously the probability of declining public support for international development unless new strategies were considered.

OECD figures indicate, however, that at least until the end of 1991, there had not been any fall in private donations to Canadian NGOs working in developing countries. Resource flows from Canadian NGOs averaged $US109 million in 1980–82 and have risen steadily since then, reaching $US270 million in 1991.[39] Nevertheless, and bearing in mind that these figures have not been corrected for inflation or for changes in exchange rates, they do not suggest increasing levels of giving. Anxiety about these levels and about likely trends is widespread.

Also persuasive is a change of mood within many NGOs. In the 1960s and much of the 1970s, Canadian NGOs could feel with some confidence that they were part of an international effort that was significantly improving the welfare and development capabilities of the poor in the Third World. This belief could be sustained in the last decade only by the wilfully naive. In country after country, living standards have fallen, basic community services have collapsed, and corruption is rampant. The NGOs have been, even at best, merely nibbling at the edges of the problem. They have checked the worst consequences of major calamities. They have extended development help to some communities and institutional support for some Third World NGOs. The need for help is still there in abundance, and the NGOs do persevere. But disillusionment and soul-searching are not surprising.

Many NGO staff members came to the view that much more than generous acts of charity were needed. Reform internationalism – the demand for international interventions to promote greater justice – at first subsided as an NGO preoccupation with the defeat by 1981 of the Third World's efforts to secure the New International Economic Order. As the depth and duration of the global crisis became apparent, NGO sympathy for new international initiatives, particularly for abrogation of Third World debt, came to the fore. At the same time, opposition quickly developed to the structural adjustment that the IMF and the World Bank were insisting on before they would extend assistance. These positions taken by Canadian NGOs were sustained and reinforced by strong Third World voices expressing similar criticisms.

This upsurge of a refurbished reform internationalism took much articulate NGO opinion in a direction quite contrary to that of CIDA. The CCIC published several highly critical status reports on international debt and on structural adjustment.[40] Ten Days for World Development focused its annual campaign on international debt for several consecutive years. The Inter-Church Fund for International Development and the Canadian Council of Churches published a severe critique of CIDA's policies four years after the Winegard Report.[41] The gap between the government and the leadership of the CCIC and those NGOs engaged with these matters had widened and deepened by the end of 1991. Divisions also increased within the CCIC between those advocating these reforms and those who were either less politicized or who had absorbed and accepted elements of Canada's new neo-conservatism.

In addition to this rejuvenated reform internationalism, expressions of solidarist internationalism also became more frequent. From this viewpoint, acquisitive greed in the rich countries and in the international economic system which they dominate causes poverty and underdevelopment. Development assistance merely helps integrate Third World economies into an international system that exploits them.[42] NGOs should concentrate on forging links with progressive social forces in the North, for this kind of strategic partnership "could mean the difference between ... survival and extinction for many Canadian NGOs."[43] It was a call to Canadian NGOs to work "on such issues as the elimination of poverty and hunger, native rights, the environment, the elimination of illiteracy and support for abused women and children in Canada"[44] and to become involved in domestic political issues.[45]

This infusion of more radical ideas did not transform the NGO community. The CCIC was giving them an airing rather than actively canvassing on their behalf. Neither the CCIC nor the few more radical NGOs can provide the analysis necessary to challenge CIDA and government policies. Those few larger NGOs that now entertain activities with reform or solidarist components add them as extras to programs that still involve primarily projects and programs. Only a handful show evidence of any significant solidarist influences.[46] The development education centres that tend to be committedly solidarist cannot finance their own activities, are dependent on CIDA to an embarrassing degree, and are politically marginal. Reinvigoration of reform internationalist ideas has contributed to the estrangement between CIDA and a number of major Canadian NGOs. It has not yet reshaped the activities of most Canadian NGOs.

David Korten has recently posited four successive generations for each NGO – the first, focused on relief and welfare; the second, on small-scale, self-reliant development; the third, on sustainable systems; and the fourth, on creation of people's movements to advocate global economic reform.[47] This classification is suggestive, but we do not find helpful the implied criticism of NGOs that fail to move promptly through the generations. Each category addresses needs that will long compel the attention of caring people.

EDGING TOWARDS A NEW RELATIONSHIP, 1991–93

In the period 1990–92, three CCIC initiatives reveal that body's desire to come to terms with both the changing role of Canadian NGOs and Canadian realities. First, the CCIC sought to enlist as members a number of major national and provincial associations that have overseas projects or might be persuaded to have them. If more trade unions, teachers' federations, nurses' associations, and similar groups were to become active in the CCIC, it could face with greater equanimity the loss of public-sector contractors, should they choose to quit, or of other members, in the event of shrinkage of the traditional NGO community.

Second, the CCIC had to respond to the major cuts that the government imposed on CIDA's budget. Though often critical of CIDA, the

NGO community still had an interest in mobilizing public opinion behind the aid program. As a result, it tempered its criticisms of CIDA. In 1991 and again in 1992, the CCIC organized public campaigns to promote support for CIDA's budget. In February 1992, it placed in 26 daily newspapers an effective four-page supplement which sought to convince readers that aid did make a difference and was in Canada's interest.

Third, Ian Smillie prepared a carefully designed proposal (*A Time to Build Up*, December 1991) to save the responsive program by transferring its budget to an independent body operating under its own act of Parliament and its own board.[48] This foundation would allocate monies to NGOs for activities presented by them and selected through a process of peer review. The Smillie Report envisioned NGOs as autonomous catalysts for strengthening civil society in the South, for building citizens' organizations, and for defending human rights. The proposals clearly challenged the determined efforts by CIDA's leadership to integrate aid policy and tighten policy control over NGOs' use of CIDA funds. Nevertheless, the proposals were consistent with the assumption fundamental to the responsive program – that there is intrinsic value to CIDA-assisted, autonomous NGO programs of development assistance and to the resulting pluralism of development experience and ideas.

Early in 1992, it became clear that there would be no policy statement or any consultations on the Secor Report. Instead, Marcel Massé decided to seek cabinet approval for CIDA to implement directly the management and structural changes that he felt were essential, including assertion of policy control over CIDA-assisted NGO activities. A responsive program would continue only for minor responsive activities. For the rest – the greater part of CIDA's country and regional programs – "Strategic objectives will be established, in agreement with the Minister, for each program ... CIDA will devise frameworks for development activities (the 'WHAT' to do) while letting agents (business, NGOs, institutions) determine the 'HOW' to do it."[49]

In December 1992, this proposal failed to win cabinet approval, and the cabinet requested that External Affairs quickly prepare a policy update paper to provide a framework within which the CIDA proposals could be considered. This it did by late January 1993, when the department completed "International Assistance Policy Update." Soon thereafter, Massé was transferred from CIDA, and the senior vice-president, Douglas Lindores, resigned, both in response to an effort by External Affairs to assert greater control over the foreign policy dimension of CIDA and to secure a shift of funds from CIDA to aid for eastern Europe and the former Soviet Union.[50]

The implications for Canadian NGOs seem hardly to have entered into the debate at all. The new president of CIDA announced in early April 1993 that CIDA was proceeding with only those reforms recommended in the Massé-Lindores memorandum to cabinet that deal with the organization management, but not with those that would change its relations with any of its partners, at least until consultation with those partners. To what extent CIDA's efforts to assert closer policy control over CIDA financed NGO activities have been blunted was thus, as of June 1993, still unsettled.

The CCIC, as argued above, was in 1991 and 1992 primarily trying to limit the damage to the responsive program which it felt CIDA was intent on inflicting upon it. However, in the last week of January 1993, it received a leaked copy of the "International Assistance Policy Update." This paper strongly advocated tying aid more closely to commercial and foreign policy objectives. External Affairs had wanted swift cabinet approval of the paper, and so the CCIC launched a public campaign for a full-scale review of foreign policy, which it argued could take place only after the federal election, which was finally called for 25 October 1993. As well, groups of CCIC member agencies were encouraged to examine specific issues, including humanitarian aid, human rights, and trade policy, and to formulate proposals within a context of sustainability and global security, broadly defined. The CCIC was thus not retreating into a laager mentality, concerned mainly to protect the institutional interests of its members. It was instead moving towards a direct challenge to government on a very widely defined alternative view of Canada's long-term global interests.[51]

NGO GOVERNMENT RELATIONS IN THE MID-1990S

As it moves into its fourth decade, the development enterprise has never seemed so shaky. The imagination of people in the North has been seized by the magnitude and speed of changes in Europe; by comparison, continuing underdevelopment in the South appears both intractable and of diminishing economic and strategic interest. Aid professionals, facing more difficulty in marshalling resources, proclaim the new gospel of economic liberalism and good governance while hinting that henceforth the blame for persistent poverty must be laid at the doors of the developing world itself, for refusing, postponing, or botching full application of the "stiff medicine" prescribed for it by donors. At least three daunting issues face Canadian NGOs.

First, twenty years of steady growth has left NGOs ill-prepared for the rethinking and restructuring that now appear necessary and inevitable.

Reduced budgets are a symptom, not the cause, of these changes. Coalitions and inter-agency funding mechanisms have been one source of innovation and as such have benefited both CIDA and NGOs. However, they represent an additional, costly layer of administration inserted between CIDA and the ultimate beneficiaries, and they transfer significant management responsibilities from CIDA to the NGOs. Since most agencies have not developed a strategic approach to their involvement in coalitions, these additional tasks have gone to already overworked staff, without in most cases any diminution of project administration. Such coalitions will probably fall victim to resurgent agency self-interest.

CIDA "responsive" funding of any individual NGO has been shaped by history, by fund-raising capacity (a maximum 50:50 ratio of government funding overall has been the rule, though sometimes ignored), and – exceptionally – by organizational evaluations. Although NGOs have in the past expressed concern about the lack of transparency around funding decisions, this issue is likely to become more heated as the pie to be divided shrinks. Will coalitions and CIDA-inspired endeavours continue to receive preferential treatment? Will new claimants such as the labour "solidarity" or humanity funds be treated as equals of older organizations? Will program innovation or effectiveness have more weight than fund-raising ability? Or will the minister make the final decision on an agency-by-agency basis, as the practice has been in allocations to larger agencies to date? Both CIDA and the NGOs have alternatives that they wish to see put in place. CIDA wants a system of agency pre-selection that will ensure the loyalty of the agencies to CIDA's policy objectives; the CCIC is proposing instead hands-off allocation of funding based on peer review. The one would maximize control; the other, autonomy.

Second, NGOs must address the notion of partnership. For the government, "partnership," as defined in *Sharing Our Future*, referred indiscriminately to cooperation with any external body involved in the aid program, whether multilateral, private sector, NGO, or NGI. *Sharing Our Future* unambiguously states that partnership is one of the key operating principles of the aid program: "although the Government may participate in shaping policy and programmes, decision-making power and questions of eligibility will fundamentally rest with the partners on the basis of their own criteria." Although the wording suggested a mutual relationship based on commonly agreed objectives, in practice CIDA officials often confuse exchange of information with consultation, and consultation with partnership. The CIDA discourse routinely (and revealingly) talks of "using" partners to accomplish one or another of CIDA's objectives.

Partnership, presupposing as it does basic agreement on aims and methods, may not be the best term to describe the government-NGO relationship. It would be difficult, for example, for NGOs to pursue policy advocacy or offer overt criticism within a "partnership,"which at the least implies shared power and in consequence collegial responsibility. And is it realistic to expect that the standard practices of government decision-making, particularly in sensitive areas of foreign policy, will be opened up to NGO involvement sufficiently to allow us to talk of "shared" power? If not, then the government and the non-government sector are perhaps allies, rather than partners.

NGOs face demands from new and more confident Southern organizations to cast off an outworn charity approach and to seek real change in international economic and political relations. These demands co-exist uneasily with the liberal internationalism that underpins their work and created dilemmas for many in their relations with their donor public and with the government. Will their donors continue to support organizations that see their mission not just as charity and relief but as promoting change that must necessarily shift more power to the poor?

While many, perhaps most, NGOs are prepared to accept a subordinate role (as indicated by the many purely contractual relationships set up in recent years), is it truly in the long-term best interest of either CIDA or the NGO community as a whole for NGOs to abdicate the role of critic, gadfly, counter-model? NGOs have received mixed messages. They are told that not only will policy dialogue (and implicitly, therefore, dissent) be tolerated, it will be encouraged. Early in 1991, for example, Marcel Massé was quoted as saying: "NGOs have to get on the policy trail; the Government will just have to learn to live with criticism." He repeated this message on several occasions. Yet, as we have seen, CIDA is seeking more control rather than more openness.

Third, as realization grows that significant development cannot and will not be the product of "aid" alone, however well intentioned or well administered, NGOs find themselves in a curious paradox. For decades, they have championed people liberating themselves from the shackles of ignorance, disease, and exploitation in order to realize their full potential – a process in which aid can clearly help but is not the major force. Now the aid establishment is echoing their cry for women's emancipation, control of arms spending, respect for human rights, and democratic norms as prerequisites to development. And yet many NGOs are reluctant to join the debate, seemingly padlocked to a treadmill of fund raising, poverty evangelism, and project administration. At the moment of vindication, are Canadian NGOs fated to be left behind by governments and international organizations and by a public grown sceptical of strident appeals and claims?

Posing these sorts of questions will not make for easy relations between NGOs and CIDA or other donor organizations. But there are grounds for an effective alliance in which each side has a distinct and different role to play. CIDA's mandate is to administer Canada's aid program, within the parameters of Canadian foreign policy and commercial and other interests. Members of its staff struggle to ensure the pre-eminence of developmental priorities, but other government departments are by no means prepared to accept CIDA's assertion of leadership. It has little ability to communicate its message publicly, and – as its appearances before the Public Accounts Committee of the House of Commons attest – its relations with MPs are adversarial. CIDA badly needs the public support of the NGO community.

NGOs, though, are being challenged by their own convictions and by their Third World counterparts to be more than aid administrators and public advocates for CIDA. Fostering and strengthening links between people and institutions in Canada and the Third World, helping to build healthy, pluralistic civil societies, and projecting Canadian values of tolerance and respect for human rights are all critical matters for development and for emergence of a more just and peaceful global order. An alliance between the government and non-government actors in Canada's international development effort is not only possible, it is essential. But that alliance must be based on understanding and acceptance of the distinctive contribution of each participant and recognition on both sides that debate about the ends and the means of development is simply an acceptance of the diversity of human values and experience.

NOTES

1 A recent study estimated that by 1985 nearly 60 per cent of Canadian NGO expenditure overseas was on development projects, with 10 per cent going to emergency and relief assistance, 13 per cent to placement of Canadians overseas, 8 per cent to material assistance, and 9 per cent to child and family sponsorship. As many of the overseas placements were involved in development projects and some of the material assistance also went to them, over 70 per cent was devoted to development. See Tim Brodhead and Brent Herbert-Copley, *Bridges of Hope?: Canadian Voluntary Agencies and the Third World* (Ottawa: North-South Institute 1988), 12–17.

2 Ibid., 20–2.

3 Ibid., 22, 24.

4 Canadian University Service Overseas (CUSO) was created in 1961 to recruit and arrange overseas placement of hundreds of young Canadian

volunteers. It quickly became very dependent on CIDA funding and is treated by CIDA as a non-government institution. World University Service of Canada (WUSC) in its early years operated as a traditional NGO but since 1975 has diversified its funding within CIDA through competitive bidding on bilateral contracts and through country-focus mechanisms, on which more below. WUSC has also competed successfully and increasingly for funding from multilateral donor sources, such as the World Bank, the World Food Programme and the United Nations High Commissioner for Refugees. A. John Watson, "Diversity of Funding Channels," presentation to an NGO/CIDA consultation, c. 1990.

5 C. Francis Folz, *The Future of the International Development Executives Association* (Ottawa: C.F. Folz Consulting 1992), 24.

6 The South African Education Trust Fund was set up at the direct encouragement of the secretary of state for external affairs when he wanted to demonstrate greater support for the education of Africans in South Africa but did not wish to use for this purpose any existing NGOs or coalition thereof. The reason for this approach was probably partly political and partly administrative.

7 Canada and other Western governments continue to send an increasing number of technical assistance personnel as part of their overseas development assistance. Such personnel from Canada grew in number from 2,057 in 1980 to 4,562 in 1989; OECD, Development Assistance Committee (DAC), *Development Cooperation, 1992 Report* (Paris: OECD 1992), 209. This increase reflects both overall growth in the value of Canadian aid and CIDA's increasing reluctance to support projects that do not involve Canadian personnel. CIDA sought efficiency and, for trade and political reasons, stronger links between Canada and recipient countries.

8 As quoted in Brodhead and Herbert-Copley, *Bridges of Hope*, 41.

9 The maximum overall total contribution that any NGO could receive could not be greater them the funding raised by the NGO for its development activities.

10 We are grateful to CIDA's "statistical data bank" – Corporate Memory (1992) – for these figures.

11 CIDA, *Annual Report 1989–90* (Ottawa: Minister of Supply and Services 1991), 68.

12 Secoma Ltd and Edpra Ltd, *Evaluation of CIDA's Non-governmental Organizational Program* (Hull: CIDA 1992), 21. The OECD's DAC estimated for 1985 that 45 per cent of Canadian NGO expenditures were government funded; Hendrik Van Der Heijen, "The Reconciliation of NGO Autonomy Program Integrity and Operational Effectiveness with Accountability to Donors," in *World Development* 15 (autumn 1987), 105.

13 Folz, *Future*, 5. For 10 of these, 80 per cent of their revenues came from government – Aga Khan Foundation, Canada World Youth, Canadian Hunger Foundation, Canadian Red Cross Society, CARE Canada, CECI, CODE, CUSO, OCSD, and WUSC; ibid., 24.

14 Brodhead and Herbert-Copley, *Bridges of Hope*, 56–7.

15 See Ronald Manzer, *Public Policies and Political Development in Canada* (Toronto: University of Toronto Press 1985). Cranford Pratt applies this analysis to Canadian views on global poverty in "Canada: An Eroding and Limited Internationalism," in C. Pratt, ed., *Internationalism under Strain: The North-South Policies of Canada, The Netherlands, Norway, and Sweden* (Toronto: University of Toronto Press 1989), 49–63.

16 In February 1982, Massé explained that country focus "consists in defining what the objectives of our intervention in a given country should be, and then determining which channel of intervention available to the Agency is the most efficient. Then we choose it, we fund it and we hope it happens." Quoted in Brodhead and Herbert-Copley, *Bridges of Hope*, 59.

17 Kendel Rust, director of the Program Support Unit of the NGO division, generously provided the factual information in this and the next several paragraphs.

18 For an informed discussion of the growth of cooperative coalitions, see *Mind If I Cut In? The Report of the CCIC Task Force on CIDA-NGO Funding Relations* (Ottawa: CCIC 1988).

19 Secoma Ltd and Edpra Ltd, *Evaluation*, 20.

20 This is discussed fully by Marcia Burdette in chapter 8 in this volume. Most commentators agree on the importance of this new policy. See, for example, Andrew Clark, *Mosaic or Patchwork: Canadian Policy towards Sub-Saharan Africa in the 1990's* (Ottawa: North-South Institute 1991); Robert Clark, "Overseas Development Assistance: The Neo-Conservative Challenge," in Maureen Molet and Fen Osler Hampson, eds., *Canada among Nations 1989: The Challenge of Change 1989* (Ottawa: Carleton University Press 1990), 193–206; and Canadian Council of Churches and the Inter-Church Fund for International Development, *Diminishing Our Future. CIDA: Four Years after Winegard* (Toronto: Council and Fund 1991).

21 Massé made specific and strong reference to this in a speech to the Canadian executive directors of the international financial institutions meeting in Ottawa, 29 and 30 October 1990.

22 Groupe Secor, Strategic Management Review: Working Document (also called "Secor Report"), (9 October 1991). For a fuller critical analysis of this report, see C. Pratt, "Towards a Neo-conservative Transformation of Canadian International Development Assistance: The Secor Report on CIDA," *International Journal* 47 no. 3 (summer 1992), 595–613.

23 Secor Report, 70/4.

24 John Watson reported in 1991: "recent developments seem to indicate it has been decided at the political level to roll back the use of NGOs and institutions as aid delivery channels for bilateral projects even in those sectors, such as education and training, which have traditionally been viewed as proper realms of NGO activity." Watson, "Diversity," 3.

25 Author's interview, CIDA, October 1991.

26 This higher ratio was already available as an encouragement for projects that entailed cooperation among NGOs that extended beyond the merely financial.

27 CIDA is not always successful in these politically sensitive initiatives. In the Philippines in 1986–87, its officials helped put together a development coalition in Negros province. They misjudged the local situation, and the coalition was in fact dominated by landlords and boycotted by popular organizations. Author's interviews, CIDA, September–October 1991.

28 CECI, though a public-service contractor, has critized some of CIDA's policies, while CARE, despite its strong constituency, has avoided public discussion of CIDA's policies.

29 Much of the information on AEA is drawn from Ann Qualman, Jean Brodeur, and Al Doerksen, "An Assessment of African Emergency Aid (AEA)," mimeo (Ottawa: CCIC, n.d. [1987]), 85 and 12 annexes.

30 Partnership: Matching Rhetoric to Reality, an NGO Discussion Paper (Ottawa: Partnership Africa Canada 1989), 9.

31 Qualman, Brodeur, and Doerksen, "Assessment," 2 and annexes 3 and 5.

32 From Coordination to Collaboration (Ottawa: CCIC, September 1989), app. 4.

33 Ibid.

34 From Coordination to Collaboration, app. 4.

35 The story of CUSO's involvement with the liberation movements of southern Africa and CIDA's extreme caution about giving any help to CUSO is told in interesting detail in Christopher Neal, David Beer, John van Mossel, John Saxby, and Joan Anne Nolan, "CUSO and Liberation Movements in Southern Africa: An Appeal for Solidarity," in Robert Miller, ed., Aid as Peacemaker: Canadian Development Assistance and Third World Conflict (Ottawa: Carleton University Press 1992), 123–44.

36 For details, see a series of CCIC papers: The Central American Peace Process: A Study of Canadian Options. Synthesis Report (c. 1988–89); Creative Tension: Canadian NGOs and CIDA: Towards a New Era. A Discussion Paper (January 1990); and Canadian NGO Options in the Context of the Central American Peace Process, Workshop Report, 22–24 February 1990.

37 These three points seem to be the most frequently voiced recommendations to emerge from the substantial number of consultations that have brought together Canadian and Third World NGOs. There are published reports of some of those consultations. See, for example, *Strategic Analysis of Development Partnerships in Asia: Report of a Regional Consultation on Canadian-Asian-NGO Partnerships* (Manila: ANGOC Secretariat 1990) and "Challenges for Partnership in Development in the '90's, mimeo (Toronto: Inter-Church Fund for International Development 1990).

38 This report was prepared in 1989–90 by Synergistics, Canadian communications consultants. Extracts from it appear in CCIC, *The Critical 90's: CCIC Organizational Review* (Ottawa: CCIC, November 1990), 8–16.

39 OECD, *Development Cooperation, 1992 Report* (Paris OECD 1992), A-76.

40 CCIC, *Aid and the Why Reflex* and *Confronting Debt and Structural Adjustment*, Status Reports No. 1 and No. 3 (n.d. [1991]).

41 Council and Fund, *Diminishing Our Future.*

42 This viewpoint is argued by Brian Murphy in his "Canadian NGOs and the Politics of Participation," in James Swift and Brian Tomlinson, eds., *Conflicts of Interest: Canada and the Third World* (Toronto: Between the Lines 1991), 161–211.

43 CCIC, "The North-South Dialogue: NGOs in the 1990s," *Status Report No. 2* (n.d. [1991]), 4.

44 Ibid.

45 CCIC, *The Critical '90s*, 19–20.

46 Brian Murphy, though championing this position, concedes as much. "Canadian NGOs," 202.

47 David Korten, *Getting to the 21st Century: Voluntary Action and the Global Agenda* (West Hartford, Conn.: Kumarian Press 1990), 114–28.

48 These proposals are made in a report commissioned by the CCIC; Ian Smillie, *A Time to Build Up: New Forms of Cooperation between NGOs and CIDA* (Ottawa: CCIC, December 1991).

49 The quotation is from "Aide Memoire to the Members of the Cabinet Committee on Foreign and Defence Policy," which came into the author's possession in January 1992.

50 These developments are discussed more fully below in chapter 13, pp. 358–60.

51 A vigorous statement of this challenge is provided by Betty Plewes, president of the CCIC, in her "Preparing for the 21st Century: Why Canada Needs a Foreign Policy Review" *Canadian Foreign Policy* 1 no. 2 (spring 1993), 103–7.

PART TWO
Major Issues of Canadian Aid Policy

5 The Choice of Bilateral Aid Recipients

DAVID R. MORRISON

By the mid-1970s, Canada's bilateral aid program, once concentrated highly in three countries in the Indian subcontinent, was dispersed widely among almost ninety countries in Asia, Africa, and the Americas. Although the choice of recipients reflected foreign and domestic policy considerations that had little to do with levels of development, the proportion of allocations to the least developed and other low-income countries was well above the average of Western donors in the Development Assistance Committee (DAC) of the OECD.[1] A major policy review leading up to publication in 1975 of CIDA's *Strategy for International Development Cooperation 1975–1980* attempted to devise developmentally oriented criteria for recipients' eligibility and ways of achieving more focused effort in fewer countries. Since that time, formal commitments to concentrate Canada's official development assistance (ODA) in fewer recipients and to channel the bulk of it to the poorest countries and peoples have been somewhat in conflict with long-standing pressures to make aid serve Canadian commercial and political objectives. These pressures became more intense in the late 1970s and the 1980s. By the early 1990s, there were more than 110 national and regional recipients of government-to-government aid,[2] there was less concentration than in the mid-1970s, and a smaller proportion was flowing to low-income countries. Fuelled by geopolitical changes and budget cuts the issue of country concentration was assuming heightened prominence, and hard choices were being made, some at the expense of the poorest and least developed countries.

A GLOBAL BILATERAL PROGRAM[3]

When CIDA established a task force in 1974 to examine eligibility and concentration, the geographical spread of Canada's bilateral ODA was unusual among DAC donors. Belgium, Britain, France, the Netherlands, and other ex-colonial powers channelled their efforts largely within their former empires and spheres of influence. Japan, the Nordic countries, Australia, and other large and small donors tended to specialize along regional or ideological lines. Canada's global reach resembled that of a superpower and a major power – the United States and the Federal Republic of Germany – but without anything approaching either's economic clout or international political interests.

A "lively anti-Communist instinct and an exhilarating vision of a free, multi-racial Commonwealth"[4] underpinned Canada's decision in 1950 to participate in the Colombo Plan for Co-operative Economic Development in South and Southeast Asia. Initially a Commonwealth venture, the plan was soon broadened to include the United States as a major donor and several non-Commonwealth states in the region as recipients. However, over 95 per cent of Canadian bilateral ODA up to 1962–63 went to India, Pakistan, and Ceylon (Sri Lanka). Malaysia received just over 1 per cent, and even smaller proportions were directed elsewhere. No non-Commonwealth Asian country was designated for more than marginal support until Pierre Trudeau's foreign policy review in 1969–70 recommended an enlarged presence in Indonesia.

While Commonwealth ties circumscribed a highly concentrated Canadian bilateral aid program in Asia, the tremendous growth of new club members in the wake of rapid decolonization in Africa, the Caribbean, and the Pacific implied a dramatic increase in the number of recipient countries, if membership in the Commonwealth continued to be a primary criterion. By and large, that proved to be the case. New programs were started in Ghana and the British West Indies Federation (as it then was) in 1958; by 1970, there were 15 national and regional Commonwealth recipients in Africa and 12 in the Caribbean.

The coincident timing of Ottawa's new Commonwealth initiatives, Quebec's "Quiet Revolution," and decolonization within the African empires of France and Belgium provided the context for critical commentary among journalists and intellectuals in Quebec. "Le Commonwealth n'est pas l'humanité," wrote André Laurendeau in 1960.[5] A modest technical assistance program in francophone Africa was initiated in 1961 and expanded in 1964 as an explicit component of the Pearson government's policy of bilingualism and biculturalism.

Then, in the late 1960s, the region became a major diplomatic battle-ground in the conflict between Ottawa and Quebec over the latter's efforts to obtain international recognition. Douglas Anglin suggested that Ottawa, in setting out "to buy Francophone African goodwill with aid offers," embarked upon "perhaps the most dramatic new direction in foreign policy ever undertaken by a Canadian government."[6] There were 21 francophone African recipients of Canadian bilateral aid by 1970.

Canada resisted for some time American blandishments to become more involved in the Western Hemisphere outside of the Commonwealth Caribbean. However, the government decided in 1963 to develop a loan program in Latin America under the auspices of the Inter-American Development Bank (IDB). Business interest in securing capital projects under the IDB was soon matched by growing pressure from religious groups for a Canadian technical assistance program. Trudeau's foreign policy review led to establishment of a full bilateral program in 1970.

While the actual mix of bilateral recipients evolved through accident and design, rapid proliferation was assured not only by a growing aid budget but also by the underlying political calculus in place by the late 1960s – the Commonwealth-plus in Asia, a balance between Commonwealth and francophone states in Africa, and Commonwealth and broader responsibilities within the Western Hemisphere. What the Economic Council of Canada later labelled the "'diplomatic calling-card' aspect of aid"[7] – small amounts of aid for a large number of countries – was common enough among donors. However, with the exception of India and Pakistan (where Canadian bilateral ODA was small in comparison with total efforts by donors), the wide dispersal was also characterized by low concentration among a designated group of high-priority recipients. Another factor that fostered dispersal was the limited range of capabilities that the highly tied Canadian program was able to offer; more often than not in the 1950s and 1960s, Canada had to seek recipients for its aid rather than vice versa.

CONCENTRATION AND ELIGIBILITY CRITERIA: AN EMERGING AGENDA

Although politicians, diplomats, and aid bureaucrats were all actively engaged in playing through the underlying political calculus and stimulating the proliferation of bilateral recipients, anxiety began to develop in some quarters about the diminishing concentration of the aid program and the absence of any explicit criteria for country selection that consciously weighed developmental as well as foreign and domestic political and economic considerations. Herb Moran, director general of the External Aid Office from 1960 to 1966, was concerned about the growing administrative burden on the aid program and the irrationality of simply allowing the pressures at work to drive proliferation. He sought and achieved support for a formal policy endorsing concentration. A cabinet directive of April 1966 indicated that "Canadian aid should be channelled largely to countries where major Canadian interests were involved and where such assistance would clearly contribute to the effectiveness of development efforts."[8] No indication was given, however, about how "major Canadian interests" or "the effectiveness of development efforts" were to be defined or measured.

Maurice Strong, Moran's successor, was temperamentally suited to build, not contain, and build he did, transforming the External Aid Office into the Canadian International Development Agency (CIDA) in 1968 and presiding as president until 1970. During his term, Canada became a major player in francophone Africa, developed the new bilateral program in Latin America, and increased considerably the number of recipient countries. Nonetheless, CIDA's annual report for 1968–69 emphasized the government's policy of achieving greater effectiveness through concentration.[9] The DAC's annual report for 1969 took the claim at face value and listed Canada alongside Japan and the Scandinavian countries as donors that "have decided to concentrate their aid on a few selected countries of 'first choice'."[10] The allocations memorandum to the cabinet for 1968–69 actually announced phasing out of programs "of marginal interest." As a CIDA task force on eligibility reported in 1974, however, "the recommended 'phasing out' of countries was never effected, apparently because of the political difficulty of withdrawing completely from countries where an aid program, even of modest proportions, already existed. Consequently, ... modest programs were maintained in most previously eligible nations until the questions of eligibility and allocation could be dealt with by the Policy Review of 1970."[11]

CIDA took the lead in preparing *International Development*, one of six booklets making up *Foreign Policy for Canadians*, published after the foreign policy review of 1969–70. The document cited as principles to inform decisions on eligibility and allocation historically based special concern, degree of poverty, closeness to a self-sustaining level of growth, developmental performance, availability of good projects and programs to match Canadian expertise, and concentration in the interests of improving effectiveness and impact. It offered no guidance on how to attach relative weights to these elements, apart from the comment that "each leads to difficult anomalies if used as a sole criterion." A commitment was made to channel approximately 80 per cent of bilateral funds over the next three to five years to an unspecified number of "countries of concentration."[12]

Soon after the foreign policy review, the first annual report published during Paul Gérin-Lajoie's tenure as CIDA's president (1970–77) claimed that the criteria in *International Development* "have been consciously applied" to the new Latin American program. Backpedalling on the commitment to concentration, the report also indicated that francophone Africa "is now regarded in principle as an area of concentration without distinction between countries," as, "to a lesser degree, is Latin America." The addition of Indonesia was reported, along with the longest list to date of bilateral recipients.[13]

In March 1972, the cabinet called for action to be concentrated in fewer countries. CIDA's allocations memorandum for 1972–73 suggested three criteria for declaring recipients ineligible – high GNP per capita, large revenues from oil sales, and persistent slowness in planning and implementation of projects. These factors were at best tangential, however, when the 1973–74 eligibility list deleted occasional recipients that had "no permanent place in the scheme of Canadian assistance."[14] George Cunningham, in his comparative study of aid donors, reported: "CIDA officials acknowledge ... that the idea of countries of concentration, which was new to Canada until a few years ago, is manifested more in intention than in fact."[15]

THE TASK FORCE ON ELIGIBILITY AND THE STRATEGY FOR 1975–80

In response to the contradictory pressures for proliferation and concentration, CIDA set up a task force on country eligibility to develop guidelines for a strategy for the years 1975–80. Its report reviewed the criteria in the 1970 and 1972–73 documents and listed other factors that had been raised during interdepartmental discussions: "commitment to development, population size, the presence/absence of clear Canadian commercial and political interests, a Canadian administrative capacity in the field, the difficulties of dealing with a recipient government considered repressive or corrupt." The authors found that "some countries have been declared eligible on the basis of low per capita GNP and evidence of firm commitment to development; others were declared eligible in spite of the fact they clearly did not qualify for assistance according to the same criteria." Several decisions had clearly contradicted "general statements concerning the primacy of development." The task force summarized its conclusions about the past as follows:

The decision-making process has been informed by various developmental, political and commercial considerations introduced from time to time on an ad hoc, case-by-case basis.

No standard weightings have been applied to the argumentation of various departments for the inclusion/exclusion of countries; the result has been inconsistency and sometimes outright contradiction in discussions on eligibility.

It has been relatively easier to add a country to the eligibility list than to remove the same country or another.

A variety of development "criteria" appear and re-appear in such discussions but they have never been applied on an across-the-board, systematic, and consistent basis. They do however provide a guide to the criteria which the Canadian Government has considered relevant to the problem of eligibility.[16]

The task force set out "to render more explicit and systematic the assumptions and logical processes underlying decisions on eligibility and allocations, to disentangle and examine their development, political and commercial elements, and, finally, to illuminate and systematize future decisions."[17] It based its analysis on two premises – "that the differing impact of the energy crisis has highlighted *the need for the community of donors to channel both emergency and longer term aid to those countries which need it most*" and that, while other objectives were not always mutually consistent with the paramount purpose of ODA to foster development, CIDA's developmental mission could be pursued more effectively during the process of "blending" objectives if development criteria were clearly formulated and could be measured with reasonable ease and precision.[18]

While conceding that External Affairs and Industry, Trade and Commerce would push other concerns in future deliberations, the task force argued that decisions on eligibility and allocations should be informed foremost by developmental need, as defined by level of per capita income, social indicators, an assessment of development effort and commitment and, to the extent possible, a forecast of future prospects and availability of foreign exchange. Both the "matching" of recipients' needs with Canadian capacities and a country's ability to plan and implement effective development programs, while germane, were best left to annual country programming exercises rather than to decisions on eligibility.

Using classification schema on levels of development and GNP per capita, the authors noted that the bulk of Canada's bilateral ODA had gone to the poorest countries: "*The assumption of the Task Force has been that a substantial drift 'upward' from* CIDA's *historical category shares (i.e., in favour of the relatively well-off nations) would be a regressive step,* tantamount to a transfer of resources from the Maritimes to Alberta."[19] They recommended, therefore, that the bulk of bilateral funds be directed to developing countries with annual incomes of under $200 per capita (in 1971 $US), that 20 per cent of the program be devoted to the least developed countries (LLDCs) by 1980,[20] and that the portion of CIDA disbursements going to "upper developing countries" (UDCs – those with per capita annual incomes in excess of $375) not exceed 8 per cent. The task force also suggested that the distribution of bilateral aid should fall within ranges of 40–45 per cent for Asia, 37–43 per cent for Africa, and 9–12 per cent for the Americas (close to the recent experience but skewed slightly towards Africa as generally a lower-income region).

The report made a strong case for greater concentration among fewer recipients and suggested reducing the number of countries receiving regular and significant bilateral assistance from 67 to 50 by 1980. It recommended dropping recipients from the UDC category – first, those with below-average developmental performance and those with good foreign exchange prospects. Jamaica, which had had especially high priority (and kept it), was cited for possible deletion, along with Chile, Costa Rica, Gabon, and Trinidad and Tobago. In order to ease the transition and – one might add – maintain the "diplomatic calling card" aspect of aid, the task force recommended that up to $200,000 a year be made available to non-program countries, including those not currently in receipt of Canadian grants or loans. Allowing for sensitivity to performance and availability of foreign exchange, larger allocations were recommended for programs lower down the development index. It was proposed as well that funding be related to population, with larger countries receiving higher amounts, though not in direct proportion to population.

The work of the task force fed into the *Strategy for International Development Cooperation 1975–1980*, which was published in 1975 after an intensive interdepartmental process that diluted the developmental thrusts of earlier drafts developed within CIDA.[21] Industry, Trade and Commerce made an especially strong pitch for orienting more of the aid budget towards middle and upper-income developing countries, where Canadian commercial opportunities were more promising. Both Prime Minister Trudeau and Secretary of State for External Affairs Allan MacEachen intervened to ensure that the balance was not tipped in the direction of greater commercial orientation.[22] As a result, little was changed from the status quo. The *Strategy* promised to direct the most assistance to nations "at the lower end of the development scale" and on meeting the basic needs of "the least privileged sections of the population in recipient countries." "Particular attention will be given to the hardcore least developed countries identified by the United Nations."[23] However, up to 10 per cent (rather than a limit of 8 per cent) "will be allocated to upper income developing countries," defined as those with per capita annual incomes of more than $US375. (External Affairs had objected to the lower ceiling, fearing that it threatened the Caribbean program.[24]) No reference was made to any ranges for the major geographical areas.

The *Strategy* also made a commitment to attend particularly strongly to "a limited number of countries selected on the basis of need, commitment to development, general Canadian interests and the geographic distribution of other donors' bilateral assistance." Although the criteria were focused more clearly on development than those in the 1970 policy, the temporizing reference to "general Canadian interests" left a question mark about operational significance. In a further concession to trade promotion, one statement indicated that the government would occasionally provide "a positive response to development projects that are submitted for Canadian consideration and are outside the ambit of regular programs." The document did not propose a number for program countries (40 and 50 were used in earlier drafts) but included the proposal to make available up to $200,000 a year to non-program countries.[25]

AID DISTRIBUTION UNDER GÉRIN-LAJOIE, 1970–77

The bilateral program doubled in size to over $500 million during the presidency of Paul Gérin-Lajoie, while total Canadian aid spending almost tripled, to just under $1 billion. It was a period of rapid growth and innovative rethinking about policy, but also of organizational turmoil within CIDA and of managerial chaos, as program growth outstripped the capacity of administrative and financial systems. Total allocations to the LLDCs did increase from 12 per cent of bilateral aid in 1972 to 18.9 per cent in 1975 and, with classification of Bangladesh as an LLDC, to 28.1 per cent in 1976. CIDA informed the DAC in 1976 that five-year indicative planning figures for 1977–82 would produce a distribution that would channel 79.3 per cent to countries with an annual GNP per capita of less than US $200 in 1973, 11.0 per cent to countries in the $200–$375 range, and 9.7 per cent to those above $375. This last group was actually allocated 10.6 per cent in 1975 – down, CIDA reported, from 17 per cent in 1970–71.[26]

Stepping back from the aggregate numbers to look at distributional shifts among recipients, we find it more difficult to detect much coherence in patterns over the 1970s if we focus on level of development. Most oil and gas producers – Algeria, Ecuador, Nigeria, and Trinidad and Tobago – experienced a noticeable decline, but Indonesia emerged as a major recipient. Some LLDCs – Malawi, Tanzania, and the countries of the Sahel – were allocated more than previously, while programming commenced in Haiti and Nepal.[27] However, major flows to middle-income countries continued in such cases as Tunisia and Jamaica (the latter being in straitened financial circumstances) or increased substantially in others such as Colombia.

The task force had identified 67 active recipients and suggested pruning them to 50. During the strategy process, even greater reductions were mooted. The compromise at the practical level, however, was to divide the list into "program countries," for which there was to be sustained planning, and "project countries" without full programming, where projects were to be approved case by case. In 1975–76, there were 34 program and 31 project countries. A year later, there were 26 program countries – with the apparent reduction achieved largely by treating groupings of nations in some regions as "programming units" (Botswana-Lesotho-Swaziland, the Leeward and Windward Islands, and the Sahel).[28]

The new classification promoted sharper delineation between program and project countries, and some time later about 80 per cent of bilateral aid was going to the former, 15 per cent to the latter, and 5 per cent to a new category of "other." For the top ten recipients, however, the bilateral program became less intensive during the 1970s. This group received 64.3 per cent in 1975–76, compared to 74.2 per cent in 1970–71 (see Table 1). By 1980–81 – still within a five-year planning cycle begun while Gérin-Lajoie was president – the figure was down to 52.9 per cent. In its "Final Report Card" on the 1975 *Strategy*, the North-South Institute assigned "F" – its lowest grade – to CIDA on the commitment to achieve greater developmental impact through concentration: "All efforts in this direction seem to run afoul of either the general diplomatic embarrassment that would be involved in cutting countries off, or a specific commercial, political or developmental objective of one of the departments or agencies involved in recommending eligible countries."[29]

Although practice did not live up to rhetoric, there was a further, specific reason for this change – a dramatic drop in Canadian ODA to India. India's pre-eminence within the bilateral program would probably have continued a gradual decline, especially since an External

Table 1
Top ten recipients of Canadian bilateral development assistance ($million), selected years, 1970–71 to 1989–90

	1970–71		1975–76		1980–81		1985–86		1989–90	
	India	103.14	India	98.91	Bangladesh	74.40	Bangladesh	100.11	Bangladesh	125.33
	Pakistan	47.50	Pakistan	63.94	Pakistan	38.13	Indonesia	74.94	Indonesia	52.37
	Turkey	8.00	Indonesia	36.70	Sri Lanka	37.67	Pakistan	66.67	SADCC*	39.10
	Ghana	7.01	Bangladesh	29.48	India	29.50	India	45.49	Pakistan	36.45
	Nigeria	6.63	Tanzania	24.38	Tanzania	29.20	Jamaica	28.78	China	35.20
	Tunisia	5.49	Ghana	17.63	Egypt	22.11	Sri Lanka	26.52	Jamaica	33.34
	Sri Lanka	5.18	Niger	17.48	Cameroon	20.16	Niger	26.37	Cameroon	32.98
	Morocco	4.77	Tunisia	16.42	Sahel	19.64	Tanzania	24.29	Ghana	32.60
	Guyana	4.18	EAC†	15.73	Turkey	18.98	Kenya	22.42	Tanzania	30.57
	Algeria	4.01	Malawi	14.91	Indonesia	17.95	Senegal	20.58	Morocoo	28.38
Total to top ten		195.91		335.48		307.74		436.17		446.32
Total bilateral		264.20		521.70		581.50		816.20		1,026.30
% to top ten		74.20		64.30		52.90		53.40		43.50

Sources: CIDA, Annual Report, various years.
* Southern African Development Coordination Conference (regional projects involving 10 southern African states).
† East African Community.

Affairs review of Canadian policy towards the subcontinent in 1973 had questioned whether aid was helping Indian development.[30] Moreover, India itself had been decreasing its dependence on external assistance. The Indian government announced, however, in May 1974, that it had successfully tested a nuclear device in the Thar desert. It had given a commitment that only peaceful purposes were contemplated when it accepted CANDU technology from the Atomic Energy Co. of Canada (AECL). Prime Minister Trudeau, in the midst of an election campaign, deplored the action and announced immediate suspension of nuclear aid. Other ongoing projects were allowed to continue, but severe constraints were placed on initiating new projects until 1979.[31] The effect on the balance between Asia and Africa is clear in Table 2.

Conflict within the Indian subcontinent also altered the configuration of the bilateral program during the 1970s. The civil war in Pakistan raised for Canada a dilemma (as civil strife had earlier in Nigeria) concerning humanitarian relief to a secessionist state. While Ottawa was careful not to violate the code of non-intervention, it provided considerable support to the East Pakistani area through the Red Cross and the World Food Programme (WFP) and to refugees who fled to India.[32] However, once India's invasion ensured independence for Bangladesh, Gérin-Lajoie was quick to make a site visit, aid workers returned to projects, and new forms of assistance were provided. Bangladesh became the largest recipient of Canadian ODA by 1977–78. Normal relations were restored with Pakistan, which continued to secure substantial Canadian programming.

Other political factors shaped the bilateral program during the early to mid 1970s. Canadian advisers were withdrawn from Idi Amin's Uganda in 1972 on grounds that their security was threatened. Pressure from non-governmental organizations (NGOs) and support groups for non-military assistance to southern African liberation movements, while opposed strongly by some Conservative members of Parliament, eventually culminated in a decision to provide funding through the NGO program.[33] In addition, aid was stepped up to the "front-line" states – one of the reasons why Tanzania emerged with the largest Canadian aid program in anglophone Africa. (Other factors were its status as an LLDC, Trudeau's friendship with President Julius Nyerere, the prominence within CIDA of an ex-Tanzanian, and the international aid establishment's enthusiastic embrace of Tanzania's experiment in socialism and self-reliance.) A bilateral program was initiated in Cuba in 1973 and then cancelled amid parliamentary and media criticism of Fidel Castro's decision to send Cuban troops to support regimes in Angola and Ethiopia.

Table 2
Percentage distribution of Canadian bilateral development assistance,* cumulative totals, 1950–51 to 1989–90

Period	Asia	Anglophone Africa	Francophone Africa	Commonwealth Caribbean	Latin America	Misc.	Totals
1950–51 to 1959–60	99.9 (348.7)	0.03 (0.1)	–	0.1 0.3	–	–	(349.1)
1960–61 to 1964–65	84.0 (244.3)	5.8 (16.9)	0.5 (1.6)	6.2 (17.9)	3.4 (10.0)	– (0.1)	(290.8)
1965–66 to 1969–70	66.9 (641.3)	10.3 (99.0)	8.2 (79.3)	9.0 (86.6)	5.8 (52.8)	–	(959.0)
1970–71 to 1974–75	55.7 (953.7)	17.7 (302.7)	17.5 (299.1)	4.8 (82.9)	3.8 (64.9)	0.6 (9.6)	(1,712.9)
1975–76 to 1979–80	44.8 (1,210.7)	21.1 (569.5)	20.5 (553.8)	4.9 (134.4)	6.8 (183.2)	1.9 (50.4)	(2,702.0)
1980–81 to 1984–85	40.7 (1,434.7)	23.7 (836.5)	21.6 (760.7)	5.1 (179.0)	6.5 (229.6)	2.3 (81.7)	(3,522.2)
1985–86 to 1989–90	38.1 (1,938.4)	24.3 (1,236.8)	20.4 (1,036.1)	8.5 (430.8)	6.6 (334.4)	2.1 (111.2)	(5,087.7)
All years	46.3 (6,777.8)	20.9 (3,061.5)	18.7 (2,730.6)	6.4 (931.9)	6.0 (874.9)	1.7 (253.0)	(14,629.7)

Sources: CIDA, Annual Report, various years. Data up to 1969–70 are for allocations; those for 1970–71 and later are for disbursements. Figures in parentheses are in $million.
* "Asia" includes Turkey and Oceania. With the addition of Egypt, Ethiopia, Jordan, Mozambique, and so on, "Commonwealth Africa" was restyled "Anglophone Africa," somewhat of a misnomer. CIDA has not retained the Commonwealth Caribbean–Latin America distinction, but the data have been calculated in a way that maintains it. "Miscellaneous" includes modest contributions to European recipients and bilateral aid not allocatable by country; data before 1970–71 exclude emergency relief and the Commonwealth Scholarship Program.

THE LATE 1970S: ODA DISTRIBUTION AND
"NATIONAL INTERESTS"

Michel Dupuy began a three-year term as president of CIDA in 1977 after a long career at External Affairs. Following increasingly tense interdepartmental conflict during Gérin-Lajoie's presidency, Dupuy was asked to integrate CIDA more closely within the foreign policy apparatus. In "Directions for the Agency," circulated within CIDA in December 1977, the new president suggested that the "recent evolution of the Canadian economy as well as its short and medium term prospects require that CIDA strive to ensure that its activities maintain or generate employment and economic benefits in our own country. We must also aim at strengthening mutually beneficial bilateral relationships between our developing partners and Canada." The message was not new, nor was the notion of complementarity that was embedded in the reminder that "this goal must be achieved while not neglecting our essential mandate which is international development."[34] However, there was much heavier emphasis on commercial and foreign policy objectives than in any previous official statements or commentaries (whether internal or external). This increased emphasis certainly marked an acceleration of the assault on what Cranford Pratt has called the humane internationalist tradition in Canadian foreign policy.

Another indication of this realignment of bureaucratic forces came in the assertion of a leading role by External Affairs in the next round of policy development on criteria for eligibility. In 1978, External Affairs set up and chaired a task force of representatives from Industry, Trade and Commerce, Finance, the Treasury Board and the Privy Council Office as well as CIDA. The task force concluded that too much stress had been placed on LLDCs and too little on overall foreign policy objectives. A suggested formula would weight eligibility according to a ratio of 40:25:20:15 for need, political relations with Canada, economic performance, and commercial relations, respectively. The Interdepartmental Committee on Economic Relations with Developing Countries (ICERDC), also chaired by External Affairs, approved the proposal and endorsed focusing aid more on bilateral relations with particular developing countries, especially those in the middle per-capita income range. Despite these directives, however, the official list of core (program) and non-core (project) countries that emerged from the exercise reflected little change from the the status quo (see Table 3). A senior CIDA official who participated in the process recalled to the author that bargaining over the formula was long and hard, but that "we ended up getting the numbers right."

Table 3
Core/category I and non-core/category II countries, 1978, 1981, 1986

Category	Asia			Americas		
	1978	1981	1986	1978	1981	1986
Core (1978); I (1982), (1986)	Bangladesh India Indonesia Nepal Pakistan Sri Lanka	Bangladesh China India Indonesia Nepal Pakistan Sri Lanka Thailand	Bangladesh China India Indonesia Nepal Pakistan Philippines Sri Lanka Thailand	Belize Bolivia Colombia El Salvador Guyana Haiti Honduras Jamaica Leewards and Windwards Peru	Colombia Guyana Haiti Honduras Jamaica Leewards and Windwards Peru	Colombia Guyana Haiti Honduras* Jamaica Leewards and Windwards Peru
Non-core (1978); IIA and IIB (1982); II (1986)	Malaysia Philippines	IIA Malaysia IIB Thailand Turkey	Malaysia Regional Philippines Singapore	Barbados Brazil Dominican Republic Ecuador Guatemala Trinidad and Tobago	IIA Barbados Brazil Costa Rica Dominican Republic Ecuador Panama Trinidad IIB Belize El Salvador Guatemala	Barbados Brazil Caricom Costa Rica Dominican Republic Ecuador El Salvador Guatemala Nicaragua Panama Regional

	Anglophone Africa			Francophone Africa		
Category	*1978*	*1981*	*1986*	*1978*	*1981*	*1986*
Core (1978); I (1982), (1986)	Botswana Ghana Kenya Lesotho Malawi Sudan Swaziland Tanzania Zambia	Botswana Egypt Ghana Kenya Lesotho Swaziland Tanzania Zambia Zimbabwe	Egypt Ghana Kenya SADCC Tanzania Zambia Zimbabwe	Cameroon Guinea Ivory Coast Mali Morocco Niger Sahel Regional Senegal Upper Volta	Cameroon Guinea Ivory Coast Rwanda Sahel – Mali – Niger – Upper Volta Senegal Zaire	Cameroon Guinea† Ivory Coast Rwanda Sahel – Burkina Faso – Mali – Niger – Regional Senegal Zaire
Non-core (1978); IIA and IIB (1982); II (1986)	Egypt Ethiopia Nigeria Sierra Leone Uganda	IIA Nigeria IIB Malawi Sudan	Botswana Ethiopia Jordan Lesotho Malawi Nigeria Sudan Swaziland Uganda	Algeria Benin Congo Madagascar Rwanda Togo Tunisia	IIA Algeria Gabon Morocco Tunisia IIB Benin Togo	Algeria Gabon Morocco Regional Togo

Sources: Adapted from CIDA, Bilateral Overview 1980/81, typescript, March 1980, 21–22, 26–27; Canadian Council for International Cooperation, Excerpts from a CIDA Paper on the "Agency Programming Framework (APF)," December 1981, Annex A; CIDA, DAC Aid Review, 1983, 1984, 17–18; CIDA, A Briefing Book for Parliamentarians, 1986, 48–49. Underlining indicates a position different from the preceding or succeeding one.

* Subsequently expanded to include all Central American republics in a core region.

† Subsequently dropped; see Groupe Secor, Strategic Management Review: Working Document (9 October 1991), 22/1.

Concern that aid be used more effectively in the service of Canada's economic and political interests continued to mount in the late 1970s. There was also greater pressure from Canadian business to harness aid more directly to commercial interests. This was a major issue for the Export Promotion Review Committee, chaired by Roger Hatch and made up of leading business executives appointed by the minister of industry, trade, and commerce at the end of 1978 to examine ways of improving government export promotion and support services. A few months later, the Liberal government was defeated at the polls, and the committee did much of its work under the Conservatives (1979–80), reporting just before Joe Clark's government fell.

The Hatch Report (*Strengthening Canada Abroad*) stated bluntly: "In the view of the business community, [CIDA] has, especially since 1970, taken an overly philanthropic giveaway approach to aid." Arguing that Canada could do more for development by integrating its aid activities with its trade strategy, Hatch called for a larger bilateral program that would come from reduced contributions to multilateral institutions. Existing bilateral ODA was dispersed too widely and oriented too strongly towards nations that "are too underdeveloped for much meaningful trade to result." Therefore, Hatch argued, resources should be concentrated in "fewer countries to whom Canada's technical capabilities are most useful, and with whom there is trade potential."[35]

Secretary of State for External Affairs Flora MacDonald had earlier questioned publicly the orientation of Canada's development assistance – among them, whether greater effort ought to go into fostering mutually beneficial relations with higher-income developing countries.[36] She asked External Affairs and CIDA to undertake reviews of foreign policy and the aid program. As it happened, the government fell before the review had progressed beyond preparation of in-house discussion papers.[37] The "Aid Policy" paper was discursive and open-ended, raising questions rather than making concrete suggestions for what was then envisaged as a later product – a strategy for the 1980s. However, its ethos reflected the recent shift in official thinking away from the primacy of development (however qualified) to an External Affairs perspective emphasizing ODA as an instrument of foreign and domestic policy.

The "Aid Policy" text made the usual points about the desirability of concentration and suggested need, developmental effort, and Canadian interests as "the types of criteria" that could be taken into account. On geographical distribution, it noted that current patterns reflected a long, evolutionary process in which Africa and Asia had come into rough balance following the decline in aid to India. The paper took no position on other eligibility and allocation matters but flagged clearly the question of what "balance" Canada should achieve between "the poorest countries as compared with the middle-income countries." The text observed that need in LLDCs was great but that, even where the commitment was strong, aid tended to have a "lesser impact" than in other developing countries. While recognizing growing diversity among middle-income nations and their "complex and more intensive forms of relations with the outside world," the paper put the case for development assistance to many of them. Moreover, the "needs of middle income countries are more in line with the Canadian commercial capabilities, and a reasonable amount of aid from Canada can be useful to reinforce the maturing economic and political relationships we wish to develop with them."[38]

A NEW ELIGIBILITY FRAMEWORK

Shortly after he returned as prime minister early in 1980, Pierre Trudeau launched a major campaign to persuade other Western governments to take seriously the Brandt Report's call for a much more sustained initiative in international development. In an effort to stimulate Canadian awareness of the issues involved, he set up a Parliamentary Task Force on North-South Relations. The task force issued a wide-ranging report in December 1980. It made a plea to put some order into the objectives of aid and addressed the question of "balance" posed in the aid policy paper of 1979: "The concept of development assistance is hardly thirty years old. The reasons given for it have been many and varied. Some have argued that it is a way to promote trade. Others have seen it as a means to win friends and frustrate adversaries. Still others want aid to promote their particular concerns or values in developing countries. We think it is time to say simply that *aid is to aid.* Its purpose is to promote human and economic development and to alleviate suffering."

The report recommended that meeting basic human needs be "reaffirmed and strengthened" as a central objective and that the priority on assisting the poorest countries be upheld.[39] The government's official response was laudatory and positive, and it accepted most recommendations with few reservations. It avoided the issue of the primacy of development in the aid program, however, instead affirming that Canada's overall relations with the developing world would continue to be governed by "mutuality of interests" and "humanitarian need."[40] Soon thereafter, at the UN Conference on LLDCs in Paris in 1981, the government did reassert a commitment to the least developed, promising to raise their share of total Canadian aid to 0.15 per cent of GNP, an increase from the then current level of 0.11 per cent.[41]

Meanwhile, although the government was not prepared to endorse all of the recommendations of the Hatch Report for tying aid more strongly to domestic commercial goals, it did agree to boost the share of bilateral at the expense of multilateral ODA for the period 1981–86 "as a means of improving the commercial benefits derived from aid."[42] This two-track policy maintained the commitment to channel the bulk of Canada's ODA to low-income nations including LLDCs but also directed more effort towards strengthening aid and other relations with selected middle-income countries, some of them "program countries" and others not. A new eligibility framework reflecting this approach was approved by the cabinet in 1981. It became part of a larger conceptual-cum-organizational initiative taken by Marcel Massé during his first term as president (1980–82), and, like other innovations during that period, it bore the imprint of a president committed to revitalizing CIDA's developmental mission in a way that was carefully attuned to the political and bureaucratic constraints confronting the agency.

The new eligibility framework refined existing distinctions, classifying countries as I (Core), II-A (Middle Income Non-Core), II-B (Transitional), and III.[43]

- I: major recipients of Canadian ODA; multi-year programming; all aid instruments and delivery channels used
- II-A: development assistance to middle-income countries provided in ways that strengthen long-term political and commercial links; selected instruments; flexible response to opportunities with a minimal administrative burden; broadly defined strategy worked out for each geographical area without multi-year program planning
- II-B: Recipients moving up to core or down to III; selective instruments; only exceptional use of traditional bilateral approaches
- III: minimal presence through strictly responsive programming – Mission Administered Funds, Special Program channels and, where appropriate, food aid

The planned shares for the three categories (I, II, and III) were 75, 20, and 5 per cent, respectively. Since program countries as a group had typically received 80 per cent, this distribution moved them downwards, presumably to create more scope for initiatives in middle-income (II-A) states. Table 3 lists recipients in categories I and II and highlights changes between 1978 and 1981 and later. (By 1986, the distinction between II-A and II-B had been dropped.)

The strengthening of political and commercial links required redefinition of the commitment in Gérin-Lajoie's strategy not to exceed 10 per cent for states with annual per capita incomes of $375 or more (1973 US dollars). Beginning in 1978, CIDA experimented with different databases in its annual DAC reviews. A bilateral distribution based on 1976 US dollars showed that 25.7 per cent went in 1978 to recipients with annual per capita incomes greater than $US400. Nations with annual per capita incomes of more than $450 (US 1978) received 23.0 and 19.9 per cent in 1979 and 1980, respectively. The following year, $625 (US 1978) was picked as a standard. Its use saw allocations to "middle income countries" in 1980 drop to 10.3 per cent; by the same standard, they jumped to 16.3 per cent in 1981. Under Massé, the $625 (US 1978) measure was adopted as a norm, along with a policy of giving at least 80 per cent of government-to-government (conventional bilateral) aid to recipients with annual per capita incomes falling below that threshold. A performance yardstick was also adopted for geographical distribution: 42 per cent to each of Africa and Asia, and 16 per cent to the Americas.[44]

A NEW GOVERNMENT AND A NEW AID STRATEGY

The election of a majority Conservative government in September 1984 raised fears within the Canadian international development community that right-wing Tories might seize the agenda and act out the frustrations about CIDA that they had been venting for years. There was a palpable sense of relief when Brian Mulroney appointed as secretary of state for external affairs Joe Clark, rather than Sinclair Stevens, who had been the External Affairs critic in opposition and during the election campaign. In his first press briefing after the appointment, Clark suggested that "Canadian foreign policy under the new Conservative government will place a 'very high emphasis' on international trade."[45] Pending review of all aspects of foreign policy, however, he indicated that the essentials of the aid program would stay in place.

The outpouring of support from Canadians for victims of African drought in 1984–85 and questioning about how to move beyond relief to lasting development in sub-Saharan Africa created the context for an announcement by William Winegard, MP, that the House of Commons Standing Committee on External Affairs and International Trade (SCEAIT) would review in depth all aspects of Canada's development assistance. The Winegard Committee's report (*For Whose Benefit?*), tabled two years later, acknowledged that CIDA had evolved into an efficient, professional, and well-managed bureaucracy, but one that was uncertain of its role. CIDA had many accomplishments to its credit, but "the aid program continues to betray an ambivalence of purpose and design ... [It] needs a fresh jolt of political energy ... to adapt to the realities of the 1990s and beyond." Aid ought to be "about human development," and "it should help those most in need."[47]

In its thorough review of policy issues, the committee tackled the thorny question of how to focus Canadian aid. It subjected the existing three-tier scheme to harsh criticism: "At best, the country classification system as now constituted is over-extended and betrays a confusion of objectives. It almost invites being held hostage to foreign policy considerations that may have little to do with the basic purposes of the aid program in reaching the poor and promoting self-reliant human development. Rather than bringing clarity and focus to Canada's ODA, the multiplication of categories tends to make our aid efforts appear less concentrated than they really are. It is an exercise that lacks discipline and transparency."[48]

It questioned inclusion of certain countries in category I in the light of other priorities, as it did the absence of any apparent rationale for distinguishing between categories II and III. It recommended abolition of the existing system and designation of no more than 30 core program countries (exclusive of regional groupings) on the basis of development criteria such as absolute need, Canada's experience with the country as an aid partner, the compatibility of the country's development priorities with those of Canada, the demonstrated capacity to use aid effectively (especially for the poor), and respect shown for human rights in the broadest sense. Of direct bilateral ODA, four-fifths ought to go to core countries, with the remaining fifth available project by project to all other developing countries.[49]

The committee supported the existing commitment of 80 per cent of bilateral aid to low-income countries and 0.15 per cent of annual GNP in overall flows to the least developed. It recognized the shift towards Africa of the mid-1980s, which was appropriate in terms of a generally strong anti-poverty orientation, but "we would not want the regional distribution of funds to become unbalanced in ways that might neglect areas less in the public spotlight. Our aid to Asia, the continent that is home to most of the world's poorest people, is already very low on a per capita basis." The existing level of support for the Americas was endorsed.[50]

The government's new aid strategy for the 1990s, *Sharing Our Future*, released in March 1988, abolished eligibility categories and declared that all independent developing countries as defined by the DAC would be eligible for all forms of Canadian ODA unless expressly excluded for political, human rights, or economic reasons.[51] Ironically, in view of the committee's desire to make CIDA's policies more transparent, the government was actually able to remove from the public domain information about eligibility priorities (apparent on the old list), leaving as the only source the completely confidential five-year bilateral planning figures approved each year by cabinet.[52] At least ex post accountability was offered, however, by provision of a number of overlapping quantitative targets for bilateral assistance for the next five years: 75 per cent on 30 countries or regional groupings; 45 per cent on Africa, 39 per cent for Asia, and 16 per cent for the Americas; 65 per cent to developing countries in the Commonwealth and la Francophonie; and 75 per cent to low-income and small island states.[53]

Not surprising, in view of the pressure for proliferation, assistance to the top 30 recipients fell short by 5 per cent of what Winegard recommended. Moreover, in moving away from the existing policy (supported by SCEAIT) of channelling 80 per cent of bilateral allocations to low-income countries towards 75 per cent for these nations and small island states (which included Jamaica, a major middle-income recipient), the strategy immediately raised a question about the depth of the government's formal commitment to the poorest countries. One further target – 50 per cent of total aid to Africa and the LLDCs of Asia and the Americas – was phrased less categorically than the others ("efforts will be made"). The existing commitment to channel 0.15 per cent of GNP to LLDCs was reaffirmed.[54]

Sharing Our Future outlined yet another set of criteria for eligibility – a recipient's needs; its willingness and capacity to manage aid effectively; the quality of its economic and social policies, or its seriousness about improving its policies; Canada's political and economic relations with the country; the recipient's human rights record; and its involvement of the population in the development process.[55] The last reference was new, the link between aid and policy conditionality was stronger than in *For Whose Benefit?*, and there was much less explicit focus on alleviation of poverty.

BILATERAL AID IN THE 1980s

The level of development of ODA recipients and the move towards expanded economic and political ties with selected low- and middle-income states influenced decisions for eligibility and allocation in the 1980s. As can be seen in Table 3, six core countries/programming units were added – China, Egypt, the Philippines, SADCC (the Southern African Development Coordination Conference), Thailand, and Zimbabwe. The five other Central American republics joined Honduras as a core region. Guinea was the only deletion from the list of high-priority recipients.

Three factors – support for the front-line states facing South Africa's apartheid regime, the Commonwealth link, and the prospect of expanded relations with one of the more developed countries in sub-Saharan Africa – contributed to an immediate decision to establish a sizeable program in Zimbabwe as soon as Robert Mugabe achieved political power in 1980. The launching in 1983 of a major program within the SADCC framework was riskier and less predictable. SADCC was established in 1980 as a partnership among front-line states eager to reduce their dependence on South Africa and to accelerate their economic development through coordinated regional efforts. Angola, Botswana, Lesotho, Malawi, Mozambique, Swaziland, Tanzania, Zambia, and Zimbabwe are members. Canada's 1983 decision, later endorsed by Brian Mulroney's government, has led to its having the largest presence of any bilateral donor in regional projects aimed at reconstructing and developing transportation, communications, and energy infrastructures and at strengthening human resources and institutions. Major core programs were retained in Tanzania, Zambia, and Zimbabwe, but "Botswana-Lesotho-Swaziland" was shifted to non-core, except insofar as they formed part of SADCC projects. By the end of the decade, SADCC ranked as Canada's largest recipient in Africa and third overall, behind Bangladesh and Indonesia (see Table 1).

CIDA's annual report for 1979–80 noted that Egypt "is of special interest in that the relatively high level of that country's economy can cause significant commercial benefits to accrue to Canada."[56] Egypt was elevated to category 1 in 1981. Mutual interests inspired addition of China and Thailand to Indonesia as Asian countries targeted for development of links with Canada. The choice of China, as a low-income state, could also be justified (like Indonesia) in terms of directive the bulk of bilateral ODA to the poorest. The new Thai and Chinese programs and a revamped one in Indonesia were designed when the international aid establishment was questioning the value of mega-projects. They bore the imprint of Marcel Massé's belief that concentration on longer-term human resource development and strategic "networking" with local elites would more effectively reconcile developmental objectives and Canadian interests.

The defeat of Ferdinand Marcos's regime in 1986 prompted a quick decision to indicate Canada's support for democracy in the Philippines and earmark that nation for a longer-term relationship. By 1989–90, both China and the Philippines were receiving more government-to-government assistance than India and Sri Lanka. The jump in aid to the Philippines was the most dramatic in the history of the aid program – from virtually none in 1985–86 to a promise in the following year of over $20 million per annum.

There were no classification changes in the Americas beyond redefinition late in the decade of all of Central America as a core region.

Jamaica and Peru, both struggling with high debt loads and deteriorating social conditions, emerged as major recipients. In Jamaica, disbursements in 1989–90 made it the sixth-biggest program overall and larger than any one African country. Although Canadian assistance has not especially had a bias towards small countries, Jamaica does stand out as a dramatic exception. The $33 million allocated in that year amounted to approximately $13.70 per person, compared to $1.15 per person in Bangladesh, which, at $125 million, was the largest recipient!

While no other countries attained core status, Ethiopia, Mozambique, and Sudan – all racked by civil strife, periodic drought and famine, and desperate poverty – received major increases in bilateral ODA, while Mozambique secured further support through the SADCC initiative. Modest programming was started again in Uganda after Yoweri Museveni restored relative stability in 1986. Jordan moved from category III to II and began getting Canadian aid for the first time ever, following a trade and aid mission led by Joe Clark to the Middle East in 1986.

As chapter 8, below, documents, NGOs, church and support groups, and the media exhibited lively concern about the link between external aid and human rights during the 1980s. The Liberal government suspended ODA to Guatemala and El Salvador in 1981 on the grounds that escalating violence under military regimes made aid work impossible. Modest programming was restored in El Salvador in 1984 and Guatemala in 1987 after controversial elections brought civilians to power. Both actions led to sharp criticism, as did Canada's larger presence in Honduras at a time when American support for the Nicaraguan contras was turning it into an armed camp. Human rights abuses and civil strife prompted questioning at various times of Canada's aid to Ethiopia, Guyana, Haiti, Indonesia, the Philippines, Sri Lanka, Sudan, Zaïre, and, after the military suppression of the pro-democracy movement in Tianamen Square, China.

On aid distribution by national income level, Table 4 shows that between 1979–80 and 1989–90 bilateral flows to LLDCs increased less rapidly than those to other recipients. Between 1979–80 and 1984–85, the share obtained by middle-income countries increased by more than 3 per cent, virtually all at the expense of LLDCs. The proportions changed little between 1984–85 and 1989–90, in part because the official emphasis on selected low- and middle-income recipients was offset by continuing large shipments of food aid to Bangladesh and the poorer African countries. Nevertheless, of the top ten recipients in 1989–90 (see Table 1), three were in the middle-income group (Cameroon, Jamaica, and Morocco) and a fourth (Indonesia) was at

Table 4
Percentage distribution of allocable Canadian bilateral aid by income level of
recipient countries, 1979–80, 1984–85, 1989–90, and percentage increases,
1979–80 to 1989–90

	% distribution			% increase
Income level	1979–80	1984–85	1989–90	1979–80 to 1989–90
Least developed	39.5	35.6	35.7	44.9
	(227.5)	(296.5)	(329.6)	
Other low-income	42.4	42.5	42.6	60.6
	(244.8)	(354.2)	(393.2)	
Middle-income	18.1	21.9	21.7	91.8
	(102.5)	(182.2)	(200.4)	

Sources: Adapted from CIDA, Annual Report, 1981–82, 1985–86, 1989–90, using the World Bank's
classification of countries by income level. The figures in parentheses are in $million.

the top of the low-income category, as was Egypt, which stood eleventh.[57] Moreover, while the official target of 0.15 per cent of GNP for LLDCs was achieved in 1985,[58] the level fell to 0.11 per cent in 1989 and further thereafter, as the total volume of Canadian aid as a percentage of GNP shrank in the wake of budget cuts in the late 1980s and early 1990s.

The bilateral program was less concentrated among the top 10 recipients in 1989–90 (43.5 per cent) than in 1980–81 (52.9 per cent), continuing a trend of the 1970s (see Table 1). The two-track policy that emerged at the beginning of the decade may have increased the shares of Asia and the Americas at the expense of Africa. Table 2, however, reflects Canada's positive response to deteriorating conditions in sub-Saharan Africa, which forestalled that outcome; a further shift from Asia to Africa occurred. The share allocated to the Americas, especially the Commonwealth Caribbean, did, however, grow in the late 1980s.

INTO THE 1990S: CUTBACKS, CONCENTRATION, AND CHOICES

Although the balance in ODA allocations between support for the poorest countries and pursuit of other foreign and economic policy goals shifted somewhat towards the latter during the 1980s, an expanding budget facilitated maintenance of a two-track strategy that still favoured low-income countries. It also permitted further expansion in the number of aid recipients. That context began to change, however, in the wake of a succession of deep cuts in planned ODA expenditures beginning in 1989–90 and an absolute reduction in 1993–94. The rationale offered during both the boom of the late 1980s and the recession that followed was the need for deficit reduction, but the effect on the aid budget was disproportionately severe. The collapse of communism affected allocations as well – there were new calls for economic assistance to eastern Europe and the former Soviet Union, and the end of the Cold War raised questions about the role of aid to the South. Yet another pressure for change emerged from the rise of regional trading blocs and the prospect of closer trading links for Canada with Mexico and other Latin American states; in 1991, the cabinet approved a shift of 2 per cent in the shares of bilateral funds from Asia (39 to 37 per cent) to the Americas (16 to 18 per cent).[59]

This changing situation provided the backdrop for a strategic management review of CIDA. It was initiated at the political level but was seen by Marcel Massé (who returned as president in 1989) as an opportunity to redirect the agency from being largely an overseer of aid projects towards development of a much more policy-oriented programming capacity. In a detailed report (Strategic Management Review) made public late in 1991, Groupe Secor, the consulting firm engaged for the first phase of the review, concluded that CIDA was stretching its human and financial resources far too thinly in terms of geographical spread, sectors, channels, programs, and projects. It drew renewed attention to the wide dispersal of recipient countries, which was costly in both financial and administrative terms. The document prepared by Groupe Secor noted the limited degree to which bilateral aid in 1989–90 was concentrated in core countries – 65 per cent in anglophone Africa, 74 per cent in francophone Africa, and 69 per cent in the Americas. Resources were highly focused only in Asia (95 per cent).[60] The review suggested that these characteristics resulted in a low level of leverage or "aid related influence" in comparison with the bilateral programs of most other donor countries.

The review's conception of leverage is open to debate on many fronts, not least the proxy measure that it employed – the percentage of recipients to which a donor country delivers 10 per cent or more of total bilateral ODA.[61] Nevertheless, the document conveyed some revealing data. Canada's "leverage index" for the period 1987–89 (12 per cent) was among the lowest of the DAC and substantially below that of other mid-range donors such as Australia, Italy, the Netherlands, Sweden and the United Kingdom. Moreover, of the 13 countries in which Canada achieved the 10 per cent threshold, only Bangladesh and Ghana were outside the Americas (where the so-called leveraged recipients were either small or, as in the case of Colombia, received little aid).[62] While recognizing that eligibility was a matter for the cabinet to determine, the review strongly supported geographical and other forms of concentration as means of enabling "CIDA to better allocate its resources, enhance its leverage in the aid industry and improve its performance in delivering aid."[63] The second phase of the strategic management review, an internal process within CIDA, endorsed concentration as an essential component in any restructuring of activities.

Meanwhile, pressure to focus mounted after the government announced in February 1991 creation of a single funding framework for ODA and various ad hoc support programs for eastern Europe and the former Soviet republics. Initially, the ad hoc support took less than 5 per cent of the new International Assistance Envelope (IAE). In the 1992–93 fiscal year, however, a 3 per cent increase in the IAE (well below the earlier planned level) was divided equally between ODA and these new programs. The IAE was then cut by 10 per cent for 1993–94, but $47 million was added to the $100 million provision for eastern Europe and the former Soviet Union, "thus implying an even sharper cut to the developing countries component (ODA) of the Envelope."[64] The Department of External Affairs – now External Affairs and International Trade Canada (EAITC) – took on the new eastern European programs.

In the fall of 1992, CIDA sought cabinet approval for a much-delayed submission setting forth proposals from the strategic management review, including greater geographical concentration. Officials at EAITC prevented consideration, arguing that much had changed internationally since publication of *Sharing Our Future* in 1988 and that a review of all aspects of Canada's international assistance policies should occur before CIDA's programming was changed in ways that might now not make sense. The budget cuts for 1993–94 and beyond, announced in December 1992, further spurred preparation within EAITC of an "International Assistance Policy Update." A draft of the document, leaked to the public at the end of January 1993, created an immediate uproar among concerned parliamentarians and members of the NGO community.

As noted in chapter 13, below, the policy update recommended dramatic deviation in the balance of policy, away from the long-term anti-poverty and developmental goals of *Sharing Our Future* and towards a much shorter-run preoccupation with foreign and commercial policy goals. With respect to geographical spread and concentration, the draft advocated a "shift from global coverage to strategic intervention" at "acupuncture points where Canada can achieve maximum influence." A "credible commitment to development cooperation in a climate of budgetary restraint" required narrowing the focus to a few key countries and regions "of long-term strategic interest to Canada," chosen on the basis of foreign policy priorities, "including development objectives." Besides envisaging increased assistance to eastern Europe and the former Soviet republics, the update proposed cutting out fully two-thirds of the 56 countries for which CIDA had planning figures, including approximately half of the core recipients. Of the 14 to 18 remaining, only 8 to 10 would be "development assistance countries" for purposes of "traditional CIDA multi-dimensional" programming. The other six to eight would be "economic cooperation countries" targeted for "mutually beneficial trade development relationships" and "long-term market penetration" by the Canadian private sector. Depending on the funding chosen, the latter would receive between 40 and 60 per cent of the funds earmarked for the two categories.[65]

Given the awkward timing of the leak – in the year of a federal election – the government responded to public pressure by postponing the policy review until there was an opportunity for an open consultative process. Choices about recipients were made, however, in the wake of the 10 per cent budget cut for 1993–94. The choices were not as drastic as those advocated in the draft policy update, but some were made with sufficient finality to foreclose future public discussion. While spread evenly over each of the geographical branches, the actual year-by-year reduction for CIDA's bilateral programs – 4.6 percent – was not distributed equally within the regions. Within Asia, already the area of greatest concentration, planned disbursements to Sri Lanka (racked by civil strife) continued to fall and some marginal country programs were dropped; for the most part, allocations to each major recipient were trimmed in preference to dropping any one of them. In the Americas, "mutual interest" in South America meant that cuts were heaviest in Central America and especially the Caribbean, but no core country or region was eliminated.

In terms of the choice of Canada's bilateral recipients, the most severe budgetary repercussions were felt in sub-Saharan Africa. Soon after merger of the old anglophone Africa and francophone Africa programs in 1991, the new Africa and Middle East Branch had produced a strategy paper, "Africa 21," which projected a vision of a more united, democratic, and entrepreneurial Africa in the twenty-first century. It called upon CIDA to play a "catalytic role" in support of greater regional integration and to reorient programming more along regional lines.[66] Then, faced with reduced commitments in 1993, the branch chose to phase out bilateral assistance in East and Central Africa rather than taking an across-the-board approach.[67] Of the five long-standing core countries in the region – Cameroon, Kenya, Rwanda, Tanzania, and Zaire – three had already experienced suspension (Zaire) or curtailment (Kenya and Rwanda) of Canadian aid in response to human rights abuses and political unrest. However, the decision to drop Tanzania, the largest country program in Africa since the mid-1970s, was a shock. By withdrawing from Ethiopia as well, CIDA was thereby terminating bilateral programming in the world's second- and third-poorest countries in terms of per capita annual income. In contrast, even within the region, Cameroon, a middle-income nation, was spared somewhat (in part because of its bilingual status), while the somewhat smaller program in Gabon, an even wealthier country, was unaffected.[68]

SUMMARY AND CONCLUSIONS

The political calculus that shaped distribution of Canadian aid – especially the large initial allocations to the Indian subcontinent and then the major expansion into sub-Saharan Africa – skewed bilateral allocations towards lower-income countries. When greater sensitivity to the plight of the least developed and those most affected by the energy and food crises of the early 1970s gave rise to pressures to hold donors accountable on these matters, Canada was able to say that the bulk of its ODA went to LLDCs and other low-income recipients. Efforts by CIDA's planners to entrench this as policy and to secure a new, more development-oriented framework of eligibility were challenged by other bureaucrats who wanted aid distribution better to reflect trade and diplomatic priorities. While interdepartmental rivalry and inertia within the agency itself precluded much change, enshrinement of the status quo in the *Strategy for International Development Cooperation 1975–1980* helped to contain a determined effort from the late 1970s onwards to link aid allocations to trade promotion. What then emerged was a two-track approach, which maintained the commitment to the poorest countries but focused more energy on developing longer-term relations with middle and selected low-income recipients, especially in Asia.

Although promoters of a stronger aid-trade link looked to Asia for opportunities, especially after the debt crisis stopped growth in Latin America, the historical trend in allocations was for Africa to gain relatively at the expense of Asia (see Table 2). This process was accelerated when aid to India dropped markedly after that country's explosion of a nuclear device using Canadian technology in 1974. It continued in the 1980s when aid to sub-Saharan Africa grew in the wake of the 1984–85 famine and support was stepped up for the front-line states and regional cooperation in southern Africa.

"We envy the Swedes and the Danes," a long-serving CIDA person told the author in 1990 when commenting on Canada's extraordinary range of recipients, its wide geopolitical dispersal of bilateral funds, its lack of regional concentration, and its relatively marginal aid presence even in core countries. As we have seen, the proliferation of ODA partners can be understood in terms of the foreign and domestic political goals that spawned a global program before any efforts were made to rationalize decision making on eligibility and allocations. Once the distributional pattern was established, inertia and an expanding aid budget (albeit below promised levels) ensured relative stability until the end of the 1980s. Changes, mostly additive, occurred largely as responses to crises and/or opportunities such as the African famine, China's opening to the West, and the fall of Marcos.

In the 1990s, however, the issues of geographical concentration and focus became salient as never before when the Conservative government's spending cuts imposed a heavy burden on the ODA budget. The pressure has been heightened by competing demands for economic assistance from eastern Europe and the former Soviet Union. Moreover, given structural dislocations and recession within the Canadian economy, the government was trying to exact more of a pay-off from the aid program for its "prosperity initiative," even as it reduced resources. The two-track strategy is unlikely to be abandoned, but, as the recent cuts in its African programming demonstrated, Canada's commitment to the poorest countries of the South is increasingly at risk.

NOTES

1 In 1974, Canada sent 17.5 and 61.0 per cent of its official development assistance to the least developed and to other low-income countries, respectively. The DAC averages were 9.9 and 54.6 per cent, respectively. Organisation for Economic Co-operation and Development (OECD), *Development Co-operation: Efforts and Policies of the Members of the Development Assistance Committee 1990* (Paris: OECD 1990), 233–41.

2 In 1990–91, bilateral funds were allocated to 108 countries and to regional programs in southern and western Africa, Southeast Asia, and the Caribbean. Canadian International Development Agency (CIDA), *Annual Report 1990–91*, S9–S20. This chapter is concerned only with government-to-government aid, but the total number of country and regional recipients of Canadian ODA from all channels (including multilateral, non-governmental organizations, and business cooperation programs) in 1991 was 158. See Groupe Secor, Strategic Management Review: Working Document (9 October 1991), 13/1.

3 This section is a brief summary of material on geographical distribution in the author's forthcoming book on the history of CIDA and the Canadian development assistance program.

4 Keith Spicer, *A Samaritan State? External Aid in Canada's Foreign Policy* (Toronto: University of Toronto Press 1966), 3.

5 Ibid., 56.

6 Douglas Anglin, "Canada and Africa: The Trudeau Years," *Africa Contemporary Record*, 1983–84, A189.

7 Economic Council of Canada, *For a Common Future: A Study of Canada's Relations with Developing Countries* (Hull: Supply and Services 1978), 98.

8 CIDA, Report of the Strategy Task Force on Eligibility, Strategy 1975–1980, Key Policy Papers, vol. 1, typescript, September 1974, 10.

9 CIDA, *Annual Review 1968–69*, 9.

10 OECD, *Development Assistance 1969*, 161.

11 CIDA, Key Policy Papers, 11.

12 Deparment of External Affairs, *International Development: Foreign Policy for Canadians* (Ottawa 1970), 18–19.

13 CIDA, *Annual Review 1970–71*, 14.

14 CIDA, Key Policy Papers, 12–13; quotation from 12. The countries deleted were Bolivia, Brunei, Burundi, Central African Republic, Cyprus, Dominican Republic, Fiji, Gambia, Guinea, Hong Kong, Maldives, Paraguay, Philippines, Sierra Leone, Singapore, Somalia, South Korea, and Western Samoa. Of these, only Bolivia, Guinea, and the Philippines subsequently made a "comeback" of any significance.

15 George Cunningham, *The Management of Aid Agencies* (London: Croon Helm 1974), 129–30.

16 CIDA, Key Policy Papers, 13–14.

17 Ibid., 15.

18 Ibid., 1–3.

19 Ibid., 32.

20 Following the appeal launched at UNCTAD III in 1972 to pay attention to the special needs of the least developed, another agency task force had already made a number of recommendations for increasing the size and quality of CIDA's economic and social assistance to the 25 countries so identified. See CIDA, Report of the Action Committee on the Least Developed Countries, typescript, January 1973.

21 See Glyn R. Berry, "Bureaucratic Politics and Canadian Economic Policies Affecting the Developing Countries – the Case of the Strategy for International Development Cooperation 1975–1980," PhD dissertation, Dalhousie University, 1981.

22 Ibid., 326 and 335.

23 CIDA, *Strategy for International Development Cooperation 1975–1980* (Ottawa: CIDA 1975) 23 and 25.

24 Berry, "Bureaucratic Politics," 356.

25 CIDA, *Strategy*, 27.

26 CIDA, *Annual Aid Review to DAC 1972*, 18; *1975*, 12; and *1976*, 8.

27 Gérin-Lajoie insisted that Haiti be included in the Latin American program. It was the only independent French-speaking country in the Western Hemisphere and the least developed. He encountered strong objections from the people in CIDA's Planning Division who doubted that it would be possible to do much meaningful development work under the corrupt and dictatorial regime of "Papa Doc" Duvalier (author's interview). The sceptical position was by and large vindicated.

28 CIDA, *Annual Aid Review 1975–76*, 25 and 27; *Annual Aid Review to DAC 1976*, 7.

29 North-South Institute, *In the Canadian Interest? Third World Development in the 1980s* (Ottawa: North-South Institute 1980), 11–12.

30 J.L. Granatstein and Robert Bothwell, *Pirouette: Pierre Trudeau and Canadian Foreign Policy* (Toronto: University of Toronto Press 1990), 294.

31 Réal P. Lavergne, "Determinants of Canadian Aid Policy," in O. Stokke, ed., *Western Middle Powers and Global Poverty* (Uppsala: Scandinavian Institute of African Studies 1989), 60.

32 See Patricia Jean Appavoo, "The Small State as Donor: Canadian and Swedish Development Assistance Policies, 1960–1976," PhD dissertation, University of Toronto, 1988, 184–9.

33 See CIDA, *Annual Review 1972–73*, 24; Appavoo, "The Small State," 189–95; and Paul Ladouceur, "Humanitarian Aid for Southern Africa," in Douglas Anglin et al., eds., *Canada, Scandinanvia and Southern Africa* (Uppsala: Scandinavian Institute of African Affairs 1978), 85–102.

34 CIDA, President's Office, Directions for the Agency, 7 December 1977.

35 Department of Industry, Trade and Commerce, *Strengthening Canada Abroad: Final Report of the Export Promotion Review Committee*, (Ottawa 1979), 35–36.

36 See "MacDonald Pledges New Direction in Foreign Aid Policy," *Ottawa Journal*, 20 August 1979.

37 Dated 30 November 1979, they were published, after the Liberals returned to power, in House of Commons, *Proceedings*, Parliamentary Task Force on North-South Relations, 10 June 1980, 3A, 28–195.

38 Ibid., 172–5; quotations on 173 and 175.

39 House of Commons, Parliamentary Task Force on North-South Relations, *Report to the House of Commons on the Relations between Developed and Developing Countries*, 1980, 37 and 39.

40 External Affairs, Government Response to the Report of the Parliamentary Task Force on North-South Relations, 15 June 1981, 1.

41 CIDA, *Annual Aid Review to DAC 1981*, 25; *1983*, 16.

42 Department of External Affairs, *A Review of Canadian Trade Policy* (Ottawa 1983), 163.

43 Canadian Council for International Co-operation (CCIC), Excerpts from a CIDA Paper on the Agency Programming Framework, Ottawa, December 1981, 3–5. The category descriptions are my summaries.

44 Reported in and calculated from CIDA, *Annual Aid Review to DAC 1978*, 16; *1979*, 21; *1980*, 18; *1981*, 26.

45 *Ottawa Citizen*, 18 September 1984.

46 House of Commons, Standing Committee on External Affairs and National Defence, *The Second Report to the House (Response to the Report of the Honourable David MacDonald on the African Famine)*, *Proceedings*, 18–19 April 1985, 14, 3–14.

47 House of Commons, Standing Committee on External Affairs and International Trade (SCEAIT), *For Whose Benefit? Report of the Standing Committee on External Affairs and International Trade on Canada's Official Development Assistance Policies and Programs* (Ottawa: Supply and Services 1987), 3 and 12.

48 Ibid., 65.

49 Ibid., 66–7.

50 Ibid., 61.

51 CIDA, *Sharing Our Future: Canada's International Development Assistance* (Hull: Supply and Services 1987), 28. With respect to level of economic development, any country that "has been 'graduated'" from World Bank lending would "normally" be excluded. As before, European countries still officially classified as developing – such as Greece, Portugal, and Yugoslavia – would be excluded. The "independent" criterion would be qualified, as in the past, to permit inclusion of some of Britain's few remaining Caribbean dependencies.

52 Groupe Secor's management review of CIDA provided a snapshot of CIDA's core countries, which showed that the list had been changed only slightly since it was last published in 1986. Guinea was dropped from francophone Africa, and Honduras was merged into a core region encompassing all six Central American republics. See Groupe Secor, Strategic Management Review, 13/1–34/1. See Table 3 for the 1986 list.

53 CIDA, *Sharing Our Future*, 30.

54 Ibid., 30 and 22.

55 Ibid., 30.

56 CIDA, *Annual Report 1979–80*, 14.

57 Moreover, 16 of the top 40 recipients over 1988–91 were in the middle-income category. Andrew Clarke undertook a statistical analysis of

Canadian bilateral aid to these countries and found no statistically significant relationship between the amount of that aid and a country's per
capita annual income or its ranking in the UNDP's Human Development
Index. See Clarke, "ODA Analyzed: Another Canadian Aid Paradox?"
Review (Ottawa: North-South Institute, fall 1992), 7–8.
58 CIDA, *Annual Aid Review to DAC 1985*, 7.
59 CIDA, *Annual Aid Review to DAC 1991*, 22.
60 Groupe Secor, Strategic Management Review, 36/1.
61 Ibid., 92/1.
62 Ibid., 97/1–115/1.
63 Ibid., 8/4.
64 Andrew Clark, "Secret Paper Steers Aid Policy Changes," *Review* (Ottawa:
North-South Institute, spring 1993), 1.
65 External Affairs, "International Assistance Policy Update," typescript,
January 1993.
66 CIDA, Africa and Middle East Branch, *Africa 21: A Vision of Africa in the
21st Century* (October 1991).
67 The Maghreb and the Middle East were exempted on grounds of foreign
policy (Canada's involvement in the peace process) and commercial
interest. While all of the sub-Saharan programs have been focused on long-
term development and alleviation of poverty, Canada's support for
a democratic transition in South Africa and long-term mutual interest ensured a continuing commitment to southern Africa. The anglophone/
francophone mix was an important factor in the decision to maintain a
presence in West Africa.
68 See material distributed by CIDA to the Standing Committee on External
Affairs and International Trade, 20 April 1993. The countries dropped
for purposes of bilateral programming were promised access to new but
limited "thematic" funds in the areas of private-sector development
and human rights, democratic development, and good government. In
addition, Tanzania will remain eligible for regional funds channelled
through the Southern Africa Development Community (created in 1992
as a successor to SADCC).

6 An Institutional Analysis of CIDA

PHILLIP RAWKINS

INTRODUCTION

The central concern of this chapter is CIDA's complex organization and the dynamics internal to the agency and underlining its relations with other elements of the government of Canada. This approach provides a vantage-point from which we may better understand the efforts of CIDA and its senior management to ensure organizational survival in difficult times. It also seeks to balance a focus on senior management with consideration of the perspective of those at the working level in the agency. "Top-down" and "bottom-up" views will be brought together in an examination of the interaction of efforts at reform and the priorities of those directly responsible for day-to-day implementation of the development assistance program.

The analysis presented here represents an effort to answer the question "how does CIDA work?" A critical element of the answer is recognition that "CIDA" is not a seamless web, but rather a loose collection of task-oriented units, with a large measure of autonomy in decision-making at the operating level. How well the agency works depends not so much on formal rules and regulations as on the culture of the organization; the common understandings of senior and middle management, the program officers, and other staff members; and the general sense of purpose and direction that informs the agency's activities. Much depends on the ability of senior management to balance the need to demonstrate understanding of the culture and cherished values of the organization with an ability to set clear directions and determine new goals without being held back by the pull of habit and tradition. At the time of writing, the agency is in the midst of an effort by senior management to restructure the organization and transform management processes and the mix of activities that makes up the workload of those at both managerial and operating levels.

For CIDA, as with other public organizations, there are three central problems to address, which, when met successfully, will provide a basis for ensuring organizational success. The way in which senior management characteristically deals with these issues will also reveal a great deal about the nature of the organization and its capacity to respond to new challenges.[1] First, managers must decide how to perform their critical task: emphasizing and rewarding those types of behaviour, which, if successfully performed by key organizational members, would enable the organization to deal effectively with the critical and potentially threatening elements of the environment in which it operates. Second, they must decide how the critical task is to be performed, build and internalize a sense of mission, and give employees a sense of pride in, and identification with, what the organization does and the manner in which it carries out its work. Third, they must achieve a reasonable degree of autonomy (and support from above) in carrying out their activities.

This book represents an effort to address Canada's performance as a contributor to the practice of nurturing development. What this chapter seeks to do is to demonstrate that CIDA is far more than a passive tool for management and delivery of an aid program. It is an active participant in the shaping of policy and practice. Hence its character and organizational priorities will have considerable effect on the character and quality of the Canadian Development Assistance Program.

This chapter seeks to assess the capacity of CIDA as a public agency to undertake and manage the environment in which it operates, while pursuing objectives intended to strengthen its standing in government, with Parliament, and with the public and thus to secure its hold on the resources that it requires to survive and proper. At the same time, attention will also be given to the organization's efforts to instill and maintain a sense of mission and commitment in its employees in the context of considerable internal and external change and to obtain the necessary degree of autonomy within government to define objectives and develop its strategy to achieve them. How the agency has tackled these issues has affected the character of the Canadian aid program and its developmental results.

The role of deputy minister in the Canadian political system is one of considerable importance. In the case of CIDA, the senior civil servant has the title "President," suggesting an unusual degree of independence. The role of the president is to mediate between CIDA and the government of Canada and, on a day-to-day basis, to represent the agency in its dealings with developing countries and other donor agencies. Most critical is the capacity of the agency's chief executive officer to secure the resources and space for manoeuvre in government essential to the fortunes of CIDA and its work-force. The president must also play the central role in determining broad directions, while demonstrating to the staff empathy with the central values of the agency. The capacity to perform the various facets of the role and to allocate resources judiciously to the agency's major tasks has varied among the individuals who have held the position.

In the years since 1985, in the context of fiscal restraint, a public service undergoing contraction, and a government committed to a specific political agenda, the effectiveness of the president has become even more central to CIDA's fortunes. Thus a good deal of attention will necessarily be given to the agenda and the impact of successive presidents, particularly Marcel Massé during his second term, from 1989 to March 1993. It was Massé who determined that CIDA must undertake a series of major structural and policy adjustments to maintain a credible position among major donors. The focus of this chapter is on the character of the agency as he found it in 1989 and on his vision and the effects of efforts by senior managers under his leadership to translate that vision into a plan of action.

In the 1990s, the whole apparatus of "foreign aid" is undergoing scrutiny on a global basis. Difficult questions are being asked about the purpose and effectiveness of aid. In Canada, the fight against the deficit takes priority over the government's promises of development assistance. All of this simply reinforces the reality that CIDA is not immortal. Government departments and public agencies, in Ottawa as elsewhere, flourish, struggle, and sometimes disappear. Failure to adjust to changes in the environment is probably at the root of a majority of cases of "organizational death."[2] The challenge is to adapt or die, and CIDA perceives itself to be embarked on a strategy through which it hopes to secure its future.

CIDA IN ITS ENVIRONMENT

CIDA began as a highly dependent organization. As its budget grew during the 1970s, so other departments' interest in the aid program expanded. In these early years, many members of the CIDA management team came from External Affairs and other parts of government. In terms of their further advancement, they had little apparent incentive to encourage the agency to take a more independent path.[3] In any case, the need to win the approval of the central agencies was vital to securing continuing growth in the aid budget and hence to gaining credibility in the eyes of government-at-large, with international organizations, and with the governments of developing countries. In the case of CIDA, while its "parent" ministry, External Affairs, is obviously crucial, just as important has been the disposition of the Prime Minister's Office (PMO), the Privy Council Office (PCO), the Treasury Board, and the Department of Finance. The logical way to secure support from the centres of bureaucratic power was to accept, at least in part, the agendas of others.

Through the first dozen years of its existence, rapid growth in the aid budget and much slower increases in staffing levels left CIDA little opportunity for quiet reflection on its development objectives. At the working level, officers were minimally affected by higher-level discussions. At the project and country program level, there was far less need for interdepartmental consultation than would be the case in the 1980s. The agency's resources were expanding rapidly, but it had little ability to channel these resources in a deliberate and measured way.

The Winegard Report – For Whose Benefit? (1987) – a major parliamentary study of Canadian development assistance, suggests that by the 1980s CIDA "had entered something akin to a mid-life crisis."[4] This reflected a more general sense among those associated with the aid program that "something was wrong." The report recommended that CIDA emphasize aid to the poorest, put development priorities first, establish an advisory council, put in place an ODA charter, and mandate a "floor" to ODA as a percentage of GNP, all in an effort to shore up the aid program and to maintain Canada's "constructive internationalism." These proposals, along with concerns expressed about the ambivalence of the purpose and design of the aid program, directly addressed a sense of drift observed by many CIDA officers as well as outsiders.

In order to understand these concerns, we should look more closely at the operational pressures that had formed the agency. During the 1970s, CIDA's primary operational problem was simply the handling of disbursements – getting the money spent. The second challenge was to respond to recipients' concerns, as well as commercial and foreign policy demands. As a former vice-president recalls, CIDA responded to the rapid growth in aid budgets in three ways: by increased allocations to international financial institutions (IFIs) and multilateral agencies (a cheque-writing operation), by expanding food aid and extending large lines of credit to Asia (commodity funds), and elsewhere by emphasizing infrastructure projects that spent more money.[5] Another senior administrator of the time commented: "We had a great deal of money and very little knowledge of where the money went. There was very little formal planning or country programming and we had none of the equipment (i.e. computer based management and information systems) that we have now ... In the bilateral branches, we didn't know what our commitments were and didn't have a firm grasp on our financial planning."[6]

CIDA had sought to get by with a relatively small and centralized work-force that attempted to cope with a set of regulations designed primarily to ensure that tying requirements on Canadian "sourcing" of goods and services were met. It had paid relatively little attention to putting in place quality controls or financial systems, to developing clear guidelines, or to training project officers in program and project management. The pressure to disburse intensified in 1977–78, when a new government regulation decreed that, at the end of the fiscal year, all unspent money would be deemed to have "lapsed."[7] Almost inevitably, this precariously poised house of cards collapsed.

A devastating report by the auditor general in 1979 on CIDA's administrative practice followed other serious criticisms. A series of horror stories of expensive and poorly planned projects appeared in the media. Questions asked in Parliament added to the agency's difficulties and fuelled a search by the media for new lines of investigation. The severity of the attack "shook up the entire staff of the agency."[8]

The next several years saw the building of management systems, initially under the supervision of the Office of the Comptroller General, and the setting up of mechanisms of reporting and accountability to assure cabinet, the central agencies, and Parliament that money was being spent in the right places, through correct channels, and according to appropriate criteria. The overall result was to concentrate the attention of personnel at all levels on managing the government process, with direct management of projects assigned increasingly to the private sector and "non-profit" contractors.[9]

Despite the problems associated with what, from an organizational viewpoint, had amounted to overly rapid growth in the aid program, CIDA's work-force exhibited remarkable resilience. With rapid expansion of its budget, from the late 1960s, through the 1970s, and into the 1980s, CIDA was able to increase its personnel base substantially, recruiting directly a cadre of people who brought to the agency a commitment to development and a desire to build a career around it.

Many members of this group had prior experience in the field through working with non-governmental organizations (NGOs). Through their struggle to make sense of a program quite lacking in systems and detailed directives, it was they, essentially, who formed the culture of the organization. By the mid-1980s, this group filled many senior- and middle-management positions at CIDA.

Informally, the agency had developed a particular view of itself. There was a stubborn pride about the ability of project officers to take on substantial delegated authority and cope with adversity, impossible workloads, unmanageable guidelines, and the insensitivities of the central agencies. CIDA's people saw (and see) themselves as different, as professionals in the development field, as defenders of a mandate of development, and as participants in a shared fate. In the 1990s, as the agency accommodates itself to new organizational challenges, and financial uncertainties, there are signs that its organizational culture is weakening.

SECURING THE FOUNDATIONS:
THE EARLY 1980S

From the early 1980s onwards, CIDA has devoted a great deal of attention to strengthening support and visibility for the agency both in government and in the public eye. In the wake of the "time of troubles" of the late 1970s, during which its credibility as a soundly managed organization was badly damaged, consultations with other departments were regularized, potential conflicts within government were smoothed over, and confrontation was avoided.

The government saw and communicated the need to take remedial action to increase domestic support for the program. Continued action was also necessary to ensure that aid money was seen to be well managed. The building of close relations with domestic constituencies – the private sector, the NGOs, churches, universities and colleges, and professional associations, as well as provincial governments – received high priority. Greater attention was devoted to communicating with the citizeny at large, and the agency began to commission and to review carefully opinion polls on public support for overseas development assistance.

The strength of organizational culture and of the sense of mission among employees grew as a result of CIDA's increased capacity to manage its relations with the rest of government. With the stronger internal process and greater openness to interdepartmental consultation, the agency's earlier difficulties with External Affairs, Finance, and the Treasury Board diminished. Early in her years (1983–89) as CIDA's president, Margaret Catley-Carlson was able to obtain for the agency substantially more authority over approval of contracts. Promotion of insiders as senior managers in the branches administering the bilateral aid programs may have helped build employees' confidence that those at the executive level understood the nature of the work undertaken by project officers and middle managers.

During his short initial tenure as president from 1980 to 1982, Marcel Massé also reinforced the sense of mission by leading what some remember as a continuing seminar in the President's Committee on how to tackle development. The famous "CPD Course" for country program directors held at Mont Ste-Marie is still remembered fondly as an inspirational experience by many of today's senior and middle managers.

With Massé's departure, demonstrating to the government CIDA's capacity to "deliver the goods" continued to define the agency's directions. With emphasis on handling projects efficiently, senior managers concentrated on handling the project cycle, expanding the range of delivery channels, collaborating with domestic constituencies and suppliers, and selling the program to the public.

Planning procedures improved substantially. The primitive country planning frameworks of the late 1970s – when the basic documentation was usually borrowed from the World Bank and other international agencies – were upgraded. However, Massé's aspiration to strengthen policy and planning and make the country program the focus of all agency programming, through whichever channel, was not realized. With his departure, senior management lost interest in the discipline of the country program review.

Catley-Carlson wanted to ensure that CIDA was viewed elsewhere in government as a fully cooperating and managerially competent agency. CIDA had addressed those issues quite satisfactorily. However, her conviction that CIDA was "not a policy maker, but a policy taker" seemed to many to sum up the lack of focused effort to deal with development goals. Despite general strengthening of the organization internally and the building of its credibility elsewhere in government, the sense of unease associated with what Winegard had termed the agency's mid-life crisis was palpable.

CIDA AS AID IMPLEMENTATION AGENCY

Government organizations, observed James Q. Wilson, the American scholar of public bureaucracies, tend to be driven by constraints deriving from the political process rather then by efforts to achieve goals.[10] The validity of this observation was given a substantial test in the mid-1980s. The new Conservative government requested that the Standing Committee on External Affairs and International Trade (SCEAIT) thoroughly review Canadian aid policies. William Winegard, a senior Tory backbencher, headed this committee, which included strong representation from all three parties. An enormous amount of energy – from politicians, officials, and the interested public – went into the process, which led to publication of the Winegard Report, *To Benefit a Better World*, in 1987. The government formally responded three months later and eventually released a strategy document for ODA, *Sharing Our Future*.[11]

Once *Sharing Our Future* had appeared, the Winegard Committee, concerned ministers, and CIDA itself made no serious effort to assess the agency's performance in light of the policy priorities set out. Treasury Board and CIDA agreed that some measures should be taken to aggregate statistics on expenditures to accord with the categories set out in the document and to ensure reporting on allocations against specific commitments. However, this process was later discontinued. The rationale presented in the annual allocations memorandum to cabinet is also set out in terms of the themes and categories contained in the strategy. Beyond that, no further official interest has been taken.[12] At the time of writing (May 1993), *Sharing Our Future* stands as the government's official position on ODA.

Given the preoccupation with rules and procedures, managers have every incentive to worry more about constraints than about programs' directions and to concentrate on process rather than results. It is difficult to hold a CIDA manager accountable for rural poverty or the rate of infant mortality in Bangladesh or Malawi but easy to bring her or him to account over improper procedures. The latter may well bring complaints to the minister from contractors or potential contractors. Shock waves were felt throughout the agency when it was reported that in a high-level discussion of a project evaluation a senior administrator had indicated that project team leaders (PTLs) would be held accountable (by a note in the officer's performance file) for shoddy project planning, even if the evaluation report was brought forward several years after the project's completion. A soothing circular was issued shortly afterwards.[13]

The government's predictable preoccupation with form over substance has affected priorities of management at all levels in CIDA. However, while process must often take priority, there remains a great deal of scope for determining priorities and building programs in ways not specified by the ODA policy and the preferences of the government at large. In the absence of a clear and realistic definition of policy, and because politicians and central agencies alike are not much interested in the results of development assistance, middle-level and operating managers have enjoyed a wide measure of freedom in determining objectives and formulating guidelines for making things work.

It is generally believed in the agency that the requirements of each country program are unique. This belief is strongly supported by the direct experience of those who express it. Although the enormous differences within and among geographical regions seem to confirm this argument, its strength has inhibited development of anything more than the broadest guidelines for programming. This outcome has been accepted as both inevitable and desirable by most, though not all, vice-presidents, as well as by most middle managers and project officers. It has reinforced strongly the tendency towards relatively autonomous decision making and increased resistance to central direction. Further, it has constitued a powerful weapon in the hands of the bilateral branches in restricting potential intrusions by other CIDA branches, such as Professional Services and Policy, which are in a position to take a global view of development. As well, it has limited the potential for collaboration and information sharing between the bilateral branches and the Multilateral Branch. Efforts since 1989 to change organizational structure and internal policy making represent a challenge to this state of affairs.

With its emphasis on the uniqueness of country programs and of projects – the agency's basic unit of analysis – CIDA would seem to resemble what Henry Mintzberg, following Alvin Toffler, has termed an adhocracy. In such a structure, work is conducted by teams that are built for a specific task and dissolved once the task (in this case, finalization of the project plan) is completed. The structure remains fluid because it is intended to produce unique and distinctive products.[14] Top management relies heavily on the skills and technical knowledge of those at the operating level.

In the author's view, CIDA's emphasis on "uniqueness" has overstated the reality. This notion of uniqueness includes within it a defence of development priorities. It is also a belief about the organization rather than simply a description of what it does. As such, it has served to reinforce resistance to integration and to rationalize failure to learn from experience and hence build better programs. In the 1990s, this belief is under attack, but it remains in place.

The strength of the commitment to "uniqueness" does not prevent signals on new directions getting through from senior management. Indeed, because of the importance of process and "doing it right" (rather than "doing the right thing"), channels must remain open for messages concerning the expectations of the central agencies or the "political level."

Those at the operating level must be alert to the changing sensitivities of senior management on the way to handle particular issues or relationships with external suppliers and constituencies. Such messages, however, usually convey little about programs' detailed development content. They may propose giving greater attention to the environment or primary health care but rarely contain more detailed advice.

Most vice-presidents value and support the integrity and autonomy of country programs and do not intervene in detailed planning and direction setting. This is indicative of the shared values and outlook of senior administrators and middle managers rather than of the limits of vice-presidents' power. It is also testimony to CIDA's success in socializing its middle managers into working as "development assistance professionals," whose own personal and job commitment will ensure that activities are conducted and framed appropriately. Most important, it demonstrates that the agency remains operationally driven, as it was twenty years ago. The vice-presidents who head the regional bilateral branches are part of the organizational culture and convey in a straightforward way what they expect of their staff. They receive few surprises and in return can afford to be non-interventionist.

POLICY AND INCREMENTALISM

The role of CIDA's management has been to secure the institution's boundaries while maintaining the flow of funds into programs. Generally, it has performed this task successfully, but only through considerable expenditure of time and energy. Consequently, as in many government organizations, top management must concentrate on obtaining resources and managing relations with the rest of government, leaving the middle tier and desk officers to define and implement programs.[15]

This overly simple picture minimizes the participation of senior managers in program definition; however, it does point realistically to their limited opportunities to shape *programs* directly. From 1989, under Marcel Massé and his successors, Jocelyne Bourgon and Hugette Labelle, there have been deliberate and concerted efforts, discussed below, to shift CIDA's direction, to strengthen and transform the role and accountability of senior management, and to alter the policy process.

The academic literature on CIDA has noted the dominance of outside interests – other government departments or the broad needs of the capitalist state – shaping CIDA's programming. It is important, however, to come to terms with the complexity of relationships with external forces and to recognize that government agencies are far more than merely political arenas in which contending social forces struggle for dominance. They are also collections of structures and standard operating procedures, the articulation and character of which serve to define and defend values, norms, interests, identities, and beliefs. In other words, there is a more-or-less clear set of institutional interests and concerns that become a major factor in the equation. These interests become crucial in the elaboration of programs and in determining the specific purposes that are to be met in their implementation.[16]

A key to "program survival" is "manageability," as judged by the officers at the operating level. Manageability certainly takes into account "what will fly" at the political level. However, where policies fail to provide clear guidelines on practice (as is often the case), program designers and managers must fill the gap. In doing so, they will draw on CIDA's conventions and traditions. Thus "appropriate behaviour" and "trade craft," rather than policy, guide organizational practice. In this sense, actions around programs and projects are fitted with existing formal and informal structures so as to reinforce common-sense views of soundness and viability and the professional identities of those engaged in the process.[17]

Thus when top management attempts to impose new policies or practices, it may encounter strong resistance. Such efforts are quickly transformed into discussion of process and implementation procedures. One example was the agency's response to proposed decentralization, as announced in the government's ODA strategy in 1988. For good political reasons, CIDA moved at once to act on the commitment. Discussion on implementation dealt exclusively with technical, financial, and staffing issues. Policy and objectives were left aside.

Discussion within and outside the agency (with other parts of government) focused on formal and working relations with External Affairs; budgets, personnel, and human resources; and operational requirements. Senior managers were determined to accelerate implementation, largely because they saw only a shaky commitment from Finance and Treasury Board to accepting the financial and administrative implications of the exercise. They left little room for consideration of objectives or new working priorities for officers in the decentralized posts. These issues, though addressed in the ongoing review of decentralization, did not guide implementation.

Ability to translate policy into implementation and process mechanisms is in many ways an indicator of an institution's vitality. However, for an agency dedicated to "provoking development," to quote Marcel Massé, the very strength of the organizational culture has often precluded serious, sustained analysis of the presumed development objectives associated with policy initiatives. Instead, process has come first, and process determines objectives.[18]

Because of CIDA's work style, middle managers have often seen efforts to develop policy as an inhibitor to getting on with the job. Changes – even potential ones – are a challenge to organizations, which maintain their stability by shaping the change to make it more consistent with existing procedures and practices. Priority accorded by senior management to Women in Development (WID) and environmental concerns was eventually built into the project cycle through a "checkoff" (an attachment) to project documents. PTLs are expected to indicate that they have acted to optimize the potential benefits to women resulting from the project. They are also to show how they have assessed possible environmental impact. The "checkoff" is a way of standardizing what would otherwise be a source of continuing organizational difficulties.

Preoccupation with process reflects one of the realities of a project- and disbursement-driven agency; the ordinary condition of administration is to keep things going, rather then to get things started.[19] The key job of the desk officer or PTL is to move the money and to keep the project cycle on schedule. Constant movement of paper, and facilitation of sequences of linked decisions, are crucial to coping – and to avoiding flak from above. In other words, one's job is to protect the boundaries of one's own operating space – moving troublesome items out but assuring that they do not float upstairs to disturb senior managers. This situation creates considerable pressure for the project officer to solve problems without reference above.

Officers speak wistfully of how agreeable it would be to have the time to read something about the substance of development or even to consult policy documents as they drift down through the organization. Country program directors and vice-presidents, too, have found it difficult to break away from the accumulation of documents relating to the project cycle that require urgent review and decision. These pressures limit the scope for, and possible responsiveness to, change.

In such circumstances, "lower level administrators become policy makers in that what they do operationally becomes what the policy turns out to be."[20] While this overstates the case, patterns of activity emerge from an ongoing series of small decisions around projects and programs made by project officers and country program directors within their respective areas of discretion. These become codified as routine responses and hence part of the "stuff" of organizational knowledge. Policy is then made incrementally from the pull of individual decisions towards a norm.[21] Viewed in this way, as Mintzberg and Jorgenson point out, policy is merely a "pattern in action," or consistency in action over time, rather than intended strategy. It is formed through practice rather than formulated.[22]

The agency's thinking on human resource development (HRD) took shape in this way. While CIDA, following the Winegard Report and *Sharing Our Future*, regards HRD as "the lens" through which to view development initiatives, it still lacks guidelines on how to do HRD or how to achieve its own objectives through this type of programming.

However, knowledge of "successful" projects and programs – as judged by senior managers' responses – spread through the agency. The Asia Branch and the Area Coordination Group produced "Lessons Learned" and implementation guidebooks, respectively, to assist project officers with programming in this area. Professional Services, after some seven years of work and innumerable drafts, produced an "Education and Training Sector Strategy," originally labelled "HRD Strategy." After preliminary discussion of the document at President's Committee, it was put aside.

All these efforts, along with some summary documents produced by the Evaluation Division and individual country desks, sought to build on experience. None of them formally constitutes a "policy" on HRD. Insofar as policy may be said to exist, it has followed on from implementation.[23]

Operating experience produces rules of thumb that pass into trade craft and become lore at the desk level or in informal peer networks. Eventually, these are translated into administrative guidelines at branch or agency level. This process has been surprisingly effective in translating both negative and positive experience into agency priorities, though with considerable time lag.

New thinking about development has found its way into CIDA in a variety of ways. During the 1980s, new ideas for substantive programming were brought through Professional Services and through Multilateral Branch, with its window on the IFIs and UN agencies. Fresh concepts also filtered in through the exposure of officers and senior management to discussions at working groups of the OECD's Development Assistance Committee (DAC) or special geographically and sector-focused meetings, sponsored by the World Bank or other multilateral donors.

A few "trusted consultants," along with key personnel from a handful of frequently used executing agencies, have also introduced innovative ideas, packaged into practical form.

CIDA has revealed little capacity to process and reflect on new thinking. Continuing bias towards the project as the unit of analysis has permitted initiatives to take place with surprisingly little reference to sector priorities or overall, country-level assessment of needs.[24] By 1992, however, there was evidence of substantial change.

MANAGEMENT AND THE ACCOUNTABILITY TRAP

Ironically, many of the inconsistencies and unsolved problems apparent in CIDA's administration of aid date back to the 1970s and "solutions" imposed to deal with apparently inefficient management. What happened to CIDA was merely one example of a general effort by the government to address issues of accountability. As Timothy Plumptre has argued: "If accountability is equated with control, then the solution to an 'accountability problem' is clearly to increase controls rather than to deal with the broader aspects of accountability such as clarity of reporting relationships or objectives. The Canadian government fell into this trap in the 1970s."[25] Continuing emphasis on controls by central agencies has inhibited CIDA's ability to develop a consistent approach to balancing delegation and central direction.

From the mid-1980s on, there was a good deal of internal discussion, at meetings of the President's Committee and at lower levels, of "hands-off management." In the early 1980s, CIDA could not disburse aid rapidly enough. Managers came to be valued "if they could just get their money out of the door. At that time, the [project] pipe line was empty; it is now full. We just didn't have the staff – so get your hands off and get your contractors out there to do the job."[26]

In practice, project officers and middle managers received (and still do) contradictory signals about their role. Handling disbursements and achieving cash targets were difficult but manageable and clearly defined objectives. "Hands-off" – managing the overall process while leaving "micro-management" to contractors – was a different matter. In the curious intimacy of CIDA, probably strengthened by the leadership style of the mid-1980s, there was a strong sense of personal accountability for projects. Officers felt uneasy about leaving everything to the executing agency. As one senior manager said: "PTLs are almost suicidal when their projects run into trouble – they feel a strong sense of personal commitment." However, as another experienced officer has suggested, that sense of obligation is reinforced by very real anxiety that the civil servant will be held responsible for mistakes. He wonders whether "feverish hard work, overtime, risk and creativeness [are] not also seen to be sometimes driven by fear of failure, panic at being found out as personally responsible for a foul-up, or simply the shaky insecurity of knowing that one does not know how best to do what one is doing?"[27] In summary, it was this deeply held commitment and work ethos, combined with fear of failure, rather than directives or strategic plans sent from above or formal structures, that held the agency together.

CIDA officers were encouraged to devote their attention to contracting, monitoring, and evaluation, at the expense of the "front end" of the cycle – planning and building strategic, developmental relationships (and hence country-based knowledge).[28] The results, which became apparent in the mid-1980s by the time of the Winegard

Committee's hearings, were growing incoherence and weak integration in many country programs across projects, sectors, and channels
for program delivery. At the same time, there was also room for creativity. A new attitude to working with the "voluntary" and "institutional"
sector (NGOs and NGIs, professional associations, and cooperatives,
among others) brought many Canadian organizations into the aid
program and facilitated new programming with a broader range of
recipient-country organizations. It also provided for "pluralism" of objectives – a mix of programs responding to social needs, as well as
other, "supply-driven" initiatives.

However, broadening the program base made it still harder to define
principles, make decisions on resource allocation on developmental
grounds, or set priorities. In the largest programs, funds were now deployed over a wide range of sectors, further impeding movement or setting of new priorities.

Despite all this, and precisely because of the relative power and autonomy of the bilateral branches, in some programs innovative planning became a priority for CIDA officers and middle management,
particularly in the Asia Branch. Strong support at the vice-presidential
level, throughout the 1980s, together with local circumstances and the
failure of a "trade-aid" thrust initiated in the 1970s, allowed program
entrepreneurship in such countries as Thailand and Indonesia. China,
a program initiated in the early 1980s, also became a testing ground for
new approaches. Patterns established in CIDA's programming in these
countries inspired the agency as a whole. In general, however, hands-
off management did not facilitate coherent country and sector planning. In any case, as is argued above, coherent planning was not the
expectation of senior management. Lack of clarity in defining the jobs
of managers and project officers encouraged adherence to well-set
patterns.

A hands-off style of management defies the natural inclination
of many, if not most, CIDA officers and the predominant themes in
CIDA culture. However, by the mid-1980s, reporting requirements of
the project cycle forced officers away somewhat from intervention and
the detailed counter-management of Canadian executing agencies
(CEAs).

Necessity forced the contracting out of routine management and
specialized technical work. In 1991, CIDA, with 1,150 permanent staff
members in Ottawa, was also contracting the services of about 1,000 in-
house consultants.[29] Even CIDA's sector and technical specialists, the
professional resource officers, now manage consultants and have few
opportunities to tackle substantive issues in programming or planning
directly.

Paradoxically, then, CIDA's employees, attracted because of their interest in development, have had little time and less incentive to focus on that subject. In the mid-1980s, a majority of project officers had probably been hired primarily because of their professional dedication to development and their practical experience in the field. Although more people were coming in from elsewhere in government, development remained the dominant concern in the program branches and the launching pad for a CIDA career.

This commitment to development has provided some common ground, but frequent rotation of officers to new assignments has made continuity at the project level hard to achieve. Many newly assigned officers "go by the book." As one relatively young officer, recruited in the late 1980s, reflected: "The preparation for an officer is nil – what you learn is through osmosis – talking to colleagues, sharing problems ... Things always happen revealing the problems needing attention. For most projects you have a POP (plan of operations) and/or a management plan. That is ultimately your bible ... There is a lot of policy documents from CIDA you have access to – this is how you become aware of CIDA's policies: you don't implement them directly. When you come here, nobody says to you 'Here are the basic CIDA policies.'"

There are a number of training courses available, and in 1991 and 1992, short courses were introduced on such subjects as macroeconomics and human rights; a new five-day residential course on "Sustainable Development" started in early 1992. Many courses cover use of computer information systems, project management, formulation of a project using a "work break down structure," management of a bilateral project team, and putting together of an evaluation team. But "the training courses don't give you the tools to do the job ... They are contracted to outside consultants – they don't know CIDA and its procedures or the expectations of management ... and each branch is a little kingdom."[30]

In other words, procedures and reporting structures have provided some consistency in form and approach. But much still depends on personal style and experience, the informal norms and values of the culture, and the concerns or anxieties of individual PTLs, country program directors (CPDs), and vice-presidents. In the 1990s, the picture is beginning to change. However, senior management now emphasizes policy leverage – influencing macro policies of recipient governments. How can officers "take their hands off" the mechanical or routine parts of the work and concentrate on "the levers of substance"?

Many are sceptical about the new direction because "the political level" does not seem to share the view of CIDA's management. In recent years, the public, Parliament, and the auditor general have asked that "we manage tightly." The physical proximity of the minister, and the fact that dealing with inquiries from the minister's staff takes up a great deal of the time of middle managers, reinforce the apprehension.

For many officers and middle managers, success seems to be measured in, first, "squeaky-clean" financial management, and, second sound development. A PTL still feels that he or she will be held personally responsible if a major error is made by a CEA – if, for example, an assignment of cattle arrives in port dead or expensive Canadian equipment proves ineffective. Financial difficulties experienced by both private- and voluntary-sector contractors between 1990 and 1992 exacerbated such anxieties.

There has been no redefinition of levels of responsibility and accountability to ease the move away from detailed management and towards leaving routine work to others. CIDA must, of course, take into account broader governmental considerations and barriers that may restrict senior management and perhaps challenge the position of the central agencies and, particularly, the Public Accounts Committee (PAC) of the House of Commons and the auditor-general regarding CIDA's detailed responsibility for use of program funds.

CIDA has sought a more restricted definition of its accountability, based on shared responsibility with its CEAs. Under such conditions, CIDA would regularly monitor the organization's experience and capacity to contribute to the development assistance program as well as its financial soundness and managerial competence.[31] While CIDA accepts responsibility for "overall program results," it does not view it as appropriate to assume accountability for "all discrete activities funded by CIDA resources."[32]

CIDA appears to have made, at best, modest progress towards this objective. Without a major change in accountability, its ability to move human resources away from "micro-management" will be greatly restricted.

The Groupe Secor's Strategic Management Review (1991) of CIDA had identified "the continuous pressure on CIDA for full transparency, zero defect and full compliance with public service regulations and practices" as a major reason for the "risk-averse attitude" of the agency's officers.[33] Only by breaking the cycle of overly elaborate controls will CIDA be able to redirect its program officers and middle managers towards the macro level. Without this change, senior management will be unable to carry the work-force with it as far as it would wish in building the new CIDA. In the absence of major changes in accountability, much of the rhetoric concerning this vision lacks conviction.

In the spring of 1993, the agency continues to work on clarifying new approaches to accountability and redefining relations between itself and its contractors ("principal/agent" relations). However, there has been no change in the overall system of accountability within which it must operate.

"STRATEGIC MANAGEMENT" AND ORGANIZATIONAL TRANSFORMATION

Publication of the government's ODA strategy, *Sharing Our Future*, in 1987, was an event of some importance. Unlike its predecessor, *Strategy for International Development Cooperation 1975–1980*, published in 1975, this document was built on a broad consensus, inside and outside government.

Viewed from a bureaucratic perspective, the new strategy was a considerable achievement. It represented a "reasonable" response to the major issues raised by the Winegard Report (1987). It also assisted the minister in offering a distinctive contribution to government policy and the direction of ODA. The contents of the document were built around a set of important messages and symbols directed to the domestic constituencies most relevant to the survival and prosperity of the agency. The strategy provided broad guidelines for programming and reaffirmed principles consistent with the dominant beliefs of the agency, without greatly inhibiting organizational flexibility.

Nonetheless, CIDA's employees, including several vice-presidents, saw production of the strategy as a "black box job," put together by a small group of insiders close to the president and in the minister's office. There was a good deal of muttering about lack of internal consultation, and staff members felt little sense of "ownership" of the document. The ODA charter – with the emphasis on aid to the poorest and the provision that "development priorities shall prevail" – gave officers greater confidence, however, in standing up to commercial pressures.

Three years later, many in the agency saw the strategy as "backward-looking" and, like the Winegard Report, based on "1960s thinking." Much had happened in a short time, and some in the agency saw that the laissez-faire approach of the 1980s was no longer viable. *Sharing Our Future* had not provided an operational policy framework. The reality of a highly decentralized agency operating across the globe, with a strong conviction that policies be "tailor-made" locally and incrementally, meant that policy could be little more than a loose set of guidelines and mechanisms. Publication of the ODA strategy had strengthened the organizational culture and the dominant ethos of the agency.

CIDA and the aid program had survived earlier fiscal restraint relatively unscathed. Under Brian Mulroney's government, while External

Affairs had substantially reduced staff and the scope of its activities, CIDA had escaped largely unharmed. However, from 1989 to 1991, the agency experienced three successive rounds of annual budget cuts. In 1991, in the context of a broader-based squeeze on the size of the public service, CIDA – along with the rest of the government – significantly reduced its managerial ranks. The comfort experienced by its employees, because of CIDA's apparent special protection as a place apart in government, could no longer be sustained, and this change lowered morale and self-confidence. More than forty managers and senior employees accepted generous early retirement packages in 1991. Others began looking quietly for new jobs. CIDA was no longer a place "nobody wants to leave."

With the urgency accorded to deficit reduction, and given the Conservatives' strong commitment to defence, an "easy" program to cut was the aid program, which proved vulnerable as never before. The leadership of the agency had to begin redefining its central task and attempting to deploy its resources to that end. From the time of his return to the agency in 1989, Marcel Massé devoted much of his energy to doing this, even before the extent of the crisis was apparent.

While the laissez-faire approach to development prevailed, and CIDA's main goal was seen to be in implementing and accounting for good projects, senior managers had little desire or ability to bring about significant change. The new president's first efforts in 1989–90 to alter the agency brought few results, because of the nature and strength of organizational culture and the day-to-day priorities and preoccupations of managers and employees.

Yet, by the late 1980s, other forces were reinforcing the capacity of the president to transform organizational behaviour. CIDA's increasing consultations and policy dialogue with donors about structural adjustment necessitated an improved policy capacity and revealed the agency's relative weakness in analysis.

The Asia Branch, acting alone, was emphasizing strategic decision making in the shaping of its country programs. The China Program – which Massé had helped develop – brought political and commercial benefits, along with some developmental dividends, for a relatively small investment. CPDs who moved their programs in a more "strategic," institution-building direction, with an eye to influencing recipient governments and to building long-term relationships, became role models.

Following on from where he had left off in 1982, Massé pushed the country program as the focus for policy development. He also sought to make it – rather than the project – the critical unit of analysis. Integrated country programming was a key component of his effort to make CIDA policy focused, rather than operations based.

The view of policy in the agency quickly began to change. Renewed emphasis on the country program review (as of 1991, the country policy framework, or CPF) obliged vice-presidents and CPDs to devote more resources to planning. Messages sent down through the organization emphasized the value of integrated programs and consistent policy in building organizational and programming integrity.[34]

From the fall of 1991 to the spring of 1992, a series of CPFs and regional overview or strategy papers, such as "Africa 21," went to the President's Committee. All were approved. What still remains to be seen is how these documents, which set out only the broadest of parameters for country programs or regions, will be implemented. Budget reductions and lack of funding for new activities have made it difficult to demonstrate results for the new directions. Some initiatives, however, indicate tangible, positive results.

The initial framework papers from the Asia Branch provided the model for a CPF. The president's commentary suggested that a CPF should also narrow a program's focus and its operational activities. Administrator Ronald Roskens of the US Agency for International Development (who completed his term with the ending of George Bush's presidency) had coined the phrase "focus and concentrate." Massé was sending similar messages to CIDA.

Fresh talent from outside and through lateral internal assignments has strengthened the Policy Branch. Macro-economic capacity grew in the Policy Branch and in the country program analyst positions in Bilateral. Efforts were also under way to ensure substantial representation of those with bilateral experience in the Policy Branch.

For Massé, it was vital that CIDA concentrate and regroup its resources and develop integrated views of countries and programs. Central policy themes and approaches should be reflected in country programs and in CIDA's efforts to influence the policy of recipient countries and multilateral agencies. With resource flows static or diminishing, greater external pressures from clients and "stakeholders" in the aid program, and in the context of "the G-7 view of the world," the vision from the top was that CIDA must exert greater central control in defining and acting on its priorities. Massé sought to facilitate this approach by diverting resources from programming to planning and policy making and to donor coordination. A reshaped CIDA would be judged, it was suggested, not by the dollar value of its contributions, but by the strength of its ideas.[35]

What stood in the way was a set of very strong commitments embodied and expressed in the organizational culture and the daily preoccupation with projects, selection of contractors and consultants, and managing of disbursements. Despite efforts since the early 1980s to have officers and managers concentrate on the "front end" of the program cycle, internal studies at CIDA, as well as the author's interviews, indicated that most officers remained heavily involved in project implementation and detailed management.

In his second term, Massé brought to CIDA a substantive vision of what development should look like. What the agency would need to do to build the capacity to implement this vision was less clear. From 1990 to 1992, the President's Committee was the focus of a continuing effort to work out a way to combine the president's vision of the future with both domestic political realities and CIDA's operational nature. The president clearly led from the front but came to recognize and accept the operational concerns of his vice-presidents and middle managers. In addition, the senior administration increasingly looked at strategic planning within a framework that recognized the roles of politicians and external "stakeholders." What emerged was a policy approach linked to a concept of organizational change.

Groupe Secor's Strategic Management Review, the draft report of which was discussed within the agency in the fall of 1991 and made available to the public in January 1992, became a vehicle for reshaping CIDA to fit in with the "strategic" direction currently being defined. Impetus for the study appears to have come from the minister's office. However, Groupe Secor saw the president and senior management as its client and took as a starting point the directions set out by the President's Committee in 1990. Detailed consultations with senior managers, and further refinements in their thinking, formed the basis for the report.

The process pushed the higher echelons to clarify their own thinking and define the kind of agency that they wished reorganization to produce. By the time of the President's Committee retreat in March 1991, Marcel Massé and his senior colleagues had determined that "sustainable development" would provide the framework for development of CIDA's program and initiatives. CIDA would seek to influence the policy directions of recipient countries and help strengthen their core policy-based institutions; projects and operational work would become less central. As well, the agency would also work "horizontally" in attempting to influence other areas of Canadian government policy affecting developing countries. Further, it would participate more extensively in international bodies, with a view to influencing organizational directions and setting of priorities.[36]

In order to take on these tasks, CIDA would need a new profile. Human resources and knowledge and skill requirements would be reevaluated. In bilateral programs, the agency would continue to develop projects, but not as before. In principle, CIDA would concentrate on designing the Country Policy Framework, generally allowing Canadian implementing agencies to undertake projects within the parameters set out in the framework.

The Secor Report set out an organizational and managerial plan to allow CIDA to redefine its central tasks, to reorganize its work, and to reorient the thinking and day-to-day priorities of its work-force. It aimed also to bring new thinking into a management process dominated by the rhythm of the fiscal year.

Following internal discussion of the report and perfunctory external consultations in January 1992, the senior vice-president developed a draft CIDA response. Following further talks with the minister's office and the central agencies, CIDA submitted the document in April to the minister of external relations for her consideration and approval.

At this point the agency appeared poised on the edge of fundamental change. Twenty-four years of experience had gone into moulding a strong set of beliefs and a sense of appropriate means of action. All this tradition stood in the way of a new beginning. The organizational culture was in question but had remained in place. Senior managers and others supporting the new direction began to talk openly of "foot-dragging." Citing variously public opinion polls, the transformation of the philosophy of government since the early 1980s, and changes in international politics, they asserted that CIDA must move beyond scatter-gun planning; heavy-handed, micro-management of projects; and its view that the humanitarian impulse of the public would be sufficient to secure the future of the aid program.

"Foot-dragging" stemmed not only from a preference for established ways of doing things and resentment of "top-down management," but also from strong views about how to optimize the quality of the agency's work. Many staff members believe that good development projects and programs originate in sound local knowledge, good relations in developing countries, and the designing of initiatives as "unique products" to fit local circumstances. Secor's proposals appeared to reject this view, to threaten the autonomy of project officers, and to question the validity of what was most satisfying in their work.

HIGH POLITICS AND
ORGANIZATIONAL SURVIVAL

In expectation of a relatively quick affirmative decision by the minister, in consultation with cabinet, CIDA put in place a transition team, with five senior staff members and several other experienced colleagues assigned to assist them. The team prepared papers for discussion at the President's Committee, setting out key issues involved in implementation, including establishment of a Corporate Management Branch, clarifying the mandate and function of the Policy Branch, formulation of an external consultation strategy, providing for program concentration through thematic (as opposed to sectoral) programming, and contracting.[37]

However, the minister's decision did not come. External Affairs had indicated that a number of major proposals were not "policy-neutral" but fundamentally changed "the way the agency does business" and restricted its own minister's room for manoeuvre. There was no further action for some months. Finally, the document was referred to cabinet for preliminary discussion. Other departments also had concerns regarding the suggested direction of the aid program. Consequently, the cabinet decided to request External Affairs to prepare a memorandum on the policy issues involved in consideration of institutional changes in CIDA. The department's subsequent production of an "International Assistance Policy Update" in January 1993 is dealt with in some detail below, in chapter 13. Despite CIDA's pro forma consultations with External Affairs at all stages of the Secor process, the department and the agency differed on a number of central issues.

Despite CIDA's obvious unhappiness with the "Policy Update," the two organizations are not as far apart as they might appear. CIDA's Asia Branch has consulted with External Affairs at every step in the unfolding of its strategy since 1989. The result is a common vision of the aid program as a mix of poverty alleviation and "economic cooperation," very much in tune with the themes set out in the update. Similarly, the reorganization of the Africa program in the wake of the budget cuts of December 1992 and April 1993 is entirely consistent with the priorities outlined therein.

Although the department and the agency still differ on policy, what is really at issue is autonomy. CIDA, under Massé, had sought to transform itself in a manner in conformity with the government's preferred directions. It had been an active participant in the Public Service 2000 Exercise (emphasizing managerial reform in the public service) and had sought to learn from the best practices of other elements of the government. Its extensive use of public consultation on departures in programming and in its relations with Canadian interest groups (for example, the private sector, NGOs, universities, and colleges) was also in line with the new orthodoxy in Ottawa. In so many ways, the agency's senior management was attempting to bring CIDA – always somewhat of an organization apart – into the mainstream of government. Yet, while seeking to join the mainstream, CIDA had also tried to protect its domain of development assistance policy. In this area, the reference group (at least for senior management) was in Washington, DC, with the World Bank and IMF; in New York, with UNDP and other UN agencies; and in the DAC and the Tidewater Group, the informal annual meeting of the heads of development agencies, both bilateral and multilateral. External Affairs had its view of the world rooted elsewhere.

CIDA had helped formulate the government's foreign policy framework in 1991. It described its own policy initiatives as fitting within this broad (and very general) policy framework. *Sharing Our Future* had reinforced the territorial boundaries around development assistance policy. Taken together with the new foreign policy framework, the ODA strategy was viewed as providing a protective wall within which CIDA might reconstruct its program.

For External Affairs and the government, however, dramatic changes in the world and in Canada since 1988 had resulted in a different view of ODA. In the context of successive budget cuts, by the time of the December 1992 Economic Statement, External Affairs knew that some trade-offs would have to be made and that this would necessitate "reprofiling" of ODA. If CIDA launched institutional transformation in the absence of a restating by the government of development assistance policy, it would collide head on with External Affairs, causing difficulties for ministers.

CIDA's efforts to remap its universe were entirely understandable. For some years, it had operated in a foreign policy vacuum. The foreign policy framework indicated some very general priorities and preferred themes for CIDA's relations with the developing world, but it hardly provided guidelines for action and decision making. However, just as CIDA was attempting to adjust to new realities, so was External Affairs. Joe Clark's departure from the department appeared to "unfreeeze" relations between External Affairs and development assistance, while also modifying the effective mandate of the secretary of state and the minister for external relations. External Affairs clearly had the prerogative to "intrude" into CIDA's territory but for some years had not done so. Hence the "International Assistance Policy Update" seemed a major departure in departmental relations. The fact that the document was developed by External Affairs as a basis for consultations, rather than as a joint product, says a good deal about the state of those relations.

While CIDA was devoting substantial energy to moving into the governmental mainstream, it was not paying sufficient attention to consultations and high-level working relations with External Affairs. By emphasizing its determination to be policy-oriented and knowledge-based – rather than the implementor that it had been in the 1970s and 1980s – CIDA was potentially challenging the department's authority. CIDA as a whole, unlike its own Asia Branch, had not carried External Affairs with it as it transformed itself.

Ironically, while "re-engineering" CIDA to let it cope with a changing and uncertain environment, senior management had brought new challenges to its autonomy. Efforts to modify its mission and to redefine its central tasks resulted in more visibility in the foreign policy field, which itself was changing dramatically in the wake of an end to the Cold War and the perceived challenges of economic globalization.

With the departure of Massé in March 1993, CIDA's new president, Jocelyne Bourgon, moved swiftly to restore harmonious relations with External Affairs in the aftermath of the leaked "International Assistance Policy Update," as did the department. Monique Vezina, who returned as minister to External Relations and International Development in early 1993, agreed with the president's recommendation that the agency move ahead on administrative elements of the Secor Report that were "policy-neutral" and had few implications for Canadian interest groups.[38]

Bourgon immediately set up task forces to continue the transition team's work on detailed plans for implementing administrative reform. Decisions were made to consolidate the branch structure. Perhaps most important, CIDA set up a Corporate Management Branch, broke up the Professional Services Branch, distributing its members across the agency's and created a Technical Services Unit in the Policy Branch.

This intense flurry of activity followed months of indecision and helped to defuse the anger and frustration of many working-level staff, who had been left out of major discussions and decisions. Morale, already low in early 1992, had become even worse in the following months.

CIDA remains stalled, however, in its efforts to reframe its basic policies and to move ahead with policy and systems. Major shifts in policy are unlikely until after a federal election in the fall of 1993. At that time, CIDA's proposals for internal reform may be examined in the context of restructuring of the public service and the overall direction of Canadian development assistance and/or foreign policy. CIDA can do little to influence these larger forces. The departures of the minister, president, and senior vice-president in the space of a few months were followed in April 1993 by the announcement that all vice-presidents would move to new responsibilities – mostly through rotation within the agency. These changes allowed Bourgon to demolish barriers to cross-branch cooperation and thus to define a new corporate approach to priority setting, problem solving, and setting up of programming models. Within the geographical branches, realignment into regional bureaux rather than country desks was under way in the early summer of 1993. Branch managers were reallocating human resources away from operations and into policy and planning.

Diversion of resources away from direct supervision of operations has been facilitated by cuts to the program budget. However, the distinction between policy and planning, on the one hand, and operations management (CIDA's version of the classic "staff" and "line" dichotomy), on the other hand, is likely to be difficult to formalize, particularly in view of an organizational culture that values blending of the two kinds of work.[39]

The mandate of CIDA, in the eyes of cabinet, External Affairs, and the central agencies and Parliament, is delivery of development assistance in keeping with governmental objectives. CIDA's performance will still be assessed primarily on the basis of its capacity to plan and deliver programs and spend money in the field. The agency will be obliged to implement its new vision by making a difference at the field level, not in the production of high-level policy – although one can be the means to the other.

Efforts by the agency to assert its new priorities in the face of budget cuts have been countered not by alternative statements of policy but by commercial and political pressures to favour certain projects over others. Despite internal changes in priorities, the government continues to view the aid program as before, and it acts accordingly. While CIDA is able to introduce some new programming and, in some cases, adapt existing commitments to fit with different policies, other parts of the program continue to fit poorly with the agency's altered direction.

Faced with this apparent contradiction between what the agency says it is doing and what is happening on the ground, many staff members feel that management, while playing down the importance of operations work, expects them to continue with it as before. It also expects them to equip themselves to function in the "knowledge-based" organization, but without any reduction in operational workload. There is strong resentment of the perceived division into "us" (planners and analysts) and "them" (the operations staff). In training exercises, officers feel that they are asked to take seriously ideas that they have no opportunity to apply in day-to-day work. They hesitate about "buying in" to the new directions.

Organizational change – to the extent that it has taken place – has cost an enormous amount of time and energy and led to the departure of numbers of people (and the alienation of others) who had "signed on" to a now-obsolete view of CIDA's role in the world. Further, broad-based change became apparent only in the spring of 1993, after more than three years that saw a distinct lack of fit between the stated priorities of senior management and the imperatives facing those at the working level. Systems, policies, and programs lacked synchronization. The credibility of senior managers was undermined; policy statements from the top had little resonance at the operating level.

The concentration of Jocelyne Bourgon on management and administration, rather than policy, has increased the likelihood that many of the tensions and difficulties facing those at the working level will be addressed. Attention is also likely to be given to providing stronger incentives to accept the new system and to improving internal management and development of human resources. In July 1993, only three months after taking over as president, Jocelyne Bourgon was transferred to become deputy minister of transport. Her successor, Hugette Labelle, appears committed to the same priorities as her predecessor.

The process of change embarked on by CIDA between 1989 and 1993 has been difficult and confused. The process began with an effort by CIDA to fill a policy vacuum and to reorganize itself in keeping with the new policy vision. Unfortunately, the agency lacked both the managerial capabilities to transform itself and the external support required to sustain the new direction. In 1993, organizational reform continues, but without clarity about the kind of development program the agency will deliver. Incrementally, CIDA has already begun to shift resources and reshape programs to fit with a "strategic" aid program, emphasizing action in areas where it perceives that it can influence policy or create the foundation for long-term relationships in general support of sustainable development. How much further the agency will be able to move (or will choose to move) in this direction remains to be seen.

NOTES

This chapter derives from a larger research project dealing with the aid process, based on detailed examination – primarily through intensive interviews – of CIDA and aid agencies and ministries in Japan, The Netherlands, the United Kingdom, and the United States. The author wishes to express his appreciation to officials at all levels in CIDA and other parts of government, and to well-placed informants elsewhere, for their courtesy and cooperation.

Much of the initial work was undertaken during an extended sabbatical leave. I wish to express my appreciation to Ryerson Polytechnical University in Toronto and to former colleagues and the staff at the Ryerson International Development Centre for their support. A draft of this chapter was circulated widely inside and outside CIDA in late 1991 and early 1992. I have made a number of changes as a result of readers' comments. I have also updated the text in the light of events in 1992–93.

A long conversation with Philip Quarles von Ufford of the Free University of Amsterdam assisted me in clarifying my approach. I should like to express my appreciation to Peter Morgan for a detailed commentary on the paper and for many conversations which have helped me better understand CIDA. Discussions with Charles Morrow and Pierre Beemans also assisted me greatly in the early phases of the research. None of those mentioned bears any responsibility for my interpretation. Finally, Cran Pratt has been a supportive and helpful editor – my thanks.

1 The three central problems are those specified by the American scholar James Q. Wilson in *Bureaucracy: What Government Agencies Do and Why They Do It* (New York: Basic Books 1989), 24–6. I should also like to acknowledge my debt to the work of the British sociologist Tom Burns; see especially his fine study, *The BBC: Public Institution and Private World* (London: Macmillan 1977).

2 See Herbert Kaufman, *Time, Change and Organizations*, 2nd ed. (Chatham, NJ: Chatham House 1991), chap. 1.

3 See Peter Wyse, *Canadian Foreign Aid in the 1970s: An Organizational Audit* (Montreal: McGill University, Centre for Developing Area Studies, 1983), 28–9.

4 House of Commons, Standing Committee on External Affairs and International Trade, *For Whose Benefit? Report of the Standing Committee on External Affairs and International Trade on Canada's Official Development Assistance Policies and Programs* (Winegard Report) (Ottawa: Supply and Services, May 1987), 2–3.

5 Author's interviews with a former vice-president of CIDA, 1989 and 1990.

6 Author's interview with a former senior administrator of CIDA, 1990.

7 Task Force on Canada's Official Development Assistance Program, *Study of the Policy and Organization of Canada's Official Development Aid: Report to the Minister of External Relations* (Demarais Report) (Ottawa: CIDA, 1986), 58.

8 Author's interviews with CIDA officials, past and present; quotations from Demarais Report, 57.

9 Author's interviews with members of the senior administration of the time.

10 Wilson, *Bureaucracy*, 113–26.

11 See Winegard Report; *To Benefit a Better World: Response of the Government of Canada to the Report by the Standing Committee on External Affairs and International Trade* (Ottawa: Supply and Services 1987); *Sharing Our Future: Canada's International Development Assistance* (Ottawa: Supply and Services 1987).

12 Author's interviews.

13 Private information to the author and internal documents, 1991.

14 See Henry Mintzberg, *The Structuring of Organizations*, 3rd ed. (Englewood Cliffs, NJ: Prentice Hall 1979).

15 For a useful consideration of the distinction in an aid organization between the concerns of top management and those of operating-level employees, see Philip Quarles Van Ufford, "The Hidden Crisis in Development: Development Bureaucracies in between intentions and Outcomes," in Quarles Van Ufford, Dirk Krujit and Theodore Downing, eds., *The*

Hidden Crisis in Development: Development Bureaucracies (Amsterdam: Free University Press 1988), 9–38.

16 See James March and Johan Olsen, *Rediscovering Institutions: The Organizational Basis of Politics* (New York: Free Press 1989), 17.

17 Ibid., 27–38.

18 For a related discussion, see ibid., 63.

19 See Jeffrey Pressman and Aaron Wildavsky, *Implementation: How Great Expectations in Washington Are Dashed in Oakland* (Berkeley: University of California Press 1979), 186.

20 Ibid., 173.

21 Ibid.

22 Henry Mintzberg and Jan Jorgenson, "Emergent Strategy for Public Policy," *Canadian Journal of Public Administration* 30 no. 2 (summer 1987), 214–29.

23 See the author's monograph, *Human Resource Development in the Aid Process* (Ottawa: North-South Institute, March 1993), for detailed treatment of these questions.

24 In this, CIDA has not differed greatly from other donors. See David J. Ross, "Aid Coordination," *Public Administration and Development* 10 (1990), 334; see also C. Clift, "Aid Coordination: Are There Any Lessons to Be Learned from Kenya?" *Development Policy Review* 6 (1988), 115–37.

25 Timothy W. Plumptre, *Beyond the Bottom Line: Management in Government* (Halifax: Institute for Research on Public Policy 1988), 185.

26 Author's interview with senior administrator, 1990.

27 Private communication to the author, November 1991.

28 Internal document on professional development.

29 Ibid.

30 Author's interview, 1990.

31 Author's interviews with senior officials, 1991.

32 "CIDA Accountability," document prepared for Public Accounts Committee (November 1991). On the "dialogue," see Standing Committee on Public Accounts, House of Commons, *Minutes of Proceedings and Evidence*, 19, 24, and 26 September, 24 October, and 21 November 1991.

33 See Groupe Secor, Strategic Management Review: Working Document (9 October 1991), 79/2, 7/2, 11/2; Douglas Lindores, Notes for a Statement by the Senior Vice-President to the PAC, 21 November 1991.

34 Particularly important in this regard was a statement by the president in June 1990, on the occasion of the review of the Ghana CPR – the first country (rather than regional) program to bring its review document to the President's Committee under Marcel Massé. A summary transcript of the statement was distributed throughout the agency.

35 Discussions based on the author's interpretation of interview data and on internal documents on integrated country programming.

36 CIDA Administrative Notice on the results of the President's Committee retreat, March 1991.

37 Internal (unclassified) documents, 1993, on implementation of management reform.

38 See Jocelyne Bourgon, "Notes for Remarks to an Agency Forum," 7 April 1993 (distributed 14 April 1993).

39 On the difficulties (and futility) of maintaining the "staff/line" or "advisory/operational" distinction in modern organizations, see Charles Handy, *Understanding Organizations*, 4th ed. (London: Penguin Books 1993), 266–8.

7 Export Promotion and Canadian Development Assistance

DAVID GILLIES

There are few issues more contentious in the literature on overseas development assistance (ODA) than the place of commercial interests in aid giving. Is export promotion compatible with the humanitarian foundations of development aid? Is there a trade-off among aid-giving objectives?[1] Do commercial objectives undermine aid "quality"?[2] Where one stands on the issues seems to depend on where one sits. Donor agencies and business point to mutual interests between rich and poor countries. On this view, economic self-interest is the most potent logic for helping poor countries. Fast-growing regions, such as Southeast Asia, are potentially lucrative markets for Western entrepreneurs. Aid can be a catalyst to propel growth and to introduce Western firms to new markets. By contrast, some academics, non-governmental organizations (NGOs), and Third World grass-roots organizations have long argued that commercial imperatives undermine the poverty-alleviation objectives espoused by Western donors and distort the priorities of their aid agencies.[3]

This chapter reviews the commercial aspects of Canada's aid program, paying particular attention to the evolution of government policy on tied aid and associated financing, a relatively new form of export subsidy that has been defended as a legitimate aid mechanism. It argues that the tying of Canadian aid has significantly lessened its developmental value and that associated financing is an unwarranted intrusion of commercial motives. Nevertheless, the case for deliberate "commercialization" of Canada's aid program cannot be sustained. Other determinants, including humanitarian concerns, have continued to be important. In addition, incremental erosion of the aid budget since the mid-1980s has taken primacy over all other policy considerations, including export promotion.

TIED AID: NO LONGER AN ACHILLES' HEEL

The Costs of Tied Aid

Tied aid is a device that requires a less-developed country (LDC) to spend a proportion of the aid that it receives on goods and services produced by the donor nation. This "tying" of aid diminishes its quality[4] by undercutting ODA's central purpose of tackling poverty and assisting the economic development of LDCs.[5] It lowers aid efficiency by decreasing the value of ODA to the recipient;[6] it stunts the economic opportunities of recipient-country or other LDC producers; it may tilt ODA priorities away from poverty alleviation towards foreign exchange and capital intensity; and it may favour higher-income countries or elite groups in low-income countries.[7]

A study by Canada's Treasury Board in 1976 found that "the weak competitive position of certain Canadian producers, [and] the exercise of monopolistic power by some Canadian firms ... have given rise to excess costs representing 14 per cent of bilateral disbursements."[8] For capital goods and services, excess costs reached 25 per cent of bilateral disbursements.[9]

Tied aid may give business lobbies an inroad to tilt the aid program according to their dictates. We examine the evidence for this below. Suffice it to note here the irony that commercial lobbies dedicated to freer trade are the major defenders to tied aid subsides.

Tied aid does more than simply distort donor and recipient development priorities. It also distorts trade. By subsidizing domestic producers or uncompetitive firms in declining industrial sectors, tied aid acts as a mercantilist device that deepens international protection and retards economic restructuring at home.

Export subsidies, whether given as tied aid or in new forms of associated financing, have principally benefited large firms in the manufacturing and capital goods sector. The Treasury Board's study found that aid "constitutes a significant market chiefly for a small number of large companies," with only 23 firms accounting for 75 per cent of disbursements in the study sample.[10] Major Canadian corporations, such as Bombardier, Hydro Québec, Massey Ferguson, Ontario Hydro, and "SNC-Lavalin" were at that time benefiting substantially from CIDA tied aid contracts.

Why Is Canadian Aid Tied?

Canadian governments of whatever political stripe have always said that job creation and export promotion are legitimate objectives of the aid program.[11] Tied aid has long been the principal device to ensure these immediate advantages. Three supplementary arguments are made to strengthen support for tied aid. First, the public's support for ODA is allegedly conditional on ensuring economic returns to Canada. Second, tied aid enables domestic firms to penetrate new markets and thus stimulates the Canadian economy. Third, tied aid "reflects the legitimate concern of Canadians that their tax dollars should not end up subsidizing competitors in other countries."[12]

None of these arguments is particularly compelling. First, jobs. A former CIDA president, Michel Dupuy, claimed in 1977, without supporting evidence, that tied aid had created 100,000 jobs.[13] A more recent and detailed CIDA assessment noted that of $2.2 billion in ODA disbursed in fiscal year 1985–86 some $1 billion went for procurement in Canada and that the "direct and indirect impact on the economy was some 18,000 person years of employment" and $656 million in GDP. If the "induced"[14] impact is included, ODA generated some $1.2 billion in GDP and 31,500 person-years of work.[15]

Independent research by the Economic Council of Canada, however, suggests a much smaller effect – about 10,000 to 20,000 new jobs per year.[16] Moreover, tied aid is a very costly way to create employment, compared to other government policies, such as job creation programs.[17] Direct state investment in manufacturing would have generated the same number of jobs as tied aid but at 14 per cent of the cost, while a subsidy program of the Department of Regional Economic Expansion would have done so at 13 per cent of the cost.[18]

Second, markets. Here, too, the facts belie the myths. A Treasury Board study of 1976 found that "tied aid serves to publicize Canadian technology and products, but does not necessarily generate additional sales."[19] In fact, the study could find few real costs – in lost production, balance-of-payments deficits, or market loss – from untying of aid.[20] Similarly, by comparing trends in the aid and trade patterns of France, Germany, Japan, the United States, and West Germany, Mosley found that rising "aid has no appreciable effect on trade share."[21] The question of aid and market penetration is taken up again in our discussion of associated financing.

Third, public opinion. The Canadian public has consistently preferred that aid be driven by humanitarian, not commercial motives. In a Decima Research poll in 1985, 72 per cent of respondents said that aid should not be tied to the purchase of Canadian goods and services. Only 18 per cent said that aid should be given to further economic self-interest.[22] This perspective has been sustained in CIDA's subsequent public polling. A 1988 poll found that 86 per cent of respondents mentioned a collective "responsibility to help" as the main reason for giving aid. Only 13 per cent saw trade promotion as a primary reason. Fully 67 per cent opposed tying of aid.[23] In 1990, 65 per cent of respondents opposed tying, and 84 per cent viewed "a responsibility to help" as the primary reason for giving aid.[24] In short, there has been no basis within the Canadian public for government claims that enhancing export promotion was vital to maintaining public support for development aid.

Recalcitrance and Reform

Is Canada's traditionally high tying level still the Achilles' heel of the aid program? Four points should be kept in mind before taking a position. First, tying is confined to the bilateral program and to food aid. Second, Canada's poor showing on tied aid is partly offset by the high degree of concessionality in Canadian ODA (since 1986, 100 per cent of it is in the form of grants). Third, tying does not apply to aid channelled through NGOs and multilateral agencies. In other words, a significant portion (40 per cent 1982–83) of Canada's total aid is untied. Fourth, there was a loosening of tying restrictions in the late 1980s.

Before 1987, only Austria (a very small donor) and in some years France tied a higher proportion of ODA than Canada, which long resisted domestic and international calls for a reduction in tying.[25] As Table 1 demonstrates, in the early 1980s, there were four major donors with tying levels above the DAC average: Canada, Britain, France, and the United States. By contrast, West Germany and the Scandinavian states had, and continue to maintain, consistently low levels of tied aid.

The basic rule on Canadian tied aid was laid down in 1970. It stipulated that 80 per cent of CIDA's bilateral country program budget be spent on goods and services procured in Canada. Up to 20 per cent of bilateral aid could be untied to finance local costs – a provision often honoured in the breach. Food aid, which represents about 15 per cent of the annual aid budget, has always been largely tied to Canadian procurement. A Treasury Board regulation (1984) permitted only 5 per cent of the food aid budget to be untied for purchases in third countries.[26]

Canada's intransigence on tied aid stems, in part, from the conviction of successive governments that Canadian firms are uncompetitive internationally, particularly in some Third World markets, and there-

Table 1
Tying status of ODA in selected OECD countries (percentages of gross ODA disbursements), 1982–83

Country	Tied	Untied	Multilateral
Canada	51.7	10.6	37.7
France	53.8	31.1	15.0
Japan	32.8	40.6	26.6
Netherlands	30.1	40.1	29.7
Sweden	11.9	51.3	36.8
United Kingdom	41.9	13.0	44.9
United States	41.0	23.9	35.0
West Germany	21.1	50.1	28.8
Total for DAC countries	37.2	31.5	31.2

Source: OECD, *Development Cooperation, 1985* (Paris: OECD), 227.

fore require export subsides to help maintain employment and productivity. Persistent lobbying by the business community has reinforced this perception.

In sum, tied aid has been one of the pillars of Canada's aid program, and the rationale for its continuation has taken on almost mythic proportions. But independent studies of the domestic impact of aid tying suggest that the market penetration and job-creating potential of this device has been overestimated and certainly costly in comparison to other, more direct mechanisms.

The Winegard Report (1987) on the aid program was a landmark on the road to reform. Convinced that "a high fixed tying rule carries a danger of making what Canada has to sell more important ... than what the poor want and need" and that the program's "bottom line [is] ... benefits to overseas recipients, not jobs or profits for Canadians," the authors recommended:

- that the 80 per cent rule be relaxed to allow more flexibility for local cost and LDC procurement financing;
- that up to 50 per cent of the bilateral government-to-government budget be untied;
- that tying be entirely waived for some least developed sub-Saharan recipients;
- that untying be allowed for food aid "to the extent of permitting third country purchases" from neighbouring LDCs with an exportable surplus; and

- that non-emergency food aid not exceed 10 per cent of the ODA budget.[27]

The government responded with an interim statement (*To Benefit a Better World*), followed by a comprehensive ODA "strategy" (*Sharing On Future*).[28] On aid and export promotion, the government took a somewhat equivocal position.

On the one hand, the bilateral food aid program was to remain 95 per cent tied to Canadian procurement, and only 20 per cent of multilateral food aid would be untied. Domestic considerations (the economic plight of prairie farmers and the political influence of the Department of Agriculture) may have underpinned the government's unwillingness to alter levels of tied food aid. By increasing the food aid budget by 5 per cent annually, the government acknowledged the continuing strength of the farm lobby. At the same time, it also overrode its admission "that food aid is not always the best form of development assistance, especially when it has the effect of discouraging local agricultural production."[29]

On the other hand, the government met some Winegard proposals half-way by agreeing to untie up to 50 per cent of bilateral aid to sub-Saharan African and other least-developed countries (LLDCs). It thus recognizes the importance of making greater provision for local-cost financing and procurement. But all other recipients of Canadian bilateral aid are limited to a ceiling of one-third untied. The reasons for this distinction are not elaborated, but a number of more prosperous, middle-income LDCs, such as Cameroon, Jamaica, Thailand, and Zimbabwe, are considered to have good trade potential for Canada. Maintaining a higher proportion of tied aid to these countries increases the exposure of Canadian goods and firms seeking to expand their sales. In short, creation of two tiers for "Canadian content" underlines Ottawa's continuing commitment to promoting commercial objectives through the aid program.

Reforms to tied aid, though partial, have had a visible effect. CIDA has estimated that the new untying framework would release $1.2 billion over five years.[30] And in the OECD's Development Assistance Committee (DAC), Canada is no longer among the tied aid pariahs. By 1988, Canadian bilateral ODA was only 34.5 per cent tied, well below such major donors as Italy (57.6 per cent) and the United Kingdom (46.4 per cent).[31]

In sum, while tied aid is no longer the Achilles' heel of Canada's aid program, the government has chosen damage limitation over radical dismantling of Canadian content rules. The preservation of high levels of tied food aid and two-tier bilateral tying mark the limits of Ottawa's commitment to its ODA Charter and underline the continuing pull of commercial interests on aid policy.

BUSINESS AND INDUSTRIAL COOPERATION

Another illustration of CIDA's responsiveness to business interests is the Industrial Cooperation Program (ICP). Originally a minor activity within the Special Programs Branch concerned primarily with NGOs and NGIs, in 1984 ICP became the Business Cooperation Branch.

An imaginative group of programs has been developed to induce greater collaboration by Canadian businesses with their counterparts in developing countries. Business Cooperation became the champion of commercial interests within CIDA. Its Policy and Liaison Division develops policies to increase the role of business in Canada's aid program. Its Consultant and Industrial Relations Division is CIDA's contact point with Canadian firms. In 1991, CIDA added to its growing family of business-oriented units a Private Sector Development Initiatives Fund to finance projects in countries of long-range interest to the business community. The fund will provide business with a responsive arm of its own similar to that of NGOs and educational institutions.

The contemporary prominence of the Business Cooperation Branch was achieved only gradually. The branch initially faced ambivalence within CIDA and lacklustre commercial interest. Many in CIDA recognized that the private sector would not be very interested in the poorest countries or in projects that help the poorest communities. As long as these attitudes were prominent, the work of the Industrial Cooperation Division was seen by some in CIDA as a distraction. And, indeed, spending on the work of the division was negligible until the mid-1980s. With the Conservative victory in 1984, funding for the division jumped to $28 million per annum in 1985–86 and to $62 million in 1990–91. Under the tutelage of a government committed to free markets and expanding foreign investment, the branch became, by the late 1980s, the fastest-growing activity within CIDA.

EXPORT CREDITS AND "COMMERCIALIZATION" OF ODA

Tied aid is the time-honoured way to boost exports. But during the 1980s, Western aid donors developed additional and novel ways to use aid for export promotion.[32] Described collectively as "associated financing" by the DAC, these new instruments blend ODA with commer-

Table 2
CIDA-EDC parallel financed projects: commitments ($million),
1985–91

Country	EDC portion	CIDA portion	Total cost
Asia			
Indonesia	51.2	26.4	77.6
Thailand*	17.0	5.0	22.0
Malaysia*	36.8	3.0	39.8
Philippines*	27.1	15.0	42.1
Pakistan	62.0	18.0	80.0
India*	149.0	75.0	224.0
Subtotal	343.1	142.4	485.5
Africa			
Tunisia	22.9	10.9	33.8
Morocco	18.0	7.9	25.9
Cameroon	58.2	27.1	85.3
Gabon	55.2	17.4	72.6
Rwanda	5.1	2.0	7.1
Botswana	23.2	6.2	29.4
Subtotal	182.6	71.5	254.1
Americas			
Barbados	3.9	2.1[†]	6.0
Trinidad and Tobago	6.7	5.3	12.0
Grenada	7.5	7.5	15.0
Colombia	40.0	17.5	67.5
Subtotal	58.1	32.4	90.5
Total	559.6	246.3	806.7

Source: Export Development Corp. (EDC).
Note: Some EDC figures were announced in US dollars or ECUs; conversions are based on Canadian dollars as at July 1991.
* Line of credit.
[†] Petro-Canada International Assistance Corp.

cial loans to increase the competitiveness of domestic firms seeking export markets in the Third World. The term "crédit mixte," used widely to describe such instruments, reflects the introduction of this device by France. In the 1980s, ODA began to play an important role in the financing of capital goods to the developing world.[33] Use of associated financing in Canada has sharpened policy debates, traditionally centred around tied aid, on the place of commercial objectives in the aid program.[34]

The DAC has defined associated financing to include mechanisms that associate export credits, in law or in fact, with ODA or any other official flow containing, in its first definition, a grant element of at least 20 per cent.[35] These transactions are effectively tied completely to lender procurement and may take a variety of forms, such as "mixed credits" (mixing of commercial export credits with concessional aid funds), "co-financing" (two or more agencies financing a project), or "parallel financing" (lenders' export credit and aid agencies negotiate and administer two separate transactions, with each retaining jurisdiction over its respective portion of the total package). This last mechanism, which is used most often in Canada, deflects some criticism from the aid agency, which can claim that the autonomy of the loan's "development component" shields it from the intrusion of commercial objectives.[36]

By 1983–84, Canada had emerged as the second-largest user of associated financing, accounting for 14 per cent of the DAC total. CIDA undertook 16 parallel financed projects with the Export Development Corp. between 1978 and 1984 with a total value of $1.1 billion, of which the concessional ODA component was almost $300 million, or 26.7 per cent.[37] Sectors of concentration have been transport and electrification, with some representation for mining and communications. Table 2 shows a slight falling off in associated financing, with total projects valued at $805 million between 1985 and 1991. The table also underlines the concentration on middle-income LDCs, such as Cameroon, Gabon, and Tunisia, and on poorer LDCs with good market potential, such as India and Indonesia. Note, finally, the regional concentration on Asia.

On the basis of figures for 1988–89 on associated financing (see Table 3), CIDA argues that there is now a "clear indication of Canada's shift from large infrastructure projects to human resource development, rural development and other sectors related more closely to needs of the developing countries."[38] I question this conviction below.

COSTS AND BENEFITS OF AID-BLENDED EXPORT CREDITS

OECD governments use several arguments to legitimize associated financing. First, concessional export financing is claimed as a legitimate "defence" against the predatory practices of competitors. Second, it can help established firms penetrate new markets and assist "infant industries" to establish themselves. Third, export credits allow LDC buyers to finance costly infrastructure projects which would not otherwise be possible, given their foreign exchange constraints. Fourth, the

Table 3
CIDA and EDC associated financing ($million), 1988–89*

Year	Direct CIDA contributions	EDC section 31 loans[†]
1988	30.8	124.97
1989	21.1	48.10

Source: "Annual Aid Review 1989: Memorandum of Canada to the Development Assistance Committee of the Organization for Economic Cooperation and Development" (Hull: CIDA 1989), 33.
* ODA commitments.
[†] Public funds from the Consolidated Revenue Fund. The CIDA component is concessional.

concessional component of mixed credit packages serves developmental purposes by "stretching" a limited amount of aid over a number of projects. Fifth, associated financing typically accounts for so modest a proportion of ODA that it cannot undermine the development priority of aid. Sixth, such mechanisms mirror changes in the LDCs, which are no longer a homogeneous group. Aid programs should reflect the varying needs and priorities of LDCs at different stages of economic development. Aid-blended credits, it is argued, can stimulate the industrial development of newly industrialized countries (NICs) and those lower income LDCs with growing industrial sectors. Industrial development is now viewed as a legitimate component of ODA planning for some fast-growing, middle-income LDCs – the ASEAN states, for example.[39]

There are solid reasons to justify a sceptical view of the putative domestic spin-offs of export credits and of their developmental value. Such clearly neo-protectionist devices distort market forces. Their use has created "spoiled markets" where business cannot be conducted without the use of concessional financing. Like tied aid, export credit subsidies are a costly means of creating jobs.[40]

The heart of the case against aid-blended export credits from a development perspective is that these packages are fundamentally "trade driven." Given the competitiveness of international bidding, aid agencies have little time to assess the developmental value of a project, assuming such objectives can be delineated in operational terms.

The comparatively small volume of associated financing is no reason for complacency, because governments may succumb to pressures to increase allocations to aid/trade mechanisms.[41] As worrying is the risk that an intrusion of overtly commercial objectives may distort an aid agency's priorities. As Mosley puts it: "the cutting edge of an entire aid programme may be damaged by the patent inadequacy of a small part of it."[42]

CANADA AND EXPORT CREDITS

Canada's entry into associated financing was prompted by a combination of domestic "push" and international "pull."

The world economic recession of 1981 was the main reason for a rapid global increase in export credits and associated financing. Sluggish growth, balance-of-payments deficits, and fluctuating interest rates in the North were mirrored in the South by severe foreign exchange constraints, debt rescheduling, and a reduced ability to import capital goods. In this atmosphere of intensified competition, nations felt compelled to consider these devices in order to protect markets. By 1983, export credits accounted for 8 per cent of total financial flows from OECD nations to LDCs, with Canada, the sixth-largest OECD lender, accounting for 5 per cent of total commitments. The aid component of OECD export credits rose from 31 per cent in 1981 to 38 per cent by 1983.[43]

At the same time as export credits were proliferating, lender nations recognized that these "beggar-thy-neighbour" policies could harm the international economic order. International organizations provided an obvious forum for multilateral initiatives to limit their growth.

In 1983, the OECD and its DAC negotiated the Consensus Arrangement on Guidelines for Officially Supported Export Credits, which is intended to reduce excessive and unfair bidding for major infrastructural projects. However, it is not legally binding, and voluntary adherence is not the most promising basis for cooperation.[44]

The DAC, recognizing that donors are unlikely to abandon associated financing in the short term, opted to press for greater "transparency" among donors using these devices, monitor and evaluate associated financing projects for their developmental impact, and raise the costs for donors considering aid-blended concessional financing. As already noted, the OECD-required grant element in mixed credit packages has gradually increased, from 20 to 35 per cent. While these welcome initiatives go some way towards monitoring donors' behaviour, reducing unfair practices, and limiting use of associated financing, the DAC principles limit damage rather than eliminate associated financing.

The actions of other Western competitors were undoubtedly a factor prompting Ottawa to consider associated financing, but structural weakness in the domestic economy also contributed. In addition to having an open, trade-dependent economy, a relatively small market, and a strong foreign presence in key sectors, Canada continues to experience high unemployment, reduced profitability in traditional resource industries, and declining competitiveness in the export sector. Increased concern with trade promotion and absorption of the

Table 4
Developing countries' share as a percentage of trade flows, 1987

	LDC share (exports)	LDC share (imports)	LDC share (total trade)
Canada	7.5	8.9	8.2
European Community	17.0	16.9	16.9
Japan	32.0	47.1	37.9
United States	33.0	32.1	38.5

Source: Directions of Trade Statistics Yearbook 1987 (Washington, DC: IMF, 1987).

Canadian aid program into this set of issues have preoccupied both Liberal and Conservative governments in a wider "agenda for economic renewal."[45] As is clear from Table 4, Canada has not been a significant player in the LDC market. Accordingly, expanding trade with LDCs became a key element in strengthening Canada's export performance.

EVOLUTION OF CANADA'S
ASSOCIATED FINANCING POLICY

As early as 1979, Canada's Export Review Promotion Committee was urging the government to ensure that in situations where "significant Canadian business is at risk, EDC is able to match concessional financing by using concessional rates."[46] Aid/trade instruments have been used increasingly as Canada's position in Third World markets has deteriorated.[47] This lacklustre performance has been especially marked in capital goods and equipment – a weakness that aid/trade mechanisms are designed to redress.

Strengthening Canada Abroad, the 1979 report of the Export Promotion Review Committee (Hatch Committee), contains one of the earliest, and in many ways one of the most aggressive, sets of recommendations to harness development aid in the service of trade promotion. The Hatch Report was unreservedly critical of CIDA's "overly philanthropic give-away approach to aid."[48] It argued that the proportion of multilateral aid should be halved in view of the poor record of Canadian procurement from multilateral donors, and it recommended an equivalent increase in bilateral aid. It supported CIDA's new Industrial Cooperation Division and argued in favour of EDC-CIDA parallel financing, using funds from the ODA budget.

By 1981, Pierre Trudeau's government was ready to act. It announced that $900 million in concessional funding was to be made

available over three years as a crédit mixte facility for Canadian exporters. Under section 31 of the Export Development Act, funds were
made available for transactions "in the national interest" that EDC
would not normally undertake in view of their high risk or concessional
nature. However, the facility initially proved to be a disappointment to
exporters and was rarely used because the stringency of the codes guiding application effectively prevented firms from invoking the mechanism. At this stage, Canada's associated financing was "defensively"
inspired.

At best, Canadian exporters could match the bids of their competitors, but a more aggressive mechanism would be required if Canadian
firms wanted to outbid (or rather undercut) their competitors.
Recognizing the impasse, the Liberal government began to consider a
formal aid/trade mechanism and a closer functional link between
EDC and CIDA. The potential policy options were considered by the
Mulroney government in its *Export Financing Consultation Paper* (1985).
The paper reveals an ambivalence regarding associated financing that
also pervades subsequent parliamentary and governmental analysis. It
opens with the terse observation that "the competition for export markets is tough and getting tougher." And it warns that "if Canada is to
maintain and expand its share of world markets, it is important to recognize that international competitiveness, particularly in Third World
markets," is not simply a question of price and quality. Knowledge of
the market and an "ability to provide competitive export financing" are
also important.[49]

Underpinning options considered in the consultation paper were
"perceptions in the exporting community that improvements could be
made" in the government's export financing policy by "ensuring that
commercial benefits are maximized through the use of the aid program."[50] Exporters needed a faster, more responsive, and less bureaucratic credit instrument that currently available through EDC. The
paper favoured an official aid/trade mechanism, but it also conceded
that the speed of aid/trade loan packaging would make it difficult to
screen tenders from domestic firms and ensure that the program was
not being used to subsidize uncompetitive Canadian products. Indeed
there was no assurance that an aid/trade mechanism would, in fact, increase Canadian exports to LDCs.[51] These cautionary notes are evidence of some scepticism in the Ministry of Finance towards the whole
initiative.

With the announcement of an aid/trade fund (ATF) similar to the
United Kingdom's Aid Trade Provision, Canada appeared to be
launched on a more assertive and integrated strategy of trade promo-
tional. The proposed fund was the clearest signal of the government's

intention to commercialize the aid program. Liberal Finance Minister Marc Lalonde explained the rationale for the fund in his 1984 budget speech: "Public support can do much to enhance the role which our private sector can play in international development ... The developing countries ... are experiencing unusually serious balance of payments problems which are impeding their development efforts and their capacity to import. Their decisions to undertake investments and capital projects often hinge on the availability of external financing on concessional terms. To respond to these needs, for our own benefits as well as theirs, we shall require the closer co-ordination of our development assistance and our export financing policies."[52]

Fully one-half of the projected increase in the aid program, to 0.7 per cent of GNP, was to be given over to the ATF, which on this basis might have contained as much as $900 million by 1990. ATF would be funded entirely from ODA money, thus lowering the overall costs of state-assisted export financing.[53]

Business saw the new mechanism as an improvement on earlier associated financing facilities because it did not have to fit into pre-established five-year plans for individual recipients in CIDA's bilateral program. Because speed is of the essence in competitive bidding for infrastructural projects, removal of this constraint would have allowed the government to respond quickly to exporters when a potential project was being considered, thereby giving Canada an advantage over competitors. The ATF was thus a crucial feature of more aggressive trade promotion. CIDA and Canadian firms would have been expected to work closely together to initiate project proposals rather than simply "react" by matching the offers of a competitor.

The incoming Conservatives initially endorsed ATF, renaming it the Trade and Development Facility, but they subsequently scrapped the fund in the 1986 budget as part of a plan to save $1.5 billion on aid by slowing its growth. CIDA lost the money that was to have gone to it to finance the facility.

AN AGENDA FOR REFORM?
PARLIAMENT AND EXPORT FINANCING

The prevailing ambivalence on concessional export financing was also reflected in Parliament's review of the issue. The Winegard Report of 1987 recognized that the practice distorted trade and acknowledged that parallel financing was used to finance projects "for what are essentially trade, not development, reasons." This was deemed to be "a high-stakes game in which neither Canada nor the poor are likely to win many benefits." The report also argued, however, that "there will be occasions when development can be exporter-led ... and Canada should not deal itself out through an excessive show of purity."[54]

In sum, the report defended export promotion as a legitimate policy goal as long as development objectives are not compromised. The Government's consultation paper and academic studies cast doubt on the likelihood that meaningful development criteria would be used in assessment of parallel financing. But the committee's recommendations on associated financing are less than fully consistent with its policy conclusions. The government is asked to continue in the DAC to discourage associated financing by "increasing the costs to donors and by strengthening discipline and transparency in the use of ODA to support export transactions."[55] However, deliberations by the DAC and the OECD seem to be driven more by damage limitation than real commitment to phasing out this essentially mercantilist practice.

The Winegard Committee granted that concessional funds blended with commercial loans could be reported as ODA if the projects being supported were consistent with the ODA Charter.[56] But the development priorities in the charter are too broad to offer much protection. At present, large infrastructural projects are considered to have a development component if they involve a sector receiving priority in a recipient's current national development plan. This is hardly a rigorous definition; indeed, it may encourage abuse. Moreover, if the charter is to be the standard, then much of what Canada currently reports as "associated financing" distorts proclaimed objectives because it focuses on middle-income LDCs and large infrastructural projects rather than on the "poorest countries and poorest people" emphasized in the charter. The committee's tacit approval of associated financing is at odds with its pointed recommendations to cut tied aid and with its plea that Canada relax import restrictions on LDC manufactures.

On mixed credits, the government's response is as ambivalent as the Winegard Report was vague. It continues to view these devices as a defensive safeguard to ensure that Canadian firms are not placed at a disadvantage relative to their OECD competitors. It is also confident that "help to increase Canadian exports to the Third World" can be achieved "without compromising the integrity of the aid program."[57]

The government's proposed "safeguards" amount to little substantive change in Canada's position on associated financing. The principal criterion remains that aid-blended export projects should be in a sector that has priority in the recipient government's development plan. This priority would be established by seeking endorsement from the minister of the recipient's central planning department. These "safeguards" effectively shift responsibility away from CIDA and onto the Third World government. As a result, CIDA need not examine the developmental implications of parallel financed projects.

Table 5
World Bank total contracts and contracts awarded to G-7 countries (us$millions), 1985–89

Country	1985	1986	1987	1988	1989	Total 1985–89
Canada	6.3	36.7	42.2	31.1	49.3	225.6
France	182.5	140.8	370.6	265.9	259.9	1,219.7
Italy	174.2	75.8	175.4	99.5	157.0	682.0
Japan	470.4	303.9	697.2	257.2	201.2	1,929.7
United Kingdom	158.6	89.9	195.6	400.5	192.6	1,037.3
United States	346.5	224.0	289.8	209.8	557.7	1,627.8
West Germany	315.2	230.8	344.4	560.6	325.9	1,776.9
Total for World Bank						24,710.0

Source: CIDA-IFI Data Bank, "Statistical Data Bank on the Canadian Procurement at the Multilateral Development Bank" (Hull: CIDA 1990).

The DAC secretariat also criticized Canada's concessional export financing scheme. It noted that Canada's review procedure for section 31 associated financing, "implies that there is a fundamental difference between the rigorous appraisal procedures applied to traditional projects and those to be used in assessing ODA eligibility in the case of Treasury financed mixed credits."[58] DAC's concerns apply equally to parallel financing.

EDC data reveal that while several firms have won follow-on orders as a result of aid-sweetened packages, each required another state subsidy.[59] In short, there is no evidence that associated financing can help Canadian firms generate unsubsidized "downstream" contracts.

Export promotion is important, particularly given Canada's small and declining share of LDC markets. The supposed benefits of associated financing are not clear, however, while the developmental risks are immediate and well established. It should be phased out, and some of the funds targeted for this purpose redirected to helping Canadian firms compete for contracts in the lucrative, but hitherto inadequately tapped, IFIs.

As Tables 5 and 6 underline, Canada has long had the poorest procurement record of the G-7 countries in tendering for World Bank projects. The IFIs are substantial potential "procurement pots" for Canadian firms. The World Bank's IBRD and IDA commitments for fiscal year 1989–90 were us$20.7 billion for 222 new projects. Canadian firms in this market get consulting work, but procurement in goods and equipment (which takes the lion's share of World Bank funding) is still low.[60] Similarly, although Canada is the second-largest share-

Table 6
Ratio of cash contributions (us$millions) to procurement success for G-7
countries at the World Bank, 1984–89

Country	Total cash contributions	Disbursements to firms	Ratio of disbursements to contributions*
Canada	995.6	1247.5	1.18
France	933.5	3770.8	3.79
Italy	710.1	2293.5	3.20
Japan	4667.6	6921.8	1.51
United Kingdom	1646.2	4510.0	2.49
United States	5201.4	8279.6	1.49
West Germany	2377.3	4829.9	1.95

Source: Resource Mobilization, World Bank, Washington, DC.
* An index of "returns" on contributions.
Additional notes: Contribution data are expressed for calendar years. Total
contributions include cash payments to the capital of IBRD, IDA, Special Fund,
and African Facility. Cash disbursements are to firms in supplying countries for goods
and services supplied to projects funded by the World Bank.

holder in the Asian Development Bank (among non-regional members), it won just 1.1 per cent of the bank's procurement in 1990.[61]

Tied aid and associated financing are not the only expressions of the commercial emphasis in Canada's aid program. Four other initiatives point in a similar direction. As the Winegard Report observed, "the business community is the most underutilized resource" in Canadian ODA.[62]

First, there has been a dramatic increase in co-financing of major infrastructure projects by CIDA and Arab and OPEC donors. In 1988, CIDA was involved in 35 such projects, in which total commitments were $7 billion. Canada's contribution of US$905 million made it the third-most-heavily committed of OECD donors to such financing.

Second, the Business Co-operation Branch, set up to coordinate and extend links with and services, was the most rapidly growing division in CIDA. Allocations of $27 million in 1984–85 climbed to $45 million in 1986–87. Free pre-feasibility studies, development of commercial contacts in LDCs, and assistance to Canadian firms bidding for multilateral bank tenders are among the corporate services provided by CIDA, which is increasingly acting as an economic intelligence agency for the business community. CIDA made a renewed commitment to the business sector in 1987 in Sharing Our Future. CIDA-INC, the Industrial Co-operation Program, was set to double its budget to 4 per cent of total

Table 7

CIDA's industrial cooperation with selected ASEAN countries and China (disbursements in $000), 1980–81 to 1990–91

Year	China	Indonesia	Malaysia	Thailand
1980–81	0	401	49	175
1981–82	0	323	51	170
1982–83	835	782	400	526
1983–84	775	317	201	1 823
1984–85	2,439	1,027	733	2,770
1985–86	2,297	710	812	1,590
1986–87	3,337	844	1,141	2,165
1987–88	2,988	802	1,196	2,518
1988–89	5,694	640	1,521	2,120
1989–90	4,670	1,360	1,616	2,205
1990–91	6,003	2,544	1,170	3,359

Source: CIDA, South East Asia Branch, Corporate Memory, May 1991.
Note: Figures have been rounded.

ODA by 1993. As the document notes: "This is the largest planned increase for any CIDA program."[63] Table 7 illustrates rapid expansion of industrial cooperation to ASEAN and China, markets with good potential for Canada.

Third, the new framework for recipient eligibility has raised the proportion of bilateral aid available to non–low–income countries to 25 per cent. Fourth, in addition to continuing annual consultations with major groups of exporters, CIDA has established 20 general lines of credit and "antenna offices" in southern Africa and the Caribbean to "scout" for business linkages, as well as regional information offices across Canada.

CONCLUSION

Has Canada's aid program been irrevocably commercialized in the 1980s and 1990s? The evidence is mixed. Use of parallel financing and of CIDA-INC is a bellwether of Ottawa's sensitivity to commercial interests. What UNDP calls "social priority" projects account for a very small proportion of Canadian ODA[64] while aid for "industrial development" is the fastest-growing facet of CIDA's activity.

Equally, however, the government retreated somewhat from its long-standing intransigence on tied aid and has not succumbed to calls from the business lobby to reduce multilateral and increase bilateral aid.[65] Moreover, fiscal restraint cannot be the only explanation for the tapering off in Canadian associated financing from 1985 to 1991. EDC officials concede relative lack of interest among Canadian business in exploiting the opportunities of associated financing, rather than any policy directive to phase out parallel financing. Nor can we assume that Canada has stopped associated financing. EDC's 1988 annual report suggests that increasing competition and higher Canadian interest rates call for greater use of mixed credits.[66]

The imperative of growth is the basis for the privileged position that business enjoys in making economic policy.[67] However, all domestic interest groups, NGO and commercial, have suffered from budgetary cuts to aid. An assessment of the British case is also apposite for Canada: "The business lobby demanded more tied aid ... but the government was committed to cutting spending and neither aid nor subsidies were part of its ideological baggage. So the budget was cut, severely."[68]

Since at least 1986, the principal determinant of Canada's aid budget has been control of government spending and deficit reduction.[69] All other considerations have become subordinate to these preoccupations. Thus while the business lobby initially persuaded the government to launch the Aid-Trade Fund (ATF), it fell prey to the finance ministry's budgetary cuts.

Similarly, the program of decentralization recommended by the Winegard Report and adopted by CIDA was very unpopular with the business community. Moreover, there has been a decline in infrastructure projects, which have traditionally provided contracts for Canadian business. Finally, high levels of multilateral aid have been maintained, and social safety nets have been assisted in CIDA's funding of structural adjustment in Ghana, Guyana, and elsewhere. These diverse initiatives demonstrate the continuing attention to non-commercial issues in Canada's aid program.

Since the late 1970s, CIDA has woven export promotion into a broader strategy to bolster Canada's international competitiveness. This has meant a shift from ensuring that CIDA was immediately responsive to corporate lobbying to identifying and pursuing the longer-term national economic interest. CIDA began to be integrated more closely into overall foreign policy, which, for Third World development, meant close cooperation with the IFIs' structural adjustment policies. Since the late 1980s, there have also been fitful attempts to condition Canadian aid disbursements on respect for human rights and democratic development.

In sum, the case for deliberate "commercialization" of aid is not fully proven. Aid policy is driven by competing interests – ethical, commercial, and political. Export promotion remains a powerful, but not an overriding, determinant of policy.

NOTES

1 Grant L. Reuber, "The Trade-off among Aid-Giving Objectives in Canadian Foreign Aid," in G.L. Reuber, *Canada's Political Economy* (Toronto: McGraw-Hill/Ryerson 1980), 187–96.
2 See Paul Mosley, "The Quality of Aid," *Development Policy Review* No. 2 (1982). For a dissenting view on trade-offs, see Kim Richard Nossal, "Mixed Motives Revisited: Canada's Interest in Development Assistance," *Canadian Journal of Political Science* 21 no. 1 (March 1988), 35–56.
3 This is, for example, a central theme of Robert Carty and Virginia Smith, *Perpetuating Poverty: The Political Economy of Canadian Foreign Aid* (Toronto: Between the Lines, 1981), and of Cranford Pratt, "Canadian Policy towards the Third World: Basis for an Explanation," *Studies in Political Economy* 13 (spring 1984), 27–55.
4 John Hendra, "Only 'Fit to Be Tied': A Comparison of the Canadian Tied Aid Policy with the Tied Aid Policies of Sweden, Norway and Denmark," *Canadian Journal of Development Studies* 8 no. 2 (1987), 261–81; and Paul Mosley, *Foreign Aid: Its Defence and Reform* (Sussex: Wheatsheaf 1987).
5 See, generally, Jagdish Bhagwati, "The Tying of Aid," in J. Bhagwati and R.S. Eckaus, eds., *Foreign Aid* (Harmondsworth, Middlessex: Penguin Books 1970).
6 CIDA's first president suggested that tying reduced the value of ODA by between 15 and 20 per cent. See Maurice F. Strong, "Canada's Assistance to Developing Nations," Speech given at the Vienna Institute for Development, Vienna, 1 December 1979. UNCTAD found that tied aid increased the cost of aid to Chile by 12 per cent, to Iran by 20 per cent, to Tunisia by 25–35 per cent, and to Ghana by 35 per cent. See UNCTAD, *The Cost of Aid Tying to Recipient Countries*, No. TD/7/Supp.8 (Geneva: UNCTAD 1967).
7 In Bangladesh, the "striking" aid concentration on infrastructure in a predominantly agrarian society may, in part, reflect donors' self-interest. Infrastructure provides greater ODA financial opportunities than rural and social development. Roger Erhardt, *Canadian Development Assistance to Bangladesh* (Ottawa: North-South Institute 1983), 35. In Tanzania, the benefits of Canadian bilateral aid were "to a significant extent ... directed to the urban and modern sector." Roger Young, *Canadian Development Assistance to Tanzania* (Ottawa: North-South Institute 1983), 104.
8 Treasury Board Secretariat (TBS), "The Economic Effects of Untying of Canadian Bilateral Aid" (Ottawa: Treasury Board Planning Branch 1976), 4.

9 Ibid.

10 Ibid., 25–60.

11 See for example, External Affairs, *Foreign Policy for Canadians: International Development* (Ottawa: Information Canada 1970), 10, 13, and CIDA, *Strategy for International Development Cooperation 1975–1980* (Ottawa: Queen's Printer 1975), 14, 39.

12 CIDA, *Sharing Our Future: Canada's International Development Assistance* (Hull: Supply and Services 1987), 51.

13 This section draws on Hendra, "Only 'Fit to Be Tied'."

14 "Induced" benefits refer to labour income earned from the increase in output through procurement, which is subsequently spent on the consumption of domestic goods and services. These induced benefits thus differ from wages, salaries, and profits associated directly or indirectly with initial procurements.

15 CIDA, "The National and Regional Economic Impact Assessment of Domestic Procurement for Official Development Assistance, 1985–86" (Hull: CIDA Policy Branch, June 1988). The study also found no significant impact, positive or negative, on regional economic disparities. The GDP generated from ODA domestic procurement was distributed regionally in proportions roughly equally to the distribution of overall GDP by province.

16 Keith Hay, "The Implications for the Canadian Economy of CIDA's Bilateral Tied Aid Programs" (Ottawa: Economic Council of Canada 1979), 107.

17 Peter Wyse, *Canadian Foreign Aid in the 1970s: An Organizational Audit*, Occasional Monograph Series No. 16, Centre for Developing-Area Studies (Montreal: McGill University 1983), Table 2, 4.

18 Ibid.

19 TBS, "Economic Effects," 3.

20 Ibid.,

21 Mosley, *Foreign Aid*, 221.

22 Decima Research Limited, "The Canadian Public and Foreign Policy Issues" (Toronto: Decima, 1985), 62.

23 CIDA, "Report to CIDA: Public Attitudes toward International Development Assistance" (Ottawa: Minister of Supply and Services 1988), 27, 34.

24 CIDA, "Report to CIDA: Public Attitudes toward International Development" (Ottawa: Minister of Supply and Services 1990), 12, 31.

25 For example, Canada was not prepared to sign DAC's 1974 Memorandum of Understanding, which called for partial untying of bilateral loans in favour of LDC purchases. The government ignored similar proposals in CIDA's *Strategy* (1975).

26 House of Commons, Standing Committee on Extend Affairs and International Trade (Winegard Committee) *For Whose Benefit? Report of the Standing Committee on External Affairs and International Trade on Canada's Official Development Assistance Policies and Programs* (Ottawa: Queen's Printer 1987), 36.

27 Ibid., 131–3.

28 *Canadian International Development Assistance: To Benefit a Better World. Response of the Government of Canada to the Report the Standing Committee on External Affairs and International Trade* (Ottawa: Supply and Services 1987); CIDA, *Sharing Our Future.*

29 *To Benefit a Better World,* 70.

30 "Aid Strategy Memorandum," mimeo (Hull: CIDA 1988).

31 Development Assistance Committee, *Development Co-operation, 1990 Report* (Paris: OECD, 1990), Table 6, 192. This figure is not exactly comparable with data in Table I, since DAC altered its definition of tied aid in the date 1980s.

32 Accounts of British and Scandinavian aid/trade policies are summarized in John Toye and Graham Clark, "The Aid Trade Provision: Origins, Dimensions and Possible Reforms," *Development Policy Review* 4 (September 1986); Bjorn Beckman, "Aid and Foreign Investments: The Swedish Case," *Cooperation and Conflict* 14 (1979); Stein Hansen et al., "Parallel Financing and Mixed Credits," Evaluation Report 1.89 (Oslo: Royal Norwegian Ministry of Development Cooperation 1989). A comparative study of crédit mixte in Australia, Canada, the United Kingdom, and the United States is David Birch, *Aid, Technology and Export Subsidies: Perspectives on the Political Economy of Mixed Credits* (Hants: Gower Publishers, forthcoming).

33 "Capital goods" here refers to all large-scale equipment and machinery. In relation to export credits, examples include hydro and nuclear energy, communications, railway equipment, scientific and agricultural equipment, ships, aircraft, and turnkey plants.

34 See Martin Rudner, "Trade cum Aid in Canada's Official Development Assistance Program," in B. Tomlin and M. Molot, eds., *Canada among Nations, 1986: Talking Trade* (Toronto: Lorimer 1987); and John H. Adams, *Oil and Water: Export Promotion and Development Assistance,* North-South Papers, No. 2 (Ottawa: North-South Institute 1980). In this section, I draw heavily on my article, "Commerce over Conscience: Export Promotion in Canada's Aid Programme," *International Journal* 44 no. 1 (winter 1988–89), 102–33.

35 The minimum grant portion has since increased to 35 per cent.

36 Adams, *Oil and Water,* 27, 28.

37 Gillies, "Commerce over Conscience," Table 4, 115.

38 *Annual Aid Review: Memorandum of Canada to the Development Assistance Committee of the Organization for Economic Cooperation and Development* (Hull: CIDA Policy Branch 1989), 33.

39 George Abonyi, "Aid-Trade Strategy," *Policy Options* 6 (1985).

40 See A. Raynauld, J.M. Dufour, and D. Racette, *Government Assistance to Export Financing* (Ottawa: Economic Council of Canada 1983), 53, 60, and United Kingdom, *Costs and Risks of Support for Capital Goods Exports* (London: HM Treasury and the Departments of Trade and Industry and Overseas Development Administration 1982).

41 The United Kingdom's Aid-Trade Provision began with 5 per cent of the ODA budget in 1977; by 1989, it accounted for 14 per cent.

42 Mosley, *Overseas Aid*, 228.

43 *Development Co-operation 1984* (Paris: OECD 1984), 86.

44 For more details on the OECD "Guidelines," see John Ray, "The OECD 'Consensus' on Export Credits," *World Economy* (September 1986), 295–309.

45 *An Agenda for Economic Renewal* (Ottawa: Department of Finance 1984).

46 *Strengthening Canada Abroad*, Final Report of the Export Promotion Review Committee (Ottawa: Department of Industry, Trade and Commerce 1979), 11.

47 Rudner, "Aid cum Trade."

48 Adams, *Oil and Water*, 22.

49 *Export Financing Consultation Paper* (Ottawa: Department of Finance 1985), 1.

50 Ibid., 4.

51 Ibid., 18, 19.

52 Canada, House of Commons, *Debates*, 15 February 1984.

53 Syed S. Rahman, *The Competitiveness of Canada's Officially Supported Financing System* (Ottawa: Conference Board of Canada 1985), 52.

54 Winegard Report, 40.

55 Ibid., 41.

56 Ibid., 42.

57 *To Benefit a Better World*, 60.

58 *Aid Review 1986/87: Report by the Secretariat and Questions on the Development Assistance Efforts and Policies of Canada* (Paris: DAC 1986), 22.

59 For example, a Canadian consortium including Acres, General Electric, and SNC undercut an Austrian rival for a $650-million parallel financed hydro-dam project in Himachel Pradesh, India. There was a subsequent negotiation to build a further hydro project downstream, in a $315-million parallel financed project with a $115-million concessional component.

60 For an assessment, see "Canadian Procurement at the World Bank: Report of Activities and Performance, 1989–90" (Washington, DC: Canadian

Embassy, Office for Liaison with International Financial Institutions, 1990).

61 "Canada Gets Few Contracts," *Globe and Mail*, 24 April 1991.

62 Winegard Report, 99.

63 CIDA, *Sharing Our Future*, 77.

64 About 6 per cent in 1989. UNDP, *Human Development Report, 1991* (New York and Oxford: Oxford University Press 1991), Fig. 3.5, p. 56.

65 For a review of business lobbying, see my article "Do Interest Groups Make a Difference? Domestic Influences on Canadian Development Aid Policies," in I. Brecher, ed., *Human Rights, Development and Foreign Policy: Canadian Perspectives* (Halifax: Institute for Research on Public Policy 1989), 435–66.

66 *Meeting the Global Challenge* (Ottawa: EDC 1989), 9.

67 Charles Lindblom, *Politics and Markets: The World's Political and Economic Systems* (New York: Basic Books 1977).

68 Oliver Morrisey, "The Commercialization of Aid: Business Interests and the UK Aid Budget 1978–88, *Development Policy Review* 8 (1990), 318.

69 In the 1989 budget, ODA, which accounts for just 2 per cent of government spending, bore 17 per cent of the government's total expenditure reduction. Further cuts were made in the 1990 budget. Projections for reaching an ODA: GNP ratio of 0.7 per cent by 2000 have been revised downward, to 0.46 per cent.

8 Structural Adjustment and Canadian Aid Policy

MARCIA M. BURDETTE

Since the late 1970s, many member countries of the Organisation for Economic Co-operation and Development (OECD) have been struggling with major reforms of their economies. These years saw the collapse of the Keynesian consensus in macro-economics, with "sharply reduced faith in the efficacy of policy interventions and an assertion of the superiority of market solutions" being the main features.[1] On the political front, the right-of-centre parties absorbed theories based on supply-based economics and monetarism and proposed such measures as constraints on social welfare, reduced taxes on the rich, cuts to the civil service, deregulation of the private sector, and privatization of many services that had long been in the public sector. A major thread through all these programs was belief in the ineffectiveness of the state, as well as its potentially corruptive influences, and the need to "get the state out of the economy."

In this chapter, however, we look at the structural adjustment programs (SAPs) which have been imposed on the developing world. These programs are the economic reforms that Third World countries undertake in order to receive funds directly from the World Bank and the International Monetary Fund (IMF) and sometimes, in a connected form, from bilateral donors. Some Southern countries have attempted major adjustment of their own political economies,[2] but their numbers are few. Many more have been forced to undertake reforms sponsored by the multilateral agencies and bilateral donors.

A SAP typically is embodied in an agreement between the recipient country and the IMF and is supported by the World Bank and many bilateral donors. This agreement requires a country receiving funds to adjust many aspects of its economy. The IMF and the World Bank argue that these changes increase the recipient's efficiency through changes in pricing and trade policies, in the size and structure of government expenditures, and in the extent of the government's control of productive activity. The stated purpose of these alterations is to improve balance of payments and also to "kick-start" economies into growth through fuller integration into the international marketplace, by more extensive reliance on market forces, and by significant lessening of the state's role in economic matters.

Introduction of structural adjustment within the aid arena is part of a "regime" shift of the 1980s, which had its roots in shifts in domestic policies in key Northern countries and in the policies of the Bretton Woods institutions – the World Bank and the IMF, set up in 1945 following meetings held at Bretton Woods, New Hampshire.[3] Canada began to move into line with this sea change in the mid-1980s.[4] By 1989, support for the IMF/World Bank structural adjustment policies had become a central preoccupation of the Canadian International Development Agency (CIDA). This evolution of policy was endorsed and encouraged by the departments of Finance and of External Affairs. This chapter presents the particular interplay of domestic, bureaucratic, and personal factors that occasioned CIDA's full endorsement of these policies. It provides a detailed critique of the IMF/World Bank policies and hence also of CIDA's most important policy initiative in several decades.

THE IMPACT OF THE GLOBAL CRISIS ON THE SOUTH, PARTICULARLY AFRICA AND LATIN AMERICA

The 1980s became the adjustment decade for many Third World countries. It was also the "lost decade" for many of the least developed countries (LLDCs), for they lost ground in terms of their GDP per capita, maintenance of their social and physical infrastructure, and management of their debt burdens.

For Africa, economic and political problems experienced in the 1970s greatly worsened in the 1980s, although it is not argued here that adjustment directly caused these problems.[5] GNP per capita for sub-Saharan Africa fell by an average of 2.2 per cent a year from 1982 through 1989.[6] Investment averaged only 16 per cent of GDP, bringing declines in domestic investment in productive capacity and physical infrastructure. The trade deficit for Africa's lower-income countries increased from $5.2 billion in 1980 to $6.23 billion in 1988. And their total stock of foreign debt almost trebled, from $18 billion in 1980 to $47 billion in 1989, with actual debt service absorbing 24.3 per cent of export earnings.[7] For most of the continent, economic and social conditions steadily worsened in the 1980s.

In the Americas, the debt crisis of the early 1980s was followed by stagflation. When the shocks hit, according to Edmar Bacha, "investment rates shrank, both through a direct contraction of government capital formation and a crowding out of private investment."[8] In Latin America, average consumer prices grew by an annual rate of 126.9 per cent between 1983 and 1985[9] while the annual rate of inflation for 1980–87 averaged 103.3 per cent.[10] Although some sectors of the economy did relatively well, real per capita GDP for Latin America and the Caribbean in 1988 was about 7 per cent below the level of 1980.[11] As Señora Margerita Penon de Arias, wife of the former president of Costa Rica, said in February 1991, "the people of Latin America, the majority of the people, have suffered greatly during this past decade."[12]

As governments cut expenditures, social conditions worsened in many parts of the Third World, especially for the poorest and the most vulnerable groups. One sensitive indicator of underdevelopment and lack of adequate primary health care – low birth weight – rose between 1981 and 1985 in several African countries.[13] By 1990, mortality for children under five years old in Africa stood at 178 deaths for every 1,000 live births, in comparison with 57 for Southeast Asia and 72 for Latin America and the Caribbean. In Angola, Guinea-Bissau, Malawi, Mali, Mozambique, and Sierre Leone, a quarter or more of the children die before the age of five.[14] Sub-Saharan Africa has the highest maternal mortality rate.[15]

In some places in Africa and Latin America, the state itself seemed to implode, with disillusioned and discontented civil servants providing the minimum of service, allowing generation of outside income to take precedence over the formal job. Another indicator of social stress is the rise of violence, which in many Third World countries has reached exceedingly dangerous levels. Wars in Liberia and Peru are grotesque examples of what happens when "the centre does not hold" and people's desperate poverty and lack of faith in alternatives turn them on each other.

Many governments in the South dealt with citizens' growing dissatisfaction with their economic and social plight by increasing authoritarianism. Regimes poured resources into the paramilitary, police, and army, thus taking from the state coffers money that could have gone to investment or social services.[16] It is astonishing to note that the LLDCs nearly doubled the proportion of their GNP spent on the military from 2.1 per cent in 1960 to 3.8 per cent in 1986.[17]

The economic and social decline continued for many LLDCs through the 1980s. The economic recovery of much of the North did not improve the external economic environment for most developing countries. At a minimum, less and less investment flowed into the LLDCs. Debt and debt servicing continued to grow. The terms of trade and the market share for many of these countries also declined.

For Africa, the circumstances were particularly parlous. Over the period 1981–86, the export earnings of sub-Saharan Africa dropped drastically, principally because of falling prices for primary commodities.[18] Meanwhile, debt escalated from US$72 billion in 1982 to close to $163 billion in 1990. African voices joined the Latin American chorus which had been calling since the 1970s for international action to stabilize commodity prices and to ensure more control by the South over its economic future. Instead, Southern countries in distress were offered more of the same structural adjustment/stabilization medicine, based on reforms of their domestic economies.

THE EVOLUTION OF STRUCTURAL ADJUSTMENT

Important terms for understanding the policies of stabilization and adjustment in the wider global context and the context of Canadian development policy are "conditionality" and "cross conditionality," "sectoral" versus "general" structural adjustment loans, and "human face" reforms.

In the late 1970s, the IMF came to realize that many developing countries faced chronic balance-of-payments problems. Many low-income nations needed medium- or long-term recovery plans rather than the normal short-term stabilization loans already available through the fund.[19] In 1980, the IMF introduced structural adjustment facilities (SAFs) and, later, enhanced structural adjustment facilities (ESAFs), which offered countries liquid inflows at very concessional terms if they agreed to make macro-economic policy changes that the IMF judged to be essential.

This introduction of "policy conditionality" has a strong political dimension. Because its acceptance involved some loss of national autonomy over economic decision taking, and because the required adjustment measures are sometimes painful and usually politically unpopular, governments were initially often reluctant to borrow from the IMF. Through the 1980s, few of the larger Latin American countries were willing to extend the influence of the World Bank and the IMF over their macro-economic policies.[20]

Donors also began to link their development programs and projects to acceptance of the SAF with the IMF or a structural adjustment loan

(SAL) in place with the World Bank. If that structural adjustment program (SAP) falls apart, then donors may suspend all or part of the financial flows to the recipient country, as happened in Zambia in 1987. This cross conditionality became a very powerful additional inducement to any reluctant adjusters.

In the policy conditionality of SAPs, there is a basic division of labour between the World Bank and the IMF. The latter has primary responsibility for short-term stabilization and exchange rates, and the former, for medium- and longer-term structural reform. There are, however, areas in which each institution seems to be doing the other's job, not to mention offering conflicting advice.[21]

In line with its prior activities in stabilization lending and also its general role as "banker of last resort" to members of the international community, the IMF offers short-term loans with conditionality applying to all aspects of macro-economic policy. In aid circles, the IMF was known as the "tough cop," while the bank was seen as the "soft cop."

Although the World Bank had been operating in Africa, Asia, the Caribbean, Latin America, and the Pacific for many years, it had focused on projects and technical assistance. Its entry in the early 1980s into economic policy reform involved a new and different kind of work, which is close, though not identical, to that of the IMF. World Bank loans tend to be for the longer term, and many relate to specific sectors. Often conditions are applied to a recipient country's policies or actions having to do with those sectors: these are called sector adjustment loans (SECALs). Large block program loans – structural adjustment loans (SALs) – are conditional on major macro-economic reforms.

Throughout the 1980s, SAP lending represented about a quarter of the Bank's loans. Because of the resistance of some countries, especially in Latin America, to policy conditionality, SECALs grew more popular.[22] From fiscal year 1983 to fiscal year 1987, nine Latin American nations received 17 SECALs. By 1984, adjustment lending to Latin America passed $700 million, or nearly one-quarter of the Bank's lending to the region. The quantity dipped to under $500 million in 1985 but rebounded to over $1.5 billion in 1986 and 1987.[23] Of course, an extensive or multiple set of sectoral reforms put into one economy launches an adjustment of the whole economy.

Reforms of the SAPs

By the mid- to late 1980s, many voices were raised about the distributional impact and heavy social costs of many of the stabilization/structural adjustment programs. The most vulnerable groups, the poor and the new poor,[24] women, children, and the elderly, were the main objects of concern. In two volumes of studies, UNICEF provided powerful information about the welfare of children, arguing for a "human face to structural adjustment."[25] Many donors, especially Canada, The Netherlands, and the Nordic countries, suggested that the policies of the Bretton Woods institutions should incorporate the welfare of the most vulnerable groups.[26] Other pragmatic issues, raised by an increasingly aware audience, had to do with the speed and extent of devaluation, privatization, liberalization, and removals of subsidies.

In response to the criticisms and to many operational problems, World Bank and IMF personnel altered the SAPs throughout the 1980s in terms of speed, social impact, and rigour.[27] Indeed, one can distinguish three distinct generations of SAPs in Africa.

From 1980 through 1984, the World Bank's policies and lending reflected primary concern to expand investment (both for domestic and export markets), increase efficiency, raise output, and encourage inflows of private capital. These goals, plus the technique of "negotiating" them with the recipient African state, make this early period the most orthodox. The international financial institutions (the IFIs), which include the IMF, World Bank, and regional development banks, applied to low-income countries almost as rigorous conditions as the middle-income nations. As these programs were intended to restore macro-economic balances, they can be said to be dominated more by the Fund's preoccupation with fiscal and monetary policies than with the Bank's focus on longer-term reform of the economy. Examples of these first-generation programs were the SALs for Côte d'Ivoire, Malawi, Senegal, and Zambia and Kenya's stabilization program.

In the second phase (1984–86), World Bank and IMF officials paid more attention to the social dimensions of adjustment and acknowledged that adjustment must take place over longer periods. Parallel or added-on programs to mitigate the negative effects, such as the Programme of Action to Mitigate the Social Cost of Adjustment (PAMSCAD)[28] in Ghana, were also introduced. The terms "vulnerable groups" and "targeting the poor" appeared in the Bank literature, not simply as vague concerns but as important issues to explore or attend to if the economic reforms were to succeed.[29] Second-generation programs of this sort were implemented in Ghana's second and third Emergency Recovery Programme (ERP) and in Senegal (SAL III).

In the third and present phase, from 1987 on, planners try to integrate these social concerns into the SAP itself. The World Bank says that it has designed its programs for Cameroon and Madagascar with reduction of poverty as a fundamental objective of adjustment policy, along with improved efficiency and economic growth. As an illustration of

these new, socially conscious SAPs, in 1991 Ghana provided information to the World Bank's Consultative Group considering the next ERP
in order to integrate these social concerns into its next SAP. The
Ghanaian goal, backed by a few donors such as Canada, was to make
poverty reduction and protection of vulnerable groups not just ancil-
lary concerns but central to the whole process.

The IMF and the World Bank have been responsive to some degree
to the criticisms often offered about their SAPs. Their reforms, however, occur only within the broader logic of the adjustment programs.
Adjusting countries must balance their budgets, pay their debts, expand their export earnings, and lessen the role and power of the state.
SAPs have become more flexible, but certain requirements, such as
fiscal and monetary policy, remain short term in nature.

Since 1987, the World Bank and the IMF have agreed to coordinate
their policies in regard to each country in which both are involved via
the policy framework paper (PFP) for that country. This paper is drawn
up in consultation with the ESAF- and IDA-eligible[30] country that requests a SAP. It also has to be approved by the executive boards of the
Bank and of the Fund, sitting independently. Then it becomes the basic
policy framework for economic reform, laying out the obligations for
all the parties. Although details may vary, the PFPs of most SAPs include
a familiar set of policies for the borrower to follow.

Even through the period of their own internal reforms, the World
Bank and the IMF continue to support structural adjustment. This con-
stancy seems to stem from firm belief that adjusting countries have
done better than non-adjusters.[31] Although that conclusion has been
questioned by other sources,[32] the commitment continues, as do the
SAPs.

CANADA'S CONVERSION TO
STRUCTURAL ADJUSTMENT

The Canadian policy on structural adjustment was adopted rather late
and has never been subjected to serious public debate. The election of
a Progressive Conservative government in September 1984 indicated
the ascendancy of a new policy agenda, but the implications of this for
aid emerged slowly because of the low priority of aid for the government and the even lower standing of most Third World issues. The re-
election of the Conservatives in 1988 brought intensification of their
policies, one element of which, it appears, was to realign development
assistance behind the Bretton Woods institutions. By 1990, senior
Canadian aid officials were firmly in support of the structural adjustment processes, albeit tempered by concern for the impact on vulnerable groups.[33]

The tenets of structural adjustment parallel policies undertaken at home. Many of the same phrases appear in Canadian budgetary documents about "living beyond our means" and the need to pursue areas of comparative advantage, cut back social expenditures, lessen the deficit while adjusting taxes to attract foreign investors, reduce the national debt, and so on. There was thus an easy "fit" between the IFIs' neo-conservative notions and the Tory government in Ottawa.

The Conservative government increasingly aligned Canada's foreign policy with that of the United States. Washington was heavily (though not without some divisions) committed to structural adjustment for the South. Equally, many other donors (such as Sweden), which had resisted the neo-conservative leaning of such an approach, began to express support in the late 1980s.

Structural adjustment came into prominence only gradually in public discourse on Canadian aid. It drew very minor mention in the annual aid review submitted by CIDA to the OECD's Development Assistance Committee (DAC) for 1985 and in the Hockin-Simard Report of June 1986.[34] In May 1987, the well-regarded Winegard Report[35] mentioned structural adjustment but did not give it any special emphasis. Its authors echoed UNICEF's concern about the need for a human face in its recommendation that Canadian representatives to the IFIs promote structural adjustment while showing sensitivity to the effect of economic policy conditionality on the poorest.

CIDA responded in 1987 with a new policy document, *Sharing Our Future*, in which structural adjustment emerged as one of the six priorities for Canadian aid, albeit with a caveat about social and economic effects.[36] This inclusion came as a surprise to many CIDA staff members, as structural adjustment had not been a major policy thrust.[37] Structural adjustment lending gained a toehold in budgets for adjusting countries, and a new policy began to emerge, though obscurely at first. CIDA started to express belated interest in using aid as a "policy lever" for structural adjustment – an additional way to encourage the recipient country to follow a certain set of policies.

In shaping a new Canadian policy towards structural adjustment, donors' coordination and cooperation were important. In 1986, the DAC had developed a policy statement – "Principles on Aid for Improvement of Development Policies and Programmes and Strengthened Aid Coordination." By the mid-1980s, among the members of the DAC, consensus was growing about the need for structural adjustment and policy reform for the low-income countries in particular. The World Bank and the IMF took on the task of designing these reforms; institutions such as the DAC helped coordinate donors, including Canada. At the 1988 DAC meeting, Canada was criticized for its lack of support of structural adjustment. The emergence of an international aid regime on structural adjustment required that even the countries with strong social democratic traditions had to join the consensus.

Techniques were refined to encourage donors to adhere to the new system. The new regime emerged under the direction of the World Bank (consultative groups), the UNDP (roundtables), and participants in the Paris Club – ad hoc meetings of creditor governments that began in 1956 to renegotiate debts owed to or guaranteed by official creditors. Especially at the consultative groups, where recipient countries' economic reforms were discussed, donors could question the activities built into SAPs. As a quid pro quo for being more involved in the making of policy, donors were expected to provide quick-disbursing funds to support structural adjustment, either through balance-of-payments support to the central governments or through disbursements directly to specific sectors.

Another, more human factor contributing to the switch was that many donors had lost faith in the previous models and approaches. By the mid-1980s, many Canadian aid personnel, in NGOs as well as in CIDA, plus sympathetic supporters in External Affairs and Finance, were in despair about turning around conditions for the poorest countries. Common-sense statements such as "no project, no matter how well intentioned and how hard the aid personnel work at it, can succeed for long if the overall macroeconomic policies are not right"[38] had considerable appeal.

Part of the allure of structural adjustment was its intention of dealing with the macro-economic environment, not simply individual projects. As well, it focused on Third World domestic policies rather than on unstable commodity prices, declining terms of trade, inadequate resource transfers, and rich countries barriers to LDCs' exports, all of which hurt the Third World.

In general, and for many reasons, donors, Canada included, were receptive to structural adjustment. Still, policy is always the outcome of the interplay of many actors. Although the origins of the policy lay in Washington, the new policy needed to be clearly transmitted from the Bretton Woods institutions to Ottawa.

CANADIAN INSTITUTIONAL INTERPLAY

In Canada, more than thirty federal departments and agencies or crown corporations have jurisdiction over policy issues that have an international focus.[39] However, not all of these entities are involved to the same degree and in every instance. Vis-à-vis structural adjustment, CIDA, External Affairs, and Finance are of the greatest importance.[40]

External Affairs and International Trade coordinates policy for all geographical divisions of the world. Its institutional interest is to augment Canada's good name in international circles, to aid commercial objectives, to observe international law at all times, and to make small incremental and diplomatic interventions. The hallmarks of Canadian behaviour have been mediation, persuasion, and quiet diplomacy. Canadian bureaucrats seem eager to protect the country's reputation as a "team player." By funding many countries through aid, Canada has been able to participate in many consultations, despite relatively limited funds.[41]

Under the direction of its new Conservative minister, Joe Clark, External Affairs did not give unqualified support to structural adjustment. In public speeches, Clark expressed concerns about how support for structural adjustment could affect moves towards democracy in the developing world.[42] Under his successor, Barbara McDougall, a more overtly protrade policy emerged that entailed cutting back substantially aid to several LLDCs. But in general, External Affairs has remained supportive of these major economic reform packages for the developing world, though less willing to find the capital to underwrite them.[43]

In the devolution of the policy from the IMF and World Bank to Canada, the central aid agency, CIDA, was a "policy taker, not a policy maker."[44] Through the mid- to late 1980s, a slow conversion took place within CIDA. This transmutation was related partially to internal bureaucratic constraints. Because of tight controls on hiring in the late 1980s, CIDA found itself with somewhat more money but not enough large-scale projects, programs, or personnel.[45] As project lending required more time of administrators, program lending took on greater prominence.

In 1987, within the agency, a link was gradually forged between the technique of program lending and the needs of structural adjustment programs.[46] Balance-of-payments support was merged with sectoral support to create SAP support. CIDA's bilateral program for Ghana demonstrates how this works. "Approximately 35–40 percent of cash flow for the next five-year period will be transferred as unstructured programme aid to support balance of payments ... All elements under this theme will be tied to satisfactory performance by Ghana under an internationally accepted SAP."[47] Under the presidency of Margaret Catley-Carlson, the blending of a technique (structural adjustment program support) and a need (disbursement pressures) helped win over the bureaucracy.

Once support for structural adjustment had been officially embraced in the ODA Charter (1988), CIDA's management worked to increase the staff's competence on macro-economic issues. Senior levels explained this policy to their staff members, who were specialists in project management or administration, not in macro-economic analysis. The Area Coordination Group of CIDA assembled readings on structural adjustment. It also began holding seminars on macro-economics, aided by World Bank and IMF officials. Support for structural adjustment, and its implications for CIDA budgets, were further highlighted by the growing involvement of the Department of Finance in aid policies.

In the second half of the 1980s, Finance slowly became more overt in making policy on development assistance, primarily on debt and structural adjustment. Finance has always monitored and encouraged debt repayment. It also manages financial flows to the World Bank and the IMF, whereas CIDA handles flows to the UN agencies and regional development banks.[48] For IMF-related issues, the key Canadian participants are Finance and the Bank of Canada. For the World Bank Group – the World Bank, the IDA, the Multilateral Investment Guarantee Agency, and the International Finance Corp. – a triad of CIDA, External Affairs, and Finance is involved.[49]

Finance and External Affairs were active in the special funds that the World Bank and the IMF organized in the latter half of the 1980s to provide additional finances to Africa. There was, for example, the Special African Facility in 1985, the Special Program of Action for Africa in 1987, and the provision by member states of loans and matching grants in 1988 to bring down the overall cost to recipients of funding from the IMF's Enhanced Special Adjustment Facility (ESAF).[50] Discussion of Canada's contribution to these appeals inevitably drew Finance into a more central role in the shaping of Canadian policy in these matters.

These new complexities also gave CIDA a greater opportunity to contribute to Canadian policies at the IFIs, as with the supplementation of the ESAF in 1988. Nonetheless, Finance remained prominent.[51]

Meetings concerning these large-scale financial flows brought the senior officials of adjusting Third World countries more directly into day-to-day discussions of their economic strategies and policies with the multilateral agencies and the bilateral donors. These occasions allow bilateral donors, such as CIDA, to influence elements of SAPs.

In Washington, the board of governors for the IMF meets annually to review IMF policy, but most important decisions are handled by the executive board, which has 24 members.[52] A parallel set of structures exists for the World Bank. Canada has had an executive director on both boards since their inception and also sits on the important Interim and Development committees.[53] Officially, decisions are taken by vote, but in practice they emerge usually through consensus, and hence informal influence and lobbying are more useful here than formal voting power.[54] The executive board discusses an application by a country for a structural adjustment loan. The actual terms of the policy framework papers are debated, and conditions applied.

Throughout most of the 1980s, "CIDA and most other aid agencies were accorded little opportunity to input in the design of individual adjustment programs by the IFIs or the country concerned."[55] More recently, however, CIDA has been asked to advise the executive directors concerning PFPs and adjustment programs when they come to the IMF/World Bank executive boards for approval.[56] Also, CIDA staff members make regular trips to Washington to influence general perceptions and policies and to garner information. These efforts reflect CIDA's attempts to become a "policy maker," or at least a participant in the making of policy, rather than a "policy taker."

In World Bank and IMF circles, Canadian financial officials were seen as supportive of structural adjustment programs, but acceptance of these policies at CIDA was much slower. Under Catley-Carlson's leadership, a "human face" was sought. Probably the commitment to the social amelioration package for Ghana (begun in 1985 but effected only in 1987) strengthened this side of development assistance policy towards Africa. A senior CIDA official made clear at an Ottawa seminar in February 1988 that CIDA remained sensitive to the impact of structural adjustment on the poorest.[57]

At the request of the Department of Finance, Marcel Massé, Canadian executive director to the IMF, was asked to head a donor "support group" for Guyana, which had fallen into arrears. Under Massé's direction, sufficient funds were to be collected from the donors to provide "bridging capital," allowing Guyana to pay its arrears and become eligible again for IFI concessional lending. Although this delicate task took longer than expected, Massé succeeded in the primary goals. Appointed president of CIDA in 1989, he brought back to Ottawa a fervour for structural adjustment.

A man of wide experience in Canadian government (clerk of the Privy Council and secretary of the cabinet, under-secretary of state for external affairs and president of CIDA 1980–82), Massé had five years in Washington as Canadian executive director (1984–89) that seemed to crystallize many of his ideas. Now, as president, he had room to use his considerable intellectual and negotiating skills at CIDA.

Soon after he became president, support for the SAPs toughened. In the 1989 Aid Review of Canada, done by Sweden and Japan, CIDA reinforced its position that it would not "provide aid to a sector unless certain measures [were] undertaken (e.g. appropriate tariff rates on water or electricity). In most cases, CIDA [would] condition its balance of payments assistance for structural adjustment on adherence to IMF/

World Bank adjustment programmes where monitoring is undertaken by the relevant institution, rather than have CIDA try to duplicate efforts."[58] People said less and less about the "human face."

By 1989, Canada actively supported SAPs in Bangladesh, Guyana, Jamaica, Nepal, and Philippines. Its representatives attended numerous consultative groups and roundtables. Massé's boss, Monique Landry, minister of external relations and international development, took the same line in her speeches.[59]

In that same DAC aid review for 1989, the agency announced its intention to realign "a significant part of its bilateral programs in many of the poorest countries to provide balance of payments support and structural adjustment assistance."[60] In 1989, about 43 per cent of bilateral aid was in the form of program assistance, up a bit from 1988. "Total bilateral disbursement of structural adjustment assistance ... increased from 7.3 percent in 1988/89 to 11.4 percent in 1989/90 and [was] projected to increase further in 1990/91."[61]

When parliamentarians asked for clarification in December 1989, Massé stated that 40 per cent of new bilateral ODA commitments to Africa were in the form of lines of credit or quick-disbursing assistance relevant to the region's structural adjustment requirements. About 26 per cent of new commitments in Asia and the Americas were related to structural adjustment.[62]

Assessing empirically Canadian support for structural adjustment is complicated by two factors. First, there seems to be a decision to play down any reference to CIDA's support of IMF and World Bank structural adjustment and instead to talk more loosely of support for macro-policy reform. Second, the figures presented in Tables 1 and 2, which were issued in December 1991, underrepresent Canadian support for structural adjustment.

For instance, in Tables 1 and 2, funds for a country's structural adjustment program are considered "structural adjustment disbursements" only when there is Canadian conditionality applied. Thus backing of a SAP in Bangladesh and Philippines does not appear in the official figures because Canada attached no specific conditions to its balance-of-payments support. Therefore the figures seriously understate Canadian assistance. Nonetheless they are indicative of the direction and size of these loans.

As indicated in Table 1, approvals for structural adjustment funding grew slowly from 1987–88 onwards. By 1990–91, CIDA supported six SAPs with explicit conditionality, with over 17 per cent of the value of all approvals that year. CIDA insiders suggest that the real amount of support for structural adjustment–related programs would be two to three times this figure.

Table 1
Structural adjustment approvals as a proportion of total bilateral approvals, fiscal years
1987–88 to 1990–91*

	1987–88	1988–89	1989–90	1990–91
S/A approvals (no.)	4	5	6	6
Total bilateral approvals (no.)	514	417	273	156
S/A approvals as % of total approvals	0.8 %	1.2 %	2.2 %	3.2 %
S/A approvals ($million)	85.0	113.3	126.3	154.7
Total bilateral approvals ($million)	862.3	897.9	591.4	871.7
Value of S/A approvals as % of total approvals	9.9 %	12.6 %	21.4 %	17.2 %

Source: CIDA, Policy Branch, December 1991.

* Indicative figures for CIDA activities, not final, official amounts.

According to Table 2, the largest number of disbursements, as well as the highest percentage of total disbursements, went to anglophone Africa, followed by the Americas and francophone Africa. Although Canada's report to the DAC in 1989 listed support for SAPs in Bangladesh, Nepal, and Philippines, this statistical portrayal omits Asia. Presumably CIDA's disbursements for these SAPs did not carry direct conditionality. A strong argument can be made that this sort of structural adjustment–related lending should also be included in these official figures.

Whatever the actual figures, it seems clear that there is a whole set of disbursements – called variously program assistance, structural adjustment (with conditionality), or structural adjustment–related – that adds up to considerable backing for this type of economic reform.

By 1990, for the first time, the heads of all the key institutions in Canada not only understood structural adjustment but were committed to it. An important body was resurrected, the Interdepartmental Committee for Economic Relations with Developing Countries (ICERDC), which meets to discuss issues related to debt, structural adjustment, and arrears. On that committee sit the president of CIDA and her or his vice-president for policy; the deputy ministers from External Affairs and International Trade and from Finance, accompanied by the assistant deputy ministers (ADMs) of Economic and Trade Policy at External Affairs; the Bank of Canada, through the person of the inspector general; the president of the Export Development Corp. (EDC);

Table 2
Structural adjustment disbursements ($million) as a percentage of bilateral
disbursements, fiscal years 1987–88 to 1990–91

	1987–88	1988–89	1989–90	1990–91
Americas				
Structural adjustment	0.0	3.4	14.0	18.8
Total branch	165.5	173.4	156.9	176.9
S/A as % of total	0.0 %	1.9 %	8.9 %	10.6 %
Francophone Africa				
Structural adjustment	0.0	1.8	8.5	8.9
Total branch	200.8	237.0	223.3	225.8
S/A as % of total	0.0 %	0.8 %	3.8 %	3.9 %
Anglophone Africa				
Structural adjustment	20.3	30.2	19.3	45.8
Total branch	293.7	303.6	261.8	315.0
S/A as % of total	6.9 %	9.9 %	7.4 %	14.5 %
Total bilateral				
Structural adjustment	20.3	35.4	41.9	73.5
Total bilateral	1074.7	1147.7	1000.4	1103.0
Total S/A as % of total bilateral	1.9 %	3.1 %	4.2 %	6.7 %

Source: CIDA, Policy Branch, December 1991.

and a representative of the Privy Council Office. This committee, according to insiders, endorses and reinforces CIDA's preoccupation with structural adjustment.

However, support for structural adjustment has been controversial. Many voices at home have been raised concerning the program, especially its social impact.[63] Perhaps because of that controversy, recent policy documents – for example, CIDA's Mission Statement of 1991 – avoid use of the phrase "structural adjustment." Instead, CIDA's mission is defined in terms of promoting sustainable development. That objective in turn is presented as resting on five pillars – environmental, economic, cultural, political, and social sustainability.[64] Economic sustainability includes appropriate economic policies. This can legitimately be read to mean a form of conditionality related to a country's economic policies, which for many nations translates into structural adjustment.

CIDA is now a strong supporter of this new and important component of the international aid regime. Whether this support is to be applauded or deplored depends on one's judgment of the effectiveness and the political and moral acceptability of the structural adjustment policies that Third World governments have been urged and induced into introducing. Alternatives are not dealt with here but form the central preoccupation of the ECA's African Alternative Framework to Structural Adjustment Programmes for Socio-Economic Recovery and Transformation.

CRITICAL ANALYSIS

It is important to acknowledge that there are some favourable aspects to the structural adjustment loans from the IFIs and supporting lines of credit from CIDA. Each is a quick-disbursing form of aid and often comes with specialized technical assistance to strengthen the administrative capacity of developing countries. Lessening a nation's balance-of-payments deficit is clearly essential, as those imbalances contribute to serious economic instability and deter foreign investment. In the current period of almost no new inflows of capital into debt-distressed LLDCs, SAP funds are one of the few sources of fresh capital.

Support for the SAPs rests on the belief that these major economic reforms in the long run will result in a higher rate of economic growth.[65] In normative terms, painful reform is essential to gaining eventually a better standard of living – the "trickle down" theory as applied to ODA. Our observation is that the pain is greater than estimated, the gain is more elusive than predicted, and long-term effects on the social sectors will inhibit true development.

A recent review of the experience with SAPs by one of the authors of the UNICEF "human face" appeal, Frances Stewart, pointed to the widening gap between categories of developing countries involved in SAPs. She concluded that some nations were able to combine adjustment, growth, and social progress, while others maintained social progress during the period of adjustment, without achieving much growth.[66] Some governments seem able to enact reforms well and benefit from the turnarounds in the international market enough to escape from the depths of poverty and marginality. However, the future for most LLDCs under SAPs is not so hopeful.

After a statistical evaluation of 93 countries, controlling for a variety of anomalies, a World Bank–funded research project concluded that "growth is not higher in countries recipient of IMF-WB funds."[67] Noting that accompanying structural reforms often require a relatively long period before their benefits materialize, the authors found these results unsurprising. However, their findings left in doubt the key belief concerning these rigorous policies – that they will bring about greater growth for LDCs.

Given that growth is not yet a demonstrated outcome of structural adjustment, it is important to turn to other arguments about SAPs. Supporters sometimes ask what would have happened had the SAPs not taken place, given the serious crises in external finance and internal management for many countries that turned to the IFIs – the counterfactual argument. As this is impossible to ascertain, one is left with criticisms about the SAPs' design, impact, and practical limitations.

Three types of criticism are distinguished here – the reforms' highly intrusive ideological character, the practical observation that "human face" approaches require more resources than are forthcoming, and the implicit exclusion or "blocking off" of alternative, perhaps more suitable strategies.

The Ideological Nature of the Reforms

Structural adjustment policies, either planned or fortuitous, press recipient states to dismantle protectionist policies, open up further their economies to production and investment from developed countries, and pay debts despite heavy domestic costs of doing so. The policies usually include a tipping of domestic terms of trade from urban to rural areas. These tactics can be positive for an economy in the long run if they are connected to a successful strategy for benefiting from more extensive involvement with the international economy. But the consequences of those policies go against the political logic that Third World leaders confront as they look at growing populations/urbanization and static or declining employment.

Many governments in the South have to face large numbers of very poor, unemployed, or underemployed people in the cities and towns. Although increasing prices for rural producers may attract some people back to the land, consolidation of land holdings (as in the enclosure movement in 18th-century Britain) pushes people off the land. What this influx of poor people in the urban and peri-urban centres needs is employment and basic services and infrastructure. SAPs, beginning from a logic of dismantling the state and lessening its expenditures, cut employment, slash subsidies on many commodities, and shrink basic services to people who are unable to afford fees for cost-recovery schemes, especially in medicine and education.

One has to wonder at the models that are chosen for Third World countries to emulate. During the most orthodox phase of SAPs, Chile and Uruguay in the late 1970s were held up as examples of liberalization and successful export-oriented strategies. The degree of political repression and impoverishment caused to the poorest by such policies seems to have been largely ignored.

The World Bank has cited South Korea as a model for what could be achieved through outward orientation, seemingly unaware of the dirigiste nature of this regime. The *World Development Report* for 1991 holds up Indonesia's experiences with economic growth and social-sector spending, sidestepping the serious environmental damage linked to current forestry practices and the extensive and severe violations of human rights in East Timor. The political message implicit in these choices seems not to have penetrated the halls of the World Bank and the IMF. The *Long Term Perspective Study for Africa* presented sub-Saharan Africa with the more benign model of the Nordic countries.[68] The reaction of Professor Bade Onimode of Nigeria – "It is not the business of the Bank to prescribe the Nordic model for Africa" – catches the tone of irritation and scepticism of many towards these models.[69]

At the same time, these major reform packages do not challenge or even attempt to adapt or modify international markets, especially for primary commodities, which have caused or exacerbated the economic crisis for many low-income countries. Nor do they begin from the vantage point of debt forgiveness or even substantial debt reduction. Even "strong adjusters" (World Bank parlance for governments that actively undertake adjustments and meet targets) find it difficult when higher volumes of exports produce less foreign exchange.[70] Nations that have invested heavily in export crops rather than in food production, following the rationale that their foreign exchange earnings will permit them to buy cheap food and still service their debts, may now have to rely on food aid to tide them over until another good year.

A good illustration of this dilemma is what happened to Zimbabwe in 1991 and 1992. On IFI advice, its officials sold off its stores of maize in order to avoid storage costs and also obtain foreign exchange from the sales. When the drought of 1991 stretched on and intensified in 1992, the country did not have enough food in storage for its own citizens. Because the drought also affected its most likely regional source of maize, South Africa, Zimbabwe had to spend heavily to purchase maize from long distances. Usually a surplus producer, the nation was reduced to obtaining food aid to cover its distant purchases of maize. Although the drought cannot be blamed on the IFIs, a strong recommendation to "offload" surplus stocks in drought-prone regions is subject to query.[71]

The SAPs also display gender bias. Diane Elson has carefully analysed the model: its indicators and policies, she concludes, underestimate or totally overlook the harm that it causes to women.[72] Even a relatively conservative review of this matter accepts that in the short term "the majority of potential impacts may have a disproportionate negative impact on women's employment, incomes and consumption and utilization of the goods, services and resources that are critical for their productivity."[73]

An indirect effect for women comes from slashing of state programs and from expecting families to replace these services themselves. The inability of families to provide school fees for children, for example, will increase demands on women to be available for their care during the day, without parallel lessening of the need to earn all or part of the family income.

An eloquent Third World academic raised her concerns that the World Bank's recent "discovery" of women's additional capacities could be dangerous. An eager espousal of the additional energy and creativity of women (found in recent Bank documents) might mean adding to those burdens, with fewer resources available to finance the additional needs such as care for the sick not in hospitals.[74] Reducing health care facilities can transfer the costs of care of the sick from the paid economy to the unpaid economy of the household. "The financial costs fall but the unpaid work of women in the household rises."[75] Thus the male bias in structural adjustment is another aspect of these programs' intrusive ideological character.

Practical Shortcomings: Finances

Some critics look at declining ODA and increasing Third World need. They question whether it is really possible to protect vulnerable groups and reduce poverty while initiating rigorous economic reforms, without additional massive infusions of funds. Ghana's considerable success in sustaining growth while maintaining social spending is attributable to the heavy funding from outside donors, of which Canada is one of the leading contributors.[76] The World Bank's most recent poverty alleviation policies also depend on bilateral donors supporting key social sectors. Supplementary funding on this scale cannot be expected to cover the dire needs of the more than sixty countries undertaking ESAFs, SAFs, SALs, SECALs, or stand-by agreements.

Recent Canadian budgets do not predict major increases in overall ODA or program assistance. The 10 per cent cut in development assistance announced in December 1992 pares ODA back to levels of the early 1980s, with subsequent years to be even lower. The cutting off of aid to 14 of the poorest countries may allow Canada to supply more funds to a limited number of "selected" clients – but probably not enough for Canada to gain great "leverage." Such fiscal restraint is by

no means restricted to Canada. Many DAC members, including the traditionally generous Nordics, are either paring back their ODA or redi-
recting funds to eastern Europe and the former Soviet Union, as is
Canada. So the future looks poor for additional funding and not very
good for maintenance of funding levels. There is really little chance of
major resource transfers, at least on the scale necessary to offset the
adverse social impact of structural adjustment.

Many in CIDA are well aware of this dilemma: "It is clear that with so
many countries now undertaking structural adjustment, there is very
little flexibility for increases in quantitative as opposed to qualitative
support. This makes it very difficult for CIDA to be able to provide additional resources in the short term for countries undertaking adjustment."[77] One official said about the "most successful" of the add-on
programs to mitigate the negative effects of structural adjustment in
Ghana: "we cannot afford another PAMSCAD."

How to present structural adjustment with a "human face," when SAP
policy compresses demand, thereby reducing wages and standards of
living? It is hard to imagine how demand compression could be made
compatible with reduction of poverty and lessening of inequalities.
Careful targeting of the vulnerable groups plus encouraging countries
to cut military expenditures rather than social services could soften the
impact of structural adjustment. However, in her review of SAPs up to
mid-1990, Frances Stewart concluded that neither the IMF nor the
World Bank has significantly altered the designs of its policies, despite
supposed internal reforms.[78] The hope that governments in either the
North or the South will slash military spending and pour that money
into poverty alleviation is unrealistic and naive.

Confining Third World Policy Options

A key characteristic of an aid regime is the collective agreement among
donors to act in concert. The current system permits few alternatives to
the development strategy embodied in the policy advice of the IMF, the
World Bank, and major donors. As a result, many Third World governments experience structural adjustment programs as a "narrowing
down of their range of policy options."[79]

The need for additional resource flows to all of the developing world
has been at the centre of many debates over debt and structural adjustment. Latin American countries, despite desperate economic straits,
remained net exporters of capital to creditors, both official and private,
throughout the 1980s. Because adjusting states must still meet their
debt obligations, the flow of capital continues to be negative. As the
SAPs are funded primarily through the multilateral development agen-

cies whose ground rules deny debt forgiveness, the outflow of these vital finances is likely to continue.

Again Africa's marginalization is the most extreme, except perhaps for parts of the Caribbean. Africa has received very little investment over the past 15 years. When the United Nations adopted the Programme of Action for African Economic Recovery and Development (UNPAAERD) for 1986–90,[80] delegates linked economic reforms in the low-income countries with increased overseas financial flows (ODF) from the West. A bargain was struck, if not formally, certainly implicitly. African states would implement the policy reforms being pressed upon them, and the industrial states would increase significantly their resource transfers to Africa.

Some African nations launched the reforms, others did so partially, and some dissembled. The industrialized world supplied only about half the ODA recommended, and even less in other forms of financial flows.[81] As Stephen Lewis, special adviser on Africa to the secretary general, said: "the UN programme didn't fail because it couldn't work, it failed because the international community wouldn't let it work."[82] With projections of declining ODA in the 1990s, the expensive, difficult-to-measure, and always troublesome social dimensions may receive only lip service, despite reforms to the original SAP.

Few alternatives have been permitted that bolster a nation's autonomy. Policies being insisted on by the IFIs and most bilateral donors forbid protection of infant industries. Those countries with still fragile capital goods sectors, such as Zimbabwe, will be hard pressed to defend them in an open market, because their products are rarely competitive with Western goods. Yet these industries have been central to that nation's industrial integration, which has made both agriculture and manufacturing more rational and productive.[83] Proposals to modernize Zimbabwean industry without fully liberalizing trade regulations have met with little acceptance from donors and IFIs.[84]

Another vital area is domestic production of food. Any government needs to ensure sufficient foodstuffs for its population. Many SAPs, through their insistence on investment in export crops and removal of consumer subsidies for basic foods, and also through other donors toeing the line, have undermined some governments' food security strategies.[85]

A major aspect of food security concerns availability of foreign exchange. Many Third World countries do not produce their basic food crop efficiently or adequately – for example, rice in Senegal. If there are adequate foreign earnings to buy food from neighbours or on foreign markets, such purchases can be a more effective strategy than encouraging local production. Until the collapse of the copper price in

1974–75, Zambia employed this method. However, this proposition assumes foreign exchange earnings regular enough to provide the purchased food and enough money in the hands of rural and urban poor that they can afford it. Many countries want to develop self-sufficiency in food but find that it contradicts the export orientation of a typical SAP.

The policy conditionality of the multilateral institutions' SAP programs is bolstered by the strong and growing cross conditionality of many donors. Countries undergoing these reforms must stick with the multilaterally funded program or lose very substantial amounts of bilateral monies as well.[86] In days of limited resources, furthermore, nations not structurally adjusting are squeezed out of the funding.

The major alternative, seemingly discarded, is debt forgiveness. If we look at Africa, we see a region where the debt crisis has become a "debt cancer."[87] According to Roy Culpeper, "Africans made some [US] $81 billion in service payments between 1983 and 1990. Total debt owing in 1982 was $72 billion. By 1990 it was close to $163 billion. Almost $34 billion in interest arrears piled up during the 1980s. Over half of the debt is owed directly or indirectly to governments. Instead of recognizing the problem and dealing with it, Northern governments preferred simply to convert the arrears to new loans."[88] By early 1993, sub-Saharan African debt had reached US$183.4 billion.[89]

Canada has actually been one of the most generous countries in its forgiveness of African ODA debts, but substantial amounts of commercial debt remain. A recent House of Commons subcommittee strongly and unanimously complained of official complacency over the international debt of Third World countries and urged a much stronger program of debt reduction measures.[90]

In many ways, the structural adjustment policies of the IFIs have "multilateralized" Africa's debt and made it less flexible. A remarkable change has occurred in the debt profile of Africa in the 1980s and early 1990s. By 1993, 51 per cent of that debt was owed to the multilateral agencies, in contrast to 11 per cent in 1980.[91] The unwillingness of the multilaterals to consider some form of debt forgiveness has given African countries less freedom to manoeuvre. Predictably, this will result in greater reliance on more bilateral donors, such as Canada, to pay the arrears and debts.[92]

Structural adjustment and too limited a range of debt renegotiation were part of the aid regime of the 1980s. These policies fitted very well with the neo-conservatism of many Northern states; they were less effective in helping the poorest countries of the world deal with their immediate crises or bargain for better terms and conditions of their integration into the world economy.

CONCLUSION

Structural adjustment now seems a well-entrenched and major policy of the DAC donors and multilateral agencies. Many who are concerned about the consequences for Third World development have turned to issues of how to humanize the programs in order to lessen their adverse social impact. However, structural adjustment within the new aid system rests on belief in the efficacy of the market, a diminished state, and the beneficent consequences of foreign investment. These assumptions clearly are connected to those currents of neo-conservatism in the North, and many of the same policies are being enacted in the advanced industrial world.

Even if successful, short-term balancing of low-income countries' internal and external accounts will not last for long if international trade circumstances and the international debt policies of the rich nations prevent these poorer states from investing in production for local needs as well as export. Without changes in the international terms of trade and without reduction of their debt burdens, the poor are not likely to be helped by aid donors' preoccupation with neo-conservative macro-economic policies.

In the late 1980s, Canada joined this consensus. Thus it resolved the contradiction between its obligation under its own ODA Charter to help the poorest and its support for the new aid system of structural adjustment in favour of the latter objective. In what appears to be the harder-nosed 1990s, especially if the new approach to aid and neo-conservative policies remain in ascendancy, it will hardly surprise anyone to see the concerns of the poorest people of the world slowly dropped off the Canadian aid agenda.

NOTES

1 Tony Killick, *A Reaction Too Far: Economic Theory and the Role of the State in Developing Countries* (London: Overseas Development Institute 1989), 7.

2 Zimbabwe, for example, began "home-grown" structural adjustment in the late 1980s but by the early 1990s had come under the SAP funded by the African Development Bank, the IMF, the World Bank, and bilateral donors. See Rob Davies and Tim Shaw, "The Political Economy of Adjustment in Zimbabwe: Convergence and Reform" (Ottawa: North-South Institute 1993).

3 Robert E. Wood, *From Marshall Plan to Debt Crisis: Foreign Aid and Development Choices in the World Economy* (Berkeley: University of California Press 1986), especially chap. 7, details how in the late 1970s and early 1980s aid was linked increasingly to non-aid flows and aid resources were

also restructured in the wake of the debt crisis. In particular, the IMF came to play a more central role (being among the few IFIs that had resources substantially increased), most bilateral aid flows stagnated, and multilateral development banks shifted away from soft-loan windows towards hard-loan windows and increasing speed in disbursements.

4 Wood develops this concept of an aid regime and argues that there is a "profoundly important relationship between aid, conceptualized as structured access to concessional external financing, and the basic features of the kind of development that has characterized most Third World societies and the overall world economy over the past thirty years ... This structure of aid financing has fundamentally affected the viability of alternative development choices open to Third World countries ... [which] has posed a complex combination of possibilities and constraints for Third World societies and thereby played a central role in shaping the nature of development strategies and processes." Ibid., 4.

5 Much of the evidence for this argument is drawn from Africa, because of the author's background in that region. Moreover, structural adjustment as a generic set of policy reforms also has a very African dimension.

6 United Nations Development Programme (UNDP), *Human Development Report 1991* (New York and Oxford: Oxford University Press 1991), 35.

7 "Link Adjustment to Development Goals," *Africa Recovery*, Briefing Paper 2 (August 1990), 12.

8 Edmar L. Bacha, "Latin America's Debt Crisis and Structural Adjustment: The Role of the World Bank," Departmento de Economia, Pontificia Universidade Catolica do Rio de Janeiro, Texto Para Discussao 198, mimeo (July 1988), 11.

9 Ibid., Table 3, appendix.

10 Helio Jaruaribe, "Latin America in the 1990s," *Development: Journal of the society for International Development* 3 (winter 1990), 160.

11 Dharam Ghai and Cynthia Hewitt de Alcantara, "The Crisis of the 1980s in Africa, Latin America and the Caribbean: An Overview," in Dharam Ghai, ed., *The IMF and the South: The Social Impact of Crisis and Adjustment* (London and New Jersey: ZED Books Ltd., on behalf of UNRISD and ISER/UWI 1991), 19.

12 "Proceedings of the Development Conference, New York and Washington, DC, February 1991."

13 The proportion of new-born infants with low birth weight rose in Guinea-Bissau, Rwanda, and Tanzania, among other nations, according to UNCTAD, *The Least Developed Countries 1990 Report* (New York: UN 1991), 63.

14 UNDP, *Human Development Report 1991* (New York and Oxford: Oxford University Press 1991), 35–6.

15 Ibid, 21.

16 According to the UNDP, "Military expenditures of the developing countries have increased 7.5 % a year during the past 25 years, far faster than military spending in the industrial countries. Their total expenditures multiplied nearly seven times – from [US] $24 billion in 1960 to $160 billion in 1986 – compared with a doubling for the industrial countries." UNDP, *Human Development Report 1990*, 76.

17 Ibid.

18 Roy Culpeper, *Forced Adjustment: The Export Collapse of Sub-Saharan Africa* (Ottawa: North-South Institute 1987), vi and 1–5.

19 The IMF was the leading agency for "stabilization" loans, short-term instruments to support policies that realign domestic absorption with domestic supply. Unstable commodity prices, connected to the oil shocks of the 1970s, caused serious balance-of-payments crises for many developing countries. This IMF facility was meant to provide short-term capital and encourage a country to rectify its balance of payments by reducing imports, increasing exports, lessening government deficits, curbing inflation, and so on. Performance targets would be set to measure a country's efforts. In two to three years, once the nation had been "stabilized," it would begin to repay the Fund. Lionel Demery and Tony Addison, *The Alleviation of Poverty under Structural Adjustment* (Washington, DC: World Bank 1987), 2–3.

20 Bacha, "Latin America's Debt Crisis," 22.

21 Paul Mosley and John Toye discuss the contradictions in the policies put forward by the World Bank and the IMF in the early 1980s in "The Design of Structural Adjustment Programmes," *Development Policy Review* 6 no. 4 (December 1988), 395–414. A more cynical assessment is made in "Sisters in the Wood: A Survey of the IMF and the World Bank," *Economist*, 12 October, 1991, 5–48.

22 Another reason for sectoral adjustment loans to the bigger Latin American nations was the World Bank's concern about their large and cumbersome economies and the amount of capital that economy-wide adjustment would demand. Author's interview with official from Canada's Department of Finance, 1991.

23 Bacha, "Latin America's Debt Crisis," 22.

24 Elaine Zuckerman et al., "Adjustment Programs and Social Welfare," Discussion Paper 44 (Washington, DC: World Bank 1989), 4.

25 G.A. Cornia, R. Jolly, and F. Stewart, *Adjustment with a Human Face*, 2 vols. (Oxford: Oxford University Press 1987 and 1988).

26 Author's interview with CIDA official, December 1991.

27 In 1988, the World Bank also established the Social Dimensions of Adjustment (SDA) program, focused on the worst-off continent, Africa. Sponsored jointly by the African Development Bank, the UNDP, and the World Bank, as well as several bilateral and multilateral donors, the

SDA has a research and policy function. It presents information and suggests methods for lessening the harm caused to the most vulnerable
people by the economic reforms.

28 PAMSCAD is a donor-supported program in Ghana.

29 From 1986 onwards, all SAL reports to the World Bank's president, prepared by Bank staff, have included a section discussing the social effects of the economic reforms supported by adjustment lending.

30 The International Development Association (IDA) is an affiliate of the
World Bank that offers loans on highly concessional terms and is sometimes referred to as the Bank's "soft-loan window."

31 According to World Bank, "Adjustment Lending: An Evaluation of Ten
Years of Experience," *PRS Series* 1 (Washington, DC: World Bank
1989), adjusting countries have performed better than non-adjusters.

32 For example, Riccardo Faini, Jaime de Melo, Abdelhak Senhadji, and Julie
Stanton, "Growth-Oriented Adjustment Programs: A Statistical
Analysis," in *World Development*, 19 no. 8 (1991), 957–67, and Paul Mosley,
Jane Harrigan, and John Toye, *Aid and Power: The World Bank and Policy-
Based Lending* (London: Macmillan 1990).

33 In December 1989, the new president of CIDA, Marcel Massé, made this
clear in his remarks to a parliamentary committee; House of
Commons, *Minutes of Proceedings and Evidence of the Standing Committee on
External Affairs and International Trade*, 2nd sess., 34th Parl., Issue
No. 31 (7 December 1989), 31A:4.

34 *Independence and Internationalism: Report of the Special Joint Committee of the
Senate and the House of Commons on Canada's International Relations*
(Ottawa: Supply and Services, June 1986).

35 *For Whose Benefit? Report of the Standing Committee on External Affairs and
International Trade on Canadian Overseas Development Assistance Policies
and Programs* (Ottawa: Supply and Services, May 1987).

36 CIDA, *Sharing Our Future: Canada's International Development Assistance*
(Ottawa: Supply and Services 1987); 57–8.

37 According to a senior CIDA official, between 1987 and 1989 there was
only one discussion of structural adjustment at the President's
Committee.

38 Address by Marcel Massé, President of CIDA, to a joint meeting of the
Society for International Development, the Canadian Institute for
International Affairs, and the United Nations Association of Canada,
February 1990.

39 Kim Richard Nossal, *The Politics of Canadian Foreign Policy*, 2nd ed.
(Scarborough, Ont.: Prentice-Hall Canada 1989), 203.

40 The Export Development Corp. (EDC) does play a role, but, as most of
the inflows of funds to sub-Saharan African in the 1980s were concessional, its function has been more to see if it can get paid for past loans.

Agriculture Canada is also involved, especially in food aid. The Bank of Canada also participates in these discussions of money and foreign policy, particularly with the IMF.

41 With the cutback in the number of countries and organizations that Canada funds announced in the budget of 1993, this general policy seems to be changing.

42 See speech by Joe Clark to the International Conference on Human Rights, Banff Springs Hotel, Banff, Alberta, 11 November, 1990, 5.

43 Ministry of Finance, *The Budget 1993* (26 April 1993), especially Table 3, 67, which illustrates the long-term cuts in international assistance, of which ODA proper represents a declining proportion.

44 This opinion and phrase occurred regularly in author's interviews with several CIDA senior officials in 1990 and 1991.

45 According to Groupe Secor, Strategic Management Review: Working Document (9 October 1991), 11, from 1986 to 1991 person-years for CIDA declined from 1,150 to 1,109.

46 The relative autonomy of the desk officers was crucial here, as they decide whether SAP support funds are conditional. Author's interviews with CIDA officials and desk officers.

47 CIDA's memo to the OECD, app. A; Country Programmes, Ghana, 3.1.

48 In 1989–90, Canada contributed $503.2 million to the multilateral development banks, of which $375.2 million went to the World Bank Group (identified in the same paragraph) via the Department of Finance and $128 million was channelled to the regional development banks and the International Fund for Agricultural Development. Communications Branch, CIDA, *Canada and Multilateral Development* (Hull n.d), 6.

49 Author's interview with CIDA official, December 1991, and statistics from CIDA, *Sharing Our Future*, 57–8.

50 The World Bank assembled US$1.2 billion for a Special African Facility, to which Canada contributed US$100 million. In December 1986, an agreement was reached to replenish the IDA facility to the level of US$12.4 billion for the three-year period to mid-1990. Almost 50 per cent of these funds were to be allocated to IDA-eligible countries in Africa, and Canada contributed Can$797 million. Then in December 1987, Canada pledged US$370 million to the US$6.4-billion Special Program of Action for Africa. In April 1988, Canada agreed to provide special drawing rights – US$300 million in loans and matching grants – to bring down the overall costs of ESAF funds. Statistics from CIDA, *Sharing Our Future*, 57–8, and author's interview with CIDA official, December 1991.

51 Officially, the Canadian executive directors report to Finance and the Bank of Canada. These individuals also take their instructions from External Affairs and Finance, respectively, although in 1990 CIDA began to add

a brief as well. Unofficially, the stronger hand of Finance is acknowledged.

52 As of September 1992, the number of executive board members increased to 24, with Russia and Switzerland gaining seats.

53 The Interim Committee of the board of governors for the International Monetary System is an inter-ministerial body created in 1974 to discuss important policy issues and provide advice to the IMF's board of governors. The Development Committee's full title is the Joint Ministerial Committee of the Boards of Governors of the Bank and Fund on the Transfer of Real Resources to Developing Countries. It advises the boards of both the World Bank and the IMF about the problems of and techniques for organizing flows of capital to LDCs.

54 Information on the IMF is drawn liberally from John Loxley, "The International Monetary Fund" and "The World Bank and Structural Adjustment," in *Debt and Disorder: External Financing for Development* (Boulder, Colo.: Westview Press 1986), 88–124 and 125–59, respectively.

55 Notes for remarks by Marcel Massé, President, CIDA, to the House of Commons, *Minutes and Proceedings of the Standing Committee on External Affairs and International Trade*, 2nd sess., 34th Parl., Issue No. 31 (7 December 1989), 31A:6.

56 Ibid.

57 John Sinclair, "Africa and Structural Adjustment: A Personal Perspective," in *Structural Adjustment in Africa: External Financing for Development*, seminar summary and background papers (Ottawa: North-South Institute 1988); 37–42.

58 CIDA, Policy Branch, Annual Aid Review 1989, *Memorandum of Canada to the Development Assistance Committee of the Organization for Economic Cooperation and Development*, 26.

59 For example, see Monique Landry, "Ajustement structurel et croissance des nations," address to Carleton University, Ottawa, 12 February 1990.

60 CIDA, *Annual Aid Review to the DAC*, 1989, 25.

61 Ibid, 25.

62 Marcel Massé, President, CIDA, to the House of Commons, *Minutes and Proceedings of the Standing Committee on External Affairs and International Trade*, 2nd sess., 34th Parl., Issue No. 31 (7 December 1989), 31A:4.

63 A particularly outspoken critique of policies appeared in Inter-Church Fund for International Development (ICFID), Churches' Committee on International Affairs, and Canadian Council of Churches, *Diminishing Our Future, CIDA: Four Years after Winegard*, A Report on Recent Developments in Canadian Development Assistance Policies and Practices (Toronto: ICFID, October 1991).

64 President's Notes to CIDA, mimeo, spring 1991.

65 Three documents from the World Bank in Washingon, DC – "Adjustment Lending: An Evaluation of Ten Years of Experience," *PSR Series* 1 (1989) (RAL I); *Report on Adjustment Lending II: Policies in the Recovery of Growth*, R90–51, IDA/R90–49 (1990) (RAL II); and "Adjustment Lending Policies for Sustainable Growth," *PRS Series* 14 (1990) – contain the essence of the bank's statistical backing for its continued support of structural adjustment.

66 Frances Stewart, "The Many Faces of Adjustment," paper prepared for International Conference on Policy-Based Lending, University of Manchester, 10/11 September 1990, mimeo, 44–5.

67 Faini, de Melo, Senhadji, and Stanton, "Growth-Oriented Adjustment Programs," 957–8.

68 World Bank, *Sub-Saharan Africa: From Crisis to Sustainable Growth, a Long Term Perspective Study* (Washington, DC: World Bank 1989), 186–7.

69 "World Bank's Long-term Perspective Study on Africa: An African Critique," *Third World Economics* 16 no. 30 (April 1991), 12–15.

70 In 1989–90, Côte d'Ivoire increased its export volume of cocoa only to realize less export revenue because of the sharp fall in prices.

71 Organisation of Rural Associations for Progress, *The 1992 Drought and the Structural Adjustment Programme in Zimbabwe: Preliminary Report* (April 1992).

72 Diane Elson, "The Male Bias in Macroeconomics: The Case of Structural Adjustment," in D. Elson, ed., *The Male Bias in the Development Process* (Manchester: Manchester University Press 1991), 164–90.

73 Susan Joekes, Margaret Lycette, Lisa McGowan, and Karen Searle, *Women and Structural Adjustment: Part II, Technical Document*, prepared by the International Center for Research on Women, Washington, DC, for meeting of the DAC's Women in Development Expert Group, Paris, 18 April 1988, 32.

74 Zenebeworke Tadesse, "Coping with Change: An Overview of Women and the African Economy," in *The Future of Women in Development: Voices from the South*, proceedings of the Association for Women in Development Colloquium, Ottawa, 19–20 October, 1990 (Ottawa: North-South Institute 1991), 44–62.

75 Elson, "Male Bias," 178.

76 John Loxley, "Ghana: The Long Road to Recovery, 1983–1991" (Ottawa: North-South Institute 1991).

77 CIDA, *Annual Aid Review*, 1989, 26.

78 Stewart, "Many Faces of Adjustment," 44–5.

79 Jan Isaksen, "What Did UNPAAERD Accomplish? A Review of Development of African Economies, 1986–1990," mimeo (New York: UNPAAERD 1990), 15.

80 In May 1986, the African countries at the UN presented to the General Assembly the African Priority Programme for Economic Recovery (APPER), which had earlier been adopted by heads of state and government at the Organization of African Unity's summit. The UN's 1986 special session concluded with the General Assembly unanimously adopting the United Nations Programme of Action for African Economic Recovery and Development (1986–90) (UNPAAERD). Richard Jolly, "Preface" to "Report of the North South Roundtable Session on the Challenge of Africa in the 1990s" (Ottawa: North-South Institute 1991).

81 Isaksen, "What Did UNPAAERD Accomplish?" 12.

82 Victoria Brittain, "UN Session Will Test the West's Commitment to Recovering Africa's Lost Decade," *Guardian*, 28 June 1991.

83 Colin Stoneman, "The World Bank and the IMF in Zimbabwe," in Bonnie Campbell and John Loxley, eds., *Structural Adjustment in Africa* (London: Macmillan 1989), 37–66, and Colin Stoneman and Lionel Cliffe, *Zimbabwe: Politics, Economics and Society* (London: Frances Printer 1989).

84 Davies and Shaw, "The Political Economy of Adjustment in Zimbabwe."

85 Advisory Council on Rural Development, ILO, *Report II: Structural Adjustment and Its Socio-economic Effects in Rural Areas* (Geneva: ILO 1990).

86 According to the (Zimbabwe) *Herald* of 1 August 1991, the World Bank delayed approval of a US$125-million quick-disbursing loan for balance-of-payments support until it saw if Zimbabwe's 1991–92 budget was in line with the SAP being proposed. The African Development Bank was expected to release US$100 million. The donors had held up releasing their pledges, which added up to US$700 million, "preferring to see whether the Government was committed to reducing Government spending" (p. 1).

87 Roy Culpeper, "Africa's Debt Cancer," *Toronto Star*, 13 December, 1991, 16.

88 Ibid.

89 Africa Recovery, "African Debt Crisis: A Continuing Impediment to Development" (New York: United Nations 1993).

90 *Securing the Global Future: Canada's Stake in the Unfinished Business of Third World Debt*, Report of the Standing Committee on External Affairs and International Trade, June 1990.

91 Africa Recovery, "African Debt Crisis."

92 A fuller explanation of this change in Africa's debt profile and its possible results is found in OXFAM-UK, *Africa: Make or Break* (Oxford: OXFAM 1993), 11–17.

9 Aiding Rights: Canada and the Advancement of Human Dignity

T.A. KEENLEYSIDE

Taking human rights into account in the shaping of Canadian development assistance policy has become a matter of considerable public policy attention since the late 1970s. From a humane, internationalist perspective at least, aid is or should be inherently about human rights. As early as 1976, for instance, Paul Gérin-Lajoie, then president of the Canadian International Development Agency (CIDA), wrote that the central objective of aid was "the total liberation of man" – liberation, first, from hunger, disease, illiteracy, unemployment, and chronic underemployment, but liberation also from "the use of force to silence dissenters, systematic recourse to political imprisonment, and the torture of prisoners."[1] Aid and human rights are, then, inextricably linked if the function of development assistance is seen as improving the human condition in all its aspects – as "empowering" the oppressed and disadvantaged.[2]

Viewing the developmental process in this fashion is, in effect, to acknowledge that both aid donor and recipient countries have obligations arising out of international declarations and covenants pertaining to human rights and fundamental freedoms that have been widely accepted by member states of the international system. Three documents that together make up the International Bill of Human Rights are of particular importance in this respect. First, the Universal Declaration of Human Rights, adopted by the United Nations General Assembly in 1948, constitutes a broad and eloquent statement of those political, civil, economic, and social rights that were to set a "common standard" of human rights achievement for member states. Second, the

International Covenant on Civil and Political Rights of 1976 binds states immediately upon ratification to respect such rights as those to life, liberty, security of person, equality before the law, freedom from torture, freedom of religion and expression, and the right to political participation. Third, the International Covenant on Economic, Social and Cultural Rights commits states to take steps to achieve "progressively" the right of everyone to, among other things, an adequate standard of living, including adequate food, clothing, housing, and medical and social services; the right to education; and the right to participate freely in the cultural life of the community.

While these standards govern the behaviour of states in their internal affairs, it has come to be recognized that states also have obligations to foster and protect at least the most basic of these rights outside their own jurisdictions.[3] That has been reflected in the expanding activity of the United Nations since 1971 in investigating complaints about rights violations within member states and in making recommendations in confidence for corrective action. The specific international responsibilities of states arising out of the International Bill of Human Rights are admittedly ambiguous. However, with respect to the Covenant on Economic, Social and Cultural Rights, it can reasonably be argued that in order for Canadian development assistance to be consistent with its standards, Canada has at least a minimal responsibility to ensure that its aid is not used to deny citizens of recipient countries basic economic, social, and cultural rights – that, for example, Canadian aid is not channelled to benefit a favoured religious or ethnic group within that society, at the expense of other groups. Further, in more positive terms, Canadian aid, to be consistent with the covenant, should be concentrated on meeting the needs of the most disadvantaged in the poorest countries[4] – on ensuring that they have adequate access to food, medical care, clothing, shelter, and education. That in turn means selecting as its primary aid partners those countries that take seriously their own obligations under the covenant to meet the basic needs of their citizenry.

In theory at least, since its adoption of the development strategy for 1975–80, CIDA's program has aimed at meeting basic economic and social rights by concentrating on "those countries which are at the lower end of the development scale" and on "the critical problems of their poor majority."[5] This alleged Canadian commitment to poverty-focused development assistance was reiterated in 1988 in CIDA's latest statement of aid strategy, *Sharing Our Future*, which proclaimed that "the primary purpose of Canadian official development assistance is to help the poorest countries and people in the world."[6]

The extent to which Canadian aid has lived up to this professed objective and is thus consistent with Canada's obligations under the International Covenant on Economic, Social and Cultural Rights is an underlying theme of this volume and not the specific focus of this chapter. However, less than one-quarter of Canadian aid flows to the 42 least-developed countries (LLDCs) as classified by the United Nations; just five of Canada's top 20 aid recipients over the period from 1988–89 to 1990–91[7] were in this group; in March 1993 it was reported that CIDA was terminating bilateral aid to six sub-Saharan African countries that are among the world's least developed;[8] and only a very modest proportion of Canadian assistance in any event "goes to meet basic human needs."[9] It must therefore be said that the achievement of fundamental economic and social rights in developing countries enjoys limited status among the range of objectives of Canadian aid.

The Covenant on Civil and Political Rights commits Canada at the very least to a minimal obligation to ensure that its aid does not enhance the capacity of recipient governments to repress their citizens – that aid is not used, for instance, to improve police and military equipment and communications in countries where arbitrary arrest and protracted imprisonment without trial are widespread. Some would interpret the covenant as bestowing upon Canada an additional obligation not to add to the strength and prestige of governments that grossly and systematically abuse their citizens' rights by providing them with all the normal channels of government-to-government aid. Finally, in a more positive vein, the covenant obliges Canada to enhance observance of civil and political rights by, for example, increasing aid to states with good and/or improving rights records and by selecting projects that are likely to make a contribution to human rights observance. The latter might include projects that facilitate political participation in decision making by those affected by the developmental process as well as projects aimed at curbing physical abuses of citizens through provision of legal, judicial, and police training or support to agencies monitoring human rights.

It is thus clear that the documents that make up the International Bill of Rights detail a panoply of civil, political, economic, social, and cultural rights that have pertinence to Canadian development assistance. Further, it is common practice to assert that these rights are indivisible and interdependent and that all must thus be accorded equal attention in the making of government policy and more particularly in the shaping of aid decisions. When civil and political rights are not respected, the poor in particular in developing countries lack the opportunity to participate freely and without fear in the making of decisions that will ensure that their needs are effectively met. However, when their economic, social, and cultural rights are unfulfilled, these same people are deprived of the physical and psychological capacity to wrestle for the exercise of their political and civil rights.[10]

It is, then, fair to say that all human rights should be taken into account in Canadian aid policy, especially in terms of influencing selection of specific aid channels and projects that will advance various rights and will thus contribute to the development of human beings in toto. However, as David Gillies has pointed out, "Canadian policy-makers evaluating complex human rights conditions in the developing world will be paralyzed if equal attention and equal weighting is to be given to the approximately 60 separate rights entrenched in the International Bill."[11] Thus, when it comes to making crucial aid decisions – including the negative ones of where aid should be curtailed or terminated because of gross and persistent human rights violations and what countries require close monitoring of the aid provided – there is a strong case for focusing on a narrow core of "first priority" rights. The absence of these basic security and subsistence rights makes the holding of any other rights largely meaningless. They are, in other words, rights without which it is impossible for any individual to live a life of dignity and worth. They are also rights that should not be infringed under any circumstances, even in a public emergency such as a civil or international war or a national economic calamity, although such circumstances might justify suspension of other rights, including making progress towards achieving the economic, social, and cultural rights enumerated in the international bill. At a minimum, these basic security and subsistence rights, the sanctity of which is almost universally recognized in theory if not in practice,[12] include the rights to freedom from arbitrary arrest and protracted detention without trial, freedom from torture or other forms of cruel and inhumane treatment, freedom from extra-judicial execution, and freedom from deliberate denial of the means of sustaining life, including the withholding of food and medical treatment.[13]

As discussed below, Ottawa has never identified the specific rights that are taken into account in decision making about aid and Canadian foreign policy generally. It is, however, the contention of this chapter that the basic security and subsistence rights should be acknowledged by the government as the principal, though not the exclusive, focus of Canadian human rights policy as it pertains to aid, especially in determining eligibility for Canadian aid. The assessment below of Canada's aid–human rights policy has been written from this perspective.

One additional introductory comment must be made. Canada's aid program is only one of a variety of instruments available to the government to help advance universal respect for fundamental human rights, and it cannot be relied on to the exclusion of others. To do so could, indeed, lend a racist character to Canadian policy, with the government focusing essentially on non-white developing countries while ignoring violations elsewhere. Further, not all developing countries receive aid from Canada, so that the Canadian government could legitimately be charged with discriminating even among developing countries if this were the only tool employed. Thus, while this chapter deals mainly with aid, Ottawa can use aid legitimately to influence the human rights practices of other governments only along with other foreign policy instruments, with the choice depending on Canada's relations with each state in question and the seriousness of the abuses in each instance.[14]

CANADIAN POLICY TO 1987

Until the late 1970s, Canadian governments generally shied away from explicit references to human rights criteria applying to Canadian development assistance. For instance, Ottawa's 1975–80 aid strategy document made not a single reference to "human rights."[15] When confronted with suggestions from Parliament or elsewhere that aid be made conditional on satisfactory observance of human rights, the government tended to react negatively.[16] However, in 1978, faced with increased preoccupation with this issue on the part of Parliament, interest groups, the media, and a number of specialists in Canada's international relations,[17] it adopted a more forthcoming, though still cautious position. In an address in October 1978, Secretary of State for External Affairs Don Jamieson reiterated the usual assertion that Canadian aid is "designed to help meet the basic human needs of the poorest people in the poorest countries" and by inference should not, therefore, in most circumstances be affected by human rights criteria. He then declared: "Human-rights considerations are, nonetheless, a factor in determining levels of aid and the orientation of programs." He added that "on a few occasions when the human-rights situation in a country has deteriorated to a stage where the effective implementation of the aid program is made extremely difficult, Canadian assistance has been suspended or not renewed."[18] Similar positions were adopted by the government of Joe Clark in 1979–80[19] and by that of Pierre Trudeau from 1980.[20] In 1981, however, another consideration that could precipitate aid strictures was cited: military intervention by a recipient state in the affairs of other countries. Secretary of State for External Affairs Mark MacGuigan stated that Canada had "withdrawn aid programs from those countries where scarce resources" were "diverted to war and conquest."[21]

The early statements of Brian Mulroney's government indicated continuation of past policy – action should be taken only in extreme cases, principally (although not all statements were explicit on this point) when breakdown in order rendered continuation of aid ineffectual. A CIDA document of 1984, however, once again hinted at an aid-rights link in less extreme situations, stating that "the nature and extent of our program" is affected by "the human rights records of development partners."[22] The generally restricted approach continued to be justified most frequently on the grounds that the principal function of Canadian aid was to end "the crushing oppression of poverty"[23] and that the victims of oppression should not, therefore, be "doubly penalized by the withdrawal of ODA programmes."[24]

There were several cases of curtailment of government-to-government assistance, purportedly for human rights reasons, up to 1987. However, such action was halting, inconsistent, and ambiguous concerning the actual role of violations in prompting action.

The first identifiable case, that of Indonesia, is illustrative of influences that have shaped Canadian policy ever since. Starting in the 1964–65 fiscal year, Canadian food aid to that nation was terminated for two years, and no new capital projects or commodity shipments were undertaken in 1965–66.[25] Although Ottawa was never publicly explicit about the reasons for this suspension, it was apparently caused by Indonesia's unprovoked military assault on its neighbour, Malaysia, in violation of such principles as the territorial sovereignty of states and the right of self-determination of peoples, and by parliamentary criticism over Canada's providing aid to a state diverting its resources from development to finance external aggression.[26] In short, the suspension was prompted by considerations that Canada set out only officially in the statement of 1981 referred to above.

Canadian aid to Indonesia at this time was extremely limited and confined largely to food aid. Indeed, bilateral economic and political relations were generally insignificant because of the anti-Western orientation of the Sukarno government and its chaotic management of its economy. However, following Sukarno's fall in 1965 and a gradual shift towards the West under his successor, Suharto, the country took on new political and commercial importance to Canada, and this was reflected in the decision announced in 1979 "to concentrate more funds for development programmes" in Indonesia.[27] Since that time, Indonesia has been a major beneficiary of Canadian aid. Based on government-to-government disbursements over the three fiscal years from 1984–85 to 1986–87, it ranked fourth among recipients. Yet, throughout the period under review, Indonesia was a serious violator of human rights, resorting frequently to arbitrary arrest, protracted detention without trial, torture, and extra-judicial killings.[28] Most disturbing was its treatment of the former Portuguese colony of East Timor, which it invaded and occupied in 1975. One-third of East Timor's population is estimated to have perished as a result of starvation and indiscriminate killings by the occupying army.[29]

There is no evidence to 1987 that Indonesia's gross and persistent violations of basic security and subsistence rights affected the amount or character of Canadian aid to its regime. Canada's program was not only substantial throughout the 1970s and 1980s, but it entailed sizeable capital equipment purchases and support for large-scale infrastructural projects,[30] forms of aid that arguably lent legitimacy to the Suharto government. Moreover, the decision to maintain aid without any strictures or monitoring of human rights, despite the 1975 invasion of East Timor, was strikingly inconsistent with the posture adopted in the face of the far less destructive assault on Malaysia in the mid-1960's. Canada's policy thus made a mockery of the government's assertion in 1981 about withdrawing "aid programs from those countries whose scarce resources are diverted to war and conquest."

Elsewhere in Asia, aid to Pol Pot's regime in Cambodia (Kampuchea), which tortured, murdered, and starved to death from one to three million pruported opponents, was halted in 1977. However, as in Indonesia in the mid-1960s, it was never stated explicitly that termination was because of human rights violations rather than simply because of the practical difficulties of implementing a program under extremely adverse conditions. Once again, too, the level of Canadian aid had been minimal.

In response to Vietnam's invasion of Cambodia (which resulted in the toppling of Pol Pot), Canada stopped its very modest bilateral program in Vietnam in keeping with the policy of not tolerating external aggression. Not only did the Canadian action apply to bilateral food aid, but the government directed that its contributions to the multilateral World Food Programme not be designated for Vietnam.[31] This approach was not consistent with Canada's frequently reiterated position that humanitarian aid that is able to address the needs of the most disadvantaged, food in particular, should not be withheld even in states that seriously abuse human rights.[32]

Following the Soviet Union's invasion of Afghanistan, Canada decided in January 1980 not to recognize the new regime installed by the USSR and terminated its limited bilateral aid program. Political/security and human rights considerations were, according to officials, interwoven in this instance, although a rationale was never given publicly.

Finally, with respect to Asia, on the basis of a regional program review, it was decided in 1984 not to provide "any significant government-to-government aid" to Ferdinand Marcos's government in Philippines. Implicit in the review was the notion that democracy had to be restored and the human rights situation in general had to improve before a limited bilateral program could be expanded. Following overthrow of Marcos in 1986 and restoration of constitutional democracy under Corazon Aquino, with a temporary increase in respect for basic human rights, Canada designated Philippines a major program country and committed itself to provision of $100 million in assistance over five years.[33]

In Africa, almost all bilateral aid to Uganda was suspended in January 1973.[34] Violations of basic security rights by Idi Amin's regime were clearly appalling, and it had been universally condemned for its atrocities. However, Canadian aid was suspended not specifically for human rights reasons, but because of the chaos in Uganda, which made assistance ineffective and jeopardized the lives of Canadian aid workers.[35] Following ouster of Amin in April 1979, and with the promise of improved human rights observance, Canada recommenced bilateral aid. In fact, for several years, there was little improvement. Canadian aid remained limited (as in reality it had always been) and channelled largely through non-governmental organizations (NGOs) in order to bypass the government and reach directly those most in need.

The first instance of Canadian action with regard to Latin America was withdrawal of bilateral aid to Chile following the 1973 coup which toppled Salvador Allende's democratically elected government and replaced it with Augusto Pinochet's repressive regime, which for many years thereafter committed gross violations of basic security and other civil and political rights. However, once again Canada acted quietly, making no public statement to the effect that this initiative was prompted by human rights considerations. Further, as in the other cutbacks, the aid program in Chile had always been small. In this instance, perhaps the best way for Canada to have registered its displeasure would have been to terminate Export Development Corp. (EDC) loans to Chile to finance imports from Canada, as well as insurance to Canadian exporters against commercial risks. No such action was, however, taken, and, indeed, the EDC's involvement in Chile actually increased following the 1973 coup.[36]

In 1978, CIDA's modest bilateral program in Cuba, set up only three years earlier, was terminated. The ostensible reason was Cuba's military involvement in Angola, which, according to Ottawa, indicated that it had "no more need for Canadian aid, given its new priorities."[37] As with Chile, however, Canada continued to make available to Cuba the facilities of the EDC, so that no consistent signal was communicated to Fidel Castro's regime regarding its behaviour.

Two of the most widely publicized cases of Canadian punitive action were the decisions taken in March 1981 to suspend planning for new bilateral projects in El Salvador and to allow the program in Guatemala to run out.[38] In both countries, there had for some time been widespread abuses of basic security rights, justifying such action on Canada's part. However, the administrative impossibility of carrying out the programs and the risks to Canadian field personnel under prevailing circumstances prompted curtailment of aid. The human rights rationale was employed only ex post facto, in the face of growing interest in aid-rights linkage.[39] Once again, suspensions did not entail a clear message to the regimes that their human rights records were unacceptable. In the case of Guatemala, like that of Chile, continuation of EDC loans and insurance, public-sector economic ties that had long been more significant than Canada's very limited aid program, showed Canada's ambiguity.

In December 1984, Ottawa announced resumption of direct developmental assistance to El Salvador, justifying this reversal of policy on the grounds that the human rights situation had improved.[40] Further, following restoration of civilian rule in Guatemala in 1986 and alleged improvement in respect for basic human rights, Ottawa announced in November 1987 that aid to this country would also recommence.[41] Both decisions sparked considerable criticism in Canada by NGOs, the media, and concerned individual observers who claimed that any human rights observance was at best short-lived and that torture, extrajudicial killings, and other violations of basic security rights remained endemic.[42]

Finally, in September 1983, Canada terminated its very small program in Suriname because of the repression that followed a 1982 coup, leading to liquidation of much of the political opposition. In this instance, human rights violations seem to have been the principal reason why Canada acted, although no public statement was made to that effect. In any event, Canadian aid was so limited that this initiative constituted merely a symbolic gesture.

Looking next at the avoidance of aid projects that contribute to human rights transgressions, only two clear examples were identifiable up to 1987. In November 1980, newsprint was removed from the list of commodities eligible for purchase under a line of credit to Guyana, when it became clear that the newspring was not reaching the opposition press. And, in 1984, Canada placed on indefinite hold its contribution to a massive dam and irrigation scheme in Sri Lanka when it learned that the recipient government intended to use the project in a racially discriminatory manner. Sri Lanka planned to resettle members of the Sinhalese majority community on the land irrigated by the project at the expense of Tamils, the dominant community in the affected province.[43]

As for positive shaping of Canadian aid in recipient countries so as to encourage human rights observance, up to 1987 Canada made the greatest progress perhaps in the domain of women's rights, via its Women in Development section, but this is the subject of another chapter. In Guyana, mission-administered funds[44] were used for provision of legal materials to the Supreme Court library and to the Guyana Human Rights Commission. Nigeria and Sri Lanka received grants to establish ombudsmen offices, and in rural areas of Africa CIDA sponsored workshops on legal services.[45] In 1984, Ottawa launched a program for the restructuring of Grenada's police force, entailing provision of equipment as well as an advisory service for police training and curriculum planning.[46]

In sum, until 1987, Canadian action was predominantly punitive in nature, bringing suspension of government-to-government assistance in perceived "worst case" situations. In most such instances, however, lack of explicit condemnation of human rights abuses sent an ambiguous message to the states in question. There was also obvious inconsistency in Canadian actions. Aid to Communist or strongly anti-Western countries (Indonesia in 1964 and Vietnam and Cuba) was terminated when they engaged in military interventions, but not to pro-Western states guilty of similar offences (Indonesia in the 1970s and 1980s and Honduras, which in the 1980s served as a base for a convert US war against Nicaragua). Countries such as Chile, Cuba, and Guatemala had their bilateral aid from Canada cut, but not their access to EDC facilities, which for all three amounted to a more significant public-sector economic link with Canada than development assistance. In all cases of suspended aid, the programs were small and Canada's other interests – commercial, political, and strategic – were also limited, so that no important Canadian relations were jeopardized.[47]

With Canada reluctant to act against major aid recipients that grossly abused fundamental human rights, it is not surprising that a study at the end of this period (from 1984–5 to 1986–7) found that 70 per cent of Canadian bilateral aid went to countries with violations of basic security rights ranging from serious to extreme (classified in categories 3 to 5 on a five-point, descending human rights scale). Further, almost half of Canadian aid went to 18 states in categories 4 and 5 – particularly severe offenders – including Bangladesh, India, Pakistan, and Indonesia, the four top-ranked recipients, and Sri Lanka (6th) and

Zaïre (11th), all of which appeared in category 4.[48] Yet this study acknowledged that to have suspended aid to all these countries would not have been sensible. Canada's aid program would as a result have been decimated. Further, much of the aid provided to these serious abusers was arguably being used to good developmental effect.

What was then and is still called for in such states was not the blunt instrument of termination, but a subtle response, with careful monitoring to phase out and/or not commence projects that might in any way contribute to human rights abuses and to identify others that might make a constructive contribution in this domain in the future. However, as the above review of Canadian aid indicates, before 1987 this type of filtering occurred only on a limited, ad hoc basis. Some officers, sensitive to human rights considerations, may have engaged in such a process informally or unconsciously. However, apart from the area of women in development, there was no institutionalized project-by-project assessment that applied a broad range of human rights criteria.

CANADIAN POLICY SINCE 1987

Societal pressure for a stronger human rights dimension to Canadian foreign policy grew during the 1980s. Moreover, two parliamentary committees, which reported in 1986 and 1987, gave particular attention to this subject in relation to the Canadian aid program.[49] Obliged to respond to the specific recommendations of these committees, Ottawa set out an expanded and more explicit aid–human rights policy in three documents released in 1987 and 1988.[50] It declared that "a basic principle" of Canadian foreign policy was "the promotion and protection of human rights" and that, accordingly, the human rights policies and practices of states would be "concrete factors in decision-making on aid determination." Therefore cabinet was to start giving annual consideration to information on the human rights situation in potential recipient countries in making decisions about eligibility and levels and types of aid to be provided. The government declared that "in countries where violations of human rights are systematic, gross and continuous, and where it cannot be ensured that Canadian assistance reaches the people for whom it is intended, government-to-government (bilateral) aid will be reduced or denied" and channelled unstead through NGOs "working at the grassroots level." Nations improving respect for human rights would be rewarded with increased funding. All states, including, with ministerial permission, even those not entitled to bilateral aid, would be eligible for emergency humanitarian aid in times of crisis, such as famine, epidemic, or civil war.[51]

These and subsequent policy statements reiterated Ottawa's traditional position that the victims of human rights violations must not be doubly penalized by denial of assistance as well as its view that a constructive approach to human rights, rather than a punitive one, was more likely to yield results.[52]

Late in 1991, there was a new infusion of political energy to the government's rhetorical commitment on this issue when Prime Minister Mulroney made human rights a central focus of the Commonwealth Conference in Harare, Zimbabwe, in October and of the summit of la Francophonie in Paris in November. In Harare, he asserted that "Canada will not subsidize repression and the stifling of democracy. We shall increasingly be channelling our development assistance to those countries which show respect for fundamental rights and freedoms."[53] In Paris, the prime minister indicated that Canada would change the amounts spent in repressive states "very substantially and funnel more modest amounts through non-governmental organizations."[54] Further, an External Affairs document released in December advanced "securing democracy and respect for human values" as one of three broad directions for future Canadian foreign policy.[55] In a major address the same month, Secretary of State for External Affairs Barbara McDougall asserted that "Canada will have no qualms in refusing to support abusive, corrupt and aggressive regimes that use their power to suppress their own citizens."[56]

This stronger focus on human rights in relation to development assistance is consistent with an apparent trend among donor countries, reflected in simultaneous suspension by a number of states in 1991 of aid to Haiti, Kenya, and Zaïre, principally because of violations of human rights. It is a development that has no doubt been encouraged by the embracing of democracy by the countries of eastern Europe and the former republics of the Soviet Union and by the ending of the Cold War, which has removed many of the political-strategic considerations that previously inhibited states from taking initiatives that might alienate erstwhile friends and allies in the Third World.

Since 1987, Canada has taken several concrete steps to implement its new aid-rights policy. A human rights unit (for some time a one-person operation) was created within CIDA, and the Policy Branch was designated as "responsible for ensuring that development assistance programs are consistent with Canada's overall foreign policy concern for human rights."[57] In January 1993, the human rights unit became the Good Governance and Human Rights Policies Division, responsible for coordinating development of policies and implementation strategies related to good governance, human rights, and democratic development.[58] A training program in human rights for officers of CIDA and

External Affairs was established.[59] A manual on human rights reporting was distributed to Canada's missions abroad, and posts began annually to file human rights information for Ottawa.

Canada was "instrumental" in bringing into being a "voluntary fund at the UN for providing technical assistance in the area of human rights." It also won approval for creation of a Unit for the Promotion of Democracy within the Organization of American States (OAS) and proposed a similar structure for the Agence de Coopération culturelle et technique. In the Commonwealth, it has attempted to make human rights a primary focus of the organization and of its technical cooperation programs.[60] Finally, and perhaps most important, an International Centre for Human Rights and Democratic Development, under the presidency of former NDP federal leader Ed Broadbent and located in Montreal, opened in 1990 "to help establish and strengthen institutions, programs and activities that promote internationally recognized human rights."[61]

Cumulatively, these developments represent a significant change over the situation up to 1987. The policy positions and institutional structures now in place may enable Canada to pursue an aid-rights policy that is more than rhetorical or symbolic and that represents a genuine, creative, and forceful commitment to the pursuit of global justice. There is no question, too, that as a result of these new departures, larger numbers of officers at CIDA and External Affairs have become alert to human rights issues and accept, if sometimes sceptically, their responsibility to address this dimension of policy. Nevertheless, how seriously the announced policies are being taken and how fully the new institutions will be able to fulfil their potential remain uncertain.

It was not encouraging to have Monique Landry, minister for external relations and international development, state in June 1989 that the cabinet was not considering human rights records as it decided how much aid to give recipient states in the coming year.[62] The extent to which the situation has changed since that time is unclear. While annual country reports are now available for ministerial review, the secrecy of cabinet deliberations makes it impossible to discern what use is being made of them. The analysis below does indicate, however, that they have not shifted the flow of Canadian aid away from serious rights offenders and towards those with commendable records.

CIDA's Good Governance and Human Rights Policies Division, while having an enlarged staff of four and an enhanced potential to influence policy, still lacks the human resources and mandate to review country programs and specific projects on the basis of clearly designed human rights criteria, as was recommended by the Standing Committee on External Affairs and International Trade in the

Winegard Report (1987).[63] The onus in this respect thus still rests with country desk officers, but their good intentions may well be undone elsewhere in the decision-making process as bureaucrats and their political masters weigh the implications of acting out of human rights considerations on other national interests.

The International Centre for Human Rights and Democratic Development made a promising start in October 1990, when it announced the first 13 projects to be supported. The initial interest was largely in Latin America and the Caribbean and included assistance to human rights institutes and commissions, legal services offices, and human rights conferences in Brazil, Costa Rica, El Salvador, Haiti, and Mexico, as well as to projects of a regional nature. Subsequently, the centre launched projects in Asia and Africa, including assistance to a research and documentation centre on torture in Guinea, to a legal aid centre in South Africa, and to human rights activist refugees from Burma (Myanmar).[64] The centre's initial actions reflect the priority that it has set on providing support, principally via NGOs, to "front-line activities which prevent or fight human rights violations" and that "empower people and benefit in particular the poor, indigenous people, women and children."[65] It is willing to risk incurring the ire of governments in developing countries through support for organizations that challenge the status quo. That is how it should be, since the centre, operating at arm's length from the Canadian government, has greater freedom than CIDA and other governmental agencies. However, it remains to be seen whether the centre will be constrained by government if its initiatives complicate Canadian bilateral relations. With a budget of only $15 million for its first five years, the centre can undertake only so much; it can thus serve only as a supplement to, not a replacement for, related activities by CIDA and External Affairs.[66]

At the time of writing, even evidence of a new surge of political interest in an aid-rights link was cause for some anxiety. Statements by the prime minister and the secretary of state for external affairs in late 1991 seemed to emphasize punishment (suspension or termination of aid) rather than reshaping the nature of aid given to states with unacceptable records and expanding allocations to those with examplary or improving observance. Human rights considerations might thus be used inappropriately to help reduce Canadian aid during a time of economic austerity. Additional cuts in aid announced in December 1992 have only added to this anxiety.

Apart from the above qualifications, at least two omissions from Canada's aid-rights policy cause concern. First, the government rejected the recommendation of the Winegard Report for tabling an annual ODA–human rights review in Parliament.[67] Ottawa would go only so far as to undertake to provide in camera information to parliamentary committees regarding the human rights situation in recipient countries.[68] While reluctance to engage in public debate on the records of individual states may be understandable, non-governmental observers will not be able to analyse effectively the rationale underlying Canadian policy decisions and to monitor the consistency and vigour with which Ottawa pursues its aid-rights commitment.[69]

Second, this shortcoming is compounded by the fact that the government has never defined clearly the human rights violations that would trigger a policy response. Ottawa has stated simply that it would "focus on those violations of human rights which are patently systematic, gross and continuous, whether in the area of civil and political rights, or in the field of economic, social and cultural rights."[70] Its ambiguity, particularly its failure to emphasize explicitly the basic security and subsistence rights, increases the prospect of inconsistent action. Moreover, the government rejected the Winegard Report's recommendation that it adopt an objective, systematic framework for categorizing potential aid recipients by human rights record and that it pursue aid policies appropriate to each state's classification as human rights "negative," "watch," "satisfactory," or "positive."[71]

Any classification system has limitations. It could serve only as a guide to action, not as an inflexible, automatic determinant of decisions regarding expansion or contraction of assistance. After all, Canada may have varying expectations of different states, depending on their stage of evolution in respecting human rights. Whether or not a state's record is improving or deteriorating also deserves consideration. Further, there may well on occasion be compelling political/strategic or other reasons for preserving all channels of aid despite classification as "negative." Nevertheless, not to establish some type of framework as a broad policy guide is to heighten still further the prospects of inconsistent action. Countries with which Canada has important political, commercial, and developmental relations are likely to continue to be shielded from censure, while those where Canada has few if any vested interests will probably go on being singled out for punishment. Moreover, government initiatives will probably be prompted by media, parliamentary, and interest group focus on certain states rather than be based on objective, comparative assessments of the human rights situation in different countries. The following analysis of recent Canadian aid-rights initiatives reveals the consequences of the remaining deficiencies in Canadian policy.[72]

We shall look first at cases of suspension or general contraction of Canadian aid. In 1987, bilateral assistance to Fiji was quietly terminated following two military coups that had racist implications related to curbing the influence of the Indian population of the islands. These developments led to widespread calls for sanctions, especially from Canada's Commonwealth partners in Asia. Canadian assistance had, however, been minimal, averaging roughly $150,000 per year over the period from 1985–86 to 1987–88, so that the suspension had no real effect.

In 1988, the government-to-government program to Haiti was suspended after two violence-plagued elections failed to restore order and respect for basic human rights. Considerable Canadian assistance continued to flow via NGOs, targeted at helping the poorest.[73] Again, Canadian bilateral aid had been modest, averaging under $10 million per annum for several years. Following election of Jean-Bertrand Aristide's government in December 1990, with a renewed promise of greater respect for fundamental human rights, bilateral aid was restored. However, it was suspended once again in October 1991, when Canada, acting in concert with other OAS states, applied a range of economic sanctions against Haiti following a military coup that toppled President Aristide. This time, in a controversial move, Ottawa also suspended bilateral assistance executed by NGOs – the largest component of the program prior to the coup.[74] Food aid and humanitarian assistance were, however, allowed to continue.[75] In March 1993, Canada announced a contribution of $2.35 million for a joint OAS and UN observer mission to Haiti to monitor the human rights situation.[76]

In 1989, because of widespread human rights violations, Canada suspended its marginal bilateral program in Myanmar (disbursements averaged $440,000 annually over the period from 1987–88 to 1989–90) and announced that it would not forgive the country's ODA debt. However, it allowed the crown corporation Petro-Canada to continue with a $22-million drilling project in association with the military authorities.[77] This controversial involvement was finally discontinued in November 1992, but, according to Petro-Canada officials, the project ended primarily because no oil had been discovered.[78]

In 1989, Canada also threatened to suspend all but humanitarian aid to Sudan[79] in the face of gross violations of human rights and use of food as a weapon in the civil war by both government and rebel forces. While such draconian action was not taken, Canadian disbursements did decline because of difficulties in delivery.

Similarly, in Sri Lanka, the protracted civil war, with its accompanying disorder, led to steady contraction of Canadian aid to what was long one of Canada's leading recipients. Bilateral aid dropped from $34.47 million in 1987–88 to $8.72 million in 1990–91. This reduction was, however, a result as much of the civil war as of human rights violations. Nevertheless, according to officials, Sri Lanka is one country where Canada's program is assiduously monitored in terms of the human rights implications of any projects undertaken.

Aid to Malawi, which was not a significant recipient, was also reduced as of 1991 in part because of its poor human rights record, but constraints on CIDA's budget also influenced this decision.[80]

After having pursued a sizeable aid program in Zaïre through many years of gross and persistent violations of human rights, Canada, along with other donors, finally suspended bilateral aid in October 1991.[81] By that time, collapse of civil order made continuation of assistance untenable.

In November of the same year, in an effort to push President Daniel arap Moi of Kenya into holding multi-party elections and improving human rights observance in general, Canada, like other donors, made no pledge of new assistance at a consultative group meeting in Paris.[82] In March 1993, it was reported that Canadian aid to Kenya was being terminated altogether.[83] While human rights violations were a factor in the gradual reduction of aid to that country from 1989 onwards, cessation of the program in 1993 seems to have been a result principally of cuts in CIDA's budget.

Canada partially suspended aid to Peru in May 1992, following the assertion of dictatorial powers by President Alberto Fujimori and his unwillingness thereafter to show flexibility in restoring democracy.[84]

There have been three identifiable suspensions of specific projects. Disbursements from a line of credit to Burkina Faso were temporarily halted between 1989 and 1991, when two military officers who held cabinet portfolios and two other soldiers were summarily executed for allegedly plotting to overthrow the president. Overall, however, Burkina Faso preserved its status as a middle-ranking aid recipient.

In December 1991, Canada suspended approval of new development projects in Indonesia worth $30 million, to protest against dozens of killings of pro-independence demonstrators in East Timor by Indonesian authorities the preceding month. Projects under way and other new initiatives were, however, not affected.[85] While Indonesia's human rights violations, especially its persisting repression in East Timor, have generally received little international attention, the 1991 killings generated widespread media coverage, which seems to have prompted Canada's carefully measured rebuke.

China offers a rare example of an initiative against a major recipient of Canadian aid with which Canada also has other important relations. On 4 June 1989, Chinese troops fired indiscriminately at thousands of unarmed, pro-democracy demonstrators and bystanders in Tiananmen Square in the heart of Beijing. Hundreds were killed in the attack, and thousands more were arrested throughout China during the subsequent crackdown by the authorities. Many of those detained were held incommunicado and tortured. There were also reports of summary executions of some of those involved in the demonstrations, while many others received long, harsh prison sentences following secret trials.[86]

In response to these gross violations of human rights, Canada imposed a number of sanctions on China, including ones related to the aid program. On 5 June, it postponed signing of five development projects worth roughly $60 million, pending further review.[87] On 30 June, it announced its withdrawal from a further three projects worth $11 million; it said that the projects failed the test of the new criteria to be applied in screening relations with China, one of which was avoidance of programs that benefited or lent prestige to the hardline government.[88] At least one of the projects certainly fell into this category – a training program for urban traffic management; cameras for monitoring traffic, furnished under a similar British scheme, had apparently been used to spy on student demonstrators in and around Tiananmen Square.[89] As well, Canada suspended indefinitely all activity associated with the massive Three Gorges hydroelectric project.[90]

In reality, however, the aid sanctions imposed on China, like the other initiatives taken at the same time, were symbolic rather than substantive. Projects whose signings were postponed subsequently went ahead.[91] All three that were cancelled were already near completion, so that the effect of the terminations was marginal.[92] Further, they were by no means the only projects that benefited or lent prestige to the Chinese government and its repressive policies. The Three Gorges scheme, widely criticized both in and outside China as environmentally unsound, had already been placed under suspension by the Chinese government, so that the Canadian action meant little. China has increased in importance as a development partner for Canada despite its record of repression. Disbursements to China in 1990–91 amounted to $63.85 million, making in the second-largest Canadian aid recipient that year.[93]

China is thus illustrative of Ottawa's continuing reluctance to take substantive action on aid when the country in question is one with which it has important developmental and other relations. During an official visit to China in May 1986, Prime Minister Mulroney had announced doubling of CIDA's bilateral program there to $200 million for the period 1987–92.[94] Realization of this objective would have been placed in jeopardy by meaningful sanctions. Moreover, China is a significant trade partner, ranking as Canada's fifth-largest export market in 1992, and clearly Canadian aid has been designed to help promote this commercial relationship. As Secretary of State for External Affairs Joe Clark put it in his statement of 30 June 1989 regarding the situation in China, Canada has "a great deal invested in our relationship with the People's Republic."[95] Clearly, Ottawa was not prepared to allow government repression to disrupt that investment, especially when other countries were moving to restore full economic relations. A variety of considerations – intense media focus on China, lobbying by concerned groups, parliamentary preoccupation with the situation, ministerial attention to China, and actions by other states – impelled Canada towards some kind of reaction to events in China.[96] However, Canadian national interests dictated that the response be symbolic only.[97]

With Canada continuing to treat states such as China (and Indonesia) differently from those with which its relations are marginal, it is not surprising that there was little change over the period from 1988–89 to 1990–91 in the proportion of Canadian aid flowing to serious human rights abusers, compared to the years from 1984–85 to 1986–87 discussed above. Analysis of the 57 states that averaged $1 million or more in assistance each year over the later three years disclosed that 70.4 per cent of Canadian aid was disbursed to serious violators (categories 3 to 5 on the five-point scale) and 43.2 per cent to particularly abusive states (categories 4 and 5).[98]

Some countries with clear deterioration in respect for human rights increased dramatically their rankings as aid recipients. China (category 5 in this period) moved from 16th to third, and Philippines (category 4) from 44th to 13th.[99] Others whose records remained bad held their own or raised their rankings. Bangladesh (category 4), for example, stayed, as it has been for many years, the top recipient,[100] while Indonesia (category 4) moved from fourth to second.[101] Among particularly serious abusers, only Sri Lanka (category 5), which fell from sixth to 25th, and India (category 4), which plunged from second to 16th, saw marked drops in aid, but it is unclear to what extent these cutbacks were for human rights, as opposed to other reasons.[102] While a few countries with good records did rank higher as aid recipients,[103] others with satisfactory performances (for example, Botswana, Côte d'Ivoire, and Niger) declined significantly. This latter finding suggests continued absence of any concerted effort to concentrate more Canadian aid on states where exemplary levels of respect for human rights make the prospects promising for effective assistance programs.

More projects designed to improve human rights observance in developing countries have been approved in recent years. Too numerous to enumerate, they include country-specific and multi-country projects related to legal, judicial, and police training, literacy, assistance in holding elections, research and legal services to unions, provision of legal and human rights publications, and support for human rights institutes and for families of victims of oppression.[104] Within the totality of Canadian assistance, these positive projects remain, however, a very modest proportion. Further, as indicated above, the potential for expanding this type of activity remains constrained by the paucity of human resources assigned to monitoring the human rights dimension of country programs and projects.

CONCLUSION

From a halting and tentative policy in which the relevance of human rights to government action was highly ambiguous, Canada has moved to a much more assertive position concerning the place of human rights in Canadian aid policy. With introduction of cabinet review, human rights training, and country reporting, and with creation of CIDA's Good Governance and Human Rights Policies Division and of the International Centre for Human Rights and Democratic Development in Montreal, Canada has set up structures for a highly effective aid-rights policy. Yet Canada's actual performance still falls well short of the ideal. An inadequate proportion of aid goes to the poorest in the most disadvantaged countries. While Canada has implemented constructive projects aimed at enhancing certain basic rights, it has not committed enough resources to enable systematic monitoring from a human rights perspective. There is no regular filtering process for all projects before implementation to ensure not only that they have no negative human rights implications but that their effect will be positive, especially in involving those affected by the developmental process in decision making.

There is continuing reluctance to cut aid flows to abusive states that are important to Canada and a tendency to treat them differently from those abusers with which relations are marginal. The cases of China and Indonesia, contrasted with those of Fiji, Haiti, and Myanmar, are indicative. Similarly, there has been no reorientation of the flow of Canadian aid away from serious human rights offenders and towards those with good or improving records. Indeed, faced with financial constraints, CIDA will probably use cuts in programs of some states with poor records to achieve economies overall rather than to redirect funds to worthy recipients.

Canada's mixed and inconsistent record is the inevitable product of a policy that has not yet defined the basic rights abuse of which will animate responses from Canada and that eschews systematic, comparative assessments of states' human rights records as a guide to coherent and consistent action. There persists as well a tendency to see human rights in all their aspects – economic, social, and cultural, as well as civil and political – not as the very essence of what development is about, but as only one of a wide range of factors to be taken into account in aid decisions. Human rights must then vie for attention and scarce resources against such powerful and traditional determinants of policy as Canadian political, strategic, and commercial interests. Until there is a change in this perspective, human rights seem destined to remain a part-time preoccupation in the shaping of Canadian aid policy.

NOTES

1 Paul Gérin-Lajoie, *The Longest Journey* (Ottawa: CIDA 1976), 15, 17, 22.
2 On the concept of empowerment, see, among other works, Brian Tomlinson, "Development in the 1990s: Critical Reflections on Canada's Economic Relations with the Third World," in Jamie Swift and Brian Tomlinson, eds., *Conflicts of Interest: Canada and the Third World* (Toronto: Between the Lines 1991), 33–6; Rhoda E. Howard, "Civil-Political Rights and Canadian Development Assistance," and Bernard Wood, "Human Rights and Development: Reflections on Canadian Process and Policy," both in Irving Brecher, ed., *Human Rights, Development and Foreign Policy: Canadian Perspectives* (Halifax: Institute for Research on Public Policy 1989), 363–4 and 417, respectively.
3 On this concept and for references to other sources, see Robert O. Matthews and Cranford Pratt, "Introduction: Concepts and Instruments," in Robert O. Matthews and Cranford Pratt, *Human Rights in Canadian Foreign Policy* (Kingston and Montreal: McGill-Queen's University Press 1988), 6–8 and 314 note 5.
4 See Cranford Pratt, "Ethics and Foreign Policy: The Case of Canada's Development Assistance," *International Journal* 43 (spring 1988).
5 CIDA, *Strategy for International Development Cooperation 1975–1980* (Ottawa: CIDA 1975), 9, 23–5.
6 CIDA, *Sharing Our Future: Canada's International Development Assistance* (Ottawa: Supply and Services 1987), 23.
7 Calculated from CIDA annual reports, using country-to-country disbursements.
8 North-South Institute, *Review* (spring 1993), 2.
9 The director of the UN Report on Human Development, as quoted in *Globe and Mail*, 17 May 1991. See also United Nations Development Programme, *Human Development Report 1991* (New York: Oxford University Press 1991), 54.
10 Many authors have commented in this fashion on the interdependence of various rights. For a recent discussion, see Timothy P. Draimin and Liisa North, "Central America: The Challenge of Peace," in Liisa North,

ed., *Between War and Peace in Central America: Choices for Canada* (Toronto: Between the Lines 1990), 25–8.

11 David Gillies, "Human Rights and Foreign Policy: We've Only Just Begun," *Policy Options* 11 (March 1990), 8.

12 See Jack Donelly, "Cultural Relativism and Universal Human Rights," *Human Rights Quarterly* 6 (November 1984), 404.

13 For detailed discussion of the idea of basic rights, see Henry Shue, *Basic Rights: Subsistence, Affluence and U.S. Foreign Policy* (Princeton, NJ: Princeton University Press 1980). Although he arrives at a slightly different set of core rights, for a good recent treatment of the importance of establishing a priority list, see David Gillies, "Evaluating National Human Rights Performance: Priorities for the Developing World," *Bulletin of Peace Proposals* 21 (March 1990), 15–27.

14 For the range of possible instruments, see Gerald Schmitz and Victoria Berry, *Human Rights: Canadian Policy toward Developing Countries* Briefing 21 (Ottawa: North-South Institute 1988), 8, and Matthews and Pratt, "Introduction," 11–20.

15 Julian Payne, "Human Rights and Development: A Developmental Perspective." Notes for a speech by Julian H. Payne, Director General, Policy Branch, CIDA, to Canadian Institute of International Affairs Branches in Southern Ontario, 16–19 May 1988, 1.

16 Thus Prime Minister Pierre Trudeau told Parliament in 1977 that until that time Canada had "not made it a condition of our assistance to starving people in the Third World that their government be above reproach." Canada, House of Commons, *Debates*, 2 March 1977, 3574.

17 For detailed analysis of this societal pressure, see T.A. Keenleyside, "Canadian Aid and Human Rights: Forging a Link," in Brecher, ed., *Human Rights*, 330–3.

18 External Affairs, Statements and Speeches 78/13, 26 October 1978, 6.

19 "Canada in a Changing World–Part II: Canadian Aid Policy," in Canada, House of Commons, *Minutes of Proceedings and Evidence of the Standing Committee on External Affairs and National Defence*, No. 3, 10 June 1980, 176.

20 External Affairs, Statements and Speeches 83/6, 22 April 1983, 4.

21 *Debates*, 16 June 1981, 10654. See also External Affairs, Statements and Speeches 81/21, 29 July 1981, 3.

22 *Elements of Canada's Official Development Assistance Strategy* (Ottawa: CIDA 1984), 36.

23 External Affairs, Statements and Speeches 85/16, 18 October 1985, 6.

24 *Elements*, 35.

25 See Theodore Cohn, "Politics of Canadian Food Aid: The Case of South and Southeast Asia," in Theodore Cohn, Geoffrey Hainsworth, and Lorne Kavic, eds., *Canada and Southeast Asia: Perspectives and Evolution of Public Polities* (Coquitlam, BC: Kaen Publishers c. 1980), 43.

26 See, for example, *Debates*, 19 November 1964, 10301–2.

27 White Paper, *Foreign Policy for Canadians*, Pacific Booklet (Ottawa: Information Canada 1970), 20.

28 For details of the situation in Indonesia, see the annual reports of Amnesty International and also *Indonesia, an Amnesty International Report* (London: Amnesty International Publications 1977) and *Torture in the Eighties* (London: Amnesty International Publications 1984), 189–91.

29 For the situation in East Timor, see *Amnesty International, East Timor Violations of Human Rights* (London: Amnesty International Publication 1985).

30 See Martin Rudner, "Advantages of Trading with Indonesia," *Canadian Business Review* 11 (spring 1984), 26.

31 Cohn, "Politics," 48.

32 In 1990, after several years of urging by NGOs, Cambodia and Vietnam (as well as Laos) were declared eligible again for Canadian aid. External Affairs and International Trade Canada, Statement 90/25, 25 January 1990, 1–3; *Globe and Mail*, 18 May 1990.

33 See Martin Rudner, *Canada and the Philippines: The Dimensions of a Developing Relationship* (North York, Ont.: Captus Press Inc., 1990), 4–5, 52–4.

34 *Country Profile: Uganda* (Ottawa: CIDA 1982), 2.

35 This was acknowledged by officials in interviews with the author.

36 See T.A. Keenleyside and Patricia Taylor, "The Impact of Human Rights Violations on the Conduct of Canadian Bilateral Relations: A Contemporary Dilemma," *Behind the Headlines* 42 no. 2 (1984), 17–20, 22.

37 External Affairs, Statements and Speeches 82/12, 31 March 1982, 3.

38 *Debates*, 9 March 1981, 8034.

39 CIDA's annual report for 1981–82 stated: "Political turmoil and civil strife, with an inability of governments to guarantee the protection of development workers led to the suspension of CIDA bilateral programs in El Salvador and Guatemala." *Canadians in the Third World: CIDA's Year in Review 1981–82* (Ottawa: Supply and Services Canada 1983), 26. See also Margaret Catley-Carlson, in *Minutes of Proceedings and Evidence of the Standing Committee on External Affairs and National Defence*, 1st sess., 33rd Parl., Issue No. 22, 16 May 1985, 6.

40 "International Canada: The Events of December 1984 and January 1985," supplement to *International Perspectives* (March/April 1985), 10; *Globe and Mail*, 12 June and 10 July 1985; John Graham, "The Caribbean Basin: Whose Calypso?" Notes for a speech by John Graham, director general, Caribbean and Central America Bureau, External Affairs, to the Canadian Institute of International Affairs, Foreign Policy Conference, 4 May 1985, 9.

41 External Affairs, News Release, 13 November 1987.

42 See, for example, Meyer Brownstone, "Canadian Aid to El Salvador Gone

Askew?" *Globe and Mail,* 16 June 1986; Andrew Cohen, "Canadian Aid Faces Tough Choices," *Financial Post* (Toronto), 7 December 1987; Mary Morgan, "Aid Fosters Guatemalan Repression," *Winnipeg Free Press,* 12 January 1989; Amyn Sajoo, "Aiding and Abetting, Canada's Ad Hocery on Human Rights," *Policy Options* 10 (November 1989), 32; Liisa North, "Canada's Development Assistance Programs and Economic Relations with Central America," in North, ed., *Between War and Peace,* 99–104; *Report Card on the Government of Canada's Foreign Aid Program, Background Materials* (Ottawa: Canadian Council for International Cooperation, February 1991), 7–8. Since its renewal, Canadian aid to Guatemala has remained extremely limited and is channelled almost exclusively through NGOs. Bilateral aid to El Salvador, in contrast, has been relatively substantial.

43 In 1988, however, Ottawa again released funds for the project once it was satisfied that 75 per cent of those resettled in the irrigated area would be Tamils. See Schmitz and Berry, *Human Rights,* 10; *Annual Report 1987–88* (Ottawa: CIDA 1988), 57.

44 Now called the Canada Fund.

45 Howard, "Civil-Political Rights," 367.

46 "International Canada: The Events of October and November 1984," supplement to *International Perspectives* (January-February 1985), 8.

47 For a fuller explication of policy initiatives to 1987, see T.A. Keenleyside, "Development Assistance," in Matthews and Pratt, eds., *Human Rights in Canadian Foreign Policy,* 196–205.

48 T.A. Keenleyside and Nola Serkasevich, "Canada's Aid and Human Rights Observance: Measuring the Relationship," *International Journal* 45 (winter 1989–90), 158–62.

49 *Independence and Internationalism: Report of the Special Joint Committee on Canada's International Relations* (Ottawa: Supply and Services Canada 1986), 99–114; House of Commons, Standing Committee on External Affairs and International Trade (Winegard Committee) *For Whose Benefit? Report of the Standing Committee on External Affairs and International Trade on Canada's Official Development Assistance Policies and Programs* (Ottawa: Supply and Services 1987), 23–31.

50 *Canada's International Relations: Response of the Government of Canada to the Report of the Special Joint Committee of the Senate and the House of Commons* (Ottawa: Supply and Services 1986), 23–5; Canada, *Canadian International Development Assistance: To Benefit a Better World. Response of the Government of Canada to the Report of the Standing Committee on External Affairs and International Trade* (Ottawa: Supply and Services 1987), 49–56; CIDA, *Sharing Our Future,* 31–2.

51 See, in particular, CIDA, *Sharing Our Future,* 31–2.

52 Ibid., 31; External Affairs and International Trade Canada, Statement
   90/66, 11 November 1990, 3–4; Ian Ferguson, "Human Rights as
   a Factor in Canadian Foreign Policy," Notes for a speech by Ian Ferguson,
   Director, Human Rights and Social Affairs Division, External Affairs
   and International Trade Canada, to the Windsor Branch of the Canadian
   Institute of International Affairs, 14 February 1991, 10.

53 *Globe and Mail,* 17 October 1991.

54 Ibid., 22 November 1991.

55 *Foreign Policy Themes and Priorities, 1991–92 Update,* Policy Planning Staff
   (Ottawa: External Affairs and International Trade Canada, December
   1991), 11–12.

56 External Affairs Canada, Statements and Speeches 91/9, 10 December
   1991, 6, reproduced in John English and Norman Hillmer, eds.,
   Making a Difference: Canadian Foreign Policy in an Evolving World Order
   (Toronto: Lester Publishing 1992), ix–xvi. See also Monique Landry,
   *Minutes of Proceedings and Evidence of the Sub-Committee on Development and
   Human Rights of the Standing Committee on External Affairs and
   International Trade,* No. 12, 17 February 1992, 4–9.

57 Payne, "Human Rights and Development," 13.

58 Good governance and democratic development thus joined human rights
   as necessary ingredients of "political sustainability," which the government now sees as essential to "sustainable development." See "Sustainable
   Development," Discussion Paper (Ottawa: CIDA, July 1991). See also
   the CIDA-commissioned study of the North-South Institute by David Gillies
   and Gerald Schmitz, *The Challenge of Democratic Development: An
   Exploration* (Ottawa: North-South Institute, April 1991).

59 For an account of the training activities, see Allan McChesney, "Teaching
   Human Rights to Foreign Service Officers and Other Public Officials:
   Developments in Canada and Abroad," in Brecher, ed., *Human Rights,*
   179–211.

60 Ferguson, "Human Rights," 4, 10–11.

61 CIDA, *Sharing Our Future,* 32.

62 *Globe and Mail,* 9 June 1989.

63 Winegard Committee, *For Whose Benefit?,* 30.

64 For details of the centre's activities, see in particular its quarterly newsletter,
   Libertas.

65 *Statement by the Honourable Edward Broadbent* (Montreal: International
   Centre for Human Rights and Democratic Development, n.d.).

66 For an assessment of the centre, see David Gillies, "The Centre for Human
   Rights: A Distinctive Vision?" *International Perspectives,* 19 (March
   1990), 36; David Gillies, "Between Ethics and Interests: Human Rights
   in the North-South Relations of Canada, the Netherlands, and
   Norway," doctoral dissertation, McGill University, 1991, 334–8.

67 Winegard Committee, *For Whose Benefit?*, 30; Canada, *To Benefit a Better World*, 54.

68 CIDA, *Sharing Our Future*, 32.

69 For expressions of concern about the secrecy of the policy process, see Schmitz and Berry, *Human Rights*, 14; *Human Rights Considerations and Coherence in Canada's Foreign Policy*, Third Report of the Standing Committee on Human Rights and the Status of Disabled Persons (Ottawa: Supply and Services Canada, June 1990), 2–11.

70 Canada, *To Benefit a Better World*, 50.

71 Winegard Committee, *For Whose Benefit?*, 27–8. The government said that such a grid would entail subjective evaluations and would be "essentially punitive and judgmental rather than positive and developmental"; Canada, *To Benefit a Better World*, 52.

72 For a good, general critique of the government's new aid-rights policy, see Gillies, "Human Rights," 7–9.

73 CIDA, *Annual Report 1988–89* (Ottawa: CIDA 1990), 29.

74 External Affairs Canada, Statement 91/53, 4 November 1991, 1.

75 Ibid., 92/19, 19 May 1992, 3. Additional sanctions were applied against Haiti in June 1992, but none of these related to development assistance.

76 External Affairs Canada, News Release No. 58, 6 March 1992, 1–2.

77 Gillies, "Between Ethics and Interests", 316; *Calgary Herald*, 13 January and 4 May 1990.

78 *Globe and Mail*, 3 November 1992.

79 Ibid., 9 March 1989.

80 "Summary of Canadian Measures Related to Human Rights and Other Foreign Policy Concerns," prepared by Human Rights, Women's Equality and Social Affairs Division, External Affairs Canada, 1992, 10.

81 External Affairs Canada, News Release No. 240, 28 October 1991, 1.

82 "Summary of Canadian Measures," 11. See also *Globe and Mail*, 26 May and 19 October 1992.

83 *Review*, 2.

84 External Affairs Canada, Statement 92/19, 19 May 1992, 4.

85 External Affairs Canada, News Release No. 280, 9 December 1991, 1. See also *Globe and Mail*, 10 December 1991 and 4 April 1992.

86 For details, see *Amnesty International 1990 Report* (London: Amnesty International Publications 1990), 65–7.

87 External Affairs Canada, Statements and Speeches 89/16, 5 June 1989, 4.

88 Ibid., 89/18, 30 June 1989, 3–4.

89 *Globe and Mail* 7 October 1989.

90 External Affairs Canada, Statements and Speeches 89/18, 30 June 1989; 4; *Toronto Star*, 1 July 1989. In April 1992, Ottawa announced that

no more funding would be available for this project; *Globe and Mail* 6 May 1992.

91 *Globe and Mail,* 2 June 1990.

92 *Report Card,* 8.

93 CIDA, *Annual Report 1990–91* (Ottawa: CIDA 1992). EDC loans in large numbers also recommenced quickly after the June massacre, essentially unencumbered by the government's new criteria for relations; these loans were simply regularly declared to be consistent with those principles.

94 *Department of External Affairs Annual Report 1987–88* (Ottawa: Supply and Services 1988), 45.

95 External Affairs Canada, Statements and Speeches 89/18, 30 June 1989, 1.

96 The means by which a country becomes a target for strictures was described to the author by one official as the "slot machine" approach. A variety of factors along the lines of those enumerated must be simultaneously in alignment for action to occur, rather than initiatives being determined by objective human rights criteria applied uniformly to all states.

97 For other statements of this point of view, see J.T. Paltiel, "Rude Awakening: Canada and China Following Tiananmen," in Maureen Appel Molot and Fen Osler Hampson, eds., *Canada among Nations 1989: The Challenge of Change* (Ottawa: Carleton University Press 1990), 44–5; *Financial Post,* 4 June 1990.

98 The comparable figures for 1984–85 to 1986–87, based on the 58 countries that averaged over $1 million per year during this period are 70.7 per cent for states in categories 3 to 5 and 49 per cent for those in categories 4 and 5. In view of the special character of Canadian aid to South Africa, this country was omitted from the list, although it averaged over $1 million per year during the latter period. I am grateful to my graduate student Frank DeAngelis for his assistance in coding with me the top 57 recipients, using the scale in Keenleyside and Serkasevich, *Canada's Aid and Human Rights,* 150–3.

99 For Philippines, as for China, commercial and political/strategic interests, combined with a recent commitment to increase the level of Canadian disbursements, have restrained Canada from placing any restrictions on the level of bilateral aid. For that country's importance to Canada, see Rudner, *Canada and the Philippines,* 6, 10, 33.

100 A discussion paper prepared by the Asia Working Group of the Canadian Council for International Cooperation asserted that the aid that has poured into Bangladesh has done little to end poverty; rather, it has played "an important role in strengthening the political regime and in sustaining the very conditions which undermine poverty-focused

development"; "Bangladesh: Crucial Question for Canadian Aid Policy," *International Perspectives* (June 1990), 72.

101 Regarding the commercial considerations that affect Canadian policy towards Indonesia, see Kim R. Nossal, "Les droits de la personne et la politique étrangère canadienne: le cas de l'Indonésie," *Études internationales* (11 June 1980), 223–38; Theodore Cohn, "Politics of Food Aid," Lorne Kavic, "Innocents Abroad? A Review of Canadian Policies and Postures in Southeast Asia," and David Preston, "The Canada–Southeast Asia Aid and Trade Relationship: Evolution and Future Directions," in Cohn, Hainsworth, and Kavic, eds., *Canada and Southeast Asia*, 28, 36–8, 49, respectively; David Van Praagh, "Canada and Southeast Asia," in Peyton Lyon and Tareq Ismael, eds., *Canada and the Third World* (Toronto: Macmillan 1976), 334–5.

102 Kenya and Zaïre, whose aid was suspended after this period, dropped somewhat, with Kenya moving from eighth to 21st, and Zaïre, from 11th to 20th. However, Canadian aid disbursements still averaged around $20 million per year for each country during the three-year period from 1988–89 to 1990–91.

103 During the years from 1988–89 to 1990–91, Thailand was one example, moving from 22nd to 14th, but the increase was related presumably to that nation's commercial potential to Canada, not its human rights record. Further, the increase was hardly justifiable in terms of need, for Thailand is a relatively wealthy developing country.

104 For some examples, see "Human Rights and Canadian Aid Policy," Background to Development (Ottawa: CIDA, June 1992), 5.

10 Public Policy Dialogue and Canadian Aid: The Case of Central America

KATHARINE PEARSON AND
TIMOTHY DRAIMIN

Throughout the 1980s, Canadian foreign policy towards Central America was of enormous interest to thousands of Canadians.[1] Voluntary agency and church workers, teachers and students, farmers, fishers, and tradespeople travelled to the region in unprecedented numbers. Nicaragua, especially, became the focus of extensive fundraising and advocacy campaigns in Canada by non-governmental organizations (NGOs) and solidarity groups. To many Canadians, the Nicaraguan revolution of 1979, which vaulted the Sandinistas into government, began a social transformation that would, over the following decade, provide a unique opportunity to support equitable development.

From 1979 onwards, media coverage of events in the region exploded. Southam News and the *Globe and Mail*, as well as virtually all of the US television networks, sent correspondents to Central America. The growing flow into Canada of refugees escaping the region's civil strife further heightened public awareness.[2] Increased exposure translated into greater public concern about Canadian policy. According to a 1985 Decima poll, 80 per cent of Canadians believed that their country should take an interest in the crisis (26 per cent thought it very important, and 54 per cent, important).[3]

Thus Canada's official aid program for Central America was subjected to intense scrutiny. Public interest was at least partly responsible for the dramatic increase in government-to-government aid to the region from $11.3 million in 1981–82 to $19.7 million in 1989–90 (see Table 1). In addition, the Canadian International Development

Agency (CIDA) channelled over $57 million during the same period through Canadian NGOs active in that area.[4] With Central America's increasing significance for Canada came the major challenge to the government of developing effective aid and diplomatic programs in a region of severe conflict in which the United States had a high stake.

While written CIDA policy embraces laudable objectives – such as "putting poverty first," helping people to help themselves, establishing partnerships, and taking human rights into account – these were not always met in practice. Political and economic constraints diluted the developmental value of Canadian aid. Decentralization of CIDA personnel into the region, intended to reduce bureaucracy and improve programming, also led to the by-passing of Canadian NGOs in favour of direct funding of local groups, raising questions regarding the relationship between government and non-governmental groups in Canada and in Central America.

This chapter examines the evolution of Canadian aid policy towards Central America, with a primary focus on the decade 1980–90. There is greater emphasis on the years following CIDA's publication in 1988 of *Sharing Our Future*, which offered strong direction to Canada's aid policies. Examples of actual programs will be compared with stated policy objectives, with a look at the unique role played by the Canadian public in shaping some of those objectives. CIDA's frequently difficult relationship with the Canadian non-governmental community will be explored, as well as the clear link among aid, Canadian domestic and foreign policy, and international economic policy in Central America. As we shall see, by focusing on a broad aid program and on peacekeeping, Ottawa responded to strong domestic policy pressures while avoiding confrontation with US policy towards the region.

CENTRAL AMERICA IN THE 1980S

The international community paid little attention to Central America prior to the revolution that brought the leftist Sandinista Front for National Liberation (FSLN) to power in Nicaragua in 1979. Over the previous decades, acute poverty, unequal distribution of wealth and land, and a succession of authoritarian, military-dominated governments in Nicaragua, El Salvador, Guatemala, and, to a lesser extent, Honduras led to popular unrest, dislocation, and, finally, insurgency. Yet domestic policy frameworks and international aid to alleviate poverty and address some of the root causes of these crises were pitifully inadequate.

While there was greater foreign political interest in the region during the ten years in which the FSLN remained in power, as well as an

Table 1
Canada's direct aid to Central America ($000), 1981–82 to 1989–1990

Country and type of aid*	1981–82	1982–83	1983–84	1984–85	1985–86	1986–87	1987–88	1988–89	1989–90	Total
Honduras										
Gov't-to-gov't	3,248	4,829	3,230	19,356	2,939	1,780	3,740	8,893	5,410	53,425
NGO	1,542	2,845	1,987	726	720	1,620	1,960	1,799	2,100	15,299
Other	180	609	473	447	651	1,540	1,990	2,191	940	9,021
Total	4,970	8,283	5,690	20,529	4,310	4,940	7,690	12,883	8,450	77,745
Costa Rica										
Gov't-to-gov't	346	3,231	6,342	6,637	6,888	4,810	4,616	2,321	10,650	45,841
NGO	309	168	248	320	60	240	280	260	550	2,435
Other	380	1,128	1,131	1,115	1,752	10,310	16,659	11,896	3,910	48,281
Total	1,035	4,527	7,721	8,072	8,700	15,360	21,555	14,477	15,110	96,557
Nicaragua										
Gov't-to-gov't	166	1,138	6,102	6,612	6,076	3,830	9,567	8,055	2,800	44,346
NGO	1,853	1,772	2,397	1,867	877	2,630	2,530	4,473	3,250	21,649
Other	5,290	1,119	3,387	492	1,189	2,050	2,940	4,839	2,310	23,616
Total	7,309	4,029	11,886	8,971	8,142	8,510	15,037	17,367	8,360	89,611
El Salvador										
Gov't-to-gov't	6,378	712	699	683	374	6,290	6,782	647	380	22,945
NGO	415	542	1,613	912	240	1,270	750	956	1,360	8,058
Other	170	270	1,135	356	1,300	1,670	579	90	110	5,680
Total	6,963	1,524	3,447	1,951	1,914	9,230	8,111	1,693	1,850	36,683

Guatemala

Gov't-to-gov't	1,163	2,537	861	834	438	410	598	568	480	7,889
NGO	414	636	848	1,121	730	980	990	1,348	2,580	9,647
Other	215	640	166	526	816	1,720	1,090	2,392	750	8,315
Total	1,792	3,813	1,875	2,481	1,984	3,110	2,678	4,308	3,810	25,851

Totals for region

Gov't-to-gov't	11,301	12,447	17,234	34,122	16,715	17,120	25,303	20,484	19,720	174,446
NGO	4,533	5,963	7,093	4,946	2,627	6,740	6,510	8,836	9,840	57,088
Other	6,235	3,766	6,292	2,936	5,708	17,290	23,258	21,408	8,020	94,913
Total	22,069	22,176	30,619	42,004	25,050	41,150	55,071	50,728	37,580	326,447

Sources: CIDA, *Summary of Canadian Aid to Central America* (Ottawa, 1986, 1988, and 1989); CIDA, *Annual Report 1989–90*.

* "Gov't-to-gov't" includes what used to be called Mission Administered Funds (MAF), now the Canada Fund, which is administered by Canadian missions and constitutes a very small percentage of ODA. "Other" includes food aid, non-governmental institutions (NGIs), International Development Research Centre (IDRC), Petro-Canada International Assistance Corp. (PCIAC), Institutional Cooperation and Development Services Division (ICDS), Industrial Cooperation (INC), International Centre for Ocean Development (ICOD), and provincial governments.

increase in economic assistance, conditions deteriorated rather than improved. For many donors, as long as the Sandinistas governed Nicaragua, political considerations dominated economic ones, particularly in US policy towards the region, distorting aid priorities and contributing to militarization. This, along with many other factors, contributed to an overall decline in living standards in the region. According to the United Nations Development Program's *Human Development Report 1991*, in Latin America as a whole between 1980 and 1989 "production per head fell, along with living standards, and child malnutrition and infant mortality started to rise in many countries."[5] By 1989, 40 per cent of the Central American population lived in absolute poverty, 57 per cent was unemployed, and one out of every ten children died before reaching the age of five. Malnutrition and infant mortality showed a particularly alarming rise in rural areas.[6] Indeed, these years have become known as the "lost decade."

Endemic violence made the situation worse. During the 1980s, civil wars and repression cost the lives of 160,000 Central Americans and displaced two million others, within their country or externally as refugees. Although by 1990 progress was being made towards negotiating political settlements to the civil wars in El Salvador and Guatemala, the death toll remained high in these two countries. As the new decade began, human rights violations were becoming more prevalent in Honduras and Nicaragua.

This climate of conflict devastated the region's economy, which in effect stagnated between 1978 and 1990. Production suffered at the same time as prices for export commodities such as coffee, cotton, and sugar plummeted. Economic gains made in the 1960 and 1970s were wiped out. In the 1980, all the Central American countries registered negative growth in per capita annual income. Foreign debt reached $17.2 billion by the end of 1986, and interest payments equalled 40 per cent of export revenues.[7]

Costa Rica, El Salvador, Honduras, and Nicaragua implemented orthodox structural adjustment programs (SAPs) to qualify for credits and loans from the International Monetary Fund (IMF) and the World Bank. These SAPs tended further to penalize the poor, as governments cut subsidies to production of basic grains in order to force land into agro-exports, reduced spending on social programs such as health care and education, cut jobs, and encouraged market forces to determine prices. Orthodox SAPs also lowered tariff protection in order to allow foreign-produced goods into the country.

Under certain circumstances, such measures may increase efficiency in domestic industry. For Central America, given the conditions within the world's commodity market as it is currently structured, and the region's fragile and underprivileged industrial sectors, SAPs badly damaged the manufacturing base and reduced employment.

Promoters of an export-oriented economy argue that "the logic of any small, open-economy model dictates that if poverty is to be alleviated, resources must first go to generating the necessary foreign exchange surplus."[8] Export-led growth strategies in Central America, however, have tended to come at the expense of food security, as in Costa Rica, the first country in the region to undergo structural adjustment. In 1987, Costa Rica had 2,400 rice farmers; three years later, it had 350. In addition, the country was importing other staples such as corn and beans.[9] It was bowing to World Bank pressure to decrease its assistance to "inefficient" small farmers through agricultural credit and price supports. In good years, imports will doubtless be readily secured, but for a small and poor developing country, this degree of import dependence for basic food needs is clearly risky.

Costa Rica, Guatemala, and even Honduras did indeed boost their exports and thus their foreign exchange reserves, but poverty also increased and national fiscal deficits and inflation were at very high levels. According to the UN Economic Commission on Latin America and the Caribbean, at least 40 per cent of Costa Rican families lived in poverty in 1990, compared to 25 per cent in 1980.[10] In response to a question from a Canadian journalist about the role that Costa Ricans played in setting the targets for structural adjustment, a former government minister answered: "Only in the same sense that a man who is going to be executed is given the choice between poison and hanging ... We didn't have an alternative."[11]

Strong international pressure to develop functioning economies (along with the changing geopolitical climate) had another, more positive effect: it forced the governments of El Salvador and Guatemala to negotiate with their armed oppositions in order to provide "stable" conditions for international investment. These peace processes, however, are fraught with difficulty and will ultimately be unsuccessful unless they can redress some of the gross inequities that exist in both countries.

INFLUENCES ON CANADIAN AID POLICY

While Central America scarcely figured in Canadian aid policy in 1979, the situation changed rapidly through the 1980s. In response to growing public interest and attention, Secretary of State for External Affairs Allan MacEachen announced in 1982 that Canadian aid to the region would double. A Parliamentary Sub-Committee on Latin America and the Caribbean, struck in May 1981, recommended in July 1982 that Central America receive higher priority.[12] As the region became a Cold War battlefield for the United States, particularly during Ronald Reagan's presidency (1981–89), Canada chose to assign it greater significance, and two External Affairs Secretaries visited there (Allan MacEachen in 1984 and Joe Clark in 1987). Monique Vezina, minister of state for external relations, also made the journey in 1985.

At the same time, the environment for Canadian aid policy towards Central America became highly politicized. Ottawa wanted to develop a policy sensitive to public opinion, while safeguarding its relationship with the United States, especially at a time of increasing economic integration. The intensity of Washington's antipathy towards the Sandinistas in Nicaragua was not shared by the Canadian government (Canada, for example, did not join the economic embargo against that nation), but neither was there much official criticism of US policy. Instead, Canada attempted to steer a "middle course" by crafting a marketable role in support of regional peacekeeping and discreetly demonstrating some independence in foreign policy, while simultaneously avoiding a political profile that would provoke conflict with the Americans.

Joe Clark used his 1987 visit to reaffirm this "middle course," announcing new aid to Honduras (despite international concerns about its government's failure to comply with the Esquipulas Peace Accords signed the same year) and renewal of bilateral aid to Guatemala.[13] With bilateral aid going to all five countries, Canada would now be seen as a "neutral" actor in the region. Canada also contributed generously to the several UN and other international agencies attempting to alleviate the desperate circumstances of tens of thousands of refugees. All this activity opened the door for Canadian support of the Central American Peace Plan through provision of technical advice and participation in such UN initiatives as ONUCA (the UN Observer Group in Central America) and, later, ONUSAL (the UN Observer Mission to El Salvador). Charged originally with monitoring human rights, ONUSAL in early 1992 also began to help in verifying implementation of the Salvadoran Peace Accords. In December 1987, in response to controversy surrounding Joe Clark's trip to the region, the government established the House of Commons Special Committee on the Peace Process in Central America. In July 1988, the committee published its recommendations, including a call for a $100-million increase in aid over five years.[14]

CIDA decentralization and restoration in 1989 of Canada's mission in Guatemala to the status of embassy also increased this nation's visibility, promoting a more positive image with all five governments. Canada further demonstrated its interest in Latin America by joining the Organization of American States (OAS) in January 1990.

Underpinning this political strategy has been a shifting economic one. In the 1980s, aid to Central America was subject to the same set of commercial objectives that had entered into CIDA's objectives elsewhere. Capital infrastructure projects that could be supplied from Canada, and lines of credit for purchase of Canadian commodities, became prominent in the expanded program in its first years. By 1989, however, a major new influence became important, as CIDA adopted the development thinking of the IMF and the World Bank and came to regard support for structural adjustment as a first priority.[15] Canada's Central American aid program shifted increasingly to support orthodox multilateral conditionality, usually embodied in an IMF structural adjustment program. There was also greater coordination with other donors, within a shared international economic policy framework defined in neo-liberal terms.[16]

More recently, criticism of and resistance to structural adjustment programs led to a shift in the rhetoric used to explain the international aid regime.[17] It was described by Secretary of State for External Affairs Barbara McDougall in these terms: "The goal of sustainable development depends upon participatory democracy; open, market-based economic policies; sound economic management, and an orderly international trading system, which we are trying to ensure in the Uruguay Round of the multilateral (GATT) trade negotiations."[18] It seems reasonable to anticipate that the emphasis will continue to be on securing macro policy changes that will commit aid recipients to such objectives and that, if anything, the emphasis on economic "reform" is likely to become even stronger.

CIDA AND CENTRAL AMERICA IN THE 1980S

Canada organized its first high-level trade and investment mission to Central America in 1979, but in the early 1980s CIDA's aid program in the region was modest and geared principally to large infrastructure projects and provision of Canadian commodities. As public interest grew, along with demands to increase assistance, disbursements of Canadian bilateral aid[19] jumped from $11.3 million in 1981–82 to a high of $25.3 million in 1987–88 and totalled $174.4 million for the period from 1981–82 to 1989–90. Honduras received the largest amount ($53.4 million), followed by Costa Rica ($45.8 million), Nicaragua ($44.3 million), El Salvador ($22.9 million), and Guatemala ($7.9 million).

Honduras

CIDA's program in Central America in the 1980s targeted Honduras as the region's poorest country. As CIDA's only "core" country in Central America, and one of only six in Latin America and the Caribbean, Honduras qualified as a recipient of Canadian funds for multi-year development plans. Honduras received $53.4 million in bilateral aid between 1981–82 and 1989–90. Programs focused above all on infrastructure and resource management (especially forest resources), through large-scale projects that appear to have had minimal effect in reducing poverty.

One of CIDA's largest projects in Honduras during the period 1980–87 was the El Cajón hydro-electric plant. Canada contributed $18.3 million to a $794-million budget supported by a consortium of international banks and governments. It made its contribution in the form of a loan for purchase of Canadian transformers, electro-mechanical equipment, and transportation material. CIDA judged this project a "success": "With the start-up of the El Cajon power station, the country's production of electricity has doubled, saving up to US$20 million per year in oil imports and producing a further US$20 million in energy exports to neighbouring countries."[20]

Another major aid project was approved in 1986 to help the Forestry Development Corp. (COHDEFOR) manage publicly owned tropical forest reserves. One goal was to improve the living conditions of adjacent peasant communities (previous CIDA-financed forestry projects in Honduras had concentrated on industrialization and worked exclusively through COHDEFOR). However, these communities were hardly consulted at the design stage, and there was no communication mechanism in place through which they could relate to COHDEFOR. In addition, the project identified the peasants', rather than the landlords', agricultural practices as the cause of deforestation. Successive Honduran governments have been reluctant to implement the Agrarian Reform Law of 1975. As a result of unequal distribution of land, peasants are forced to cultivate hillsides and engage in "slash and burn" agriculture.[21]

While it was claimed that Canadian aid policy took into consideration the quality of a recipient government's economic and social policies, commitment to involve its population in the development process, environmental sensitivity, and respect for human rights, the

Honduran government's record in all these areas has been dubious, to say the least. The above project, while well intended, fell short of meeting Canada's own aid criteria. Subsequently, the Honduran government privatized COHDEFOR, along with fourteen other state agencies, as part of its structural adjustment. The overall program illustrates the constraints imposed by the tying of aid to purchase of Canadian goods and services and by government responsiveness to business interests.

Costa Rica

Costa Rica was the region's second-largest recipient of Canadian bilateral aid between 1981–82 and 1989–90, with a total of $45.8 million. Since that country is Central America's wealthiest, its share was clearly not determined on the basis of economic need. Rather, Canada chose to favour Costa Rica for political reasons, in order to safeguard its democratic traditions during a period of increasing regional conflict. Indeed, during the tenure of President Oscar Arias, Costa Rica played a critical role in shaping a regional peace process (Esquipulas II), for which Arias was awarded the Nobel Peace Prize in 1989. Canadian aid in the years 1980–87 included lines of credit for fertilizer and agricultural equipment. Sale of these goods generated a "counterpart fund" that was used to build low-cost rural housing. Canada also supported a scholarship program for technical and vocational training in agriculture, and Petro-Canada invested nearly $30 million in the country between 1986 and 1988.

Nicaragua

Canadian bilateral aid to Nicaragua between 1981–82 and 1989–90 totalled $44.3 million. This large amount reflected public interest and support in Canada for Nicaraguan development. Throughout the decade, Canadian groups persistently lobbied Ottawa to increase bilateral aid to Nicaragua because of its government's demonstrated capacity to "encourage grassroots participation in development efforts to improve the livelihood of the poor through redistributive reforms and the extension of basic services."[22] Large-scale projects included the Chiltepe Dairy Farm, involving export of Canadian cows and technology; a $7-million loan for potable water systems; and the Momotombo geothermal electrical generating plant, co-financed with Italy and France. In the latter case, Nicaragua received a $12-million loan to purchase Canadian equipment.

It is interesting to contrast the Momotombo electrical plant with the El Cajón dam in Honduras, also supported with Canadian bilateral funds. First, the Nicaraguan project was significantly less costly. Second, "the chances are slim that El Cajón's power will be used to advance the welfare of the majority of Hondurans. In contrast, the [Nicaraguan] government ... clearly enunciated its commitment to self-reliant development [with a] basic needs-based industrial development plan ... It may be that in the case of Momotombo and other Nicaraguan projects, CIDA ... achieved a rare mix of Canadian economic advantage and Third World social welfare."[23]

El Salvador

El Salvador received $22.9 million in Canadian bilateral aid between 1981–82 and 1989–90. With resumption in 1985 of bilateral aid (suspended in 1982), Ottawa created the El Salvador–Canada Development Fund, generated through sales of Canadian-donated fertilizer to Salvadoran middle-level agricultural producers. By terms of the bilateral aid agreement, the Salvadoran government was to place the profits from these sales into a counterpart fund to support development projects. The fund was administered by a Canadian NGO, the Canadian Hunger Foundation, new to El Salvador. Furthermore, while CIDA made the decisions, the Salvadoran Ministry of Planning was to be consulted on project approvals/rejections, and project information was to be made available to it upon request. This arrangement caused profound concern to many Salvadoran organizations and their partners in the Canadian NGO community, because of the violent and polarized situation in the country. Numerous Canadian NGOs and churches remained consistently opposed to any bilateral aid agreement with the government of El Salvador while gross and systematic violations of human rights continued.

Guatemala

Guatemala received the least amount of Canadian bilateral aid in Central America, with a total of $7.9 million – much of it in the form of Mission Administered Funds – between 1981–82 and 1989–90.[24]

NEW DIRECTIONS SINCE 1987

CIDA's aid program became more pro-active during the last half of the 1980s. In 1987, for the first time in 12 years, Ottawa produced a new aid strategy, *Sharing Our Future*, which outlined a broad range of objectives and strategies resting on such principles as putting alleviation of poverty first, helping people to help themselves, and emphasizing development priorities and partnership.[25] *Sharing Our Future* made human rights considerations an important criterion for a country's eligibility for bilateral aid. In principle, bilateral aid is to be denied or reduced to countries where violations of human rights are systematic, gross, and continuous. Additional criteria include the recipient's commitment and capacity to manage aid effectively, the quality of its economic and social policies, and its commitment to involving its population in the development process.

Sharing Our Future recommended an international aid program based on establishing peace and democratic development, while giving priority to the poor and disadvantaged. However, other factors, particularly economic considerations, have influenced these objectives. For example, tied aid, though reduced as a proportion of bilateral aid, still averaged 66 per cent in 1991–92. It resulted in several projects being concentrated in areas in which Canadian business has some degree of specialization, such as hydro-electricity, forestry, agriculture, and construction of infrastructure.[26] In addition, such a criterion reinforced reliance on the bilateral channel, requiring coordination with recipient governments in Central America, many of which have failed to implement meaningful basic needs/human development strategies.

One could also question Ottawa's record with regard to *Sharing Our Future's* recommended human rights criterion. It suspended bilateral aid to El Salvador and Guatemala in 1981 because of political instability and concern for the safety of field personnel. It renewed such aid to El Salvador in 1985 and Guatemala in 1987 because of political considerations, despite continuing and serious violations of human rights. Even while aid was suspended, Canada maintained credit assistance for trade purposes with both countries.[27] Bilateral aid to El Salvador was suspended briefly again in November 1989, after the murder of six Jesuit priests, their housekeeper, and her daughter, for which atrocity the Salvadoran military was held responsible. (These bilateral aid programs are discussed again below).

Following the broad aid objectives described in *Sharing Our Future*, CIDA published its "Central America Programme Strategy 1989–1994" in August 1990. The document represented CIDA's first attempt to define a regional approach to its bilateral programming in Central America. The program's three strategic goals were identified as economic recovery and adjustment, sustainable development of natural resources, and poverty alleviation. The document stated that, "where possible, program activities will address objectives related to more than one goal (for example, development lines of credit in support of economic adjustment in combination with counterpart fund programming for poverty alleviation)" and that "counterpart funds will concentrate on social sector programming with financing channelled through local NGOs and other local institutions." Efforts were to be made to assess the implications of human rights issues for program delivery and "the potentially positive impact on human rights of the Canadian aid program."[28] CIDA now saw its Central America program as more solidly integrated, rather than consisting of a set of discrete projects. As one Canadian aid official put it: "I would say that [we have a shift] that integrates infrastructure within a human-centred and a more rounded approach to development."[29]

Ottawa's 1991–92 Central American program had as its stated goal to "establish partnerships on many levels to support the efforts by the countries of the region to achieve sustainable economic development and political and social stability."[30] In keeping with CIDA's five-year plan for the region, first on the list of "principal areas of concentration" was "to support economic recovery and adjustment through balance-of-payments assistance." CIDA backed this type of initiative in Costa Rica, Honduras, and Nicaragua, but with conditions. As one Canadian aid official stated: "the linkage of conditionality is that if a SAP is not in implementation for reasons within the control of a government and this does not constitute sufficient commitment to reform, our conditionality allows us to withdraw our support."[31] At the same time, many Canadian aid programs were now intended to alleviate the worst effects of structural adjustment by helping the poorest segments of the population. One channel was the social investment fund set up by a government when it implemented a SAP.

Bilateral Aid since 1987

The increasing emphasis on adjustment has begun to override other policy objectives contained in Sharing Our Future. The humane internationalist approach that Canada has traditionally espoused was by 1991 being set within a more overtly orthodox, neo-liberal economic framework.[32] This preoccupation with changes in macro-economic policy became a new and major point of contention between CIDA and many of the NGOs active in Central America, who saw it as going beyond pragmatic considerations to impose on recipients a set of policies with ideological overtones.

In 1991–92 program for Central America launched a new emphasis on human resource development. Much of this emphasis, however, has been implemented through traditional means, with training programs for civil servants rather than community-based organizations. There have been exceptions, of course: in Honduras, CIDA began in 1989 to finance an integrated irrigation and agricultural development project through CUSO and the National Farmworkers Central (CNTC). This initiative contrasted with some of CIDA's earlier bilateral programming, which did not actively involve Honduran NGOs. The project was designed largely by the farmworkers themselves through the CNTC and was quite effective in reinforcing civil society (through support to a broad-based peasant organization) and meeting the needs of the poor in these communities.

Canada has also increased its use of lines of credit for purchase of particular Canadian commodities. The goods are then resold in the recipient country and the proceeds put into a counterpart fund earmarked for specified purposes, usually services to the poor. For example, recent aid programs to Nicaragua included a $15-million line of credit, with the local currency generated being paid into a social investment fund. This form of aid seems to meet several, apparently conflicting CIDA objectives at once – it generates sales for Canadian business, it assists the balance of payments of the recipient country and can therefore directly support structural adjustment, and it secures local funds for alleviation of poverty.

While Canada announced renewal of bilateral aid to Guatemala in 1987, an agreement was not signed until March 1990. The project involved $8.8 million over four years, of which $7 million was to be disbursed directly to Guatemalan "grass-roots" organizations to support development efforts of the poor. As in El Salvador, this money was administered by a Canada NGO. According to CIDA, the government of Guatemala was to be provided with only minimal information on approved projects and had no formal veto. It has, however, had the option of proposing its own municipal projects to the administering NGO.

Canada and El Salvador signed a second bilateral aid agreement in October 1990, and it covered an initial, two-year, $2-million project for "Support to Community Development." The subsequent phase was to "take very much into account the evolution of the situation of the Rights of the Person in the country, the results of the Dialogue for Peace between the Government of El Salvador and the armed opposition, and the conclusions of the next meeting of the [World Bank] Consultative Group on El Salvador."[33] Canada was to provide direct support to groups of repobladores ("repopulated") and internally displaced, as part of its commitment to the International Conference on Refugees in Central America (CIREFCA). As with the bilateral aid agreement of 1985, a Canadian NGO administered the money, but this time there was no counterpart fund involved, the Salvadoran Ministry of Planning had no formal role in project selection, and the government of El Salvador pledged to "guarantee the freedom of movement of persons, goods and equipment necessary for the realization of the project."[34]

The bilateral aid agreements signed in 1990 with El Salvador and with Guatemala were both developed in a climate of political sensitivity in Canada and in Central America. Numerous Canadian organizations had remained sharply critical of the role of the Salvadoran and Guatemalan governments with regard to the grim human rights situation in their countries. They were joined in this by the House of Commons Standing Committee on Human Rights and the Status of Disabled Persons, which commented in June 1990 that Canada was in the position of "piously condemning human rights abuses on Sundays and then carrying on business as usual – including mutually lucrative business – with human rights abusing countries, during the rest of the week."[35]

Canadian groups had actively lobbied Ottawa to suspend bilateral aid to both countries in order to avoid conferring legitimacy on governments that were showing themselves unable or unwilling to hold violators – often military or paramilitary personnel – accountable. This position was consistent with Canadian government policy as stated in *Sharing Our Future*. Ottawa responded that it did not want to "doubly penalize the poor" by withholding aid to countries where the poor are already victims of violence and dislocation. Had its motives been unaffected by political considerations, however, multilateral channels or partnership-oriented NGOs offered an alternative mechanism for delivering aid that was insulated from formal government-to-government agreements.

While political objectives ensured that Canada would re-establish bilateral aid (to "maintain a process of dialogue" with new governments and to generate an invitation to participate in peacekeeping), crafting of the agreements showed sensitivity to Canadian public opinion. In effect, Canada tacitly endorsed both governments while circumscribing their role in aid delivery.

In Nicaragua, Canada's bilateral aid program reached the end of one phase and paused while planning was under way for another during the final year of the Sandinistas' period in office. Following the elections of 1990, which the Sandinista Front lost, Canadian bilateral aid again began to flow, and so projects conceived and designed in one political context were now being implemented in a very different one, for which their appropriateness could be questioned.

Other Canadian Aid Channels

Canada's official development assistance (ODA) is disbursed also through the Industrial Cooperation program (INC), which grew from 2 per cent to 4 per cent of the ODA budget in 1989–90. Its budget for Central America expanded from $50,000 in 1985–86 to $700,000 in 1988–89. Other funding channels for Canadian ODA to the region include multilateral ones such as the UN High Commissioner for

Refugees and the World Food Programme (WFP), as well as the International Development Research Centre (IDRC), Petro-Canada International Assistance Corp. (PCIAC), and, before it was cut, the International Centre for Ocean Development.

A recent initiative is the Partnership for Democracy and Development in Central America (PDD), constituted in April 1991. It includes 30 countries, among them Canada, the United States, Japan, European states, and the countries of Central America. It has been described as "a forum through which economic assistance from developed countries and international institutions will be channelled to the region to consolidate democracy within the framework of the Initiative for the Americas proposal of U.S. President George Bush."[36] Canada hosted the second plenary meeting of this group in January 1992. Apparently the PDD does not automatically signify additional aid to the region but "is destined to play an important role in the negotiations to define Central America's participation with the world trade blocs now taking shape."[37] During its inception, however, there was little consultation with Central America NGOs and popular organizations in shaping the PDD's objectives, even though reconciliation and a strong civil society are essential to the region's democratic future.

Another aid channel is the Canadian government–funded International Centre for Human Rights and Democratic Development (ICHRDD), set up in July 1990. The centre chose Latin America as an initial area of emphasis and has supported numerous projects with human rights–related groups in Central America. At the ICHRDD's inception, many NGOs feared that CIDA would try to shift responsibility for funding projects related to human rights to the centre, despite the declaration in *Sharing Our Future* that consideration of human rights was now integral to Canadian aid policy. However, CIDA has ensured a strong component of human rights and democratic development within two important bilateral aid programs in Guatemala and El Salvador.

Decentralization

Sharing Our Future announced decentralization of CIDA's Bilateral Division personnel from headquarters in Canada to offices in the field in order to "significantly improve the quality and efficiency of Canada's assistance as well as bringing our programs closer to the people we are trying to reach – the poorest."[38] The process began in Central America in September 1989. In 1991, there were 16 Canadians and 17 local staff members representing CIDA in the region, with most in the Canadian embassy in Costa Rica, and additional representatives and support from the consulate in Honduras and the embassy in Guatemala (upgraded from consulate in September 1990 and assigned responsibility for El Salvador). Canadian Cooperation Offices in all five countries, staffed by host nationals, administer the local Canada Fund ($350,000 per country per year).

The Cooperation Offices, which in effect represent an increase in CIDA administrative personnel in the region, are treated not as an administrative expense but as bilateral aid projects, accounting for about $1.1 million of the agency's annual bilateral aid programming in Central America.[39] In addition to administering the Canada Fund, these offices are a source of information to CIDA on bilateral projects and relations with local NGOs and other social organizations. They also involve use of Canadian aid dollars to expand Canada's presence in the region (a political goal), while the government refused to open an embassy (even the "store-front" variety favoured by the United Kingdom) in important capitals such as Managua and San Salvador.

While Canadian NGOs on the whole supported a stronger Canadian diplomatic presence in Central America, they did have some misgivings about CIDA's decentralization. Initially, many Central American groups were confused about the Cooperation Offices, presuming them to be non-governmental. They saw CIDA officials more frequently than their Canadian NGO counterparts, which do not have the resources to decentralize on such a scale. Furthermore, as demands on Canadian NGOs to live up to a genuine partnership increase, CIDA attempted, in some cases, to fill the gap.

With presumably well-intentioned promises of direct funding to long-term partners of Canadian NGOs, CIDA risked undermining the traditional NGO-to-NGO relationship, which goes far beyond transfer of funds to encompass such activities as human rights support, information sharing/networking, training opportunities, and development education in Canada. One Canadian aid official in the region told a reporter: "I do not see that much difference between a Canadian NGO and a local NGO. Both can be effective and appropriate. I think the debate about this has been in Canada."[40] Canadian NGOs, after some reflection, did not oppose direct CIDA funding of overseas NGOs but remained anxious about the possible effect on their relations with their partners. These anxieties did not appear to be widely appreciated in CIDA.

THE PUBLIC'S ROLE

Canadian public interest in Central America, expressed most directly through solidarity groups, development education organizations, churches, unions, academic institutions, and international development agencies, grew dramatically throughout the 1980s. This interest was expressed initially through fund-raising to support literacy and health-care campaigns in Nicaragua. According to CIDA figures, NGOs (with matching CIDA funds) channelled $21.6 million to Nicaragua between 1981–82 and 1989–90 more than to any other country in the region. These figures do not include the large amounts of cash and in-kind donations that were not matched, such as the $2 million raised in 1987 alone by the nationwide Tools for Peace campaign. By the mid-1980s, at least 80 Canadian NGOs were funding projects in Central America.

Canadians did more than fund projects. They participated in intense lobbying campaigns to urge Ottawa to increase bilateral aid to Nicaragua, where government policy such as agrarian reform and universal literacy and health care programs favoured development. A 1986 analysis observed: "Canada's aid programme in Nicaragua, which contradicts the short-term intent of U.S. policy, is currently the chief manifestation of what can be termed the 'independence imperative' in Canada's Central American policy. The independence imperative is not often the chief consideration in Ottawa's foreign policy development. But it is always present as a factor which may be strengthened by the intervention of concerned Canadians."[41] Indeed, when Ottawa was criticized during the debate over the Canada–United States Free Trade Agreement for not having an independent foreign policy, both the prime minister and the secretary of state for external affairs alluded to Canada's relationship with Nicaragua as a key example of its independence.

Other lobbying efforts included requests that Ottawa suspend official assistance to El Salvador and Guatemala, in light of their appalling human rights records, and actively support the search for a peaceful resolution of regional conflicts. A dramatic increase in fact-finding tours to the region, involving both the public at large and elected officials, created a well-informed and vocal constituency.

Organizations such as the Inter-Church Committee on Human Rights in Latin America, the Central America Monitoring Group, the Canadian Council for International Cooperation, and Canadian-Caribbean–Central American Policy Alternatives (CAPA) have presented the Canadian government with briefs on aid, human rights, and peacekeeping. CAPA, with the support of the now defunct Canadian Institute for International Peace and Security, organized a series of successful "Round Tables" in Ottawa with academics, NGOs, and politicians from Central and South America, Canada, Europe, and the United States to study the options for peace for Central America and to encourage Canadian involvement. Canadian NGOs have also arranged numerous missions to the region involving members of Parliament and other high-profile Canadians; there were five such "Missions for Peace" organized with the support of the Canadian public, churches, and the Canadian Council for International Cooperation (CCIC) between 1985 and 1989, and the Central America Monitoring Group sent three others, in 1989, 1990, and 1993.[42]

NGOs consistently urged Ottawa to play a role in regional peacemaking and to develop an aid program that supported civil society as the bedrock of a peaceful, just, and democratic society. In fact, dozens of Canadian groups participated in a two-year process from 1988 to 1990 aimed at creating a Central America Peace and Development Fund, which would be managed by NGOs and would have allocated CIDA and NGO monies to the region. Its intention was to strengthen civil society, support refugees and displaced people, develop alternative agricultural models, and defend human rights. Programming was to be done collaboratively and was to include development education in Canada. The emphasis on civil society was explained in the following way: "A strong civil society in Central America is both the long-term guarantee for democracy and an important countervailing influence to military power in the transition to a more equitable society. Popular organizations played a key role in pressing demands for peace in the period leading up to the signing of Esquipulas II [in August 1987]. Important political processes have now emerged, led by popular organizations as they work for the longer-term development priorities which will meet the basic needs of the poor majority and help secure the 'authentic pluralistic and participatory process' called for by the Esquipulas II Accord."[43]

Unfortunately, CIDA was less than wholehearted in its support of the proposal. Some within the Canadian government saw certain NGOs as ideological and programmatic supporters of left-wing movements in Central America, to the detriment of their development objectives. These NGOs were unable to build a constructive working relationship with CIDA.

Could NGOs have prepared more effective strategies to overcome the polarization with CIDA? During the 1980s, expansion of points of dialogue helped – roundtables and more conversation between NGO and CIDA personnel in the field and in Ottawa – but did not resolve conflicting development perspectives within a politicized context. Presumably more sophisticated advocacy and liaison by NGOs could have made a difference. Such a strategy would have had to emphasize regional programming and better understanding of the broader approaches being adopted by CIDA as a whole.[44]

CONCLUSION

It is unlikely that Central America would have figured so prominently in Canada's official aid program during the 1980s were it not for significant public interest and pressure. Geographic location was a factor: thousands of Canadians were able to travel to the region, returning to constitute a well-informed, vocal, and persistent lobby. The "middle road" for aid policy towards Central America took this nation closer to Europe's Social Democrats than to the United States. Ottawa's decision to provide ongoing aid to Nicaragua was its most explicit statement of policy independence (despite the absence of public criticism of Washington's military support for the Contras). By focusing on aid, and later actively supporting regional peacekeeping, Canada was able to devise a positive strategy for avoiding direct conflict with the United States and to sidestep domestic critics who lobbied the government to play a much stronger political role. As a result, while initially reluctant to become involved, by 1990 Canada had greatly expanded its profile in Central America.

In the development of its aid policy, Ottawa never actively sought a partnership with the broad Canadian non-governmental community involved in Central America, unlike the case with the Swedish and Dutch governments. Indeed, the relationship was often adversarial, as NGOs urged Canada to take political initiatives that would put it in direct contradiction with US policy in the region. Unlike the case of southern Africa, over which there was effective convergence of views, Canadian NGOs were unable to reach an agreement with the government on Central American aid implementation. CIDA and the NGOs missed the opportunity to create innovative regional programming, which would have allowed both to respond more effectively to such events as the El Salvador peace agreements signed in January 1992. CIDA was handicapped by its retreat into defensiveness vis-à-vis NGOs. Rather than acknowledging that dialogue would have assisted programming, CIDA protected itself.[45]

Conflict creates a difficult milieu in which to implement "development" programs. Current development thinking recognizes that aid in such circumstances needs to be an explicit tool in promoting and making peace and in national reconciliation. More effective working relations with NGOs in the 1980s would have given Ottawa more direct access to innovative ideas and partnerships. This could have led in turn to a more relevant program, even in the face of powerful international and economic influences.

At a time when parameters for the international donor community are being set increasingly by neo-liberal macro-economic thinking, public policy dialogue becomes essential. In the case of Central America, a wide range of Canadian groups has attempted to facilitate debate about political influences on aid policy. Throughout the 1980s, however, Ottawa deferred to US geopolitical interests in the region, and these, in the end, proved a more important factor in shaping Canadian policy.

NOTES

1 The authors wish to thank Judy Lux and Don Cockburn for their research and editorial assistance.

2 Between 1982 and 1987, Canada admitted 20,935 Central American refugees under its annual refugee plan, the majority from El Salvador, according to *Supporting the Five: Canada and the Central American Peace Process*, report of the House of Commons Special Committee on the Peace Process in Central America, Ottawa, July 1988, 25.

3 Decima Research Ltd, Canadian Public and Foreign Policy Issues, August 1985, No. 1299, 50.

4 CIDA, *Summary of Canadian Aid to Central America*, Ottawa 1986, 1987, 1988, and 1989; CIDA, *Annual Report 1989/90*; CIDA, *Canadian Development Assistance in Latin America* (Ottawa: Supply and Services), June 1991. A portion of total non-governmental aid to Central America is unreported in CIDA statistics (those NGO projects that, for a variety of reasons, do not receive matching CIDA funds).

5 United Nations Development Program (UNDP), *Human Development Report 1991* (New York: Oxford University Press 1991), 34.

6 *Central America Report*, Guatemala City, January 1991.

7 Liisa North and Canadian-Caribbean–Central American Policy Alternatives (CAPA), eds., *Between War and Peace in Central America: Choices for Canada* (Toronto: Between the Lines 1990), 118.

8 R. Caceres and G. Irvin, "The Reconstruction of the Central American Common Market," in Irvin G. Holland and S. Holland, eds., *Central America: The Future of Economic Integration* (Westview Press, 1989), 180.

9 Robert Carty, "Case Study: CIDA in Costa Rica and the Central American Region," prepared as a background paper for *Diminishing Our Future: CIDA, Four Years after Winegard – a Report on Recent Developments in Canadian Development Assistance Policies and Practices* (Toronto: Inter-Church Fund for International Development and the Churches' Committee, International Affairs, Canadian Council of Churches, October 1991).

10 As reported by Karen Hansen-Kuhn, in "Poverty Increases in Costa Rica," *BankCheck Quarterly* 1 no. 3 (winter 1992).

11 *Diminishing Our Future*, 32. For an interesting analysis of structural adjustment in Central America, see Ian Walker, "Structural Adjustment,

Economic Integration and Development Strategy in Central America: A Survey of the Issues" mimeo, 1990.

12 Standing Committee on External Affairs and National Defence, *Canada's Relations with the Caribbean and Latin America*, report to the House of Commons, 27 July 1992.

13 The Canadian government defended its decision to renew aid to Guatemala as a means to recognize that government's positive role in the regional peace process, despite continuing, gross rotations of human rights in the country. Thus aid decisions were finally acknowledged as being influenced by political considerations, something earlier denied.

14 Special Committee, *Supporting the Five.*

15 This important policy development is discussed fully in Marcia Burdette's chapter (no. 8) in this volume. Several Canadian bilateral projects in El Salvador, Guatemala, and Honduras in the late 1980s emphasized support to the poorest and human resource development.

16 "Neo-liberal" (or "neo-conservative") economic policy emphasizes "freeing" of domestic and international markets from virtually all forms of government intervention, withdrawal of the state from most productive activities, and minimization of taxation.

17 For a full discussion of the concept of an international aid regime, see Jean-Philippe Thérien's chapter (no. 12) in this volume.

18 Statement by the Honourable Barbara McDougall, P.C., M.P., Secretary of State for External Affairs, before the United Nations General Assembly, New York, 25 September 1991.

19 "Bilateral aid" is aid delivered within the framework of a formal agreement (memorandum of understanding) between donor and recipient governments.

20 CIDA, *Annual Report 1985–86* (Ottawa: Supply and Services 1986), 32.

21 Latin America Working Group (LAWG), "Paved with Good Intentions: Canadian Aid to Honduras," *LAWG Letter* no. 44 (February 1989), 1.

22 North and CAPA, *Between War and Peace* 107–8.

23 LAWG, "Overview of Canadian Aid to Central America 1980–1985" *LAWG Letter* 9 no. 3 (February 1986), 12. An evaluation of the impact of the Momotombo project on poor Nicaraguans, now that a new government is in power, has yet to be held.

24 Mission Administered Funds (MAF), now referred to as the Canada Fund, are monies available for direct disbursement to relatively small projects at the discretion of the local Canadian diplomatic mission.

25 CIDA, *Sharing Our Future: Canada's International Development Assistance* (Ottawa: Supply and Services Canada 1987).

26 However, since publication of *Sharing Our Future*, infrastructure projects have accounted for less than half of CIDA's bilateral projects in Central America.

27 T.A. Keenleyside, "Development Assistance," in R. Matthews and C. Pratt, eds., *Human Rights and Canadian Foreign Policy* (Montreal: McGill Queen's University Press 1988), 203.

28 CIDA, Americas Branch, "Central America Programme Strategy 1989–1994" (Hull, August 1989).

29 In app. 3, "Interview with CIDA officials, San José, Costa Rica," by Robert Carty for "Costa Rica Report," a case study for *Diminishing Our Future.*

30 CIDA, Americas Branch, "Canadian Development Assistance in Latin America and the Caribbean" (Hull, June 1991).

31 Carty, "Costa Rica Report."

32 As one aid analyst noted: "These strategic directions for aid policy are not new. Canadian foreign policy and economic self-interest have always been implicit within CIDA's priorities. By 1989, however, the response to the development crisis of the past decade by the elites of the industrial countries, co-ordinated by international financial institutions, has tied Canadian aid programs more closely than ever before to the same economic policy objectives that had dramatically reduced social and economic conditions for the poor in the Third World." Brian Tomlinson, "Development in the 1990's: Critical Reflections on Canada's Economic Relations with the Third World," in Jamie Swift and Brian Tomlinson, eds., *Conflicts of Interest: Canada and the Third World* (Toronto: Between the Lines 1991), 52.

33 Memorandum of Understanding between the Government of Canada and the Government of El Salvador, October 1990.

34 This agreement provides the administering Canadian NGO with a $500,000 administration fee, or 20 per cent of the total budget, much more than the average of 14 per cent in most NGO–CIDA projects.

35 Standing Committee on Human Rights and the Status of Disabled Persons, *Human Rights Considerations and Coherence in Canadian Foreign Policy* (June 1990).

36 *Central America Report* (Guatemala City, April 1991).

37 Ibid.

38 CIDA, *Sharing Our Future*, 35. By 1992, however, the decentralization process had virtually come to an end, because of budgetary constraints and shifting CIDA priorities. Canadian CIDA personnel are to be gradually returned to Ottawa.

39 Of the total cost associated with the Canadian Cooperation Offices in Central America, only about $650,000 per year is a direct result of creation of the offices, with the balance representing aid-related costs previously incurred by Canadian diplomatic missions or elsewhere in CIDA.

40 In a recent response to Groupe Secor's report on CIDA – Strategic Management Review: Working Document (9 October 1991) – the

Canadian Council for International Cooperation (CCIC) argued for a different view of NGOs: "By casting NGOs solely as agents or implementors, Secor ignores the other dimensions of NGO work: supporting the building of stronger civil societies in southern countries, reinforcing people's capacity to articulate their needs, manage their own resources and enforce accountability on their governments"; CCIC Response to the Secor Report" (March 1992), 3–4. It follows that the logical long-term partnership is NGO to NGO, civil society to civil society, which can be reinforced but not assumed by governments.

41 LAWG, "Overview 1980–1985," 3.

42 Missions for Peace: 26 August–11 September 1985, mission to Mexico, El Salvador, Honduras, Nicaragua, Costa Rica, Washington, DC, and UN headquarters in New York; 22 November–4 December 1986, mission to Mexico, El Salvador, and UN headquarters; September 1987, mission to Nicaragua and Washington, DC; April 1988, emergency fact-finding delegation to Honduras and Nicaragua; 15–23 March 1989, mission to Mexico and El Salvador. Reports on all of the above are available through the Jesuit Centre for Social Faith and Justice, 947 Queen Street East, Toronto, Ontario, M4J 2B9.

Reports of the Central America Monitoring Group may be obtained from 1 Nicholas Street, Suite 300, Ottawa, Ontario, K1N 7B7.

43 Rick Arnold and Beverly Burke, "The Central American Peace Process: A Study of Canadian NGO Aid Options," mimeo (Ottawa: CCIC 1988), 7–8.

44 In June 1992, CIDA and the Canadian NGO community (through the CCIC) launched a process of consultation intended to forge a new and more productive relationship. Its objectives included: to provide a forum for policy dialogue on Central American development (including the foreign policy dimensions of Canadian development assistance); to review the status of Canadian development assistance programming; to identify emerging policy, program, and delivery strategies and priorities; and to identify opportunities for coordinated planning.

45 This defensive reaction was identified in Groupe Secor, Strategic Management Review, as an agency-wide problem, as was CIDA's management of its "stakeholder" relationships.

11 Canadian Development Cooperation with Asia: Strategic Objectives and Policy Goals

MARTIN RUDNER

Canadian development cooperation with Asia, as with other developing regions, takes place within a broader foreign policy framework. Figuring prominently in Canada's foreign policy regarding Asian developing countries are concerns over international politics and security, economics and trade, development, environment, energy, and social/cultural relations.[1] Domestic critics of Canadian aid policy tend to disparage any attempt to link development assistance to other foreign policy considerations, especially to commercial and trade objectives, lest the development objective be subordinated.[2] Reflecting this viewpoint, the 1987 inquiry by the House of Commons standing Committee on External Affairs and International Trade (Winegard Committee) into official development assistance (ODA) policies and programs was itself suspicious of encumbering aid policy with multiple objectives "to serve other short term interests, not all of which are consistent with the central purpose of Canada's development assistance," which is helping the poorest people and countries.[3] Yet, as regards Asia, at least, makers of Canadian aid policy continue to insist that the objectives of Canadian development assistance and other components of Canadian foreign policy are complementary – indeed, that well-managed complementarity can yield "synergy" among these objectives. They see policy complementarity not merely as a short-term expedient but as a framework for managing aid programs that assist Asian development while also helping build more extensive bilateral "linkages" between Canada and the countries concerned.

CANADIAN RESPONSE TO ASIA'S DEVELOPMENT REQUIREMENTS

About half the population of the world live in Asian developing countries. These nations differ in size, natural endowments, historical legacies, economic structures, social patterns, cultures, and political systems. Most are still predominantly rural, despite rapid urbanization. Economic activity is still largely agricultural, notwithstanding substantial industrialization. There are, across Asia, conflicts latent and overt over ethnicity and regional security, sometimes with far-reaching consequences politically and developmentally.

Asia as a whole recorded significant economic progress over recent decades. Yet despite generally impressive economic performance, widespread poverty, institutional deficiencies, and structural distortions abound, especially among the populous South Asian countries and in Communist Indochina. Per capita annual incomes for South Asia and Indochina are lower than for sub-Saharan Africa. Nearly half the developing world's poor, and almost half of those in extreme poverty, are in South Asia.[4]

The reduction of poverty is a categorical imperative for Asian development. Asia's aid requirements derive from the three development goals asserted by virtually all the governments concerned – accelerated economic growth, greater social equity, and maintenance of internal stability among diverse ethnic, religious, and regional groups. Most Asian developing countries are committed to economic reforms and restructuring to enhance their long-term growth prospects. Investment in infrastructure, economic and social, is everywhere deemed to be a prerequisite for improved development. Be that as it may, the innate weakness of government institutions at the national, sub-national, and local levels in virtually every Asian developing country is an impediment to progress. Institutional deficiencies prevent governments from implementing policies, severely constraining efforts in agriculture and rural development, infrastructure development, urbanization, education, and health care services.

Canadian aid to Asian developing countries responds simultaneously to both aspects of what CIDA has termed the "Asian duality" – massive poverty alongside accelerated industrialization. Some 20 such countries currently receive ODA from Canada.[5] CIDA deems nine of these – Bangladesh, China, India, Indonesia, Nepal, Pakistan, Philippines, Sri Lanka, and Thailand – "major" program countries. Despite recent fiscal cutbacks and a decline in Asia's relative share of total ODA, its countries still constituted the largest individual recipients of Canadian development assistance. Over and above these country-to-country aid programs, Canada contributed over $344 million in fiscal 1989–90 to Asia-related development activities through multilateral channels such as the Asian Development Bank (ASDB), the United Nations Development Programme (UNDP), the World Bank, the World Food Programme (WFP), and other international organizations.[6]

Canada's aid programs have played a strategic and catalytic role in fostering more extensive bilateral relations with Asia. The Asian developing countries by and large do not make a moral distinction between development cooperation and other dimensions of their bilateral relations with Canada. Governments in Asia do not quite comprehend the Canadian penchant for moralizing over the attributes of aid as against trade, or the agonizing over tied aid. They expect development cooperation to yield returns also to the donor. Donors' self-interest is expected, even preferred, as making clear the motives and purposes of aid. Aid recipients seem to prefer development assistance programs designed within a coherent foreign policy perspective, so that aims and objectives are explicit. They remain quite confident in their ability to evaluate any program proposal on the basis of their own development priorities. Aid is considered not simply a philanthropic transfer but also a policy instrument for promoting the developmental component of shared foreign policy goals.

CANADIAN AID STRATEGY IN ASIA

The philosophical underpinnings of Canadian development assistance underwent a far-reaching transformation during the late 1980s. CIDA's new ODA strategy, *Sharing Our Future* (1987), shifted Canada's aid effort towards development of human resources, an updated set of high-priority objectives, and partnership in program delivery.[7] The Brundtland Report of the World Commission on Environment and Development, *Our Common Future* (1987), projected a compelling global vision of economic and environmental interdependence, elevating "sustainability" to the forefront of development.[8]

The debt crisis and the immiseration of much of sub-Saharan Africa impressed upon CIDA's policy makers that the prospects for development depend more on introduction of appropriate policies – specifically, economic reforms and structural adjustments – than on mere infusions of aid. Furthermore, it had become abundantly clear to aid managers that past practices of using concessional financing to promote export markets did not gain for Canadian firms a market presence in developing countries. Instead, CIDA began to conceptualize a rather more strategic use of aid to help sustain human resource and institutional developments in recipient countries. Such an approach was also seen as a way to foster closer linkages and collaboration between developing countries and Canada. Canadian aid programming would henceforth eschew capital assistance in favour of institution-strengthening and policy support. It remains unclear, however, whether and why recipient countries would indeed invite Canadian involvement in sensitive issues of policy development if their requirements for capital assistance are no longer to be addressed.

In applying its new strategic thinking to Asia, CIDA's policy makers were concerned to address what they perceived to be a fundamental asymmetry in bilateral relations until now. From a Canadian perspective, Asian developing countries are acquiring a heightened profile as partners in trade, investment, technology transfer, and migration. Yet expanding trade and investment have not been accompanied – so far – by any significant extension of institutional connections in other areas of mutual concern, whether in the public sector, business, education, science, culture, or environmental and social affairs. This asymmetry, it is felt, limits the ability of Canada's institutions to acquire experience in Asia and militates against an expanded Canadian role in Asian development.

In order to remedy this perceived discrepancy in bilateral relations with Asia, CIDA is looking to extend the partnership approach embodied in *Sharing Our Future* into something akin to "networking" between Canadian organizations and their Asian counterparts in strategic areas of development. A CIDA strategy for Asia, formulated within the framework of the current ODA approach, emphasizes future bilateral programming towards strengthening of institutions and development of human resources. The aim is to assist Asian developing countries to strengthen their institutional capacities to plan and implement development programs. It is expected that this will also serve to build linkages between Canadian and Asian institutions for the ultimate purpose of creating sustainable bilateral relations based on shared interests and objectives.[9]

A CIDA mission statement formulated in 1991 prescribed the agency's goal as the promotion of "sustainability" – economic, social, cultural, political, and environmental – in developing nations. Towards that end, future CIDA programming will concentrate on supporting formulation and implementation by recipient countries of policies conducive to attainment of sustainability along its several dimensions.

The Asian duality – mass poverty alongside accelerated industrialization – presents differing aid requirements for the various development objectives. CIDA accordingly uses all its aid channels, deploying a wide array of transfer mechanisms for its Asia programming. The structure and composition of individual CIDA bilateral programs for Asia differ according to recipients' aid requirements. For countries suffering from widespread poverty, poverty alleviation remains a priority objective. As for the high-growth Southeast Asian economies, an effort has been made to involve Canadian economic interests with the economic developments taking place in the region. All Asia bilateral programs aim to promote more extensive country-to-country linkages among counterpart institutions in order to facilitate transition to a more mature, post-aid relationship. While programs emphasize developmental and economic objectives, CIDA's strategic approach to Asia is designed within a wider foreign policy framework, in which international peace and regional stability are a major concern. Program implementation, including selection of projects and sectors of concentration, reflects either particular propensities of CIDA country program managers, in the case of bilateral programs, or the predilections of the respective delivery channels for other forms of ODA.

CIDA bilateral programming in Asia deals with three regional groupings, each with somewhat different aid requirements arising from poverty and growth. The South Asian recipients are all low-income countries; the Southeast Asian recipients, middle-income, high-growth economies; and there is a Communist-governed grouping, made up of China, Laos, and Vietnam (with Cambodia currently in political transition). Each grouping evokes a varied and differentiated CIDA response to the duality of its aid requirements.

ODA for Poverty Alleviation: CIDA Programming in Bangladesh

The promotion of international peace and stability is a major goal of Canadian foreign policy regarding South Asia.[10] Political relations with South Asia flourished over recent decades through bilateral and regional diplomacy, the Commonwealth, humanitarian and developmental concerns, and immigration to Canada. Despite recurrent attempts to promote trade and business links with the region, the Canadian commercial presence there is still negligible. A significant share of Canada's exports to the area actually consists of aid-financed supplies. Canadian ODA dates back to the beginnings of this country's aid effort through the Colombo Plan of the early 1950s. Since then, development cooperation has been central to bilateral relations with each South Asian country.

Canadian relations with Bangladesh expressed this geo-strategic interest in a peaceful and stable South Asia, coupled with a shared concern to help relieve poverty in one of the poorest and most populous of Commonwealth nations. From the time of Bangladesh's struggle for independence, Canada displayed considerable goodwill towards it. Bangladesh's authoritarian political record and endemic corruption raised certain qualms, but the two countries maintained especially cordial diplomatic ties bilaterally and in the Commonwealth. There was, in Canada, a groundswell of public benevolence as regards humanitarian and development assistance, expressed through active Canadian non-governmental organizations (NGOs) involved in that country. In recent years, Bangladesh has become the largest recipient of Canadian ODA, country-to-country, with Canada ranking among the leading bilateral donors to Bangladesh.[11]

Poverty alleviation is the overriding objective of CIDA's bilateral development assistance for Bangladesh. Bilateral assistance has focused on food security, alleviation of rural poverty, population planning, and promotion of economic growth.[12] CIDA's support for food security includes provision of food aid along with investments in agriculture and water projects. The effort to reduce rural poverty emphasizes income-generating projects, especially those benefiting assetless women, and community-level development delivered through Canadian and indigenous NGOs. Strong emphasis is given to human resource development. Assistance is also provided for population policy through aid for family planning and improved maternal and child health care.

CIDA's support for alleviation of poverty also addresses that country's efforts at economic growth. Assistance is provided for the government's structural adjustment as well as for development of infrastructure in energy and transportation.

CIDA's new country policy framework (hitherto country program review) for Bangladesh, adopted in 1991, sets out directions for future programs. The focus remains on easing poverty, with attention especially to agriculture, population planning, and structural adjustment. As well, support will be available to help strengthen the capacity to manage natural disasters, with emphasis on environmental flood control. CIDA also intends to foster more extensive institutional links between Bangladesh and Canadian counterparts.

Canadian aid programming for Bangladesh reflects CIDA's assessment of developmental requirements for alleviation of poverty coupled with appreciation of Canada's ability to deliver effective assistance. The conceptual approach deals with support for institutions – governmental and non-governmental – and policies that promote a sustainable attack on poverty and can lead to new forms of cooperation between Bangladesh and Canada.

ODA and the High-Growth Southeast Asian Economies:
Promotion of Bilateral Link with Thailand

Canadian relations with Southeast Asia may be considered within a three-tier foreign policy framework. At one level, Canadian policy addresses the region within a broader-ranging approach to the Asia Pacific Rim. At another level, Canada relates to Southeast Asia through policy dialogue with the Association of Southeast Asian Nations (ASEAN). A third involves bilateral objectives with regard to individual countries.[13]

Canadian ODA has varied according to particular bilateral priorities and needs. At present, Canada is engaged in major aid programs in Indonesia, Philippines, and Thailand. Each country program displays its own distinctive structure and orientation. While some aid is also provided to Malaysia,[14] its scope and scale are limited and it consists of an amalgam of initiatives by CIDA, the Export Development Corp. (EDC), and the International Development Research Centre (IDRC). Although Myanmar (Burma) has the lowest per capita annual income in the region, and was recently classified as a least-developed country (LLDC), Canadian bilateral aid to that country has been curtailed on human rights grounds.[15]

CIDA's programming for Thailand exemplifies the response to accelerated industrialization. CIDA's Thailand program was conceived in the early 1980s as an experiment in integrated country programming. The strategy envisaged a 20-year time frame, during which development assistance would be used to transform the relationship from aid dependence to partnership in economic cooperation. Underlying this vision lay a long-term projection of economic performance. Thailand was expected to achieve newly industrializing country (NIC) status by the end of the present century, and CIDA accordingly adopted a holistic perspective on Thailand's development which saw poverty and social deprivation as "policy-soluble." This approach gave expression to CIDA's confidence that the Thai government's own social and community development would reduce the incidence of poverty.

During its first five years, CIDA's Thailand program concentrated on easing rural poverty, especially in the depressed northeast. More recently, support for rural development has been consolidated into two large-scale projects – the community-based Integrated Rural Development Project and the Local Development Foundation, which functions under royal patronage. In line with the goal of creating self-sustaining mechanisms to broaden cooperation between the two countries, the aid effort expanded to encompass industrial development, natural resources, and energy; economic management; development of institutions and human resources; and rural development.[16]

The centrepiece in industrial development was the Enterprise Collaboration Program, a pioneering CIDA initiative aimed at promoting commercial and technological collaboration between Canadian and then business communities. Program support for economic management would provide assistance for policy development and programs to manage the transition towards industrialization. This included technical assistance for policy planning and analysis in the National Economic and Social Development Board, Thailand's central planning agency. It also involved support for the Thailand Development Research Institute and its socio-economic research on public policy.

Support for accelerated industrialization was relevant to creation of institutions and mechanisms that could later sustain and broaden bilateral interaction with Canada after termination of CIDA's development assistance. Transition to a more mature relationship was facilitated by signing in 1988 of an Economic Co-operation Agreement, which provided an intergovernmental framework for collaboration in many policy areas. A Thai Canada Economic Cooperation Foundation, composed of influential Thai government and business personalities, was set up to superintend development of relations. Program implementation was contracted out mostly to executing agencies, thus building up institutional connections while enabling CIDA to concentrate on policy formulation and program planning so as to ensure a good "fit" between Canadian and Thai priorities.

According to the new country policy framework adopted in 1991, the current bilateral program in Thailand is expected to phase down after the mid-1990s. Even though economic development is deemed to justify "graduation" from recipient country status, some continued CIDA support may still be warranted. There may be scope for individual projects and regional-level development cooperation to help facilitate transition to a more mature relationship.

ODA as a Geo-Strategic Element in Foreign Policy: Canadian Aid to China

Canadian foreign policy with respect to China and Indochina is driven primarily by concerns of regional and global security. In addressing Communist governments generally, Canada has tended to stress development of bilateral and multilateral relations in the political, economic, social, and cultural spheres, as inducements for sustaining a stable international system. Whenever that stability was challenged, as when Vietnam invaded Cambodia or by the Tiananmen Square massacre, Canada made policy shifts and trade-offs that catered to some interests over others, but with the overriding objective of international security.

Canadian efforts at building bridges to China took on renewed vigour shortly after the end of the Cultural Revolution.[17] For many, cultivating relations with China was a prime example of an independent Canadian foreign policy. Considerable attention was paid to maintaining a vaunted "special relationship" with China. China was targeted by Canada's trade strategy as a pre-eminent export market, especially for high-technology products, despite the problematic experience of Canadian – and other foreign – firms operating there. Several provincial governments got into the act as well, among them Alberta, Ontario, and Saskatchewan, forming twinning relationships with Chinese counterparts. From the early 1980s, development assistance also became part of this cultivation of China, one whose strategic significance far outweighs its mere dollar value.

The focus of CIDA's China program has been on human resource development, with the aim of helping China acquire the knowledge and skills necessary for economic and social progress. Assistance is provided in sectors identified as areas of demonstrated Canadian capability and where there are explicit prospective "multiplier effects" for China. Creation of human and institutional ties is intended to strengthen bilateral links between the two nations.

CIDA's China program covers education and training, agricultural development, forestry, and energy development. Since 1986, it has provided aid support also for transportation and telecommunications. Work on studies for the vaunted and controversial Three Gorges Project was deferred and then suspended indefinitely as part of the limited sanctions that Canada imposed in the wake of Tiananmen Square. About 40 per cent of aid activity involves either development of human resources or management training in the sectors of concentration. Other program elements include technology transfer, technical assistance, and, occasionally, supply of equipment.

Canada's reaction to the Tiananmen Square massacre mixed remorse with Realpolitik.[18] Limited sanctions entailed cancellation of certain bilateral exchanges and cultural agreements and postponement or cancellation of some aid. Certainly there was no intention of foreclosing on relations with China. Afater an initial interval of indignation, Canada adopted a policy that differentiated, with a measure of sophistry, between China's political regime, which stood condemned, and the Chinese people, on whose behalf ties should be maintained.

Canada wanted to keep the door to China opened, to preserve connections that Canadian foreign policy considered crucial for maintaining a geo-strategic equilibrium in the Asia Pacific region.

From Aid to Economic Cooperation: Towards Linkage-Based Partnerships

CIDA's fostering of more extensive bilateral economic relations with Asian developing nations has foundered on weak Canadian business linkages with the countries concerned. Canada does not figure prominently as a source of foreign direct investment in the region. Private Canadian investment in ASEAN countries has begun to grow in recent years but still represents only a small proportion of their private capital inflows.[19] In India, out of more than 5,000 industrial agreements concluded by Indian companies between 1981 and 1989, only 52 were with Canadian firms. The low level of Canadian direct investment in Asia has generally implied a limited Canadian role in technology transfer and productive-sector development. By contrast, the experience of other international donors indicates that transfers of private-sector technological resources and management skills can often produce more benefits than equivalent flows of aid.[20]

Not all CIDA initiatives to encourage economic links necessarily involved aid-assisted export promotion. Much aid has been channelled to strengthening Asian economic and trade-related institutions and to facilitating technology transfer, through the CIDA Industrial Cooperation Program (CIDA-INC), and imports, through fostering of expanded trade and investment.[21]

For the coming decade, CIDA's policy makers foresee that Canada's future role in the Asia Pacific region will be predicated upon creation of more extensive institutional linkages with Asian developing countries. Formation of more wide-ranging links in the educational, scientific, environmental, social, and cultural spheres is considered a vital corollary to trade expansion. Canada's quest for symmetry with developing Asia could hardly be sustainable without a synergetic emergence of trade and other institutional links.

The Leadership Role of CIDA's Asia Branch Management

During the 1980s, CIDA's Asia Branch was a creative leader in the development of new thinking for Canada's ODA. It introduced new aid mechanisms and programs, experimented with new approaches to development cooperation, and sought closer synthesis between aid objectives and the overall goals of Canadian foreign policy in Asia. That innovative impulse stemmed from the branch's managerial talent at headquarters and in the field, which permitted creative responses to emerging opportunities in developing Asia.

Behind these innovations lay a vision of Asian development. As the 1980s progressed, the Asia Branch used its corporate knowledge to formulate its strategic vision of Asia's developmental dynamics, with a new perspective on future issues and trends, and to provide a context for assessing the relevance of Canadian development assistance.

Impelled to formulate programs pertinent to that vision, management embarked on pioneering initiatives, first in Southeast Asia, where accelerated industrialization required new approaches. It launched environmental initiatives, such as the Environment Management Development Program in Indonesia; collaborative mechanisms for NGO program delivery, such as the Philippine Development Assistance Program (PDAP);[22] new kinds of NGO partnerships, such as the Canada Indonesia Forum and the Philippines Canada Human Resource Development Program; and new types of economic cooperation, such as the Enterprise Collaboration Program, the Thai Canada Economic Cooperation Foundation, and the Thailand Development Research Institute. It undertook major projects in education and training, institution strengthening, human rights, rural credit, management of environment and natural resources, institutional linkages, and women in development.

In Southeast Asia and more recently in South Asia, CIDA's Asia Branch tried to put in place new institutional links between Canadian and counterpart institutions to lay the foundations for a more sustainable bilateralism. It funded establishment of the Asia Pacific Foundation as a forum for "networking" and exchanges between Canada and the countries of the Asia Pacific Rim.

As CIDA became more involved in policy-related assistance, the Asia Branch augmented its knowledge in policy areas. This served, in turn, to enhance CIDA's capacity to foster closer integration of developmental objectives into Canadian foreign policy generally.

THE FLOW OF CANADIAN ODA TO ASIA

The flow of Canadian ODA to Asia, on a country-to-country basis, has grown by more than half since the mid-1980s, even though Asia's share of total bilateral assistance actually declined. Transfer accelerated sharply as Canada's aid effort regained momentum after the cutbacks and recession of the early 1980s. Disbursements increased from $363 million in fiscal 1982–83 to over $565 million in 1988–89 and slipped to $468 million for 1989–90, the latest year for which data are available.[23] Yet the proportion of all of Canada's bilateral assistance going to Asia, which stood at one-third in 1982–83, decreased to just over 24 per cent at the end of the decade.

This same trend was apparent in the changing geographical allocation of government-to-government aid – the single largest component of Canadian ODA. Asia's allocation declined from 42 per cent of the total during the early 1980s to less than 35 per cent in 1989–90. This shift mirrored growing preoccupation with aid to Africa under Canada's new ODA strategy, notwithstanding the importance attached to Asia in Canadian foreign policy.

The cutback in aid that followed the government's economic statement of December 1992 did not affect the overall configuration of ODA to Asia. Some very small bilateral programs, such as those for Cambodia and Laos, were terminated, but otherwise CIDA managed to maintain an aid presence in all major Asian developing countries. Rather, the budget cuts were internalized by individual bilateral programs, so that certain projects and activities are no longer to be supported.

Canada's ODA in Asia uses every aid channel and transfer mechanism, though not necessarily in each nation (Table 1). Of the total Canadian country-to-country aid to Asia, 91 per cent, or $425 million, is channelled through CIDA. CIDA operates a number of transfer mechanisms, of which the bilateral government-to-government programs are the most significant by far. CIDA's bilateral channel transferred $287 million to Asia in 1989–90, representing 61 per cent of total country-to-country assistance for that geographical region. Other CIDA mechanisms involved in aid transfers to Asia include food aid (13.7 per cent of bilateral contributions in 1989–90), support for NGOs (6.2 per cent), industrial cooperation (INC) (3.7 per cent), institutional cooperation and development services (ICDS) (2.3 per cent), international humanitarian assistance (2.0 per cent), and the Canada Fund (1.4 per cent).

A smaller volume of ODA resources reaches Asia through the specialized programs of other Canadian development agencies. Support from the International Development Research Centre (IDRC) for science and technology in Asia totalled $20.3 million in 1989–90, or 4.3 per cent of total country-to-country assistance. Energy-sector assistance by the now-abolished Petro-Canada International Assistance Corp. (PCIAC) amounted to $21.9 million (4.7 per cent of total Asian country-to-country assistance). Disbursements by the International Centre for Ocean Development (ICOD) in Asia came to $220,000.

Table 1
Canadian ODA disbursements in Asia ($million), 1989–90

Country	Bila*	CF†	NGO	ICDS	INC§	Food aid	IHA‡	IDRC	PCIAC	Total
				CIDA programs						
South Asia										
Afghanistan	–	0.9	0.06	–	–	–	2.0	–	–	2.9
Bangladesh	77.6	0.4	4.1	0.4	0.01	47.3	–	0.2	–	130.1
India	22.0	0.5	7.3	1.8	3.1	0.1	–	3.3	–	38.5
Nepal	8.1	0.3	2.0	1.1	–	–	–	0.7	2.2	14.4
Pakistan	22.1	0.5	1.0	0.5	1.3	13.9	1.9	0.5	–	41.7
Sri Lanka	10.8	0.5	0.9	0.8	0.1	0.06	0.2	0.6	–	14.1
Southeast Asia										
Indonesia	51.9	0.5	4.5	1.1	1.4	–	–	1.4	–	60.8
Laos	–	–	–	–	–	0.05	–	0.03	–	0.08
Malaysia	2.3	0.3	0.1	0.6	1.6	–	–	1.6	–	6.6
Myanmar	0.7	–	1.1	–	–	–	–	–	1.3	3.1
Philippines	25.7	0.6	3.1	0.2	1.9	0.1	–	3.9	0.7	36.4
Singapore	–	0.05	–	–	0.1	–	–	0.3	–	0.5
Thailand	20.3	0.5	0.6	1.4	2.2	–	1.9	3.1	2.1	32.1
Vietnam	–	–	–	–	–	–	–	0.01	–	0.01
East Asia										
China	35.0	0.2	0.3	1.4	4.7	–	0.05	3.5	–	45.1
South Korea	d	–	–	–	0.03	–	–	0.08	–	0.06
Regional programs	9.5	0.4	2.7	0.7	0.15	–	2.2	0.1	–	15.8
Other unspecified	–	–	0.02	–	–	–	–	0.5	–	0.52
Total#	287.3	6.7	29.8	10.9	17.3	63.7	9.7	20.3	21.9	467.8

Source: CIDA, *Annual Report 1989–90*, Table M.
Note: Discrepancies in addition are caused by rounding.
* Bilateral government-to-government assistance.
† Canada Fund (ex–Mission Administered Fund).
‡ International Humanitarian Assistance.
§ Industrial Cooperation Program.
# Asia total includes $220,000 in ICOD disbursements.

Provincial-government contributions to international development through local NGOs and institutions totalled $35.5 million in 1989–90; no geographical breakdown is available.[24]

Some Canadian aid organizations and transfer mechanisms concentrate more on Asia than do others. Canada supports large and important government-to-government assistance programs across Asia, with CIDAs Asia bilateral programming representing 34.8 per cent ot total bilateral aid for 1989–90. Asia also received a relatively high proportion of PCIAC energy-sector transfers (45.6 per cent of the total), CIDA food aid (32.2 per cent), CIDA industrial cooperation activities (29.3 per cent), and embassy-managed Canada Fund disbursements (26.3 per cent).

By way of contrast, a considerably lesser share of partnership-type program funding was directed at Asia. Activities in Asian countries attracted 21.8 per cent of CIDA's NGO program funding, 18.4 per cent of IDRC research funding, and only 9.7 per cent of CIDA ICDs funding. This disproportionately low level of partnership program involvement in Asia would seem to indicate a dearth of institutional linkages with countries of that region. Because of this, a gap has loomed between the high level of government aid transfers, which are supposed to involve Canada more extensively in Asian development, and the comparatively narrow basis of Canadian interaction with the developing countries of Asia.

The major Asian recipients of Canadian ODA on a country-to-country basis for 1989–90 were Bangladesh ($130.1 million), Indonesia ($60.8 million), China ($45.1 million), Pakistan ($41.7 million), India ($38.0 million), Philippines ($36.0 million), and Thailand ($32.1 million). Indeed, these nations ranked among the leading recipients of Canada's aid generally. During the late 1980s, India (and also Sri Lanka) declined in absolute as well as relative terms, and Indonesia and Philippines gained. These changes reflected in good measure impediments to program implementation in India and Sri Lanka and the effectiveness of CIDA's new programming for Indonesia and Philippines.

Most of Canada's country-to-country ODA to Asia has gone to the poorer side of the Asian duality. Some 32 per cent of all such aid to Asia, or $151 million, went to least-developed countries (LLDCs), mainly Bangladesh and, to a lesser degree, Nepal.[25] Over four-fifths went to countries categorized as low-income. Middle-income nations received $93 million, or 19 per cent of the total. The main beneficiaries were Thailand and Philippines, where poverty alleviation was (in the case of Thailand until recently) an important component of Canadian aid programming.

CIDA considers itself as but a comparatively small-scale aid donor to Asia. Although Canadian ODA transfers have acquired a relatively high profile in some major Asian developing countries, there is considerable disparity between Canada's aid contribution and that of leading bilateral donors. Thus for Bangladesh, the leading recipient of Canadian aid, Canada ranked as the third-largest bilateral donor in 1988 (the latest year for which data are available), after Japan and the United States. ODA from Canada constituted 12.6 per cent of Bangladesh's bilateral aid receipts. Canada ranked fourth among bilateral donors in Pakistan; sixth in Indonesia, Nepal, and Sri Lanka; and ninth in India.[26] Canadian aid typically contributed between 4 and 8 per cent of total ODA receipts.

If Canada's comparatively high donor profile implies a more salient Canadian aid presence in Asian development than the dollar value of transfers alone might indicate, in reality Canadian contributions tend to be too small and too diffuse to acquire significant "leverage."[27] With cutbacks to Canada's aid budget, coupled with a shift in geographical emphasis in favour of Africa, it would seem that Canada's donor profile across Asia is destined to decline over the immediate future. For Canadian aid to remain relevant, CIDA programming will have to become more focused and targeted at particular developmental niches, where Canada can contribute advantageously to meeting specific Asian development requirements.

DELIVERY OF CANADIAN ODA TO ASIA

The Canadian aid presence in Asia encompasses a wide range of development programs and activities. Each of Canada's aid agencies and development crown corporations, including CIDA, operates according to its own program goals, operational logic, and developmental imperatives. Notwithstanding ministerial supervision and bureaucratic controls intended to ensure a modicum of policy coordination among the agencies involved, in practice there exists little if any operational coordination between CIDA and the development crown corporations such as the IDRC or with the NGO community. Despite the matching funding offered to NGOs, CIDA takes care not to encroach on their operational autonomy.[28]

CIDA's own branches have their own program mechanisms which allow virtually no scope for a common approach – say, between the bilateral Asia Branch, which manages governmental programs, on the one hand, and Special Programs, which responds to NGO initiatives, and Business Cooperation, which is responsive to Canadian private-sector proposals, on the other hand. Delivery of Canadian ODA in Asia may be likened to an Indonesian gamelin – an orchestra comprising a complex cacophony of many instruments played without seeming to adhere to a common score or a recognized conductor, but with tacit awareness of the underlying structure and harmony of purpose.

CIDA's Asia programs express the priorities and resource allocations decided in country policy frameworks. On the basis of these plans, the

Table 2
CIDA bilateral program disbursements in Asia, by sector, 1989–90

Sector	$million	Percentage
Economic sector		
Communications	5.2	1.7
Economic and financial support	55.8	17.9
Energy	62.8	20.2
Industry	8.3	2.7
Transportation	9.9	3.2
Social sector		
Education	31.5	10.1
Health and nutrition	7.1	4.1
Human resource development	22.9	7.3
Population and human settlements	17.3	5.5
Rural sector		
Agriculture	35.4	11.4
Fisheries	1.2	0.003
Forestry	4.9	1.6
Geographic and surveys	2.8	0.009
Water and sanitation	7.0	2.2
Institution strengthening		
Institutional support	7.9	2.5
Material Management		
Procurement, transportation and handling of capital goods, equipment, and commodities	25.2	8.1
Total	310.9	100.0*

Source: CIDA, *Annual Report 1989–90*, 41 (adapted).
* Discrepancy in addition caused by rounding.

agency responds to project proposals from the governments of the nations concerned. CIDA's involvement in Asia, as elsewhere, therefore reflects a conjunction of Canadian objectives and recipient-country requirements, as represented by their project proposals.

CIDA's bilateral development assistance tends to concentrate on certain selected sectors (for example, agriculture, energy, environment, human resource development, and water resource development) and activities (such as equipment supply, food aid, and training), as revealed in actual disbursement patterns. For fiscal year 1989–90, about 46 per cent of government-to-government aid consisted of economic sector assistance (Table 2). The remainder was allocated among the social sector (27 per cent), rural sector (15 per cent), and institutional support (2.5 per cent). Some 8 per cent of disbursements went for material management, covering procurement, handling, and transport of commodities and equipment delivered to projects in the various sectors in Asia.

CIDA's bilateral assistance for economic-sector activities in Asia were mostly for energy development (mainly electric power) and on general economic and financial support (Table 2). Aid of this latter sort was intended for balance of payments or structural adjustment. It would typically take the form of commodity assistance, or food aid, or, less commonly, capital equipment for development projects. Modest support was provided for communications, including telecommunications, and transportation, such as railways. Only minor amounts were expended directly on industrial-sector activities.

The main areas of activity in the social sector involved education and human resources development. Other activities supported included population policy and human settlements and health and nutrition.

CIDA's bilateral involvement in the rural sector emphasized agricultural development. As well, there was substantial activity in water and sanitation and in forestry. Some support went also to fisheries and geographical surveys, with the latter usually for environmental and natural resource management.

Institutional support covered central-government, local-government, and other public agencies charged with managing development activities consistent with CIDA's program objectives. Support for institution strengthening is intended to help increase the effectiveness of recipient-country managers in designing and implementing development mandates, while also forming institutional links with Canadian counterparts.

Data on the sectoral allocation of aid should be treated with caution, since the figures represent only the way in which individual projects have been categorized. In fact, most projects involve a host of activities, which makes a sectoral breakdown rather more complicated. For example, an institution-strengthening project might well include technical assistance ("institutional support"), training ("human resource development"), and supply of equipment; the institution concerned might be responsible for delivering basic human needs ("social sector") to the villages ("rural sector"); yet this aid would be classified simply as "institutional support."

CANADA'S RESPONSES TO ASIAN DEVELOPMENT REQUIREMENTS

Canadian bilateral aid addresses many Asian development requirements, most notably, alleviation of poverty, human resource development, integration of women in development (WID), structural adjustment and economic reform, regional development, environmental sustainability, and food security.[29] Canada transfers aid through various mechanisms – among them, technical assistance, training, project support, commodity assistance, and food aid. Most aid to Asia goes to such activities as agriculture and rural development, energy development, environmental management, higher education and professional training, industrial and infrastructure development, policy planning, and water and natural resource development.[30]

Canadian experience demonstrates broad congruence and compatibility among the various objectives of CIDA strategy, including easing of poverty, other developmental concerns, and the building of links between Canada and Asia. CIDA seeks to use aid strategically to promote development, while also sustaining the growth of country-to-country links with Asian counterparts and contributing to peace and stability in the region. There are risks, of course, of displaced priorities or blurring of objectives. Such risks are manageable, however, and CIDA's country planning processes and accountability system uphold program compliance with the goals and objectives of aid policy.

Although Canadian aid policy must accommodate a range of domestic interests and concerns, this need not divert from the development effort. If Canada has multiple objectives, so too do the developing countries. Development is a multi-dimensional process, and development assistance is called upon to respond to developing countries' requirements in many areas of need. CIDA's experience in Asia highlights the importance of programming aid delivery so as to match donors' capabilities with recipient countries requirements. The effectiveness of aid policy depends on its capacity to achieve congruence between the interests and objectives of the donor and the goals and requirements of the developing countries.

NOTES

1 For official statements of Canada's foreign policy objectives under the Progressive Conservative government, see *Competitiveness and Security: Directions for Canada's International Relations*, Presented by the Right Honourable Joe Clark, Secretary of State for External Affairs (Ottawa: Supply and Services Canada 1985), 3, and External Affairs Canada, *Canada's International Relations: Response of the Government of Canada to the Report of the Special Joint Committee of the Senate and House of Commons* (Ottawa: Supply and Services Canada 1986).

2 David R. Morrison, "Canada and North-South Conflict," in Maureen Appel Molot and Brian W. Tomlin, eds., *Canada among Nations: A World of Conflict/1987* (Toronto: James Lorimer 1988), 138.

3 Parliament, House of Commons, Standing Committee on External Affairs

and International Trade, *For Whose Benefit? Report of the Standing Committee on External Affairs and International Trade on Canada's Official Development Assistance Policies and Programs* (Ottawa: Supply and Services 1987), 12.

4 World Bank, *World Development Report 1990: Poverty* (Oxford University Press 1990), 1–2, 39–55.

5 This excludes a number of West Asian and Middle East countries (such as Jordan) to which small amounts of aid are currently being channelled and whose programs are managed by CIDA's Africa Branch and Oceania, for which no fewer than 13 island programs are managed through CIDA's Asia Branch.

6 CIDA, *Annual Report 1989–90* (Ottawa: Supply and Services 1990), Table M.

7 On the new aid strategy, see Martin Rudner, "Canada's Official Development Assistance Strategy: Process, Goals and Priorities," *Canadian Journal of Development Studies* 12 no. 1 (1991), and "New Dimensions in Canadian Development Assistance Policy," in Brian W. Tomlin and Maureen Appel Molot, eds., *Canada among Nations: The Tory Record/1988* (Toronto: James Lorimer 1989).

8 The World Commission on Environment and Development, *Our Common Future* (Brundtland Report), (Oxford University Press 1987). See also Jim MacNeill, John Cox, and David Runnalls, *CIDA and Sustainable Development* (Halifax: Institute for Research on Public Policy 1989).

9 Rudner, "New Dimensions," 51.

10 For historical accounts of Canada's relations with South Asia, see Kim Nossal, "Canada's Strategic Interests in South Asia, 1947–1987," and Chantal Tremblay, "Real and Perceived Opportunities for Economic Cooperation between Canada and South Asia," both in A.G. Rubinoff, ed., *Canada and South Asia: Issues and Opportunities* (Toronto: Centre for South Asian Studies, University of Toronto, 1988).

11 In recent years, Canada has been the third-ranking bilateral donor of ODA to Bangladesh, after Japan and the United States: CIDA, *Annual Report 1989–90*, Table U.

12 For an earlier study of Canadian aid to Bangladesh, see Roger Ehrhardt, *Canadian Development Assistance to Bangladesh* (Ottawa: North-South Institute 1983). For a more recent survey of CIDA bilateral activities in that country, see *Summary of Canadian Aid in Bangladesh*, CIDA Bangladesh Program, Asia Branch, December 1988.

13 For a review of Canadian foreign policy perspectives on Southeast Asia, see Martin Rudner, *Canada and the Philippines. The Dimensions of a Developing Relationship*, Monograph No. 1, Asian Pacific Research and Resource Centre, Carleton University, 1990, especially 10–16; H.E. English, "Canada and the United States Look West: Pacific Policy Networks," in Brian W. Tomlin and Maureen Appel Molot, eds.,

Canada among Nations: 1986/Talking Trade (Toronto: James Lorimer and Co. 1987; and Keith Hay, "Canada and ASEAN: Problems and Policies," in Maureen Appel Molot and Brian W. Tomlin, eds., *Canada among Nations: 1985 The Conservative Agenda* (Toronto: James Lorimer 1986).

14 On Canadian aid and trade relations with Malaysia, see Manfred G. Van Nostitz, "Canadian Presence in Malaysia: Evolution and Trends," and Keith Hay, "Canada and Malaysia: The Economy and the Service Sector," both in Martin Rudner, ed., *Canada Malaysia: Towards the 1990s* (Kingston, Ont.: Ronald P. Frye 1988); see also Richard Stubbs, "Canada's Relations with Malaysia: Picking Partners in ASEAN," *Pacific Affairs* vol. 63 no. 3 (1990), 351–66.

15 Martin Rudner and Susan McLellan, "Canada's Economic Relations with Southeast Asia: Federal-Provincial Dimensions of Policy," *Modern Asian Studies* 24 pt 1 (1990), 37–8.

16 EAITC, *Survey of Bilateral Economic Relations between Canada and Thailand* (Ottawa, 1990), 12–3.

17 J.T. Paltiel, "Rude Awakening: Canada and China Following Tiananmen," in Maureen Appel Molot and Fen Osler Hampson, eds., *Canada among Nations: The Challenge of Change/1990* (Ottawa: Carleton University Press 1990), 43–5.

18 J.T. Paltiel, "Rude Awakening," 50–2.

19 Conference Board of Canada, *The Asian Experience: Canadian Business Linkages with the Developing Countries*, Vol. 1, International Business Research Centre Report (Ottawa 1987); and Conference Board of Canada, *Canadian Investment in the Association of South-East Asian Nations*, International Studies and Services Development Group Report, (Ottawa 1988).

20 Alexander J. Yeats, "Development Assistance: Trade versus Aid and the Relative Performance of Industrial Countries," *World Development* 10 no. 10 (1982), 863–9.

21 On CIDA support for import facilitation, including the role of the Trade Facilitation Office Canada (TFOC) in assisting developing-country exporters gain access to the Canadian consumer market, see Rudner, "Canada's Official Development Assistance Strategy," 29–31.

22 Rudner, *Canada and the Philipines*, especially 24–5, 90, 93.

23 Data on Canadian ODA to Asia are from CIDA, *Annual Report 1989–90*, Table M.

24 A 14 per cent share of provincial-government aid went to Asia in 1987–88, the most recent year for which a geographical breakdown is available; CIDA, *Annual Report 1987–88 (Ottawa: Supply and Services 1988), Table M. On provincial-government agencies and international development assistance, see Rudner and McLellan, "Canada's Economic Relations with Southeast Asia," especially 47–51.*

25 CIDA, *Annual Report 1989–90*, Table L.

26 Ibid., Table U.

27 Aid agencies tend to gauge their role in recipient countries by their so-called leverage on developments there, as measured by, for example, acquisition of "good" projects developmentally prominent activities having high domestic priority – (local cost funding will be available) – and whose risks of failure are manageable), access to senior levels of government for consultations, and – the greatest perquisite of all – influence on policy development.

28 Tim Broadhead and Brent Herbert-Copley, with Anne-Marie Lambert, *Bridges of Hope? Canadian Voluntary Agencies and the Third World* (Ottawa: North-South Institute 1988), especially 56–70. See also *Mind If I Cut In? The Report of the CCIC Task Force on CIDA-NGO Funding Relationships* (Ottawa: Canadian Council for International Cooperation 1988).

29 CIDA, *Sharing Our Future: Canada's International Development Assistance* (Ottawa: Supply and Services 1987), especially 25.

30 For an analysis of Canada's aid presence in Asia, with a description of the various strategic approaches, program channels, and activities, by country, see Martin Rudner, "Canadian Development Assistance to Asia: Programs, Objectives and Future Trends," Working Paper No. 6 Asian Pacific Research and Resource Centre, Carleton University, Ottawa (1990).

PART THREE
Some Conclusions

12 Canadian Aid: A Comparative Analysis

JEAN-PHILIPPE THÉRIEN

This chapter compares the aid policy of Canada with that of other member states of the Development Assistance Committee (DAC) of the Organisation for Economic Cooperation and Development (OECD).[1] A comparative overview of the major components of Canada's external assistance will be followed by an attempt, by way of conclusion, to see how aid policy reflects Canada's distinct identity in the international arena. Although the comparative approach is fruitful for analysing social relationships, be they international or domestic, comparative studies on aid are curiously few and far between. Of those that exist, not all deal with Canada,[2] evidently, and, of those that at least refer to Canada, some are essentially descriptive.[3] Others are more analytical while remaining limited to a specific geographical area[4] or theme.[5] Hence few studies seek to compare Canadian aid policy comprehensively. There was a time when CIDA regularly undertook such an exercise, but this practice, a response to the interests of government policy makers, has not continued.[6]

Because it reflects national interests, aid is a political reality that has assumed a different form from one country to the next. Yet any analysis of how development assistance policies differ among developed countries also reveals their many common features. Aid is global in scope. It is an expression of objectives that are shared by the Western states at least as much as it is the product of domestic values and preferences.

The concept of "regime" helps us sort out the puzzle of international aid.[7] An international aid regime exists insofar as assistance gives rise to international, institutionalized forms of behaviour. Aid can thus be viewed as the product of an international culture based on an evolving consensus on how North-South relations are to be organized. Historically, this consensus was illustrated first by the fact that most developed countries set up almost simultaneously – in the first half of the 1960s–bureaucratic structures to administer foreign aid. Similarities in discourse also illustrate the international consensus on aid. Almost everywhere, emphasis on infrastructure projects gave way to a "basic needs" approach, then to structural adjustment, and more recently to structural adjustment "with a human face." Of course, this standardization of aid policies is linked to broader homogenization of political and economic evolution in developed countries. More specifically, however, it was spurred by the increasing role played by multilateral aid agencies and by the growing number of forums (consortia, round-tables, DAC expert groups) at which developed-country donors meet and share experiences.

This wide international consensus has not eliminated expression of national idiosyncrasies in implementation of assistance programs. The comparative approach seeks ultimately to grasp how these national factors interact with the international regime to mould each donor's policy. Here, it will enable us to see how Canada's aid policy resembles and differs from that of other developed countries. This chapter will try to show that, in the field of aid, Canada falls, broadly speaking, between the other G-7 countries (France, Germany, Italy, Japan, the United Kingdom, and the United States) and the "like-minded" countries (Denmark, The Netherlands, Norway, Sweden). The overall judgment to be brought down on Canadian assistance depends on one's standpoint. Canada certainly appears generous and forward-looking in comparison with other G-7 members. It is much less so when compared with the performance of the small northern European countries.

THE CANADIAN CONTEXT

Certain structural specificities condition Canadian aid policy. Canada, in general, has fewer immediate interests in developing countries than do most other developed countries. Geographically, it is far from the Third World. It is further from Mexico than Norway is from Turkey or Australia from Indonesia. Nor has Canada had any colonies, unlike other G-7 members and some less important powers such as The Netherlands and Belgium. These factors help explain the low volume of flows in all areas – trade, investment, culture, and migration–between Canada and developing countries. Such a context could have hampered growth in Canada's development cooperation. Instead, through a process of compensation, it seems to have made it more vigorous.

It is true that other factors were to impel Canada to set up an aid policy. In Canada, as elsewhere, aid arose to maximize national interests. Within the international system, Canada appears as a distinct middle power insofar as it is, as one cliché says, a regional power without a region.[8] Although for the past half-century Canada has attempted to overcome this handicap, there are few areas of activity, starting with military power, in which it can exert significant influence. Development aid has progressively become one of these areas. By taking advantage of its ties to the western hemisphere and its cultural links with the Commonwealth and la Francophonie, Canada has used international cooperation to diversify its external relations and globalize its presence. In Canada, probably more so than elsewhere, aid has helped consolidate the country's status within the international order.

Although Canada defines itself continually in comparison with the United States, its political culture is more impregnated with the welfare state than is its neighbour's.[9] This difference matters because, like foreign policy as a whole, aid constitutes a projection abroad of dominant national values. In Canada, the idea of redistributing national wealth holds a central place. The setting up of a reliable social-security safety net and a complex system of interprovincial transfer payments has profoundly marked Canada's identity. Not surprising, opponents of the much-debated Canada–United States Free Trade Agreement have often asserted that Canada's foremost difference from the United States lies in the nature of its social programs. Canada's ties of cooperation with the Third World clearly appear to reflect a spirit of internationalist altruism whose roots run deeper than in the United States.

Finally, the overall framework for this comparison of aid policies would be incomplete were Canada's position in the international power structure not taken into account. The most revealing indicator of this position is undoubtedly a country's economic power. In 1989, Canada accounted for 3.6 per cent of the total GNP of all DAC members, among whom it held an unchallenged seventh place.[10] It trailed far behind the sixth position, held by the United Kingdom (6.1 per cent of total DAC GNP), and was far ahead of the eighth position, held by Australia (1.9 per cent of total DAC GNP). Canada's economic ranking gives weight to the suggestion that, in development aid, it stands out among both the G-7 and the like-minded countries. For all cases, Canada's participation in the aid regime could be expected to come close to seventh place, or 3.6 per cent, depending on whether ordinal or cardinal indicators are used. Any effort above or below these thresholds should be interpreted as arising from a special political will.

VOLUME OF RESOURCES

During the 1980s, international cooperation was faced with "aid fatigue." The resources earmarked for aid increased very little overall and even decreased in 1981, 1987, and 1989.[11] Canada maintained an above-average level of aid growth among donor countries. Nevertheless, it ranked only ninth among DAC nations in increasing resources for development assistance. France, Italy, Japan, and all the like-minded countries – except The Netherlands – outperformed Canada in this area. During the decade, Canadian aid in current dollars fell only once (in 1989), and many other countries (Australia, Austria, Ireland, The Netherlands, New Zealand, Norway, Switzerland, the United Kingdom, and the United States) also reduced their assistance that same year. But, in the final analysis, Canadian policy in the 1980s was clearly influenced by the prevailing climate of inertia.

Canada was in 1989 the seventh-largest donor within the DAC, behind (in descending order by size of donation) Japan, the United States, France, West Germany, Italy, and the United Kingdom.[12] It was followed by the Netherlands, Sweden, Australia, Denmark, and Norway. Thus Canada fell squarely between the entire G-7 and the like-minded countries. Among the first seven donors in 1980, Canada is the only one to have kept its ranking. In 1984 and 1985, however, it climbed to fifth place, overtaking the United Kingdom and The Netherlands. It then fell in 1986 to eighth, behind Italy.[13] Even though burden-sharing in the aid regime will probably undergo fewer upheavals in the near future than it has over the last ten years, this does not mean that Canada will have no trouble holding onto its standing. The way things are going, it may at any time slip behind The Netherlands.

Canada's seventh place equalled 4.9 per cent of total aid from developed countries in 1989.[14] As the six largest donor states fund more than 75 per cent of total DAC aid, Canada's share evidently entitles it to no more than a secondary role. Canada's current contribution amounts furthermore to a pullback, since its share of aid was 6.6 per cent in 1975–76 and 5.6 per cent in 1984–85.[15] Ottawa insists, of course, that in relation to GNP the country continues to pay more than its fair share of funding for international aid. Canadian aid is indeed 1.36 times higher than it would be if burden sharing were proportional to GNP. Only France outdoes Canada in the G-7. Among like-minded countries, this indicator hovers around 2.5. In fact, few nations fund aid at a level lower than their GNP's proportion within DAC. However, the United States and Japan – the two largest donors – tend to act as "free riders," and so smaller countries such as Canada make up for this shortfall.

The ratio of aid to GNP is probably the indicator most often used for comparing the relative efforts of each donor. In 1970, the UN set 0.7 per cent of GNP as the aid level to be reached by developed countries. The importance that donors have or have not given to this goal when planning their aid programs is highly revealing.[16] Together with Belgium, Finland, and Italy, Canada belongs to a group of countries that have agreed to the objective of 0.7 per cent and have, at one time or another, set a target date. This stance differs from that of the like-minded countries, which have accepted and exceeded the 0.7 per cent objective. It also differs from the posture of countries which, while accepting this goal, have not set any timetable for reaching it (Australia, Austria, France, Germany, Ireland, Japan, New Zealand, and the United Kingdom). Switzerland and the United States have plainly and simply not accepted the 0.7 per cent goal.

Canada was not alone in failing to keep its promises, since Italy did the same. Canada rather stands out as the country that has most often changed official policy on this issue. After many adjustments, the latest commitment sets a goal of 0.47 per cent, to be reached by 1994–95, and leaves completely in limbo the 0.7 per cent target date.[17] Despite the justifications given, the constant revision downwards of its objectives has seriously undermined Canada's credibility in the eyes of both donor and developing countries. Canadian policy denotes an ambiguous stand, insofar as it has helped legitimize the demands of developing countries while fostering indifference towards the actual urgency of these demands. In official discourse, Canada presents itself as being receptive to the interests of developing countries. Its conduct, however, constantly fails to live up to the intentions that it proclaims. In the eyes of the Third World, Canada is ultimately seen to be empathetic but lacking in realism and political willpower.

Canada's ratio of aid to GNP has always been above the DAC average. During the 1980s, Canada's performance varied between 0.41 per cent (1982) and 0.50 per cent (1984 and 1988) while the DAC average ranged between 0.33 per cent (1989) and 0.38 per cent (1982). In 1989, Canada had an ODA : GNP ratio of 0.44 per cent, with a performance putting it in eighth place among donor countries, behind Norway, Sweden, Denmark, The Netherlands, Finland, France, and Belgium. Canada is certainly far from the forefront, since Norway devotes more than 1 per cent of its GNP to development aid. It is, however, the most generous G-7 member after France. Once again, it finds itself between the majority of G-7 donor states and the like-minded countries.

Canada's leadership within the G-7 has nevertheless been eroding. Until 1980, it held first place in its ratio of aid to GNP, but, since 1981, it has been constantly outperformed by France. As far as the government is concerned, Canada has not done so badly, if the generally hard economic times are taken into account. And, indeed, the United Kingdom, the United States, and (West) Germany have done worse.

In summary, Canada during the 1980s distinguished itself by its steady adherence to an above-average, though lacklustre policy. Although it has supported the 0.7 per cent goal in principle, it has not mustered the resolve to bring such a goal to fruition. In comparison with other members of the international community, Canada trails far behind like-minded states and is no longer even able to maintain the leading role it had exercised in the G-7. Despite the overall stagnation of capital flows in development aid, some countries such as France and Japan have bucked the trend by the relative dynamism of their development cooperation. Canada has taken a less active stand, more in line with the United Kingdom and the United States. This "anglotropism" has been a vector for an undeniable conservatism.

NON-STATE CHANNELS FOR AID

Multilateral Aid

In 1988–89, Canada devoted 32.2 per cent of its assistance to multilateral agencies, while the average for DAC members was 23.5 per cent.[18] Once again, it has found itself in a position midway between small and large donors. Canada placed sixth, behind Norway, Denmark, Finland, Austria, and Australia. It was, however, in the forefront of the G-7, with multilateral aid from the six other G-7 states varying between 9.4 per cent (France) and 27.1 per cent (Japan). With neither the sizeable financial resources nor the clout of a superpower, Canada clearly sides with the proponents of greater multilateralism. However, its support for multilateral structures and mechanisms of cooperation has been changing. From the early 1980s, the winds of bilateralism have swept strongly across Canada's entire external policy, culminating in the Canada–United States Free Trade Agreement. In development aid, Canada's traditional leading role within international organizations has steadily sagged with the relative decline of its financial input. Fifteen years ago, the country was devoting 40 per cent of its aid budget to multilateral assistance. Canadian policy has thus contributed to the overall compression of DAC multilateral aid, which dropped from an average of 33 per cent in 1980–81 to 23.5 per cent by the end of the 1980s.

Despite its decline, multilateral aid still remains a key aspect of Canadian development cooperation. Canada obviously does more than its part in sharing the burden of multilateral assistance. In 1988–89, it ensured 6.6 per cent of the funding for multilateral agencies, coming in fifth among DAC members, behind Japan, the United States, Germany, and Italy.[19] Canada's share was almost the same then as it was in the early 1980s. In terms of ranking, however, it was bumped down one place by the rise of Italy.[20] When the entire UN structure was made the butt of attacks from the United Kingdom and the United States, Canada mustered its sense of initiative. Its aid to multilateral agencies remained particularly high between 1983 and 1986. In 1985–86, its share of multilateral aid rose to 8.6 per cent, and Canada was momentarily tied with West Germany as the third-largest multilateral aid donor.

NGOs

NGOs constitute another major channel for Canadian aid. Their funding comes from two sources – private donations and government grants. According to a general trend that includes Canada, both sources are interlinked, in that the countries offering the largest government grants to NGOs are usually those with the greatest volume of private donations. In 1988, private donations collected by Canadian NGOs amounted to $218 million.[21] Canada was then in fourth place within the DAC, behind the United States, West Germany, and the United Kingdom. Canadian private aid made up 0.05 per cent of GNP in 1988, a proportion clearly above the DAC average (0.03 per cent).[22] On this score, Canada placed sixth within the DAC, behind Ireland, The Netherlands, Sweden, Norway, and West Germany. It thus trailed the majority of like-minded states but led almost all G-7 countries. Considering that the ratio of private aid to GNP probably best measures the generosity peculiar to each national political culture, the data give weight to the idea that Canada falls between G-7 countries and like-minded states in its aid performance.

Contributions from the Canadian government to NGOs amounted to $187 million in 1988–89 and put Canada, surpassed by only Japan and West Germany, in third place within the DAC.[23] In percentage of public aid granted to NGOs, Canada also came in third, behind Switzerland and the United States.[24] Canada's governmental support for NGOs has put the country on the top rung, ahead of both like-minded states and most G-7 nations. Nonetheless, the partnership forged between CIDA and NGOs raises a dilemma that concerns all donors. By encouraging private and public bodies to work closer together, it gives coherence to national policy but at the same time dilutes the independence of NGOs by increasingly subordinating them to government priorities.

ECONOMIC TERMS OF AID

Canada devoted 27.4 per cent of its aid to least-developed countries (LLDCs) in 1988–89, with the DAC average being 24.7 per cent.[25] Although it performed better than France, the United States, or Japan, it still lagged behind Denmark, Norway, and Italy. Remarkably, Canada bucked the general trend to increase aid to LLDCs during the 1980s. Whereas the average percentage of aid to LLDCs from DAC members rose measurably through the decade, Canada's fell slightly. In this respect, Canada has not been a leader. It does, however, grant aid on comparatively advantageous terms. In 1988–89, donations made up 97.8 per cent of Canada's ODA, whereas the DAC average was 75.6 per cent.[26] Eight DAC members – notably the Scandinavian states – outperformed Canada. Canada, however, has been more generous in its policy than all other G-7 members except the United Kingdom.

In analysis of the economic conditions of aid, the extent to which it is tied has traditionally provoked the most debate. The level of tied aid helps us to judge a donor's goals by showing whether it is acting to satisfy development needs or its own trading interests. Comparisons are hard to make, though, because no widely accepted definition exists of what tied aid is. Statistics available in this area should be used with some prudence.

Canada has traditionally had a very strict policy on tied aid. In the early 1980s, 60 per cent of its aid was tied, putting it in next-to-last place within the DAC, just ahead of Austria.[27] Canada projected at the time an image of a country avidly seeking to use aid as a lever for boosting exports to the Third World. This policy raised much criticism, in development circles as much as within the OECD. Canada's performance has significantly improved in recent years. In 1988, Canada rose to 11th place out of the 18 DAC members, with the percentage of its tied aid having been brought down to 34.5 per cent. Although aid from Canada certainly remained more tied than that from Denmark, The Netherlands, Norway, and Sweden, it was less so than that from France, Italy, the United Kingdom, and the United States. In the current context, Canada is one of the few countries to have reduced the extent to which its assistance is tied. Still, the recent shift in Canadian policy may not be as clearcut as it seems. Although the government admittedly came around to recognizing that its policy was too rigid, as attested by the new provisions established in the 1988 strategy, it had revised its accounting procedures in 1985 and set out a new definition of tied aid. From this date on – well before *Sharing Our Future* (1987) was released in 1988 – Canadian policy started to become more flexible. In other words, although Canadian aid is undeniably less tied than before, it is hard to measure precisely how the new policy serves Third World interests better.

BENEFICIARIES OF AID

The two major target areas for Canadian aid are sub-Saharan Africa and South Asia.[29] In 1988–89, Canada devoted 39.8 per cent of its bilateral aid to sub-Saharan Africa. With their much closer historical ties to this area, almost all European donor countries accorded it even greater relative importance in their aid programs. Canada was nonetheless above the DAC average (33.1 per cent). Moreover, Canada's conduct in sub-Saharan Africa has been relatively forward-looking. As early as 1975–76, the region received 35.6 per cent of Canadian aid, whereas the DAC average was only 23.4 per cent. Even though Canada has followed the international trend to pull out from South Asia over the past 15 years, it still maintained a sizeable presence in that part of the world as of the end of the 1980s. At that time, it placed third – behind the United Kingdom and Denmark – in the proportion of aid funnelled to that area.

Examination of the degree of overlap between recipients of Canadian aid and those of other states reveals that in 1988–89, six countries (India, Indonesia, China, Pakistan, Bangladesh, Tanzania) were among the ten main beneficiaries of aid from both Canada and DAC members.[30] Twenty years ago, only four countries fell within this zone of overlap. Although slight, this change attests to growing convergence between beneficiaries of Canadian aid and those of all DAC members taken together. It suggests growing consensus among donors on the high-priority targets for international development cooperation. Canada has in its own way helped bring this consensus about, and its assistance increasingly conforms to the standardized guidelines of the international aid regime.

Parcelled out to over one hundred developing countries, Canadian aid is striking by its high degree of dispersal. Whether one takes as a criterion for comparison the proportion of the aid budget allocated to the first recipient country or the first 25, assistance from all DAC donors in 1988–89 was more concentrated than that from Canada. This dispersal of Canadian aid obviously results from a time-honoured tradition. Nevertheless, some say that it represents a major obstacle to maximizing the effectiveness of Canada's program.[31]

The reasons for this dispersal relate to systemic and national factors. From a systemic standpoint, Canada's conduct has fallen in line with a general trend in several donor countries. During the period 1970–89, all G-7 members widened the focus of their development cooperation programs, reflecting their desire to diversify external policy. Greater dispersal of external assistance – better distribution of it among the three main continents of the developing world – would help to spread the donor country's presence. Alongside these systemic pressures, other explanatory factors arise specifically from the Canadian context. On the geopolitical front, Canada is not tied to any one area of the Third World. It is not bound by strategic interests, or by a network of post-colonial relations. Although this situation does not explain dispersal of Canadian assistance as such, it does help account for the rather unique voluntarism on which it is based.

Bereft of deep historical roots, Canada's persona in the Third World has over the last 50 years developed largely with the ebb and flow of internal demands from various interest groups.[32] Canada's status as the richest ex-dominion was the basis for its firm commitment to the Commonwealth, thus leading the country to make its first steps into the developing world in Asia, Africa, and the Caribbean. National policy on bilingualism later induced Canada to become an active promoter of la Francophonie and to set up aid programs relatively balanced between French- and English-speaking Africa. Canada's location in the western hemisphere, bolstered by increasingly large migration flows, led to sustained participation in development of the Americas. As awareness grew in the 1970s of the Pacific Rim's strategic value, Canada decided to increase its presence in Asia. Evidently, Canadian aid policy as a whole cannot be understood if no account is taken of all these historical and geographical determinants. Canada's situation is probably unique insofar as the government, with a small population and limited resources, is faced with highly diverse demands. With an extra boost of legitimacy from the official ideology of multiculturalism, the political will to strike a balance as fair as possible among all these demands explains, more than any other factor, the wide distribution of Canada's aid program.

Because its aid is so dispersed, Canada rarely tops the list of donors in any one country.[33] It has made little effort to develop a true zone of influence in which it could wield decisive power over the development policy of the countries that it assists. As common sense would suggest, the United States, Japan, and France are the ones that most often play the part of main donor. In 1988, Guyana was the only country where Canada came in first among donor states. Yet since Guyana receives little aid, there is evidently not much competition among donors. Jamaica and Colombia, where Canada came in second among aid donors, are probably the only countries of any importance where Canada could exert some influence. Elsewhere, its presence in 1988 never exceeded 15 per cent of total assistance received. In the two countries receiving the most Canadian aid – Bangladesh and Pakistan – Canada came in third place and fourth place, respectively, among donors. Its contribution, however, represented but 12.6 per cent of the total aid received by Bangladesh, and 6.4 per cent of Pakistan's.

Dispersal of assistance obviously entails some costs for Canada. It saps the country's ability to influence recipients' development policy. Moreover, it complicates coordination between Canada and other donors in their development programs. From the government's standpoint, these costs so far appear to have been lower than the benefits of aid dispersal. The most important benefit lies probably in the fact that Canada, through development cooperation, has greatly raised its international profile. Still, one may evidently wonder whether this view of matters is compatible with maximizing the effectiveness of development aid. In the final analysis, it is not surprising that the number of recipient countries has become a major issue in the current debate over the future of Canadian aid policy.[34]

AID PRIORITIES

During the 1980s, policy choices in the donor community were dominated largely by the issues of structural adjustment and poverty alleviation.[35] In the strategy released in 1988, Ottawa fell into line with this trend by making these issues the first two thematic goals of its ODA charter. Although Canada has occasionally distinguished itself by taking forward-looking positions, its leadership has been tarnished by a substantial shortfall between its intentions and its actions.

In order to compare Canada's policy priorities with those of other donor countries, we should note first the growing consensus within the international community on both the need for and the objectives of structural adjustment.[36] In the early 1980s, donors as different as Japan and Sweden identified with the culture of structural adjustment less enthusiastically, for various economic and political reasons. But as the Canadian government observed in a report on Third World debt released in 1990, donor countries now tend to agree that structural adjustment has become inevitable.[37] Within the limits of its capabilities, Canada has fostered the emergence of this international consensus. On the macro-economic level, the differences between Canada's position and that of other bilateral and multilateral donors thus boil down to a fine shade of opinion.

Among the few truly controversial subjects, alleviating the public debt load of developing countries has received most attention. Canada, like most European nations, has held to a more flexible policy than have the United States and Japan. It was one of the first to convert its entire bilateral aid program to grants. Still, it seems relatively satisfied with the status quo and has put forward no truly novel ideas, as have The Netherlands and the United Kingdom in Paris Club meetings of the leading donors.[38] Canada has sought case-by-case solutions instead of overall ones to the debt problem. In this perspective, its 1990 decision to ease terms of repayment for English-speaking Caribbean countries may be likened to efforts by the United States and France on behalf of Egypt and French-speaking Africa, respectively. In all these cases, a clientelistic approach informed decision making.

The importance given to the market in the development process is another dimension of discussions over structural adjustment where diverging views have cropped up in the donor community. Canada's stand has been closer to the American, British, and Japanese positions than to the French and Italian ones. The Canadian government has nonetheless avoided adopting a stance as radical as the one taken by the United States on reducing the state's role in the economy and privatizing government corporations en masse. In decision-making procedures relating to structural adjustment, Canada has sought to make more room for national aid agencies when programs arranged on the multilateral level are being drawn up. The World Bank, in its discourse, strongly favours greater coordination and cooperation among donors. Yet reality has not always lived up to this intention. While recognizing the pivotal role of international financial institutions (IFIs) in the adjustment process, Canada has actively promoted its views on some economic options by sharing with the World Bank its expertise on such countries as Bangladesh and Ghana.

Canada also takes pride in its having led the way – together with UNICEF and like-minded countries – to greater awareness of the impact of structural adjustment on poor populations.[39] Even though Canada converted later than like-minded countries to favouring adjustment with a human face, it has still been instrumental in helping shape dominant thinking on the supposedly automatic benefits of structural adjustment. Moreover, as illustrated by its commitment to the Program of Action to Mitigate the Social Costs of Adjustment (PAMSCAD) in Ghana and the Social Impact Amelioration Program (SIMAP) in Guyana, it was one of the first to point out the potential of NGOs for lowering the social costs of adjustment.[40] Canada's aid program, however – in comparison with those of other donor countries – does not appear to leave much room for the specific needs of populations most in need.

Of course, it is not easy to calculate – and a fortiori to compare – the proportion of aid that each donor country devotes to the fight against poverty. The UNDP has developed three indices that are all useful approximations: proportion of aid that goes to the social sector (aid social-sector ratio), proportion of social-sector aid committed to human priority areas (aid priority ratio), and a composite index based on the two previous ones and the percentage of GNP devoted to ODA (aid human expenditure ratio).[41] On the third index – the most significant – Canada came in 10th out of 12 DAC members in 1989. Its performance (0.023) was below the group average (0.026), putting it only above Italy and the United States. Not surprising, frontrunners were The Netherlands, Denmark, and Sweden. Yet Canada also lagged behind other G-7 members (France, West Germany, and the United Kingdom). The first two indices showed a similar pattern, with Canada placing ninth in expenditures for the social sector, a performance (19.9 per cent) below the DAC average (22.6 per cent). Finally, in aid expenditures for human priority needs, Canada (25.9 per cent) was also below average (at 36.6 per cent), with a ninth-place standing.

Although the data may have been arrived at through imperfect method, they suggest that Canada is not among the leading donors when it comes to working out a genuine strategy for alleviating poverty in developing countries. This situation further undermines the government's credibility, inasmuch as *Sharing Our Future* putatively made the fight against poverty the primordial goal of all Canadian assistance. Whereas, as noted above, structural adjustment and alleviation of poverty were the two major themes in the donor community during the 1980s, it seems that Canada has ultimately attached more importance to the former than to the latter.

CONCLUSION: A WAVERING LEADERSHIP

The international aid regime is based on a number of interests that Canada shares with other donors. Aid enables all developed countries to diversify their external relations and increase their presence in the Third World. It also serves to strengthen international peace and stability. Beyond these generic characteristics, Canada's assistance has of course its own peculiarities, which help define its national identity on the world stage. Its strong involvement in the Commonwealth and la Francophonie, for example, stands out prominently. Yet, according to the comparison just made, Canada's singularity arises ultimately from its lying between the G-7 and the like-minded nations in its commitment to development cooperation.

Although this conclusion needs to be qualified, it does provide a fairly good picture of Canada's international position in aid. It is based on the volume of assistance – the most decisive indicator for ranking a nation in the workings of the aid regime. On this score, Canada falls precisely midway between the G-7 and the like-minded countries. Although their significance is less clear, other indicators support the same conclusion – official assistance and private grants as a percentage of GNP, as well as multilateral aid as a proportion of assistance provided. In terms of policy goals, Canada's position on structural adjustment also appears to be a compromise between the more rigid positions of the G-7 and the more flexible ones of the like-minded countries. Canadian aid, however, does not always result from such a balancing act. In certain respects, such as cooperation with NGOs or integration of women into development, Canada has indeed led the way. In others, such as alleviation of poverty or – until recently – tied aid, it has been pulling up the rear.

The specificity of Canadian aid lies in a variety of structural and social factors. From a structural viewpoint, Canadian aid should be related to the international power structure and Canada's place in it.[42] Canada has traditionally sought a dynamic aid policy in order to raise its status in the community of nations and to legitimize its presence within the world economic elite. Shortly after the Second World War, it saw itself propelled to the forefront of the international community and has since sought to maintain this position by all means available. Therein lies, however, a task that is proving increasingly difficult, given that Canada is inexorably losing power in relation to other major industrialized countries. Few areas of foreign policy exist where Canada can exercise a determining role. It cannot lay claim to genuine leadership in the solution of regional conflicts. Nor can it play such a role in the regulation of international trading and financial systems. Even in North-South negotiations, its poorly diversified production structure and meagre trade with the Third World prevent it from being an actor of consequence and often confine it to symbolic duties.[43] Because of the shortfall between its means and its ambitions, Canada is continually having to redefine its international identity.

In concrete terms, the government has unendingly sought new openings for promoting the country's skills and resources. Development aid has steadily established itself as one such opening. In comparison with other donor countries, Canada's development cooperation has developed through an approach that has been more voluntarist and less marked by necessity. This feature is probably not unrelated to the fact that Canada is recognized worldwide for its highly progressive rhetoric. Not only has the government articulated a forward-looking discourse on such precise issues as women or human rights, but it has also enriched the overall problématique of development with concepts such as partnership and sustainability.[44] Canada resolutely seeks to project the image of a country that is prosperous, modern, and very much concerned about its international responsibilities.

Discourse aside, Canada's contribution to development assistance remains modest. There are obviously limits to Canada's generosity and interest in the Third World's demands, depending on the health of the Canadian economy and on political considerations. On the whole, Canada's aid policy goals are set in conjunction with the G-7's. Things could not be otherwise, given the importance that Canada attaches to membership in this bloc of nations. Its policy priorities could not truly depart from the dominant ideas therein. This constraint bears down all the more because the entire external policy of Canada is strongly conditioned by that of the United States. Operating in a context of limited independence, Canada aspires to exercise a credible role of intermediary between the G-7 and the like-minded countries.

Within the aid community, Canada has the unique advantage of being a borderline-member in both the G-7 and the like-minded group of nations. This situation clearly puts the country in a class of its own.[45] The government contends that the fluidity of Canada's international persona enables it to work within different coalitions. The depth of this perception, on which there is wide-ranging consensus among politicians, explains the extensive continuity of Canadian aid policy, despite changes of government. It is probably true that the constant search for a fair middle ground[46] – reflecting a political culture built on the foundation of a decentralized federal system – confers a power of mediation on this country. However, it appears also to have hampered its capabilities for innovation.

The relative dynamism of Canadian aid has, moreover, deep roots in civil society. Canada's internationalism draws on a dominant ideology which legitimizes state intervention in response to the inadequacies of the marketplace. As well, the fact that Canada is a former colony made up of immigrants from the four corners of the earth explains why the population feels particularly responsible for its external environment. This context fostered the work of NGOs. Besides helping to implement Canadian assistance, NGOs engage in lobbying and development education. It is no accident that Canada has shown leadership in development cooperation policy, especially in those areas where NGOs are active. In comparison with most European countries, in Canada international news is less abundant and the Third World holds a marginal place in national election campaigns. NGOs have therefore been decisive in the reaching of a wide-ranging social consensus on matters of aid.

In contrast to this generally rich tradition, the outlook for Canadian development cooperation today seems grim. Questioning of Canadian policy has intensified, the aid budget having been under considerable pressure since 1989.[47] The decision to reduce aid funding was in fact only a partial surprise, given that throughout the 1980s the government continually extended its timetable for reaching the goal of 0.7 per cent. Several conventional explanations are usually advanced to account for this setback. The government points to its huge deficit to justify recent compressions in aid. Some observers have noted that, as in other habitually generous countries such as The Netherlands and Sweden, in Canada, people have less enthusiasm for aid to the Third World than formerly.

These elements towards an explanation reveal but one part of why Canada has lost leadership in the field of aid. In fact, this loss cannot be dissociated from the serious identity crisis through which the country is passing. With an acuteness unmatched by any other developed country, Canada ponders its place and potential role in the emerging new world order. The identity crisis is twofold – political and economic. On the political front, because debate over the constitution has become bogged down, the very survival of the country is far from certain. Quebec's independence would inevitably bring about a fundamental review of national foreign policy, if only by delegitimizing Canada's participation in the G-7. On the economic front, the budget deficit is but the tip of the iceberg. The real problem is that since increases in productivity are weaker in Canada than elsewhere, the national economy is becoming less and less competitive. Although Canada is still the seventh-largest industrial power in the developed world, the gap separating it from the sixth-place United Kingdom grows ever wider, while the distance from eighth-place Spain continues to shrink.[48]

These tensions affect the country's foreign policy and, indirectly, its aid policy. The government is less hard-pressed to invest its energies and resources in external relations. Canada is thus inclined to adopt a low profile on the international scene. Its discreet involvement in the incredible upheavals in eastern Europe and its feeble participation in the European Bank for Reconstruction and Development attest to the pullback in Canada's foreign policy. Over the last decade, Canada has become more inward-looking. This trend may last a long time, since a genuine solution may not be found in the near future for the country's underlying problems. In such circumstances, it is unlikely that Canadian aid could again assume the importance that it once had.

NOTES

1 Even though some eastern European and developing countries also provide development aid, this comparison will be limited to countries belonging to the DAC of the OECD; they accounted for 85 per cent of

international aid each year by the end of the 1980s. In 1990, the DAC
was composed of 18 Western countries.

2 Among the best-known of these is the one by R.D. McKinlay, "The Aid
Relationship: A Foreign Policy Model and Interpretation of the
Distribution of Official Bilateral Economic Aid of the United States, the
United Kingdom, France and Germany 1960–1970," *Comparative
Political Studies* 11 no. 4 (1979); 411–63.

3 See Stephen Browne, *Foreign Aid in Practice* (London: Pinter 1990);
B. Mothander and A. Kämpe, *Policies, Procedures and Organisation of
Bilateral Development Assistance*, Report prepared for the Swedish
International Development Authority (Stockholm: SIDA 1988).

4 See Michel Houndjahoué, "À propos de la coopération dominante et
marginale: la France et le Canada en Afrique francophone," *Revue
canadienne d'études du développement* 4 no. 1 (1983); 164–73; Olav Stokke,
ed., *Western Middle Powers and Global Poverty: The Determinants of the Aid
Policies of Canada, Denmark, The Netherlands, Norway and Sweden* (Uppsala:
Scandinavian Institute of African Studies 1989).

5 L.-M. Imbeau, *Donor Aid – the Determinants of Development Allocations to Third
World Countries: A Comparative Analysis* (New York: Peter Lang 1989);
Burghard Claus et al., *Coordination of the Development Cooperation Policies
of Major OECD Donor Countries* (Berlin: German Development
Institute 1989).

6 See CIDA, Policy Branch, *Preliminary Comparison of the Performance of
Canadian Aid in 1977 with That of Other Member Countries of the OECD's
Development Aid Committee* (Hull: CIDA 1979).

7 On the concept of regime, see S. Krasner, *International Regimes* (Ithaca,
NY: Cornell University Press 1983); F. Kratochwil and J.G. Ruggie,
"International Organization: A State of the Art on an Art of the State,"
International Organization 40 no. 4 (1986), 753–75. Robert Wood has
used the notion for the analysis of development assistance in *From Marshall
Plan to Debt Crisis: Foreign Aid and Development Choices in the World
Economy* (Berkeley: University of California Press 1986).

8 See John Holmes, "Les institutions internationales et la politique
extérieure," *Études internationales* 1 no. 2 (1970), 34; and Gérard
Hervouet, "La politique étrangère canadienne dans son environnement
international et régional," in Gérard Hervouet, ed., *Les politiques
étrangères régionales du Canada: éléments et matériaux* (Quebec: CQRI–Presses
de l'Université Laval 1983), 177.

9 See Ronald Manzer, *Public Policies and Political Development in Canada*
(Toronto: University of Toronto Press 1985); and Seymour Martin
Lipset, "Valeurs et institutions au Canada et aux États-Unis," in Lauren
McKinsey et al., *Une frontière dans la tête. Culture, institutions et imaginaire
canadiens* (Montreal: Liber 1991), 95–9.

10 OECD, *Development Co-operation: 1990 Report* (Paris: OECD 1990), 189.

11 Ibid., 268.

12 Ibid., 188.

13 The fact that from 1986 onwards Italy's volume of aid has exceeded Canada's is of particular importance. Both countries are known to pursue the same goal – avoiding rock-bottom status within the G-7.

14 OECD, *Development Co-operation: 1990 Report*, 189.

15 OECD, *Twenty-five Years of Development Co-operation: A Review* (Paris: OECD 1985), 93; OECD, *Development Co-operation: 1986 Report* (Paris: OECD 1986), 224.

16 See OECD, *Development Co-operation: 1986 Report*, 75; OECD, *Development Co-operation: 1990 Report*, 136–41.

17 Department of Finance, *The Budget Tabled in the House of Commons by the Honourable Michael Wilson* (Ottawa, February 1991), 68.

18 OECD, *Development Co-operation: 1990 Report*, 193.

19 Author's calculation based on ibid., 186 and 193.

20 David Protheroe, *Canada and Multilateral Aid* (Ottawa: North-South Institute 1991), 50.

21 OECD, *Development Co-operation: 1990 Report*, 248.

22 Ibid., 190.

23 Ibid.

24 Ibid., 196, data for 1987–88.

25 Ibid., 193.

26 Ibid., 191.

27 OECD, *Development Co-operation: 1984 Report* (Paris: OECD 1984), 219.

28 OECD, *Development Co-operation: 1990 Report*, 192.

29 Ibid., 195.

30 Ibid., 223–42.

31 OECD, "Examen de l'aide du Canada par le CAD," Press release, 7 December 1990, 3.

32 See Louis Sabourin, "Le Canada et le Tiers Monde: des voix et des voies ...," in Jean-Philippe Thérien, ed., *La quête du développement. Horizons canadien et africain* (Montreal: ACFAS-GRETSE 1988), 40–1.

33 See OECD, *Geographical Distribution of Financial Flows to Developing Countries* (Paris: OECD 1991).

34 Parliament, House of Commons, Standing Committee on External Affairs and International Trade, *Minutes of Proceedings and Evidence of the Standing Committee on External Affairs and International Trade*, 34th Parl., 3rd sess., Issue No. 52 (16 February 1993), 9–10.

35 These two issues were particularly emphasized in A. Cornia, R. Jolly, and F. Stewart, *Adjustment with a Human Face* (New York: Oxford University Press 1987).

36 Claus et al., *Coordination*, 59.

37 External Affairs and International Trade Canada, *Government Response to the Report of the Standing Committee on External Affairs and International Trade Entitled: "Securing Our Global Future: Canada's Stake in the Unfinished Business of Third World Debt"* (Ottawa: Minister of Supply and Services Canada 1990), 13–14.

38 Standing Committee on External Affairs and International Trade, *Unanswered Questions/Uncertain Hopes* (Ottawa, March 1991), 15.

39 Cranford Pratt, "Towards a Neo-conservative Transformation of Canadian International Development Assistance: The SECOR Report on CIDA," *International Journal* 47 (summer 1992), 612.

40 See Conseil canadien pour la coopération internationale, *Le défi de la dette et de l'ajustement structurel,* Rapport périodique no. 3 (1991), 2.

41 United Nations Development Programme, *Human Development Report 1991* (New York: Oxford University Press 1991), 53–7.

42 For a general discussion of this question, see Bernard Wood, *The Middle Powers and the General Interest* (Ottawa: North-South Institute 1988).

43 Cranford Pratt, "Canada: An Eroding and Limited Internationalism," in Pratt, ed., *Internationalism under Strain: The North-South Policies of Canada, The Netherlands, Norway, and Sweden* (Toronto: University of Toronto Press 1989), 24–69.

44 On partnership, see CIDA, *Sharing Our Future: Canada's International Development Assistance* (Ottawa: Supply and Services 1987), 63–79; on sustainability, see CIDA, Policy Branch, *Sustainable Development: A Discussion Paper* (Hull: CIDA, March 1991).

45 Claus et al., *Coordination,* 9.

46 See Kimon Valaskakis, *Canada in the Nineties: Meltdown or Renaissance* (Ottawa: World Media Institute 1990), 83–99.

47 At the end of 1992, new cuts to the aid budget were announced by the government. These cuts, which extend to 1994–95, amount to more than $600 million. See Manon Tessier, *Canadian International Relations Chronicle: October–December 1992* (Quebec: Centre québécois de relations internationales 1993), 11.

48 When this chapter was being written, Spain did not belong to the DAC. It announced its intention to become a member in 1991. As mentioned above, Australia had until then been the eighth-largest economic power in this group.

13 Humane Internationalism and Canadian Development Assistance Policies

CRANFORD PRATT

The detailed and substantial chapters in this volume provide an opportunity to consider a major paradox in Canadian development assistance policies. The Canadian public and Parliament have supported aid for over forty years, primarily for humanitarian reasons; nevertheless, most scholarly commentators have concluded that humanitarian considerations have played little role within government in the shaping of those policies.[1] On the basis of the chapters above, we ought to be able to consider this paradox rather closely and to discuss what have in fact been the major determinants of Canadian aid policies.

THE PARADOX MORE FULLY EXPOUNDED

The Western Middle Powers Project, in which 18 scholars recently undertook a major study of the North-South policies of Canada, The Netherlands, and the Scandinavian countries,[2] concluded that humane internationalism – acceptance that the industrialized states have ethical obligations relating to global poverty – had informed public philosophy[3] in these middle powers. Though often overwhelmed by more wordly considerations, sensitivity to the development needs of the poorest countries and peoples within the Third World had by the 1970s become widespread among the citizens of these countries and provided a substantial underpinning for government policies that putatively sought to meet these needs.

Public opinion polls corroborate that, at least until recently, a substantial proportion of the Canadian public has long supported a generous Canadian aid effort. An Adcom poll in 1980 showed that 78 per cent of those interviewed agreed that the level of Canadian aid should either be kept as it was or be increased. Gallop polls from 1975 to 1981 were roughly consistent with these results.[4] This pattern continued throughout the 1980s. There has been some diminution of support since 1987, but, considering the state of the economy, the majority that continued to favour official development assistance (ODA) remained impressively high, at least until 1992. For example, in 1987, 81.3 per cent of those with an opinion on aid levels felt that they were either too low or the right amount. Four years later, although the proportion had fallen, it was, at 74.1 per cent, still remarkably high.[5]

These polls reflected a basic congruence between a humane internationalist aid policy and the liberal public philosophy[6] that was dominant in Canada at least until the mid-1980s. In addition, the fact that support for aid did not collapse in the 1980s, despite the sustained recession, suggests that the humane internationalist strand of Canadian political culture remained resilient. However, it was never so robust as to generate a politically compelling demand for a major and generous aid policy. When the government promoted such an aid policy, as to some extent it did from 1968 to 1976, it could count on public support for it. However, when the government diluted the quality of the program, after 1976, or cut ODA as a proportion of gross national product (GNP), as it has done recurrently since 1989, it could do so without serious political risk. Even substantial cuts to the aid budget announced in 1989 and again in 1992 did not generate a major popular reaction.

It is reasonable to suggest that the severe economic crisis that Canada faced in the 1980s diminished whatever political salience might have attached to the support for CIDA that the polls revealed. So also, rather perversely, did the increasing intensity of the economic and social problems faced by so many Third World countries. The buoyancy and optimism that were a feature of the great upsurge of involvement with development issues in the late 1960s and the 1970s were much harder to sustain in the 1980s. The polls themselves, by the end of the 1980s, showed that widespread support for a generous aid program might not have proven reliable under pressure. In 1988, 69 per cent of those interviewed believed that aid never reached those for whom it was intended, and 62 per cent felt that recipient governments were not really committed to helping their peoples. Two years later, these proportions were 81 per cent and 69 per cent. As well, in these same two years, first 79 per cent and then 87 per cent believed that Canada should help its own needy first.[7]

In 1992, several surveys indicated that the public was no longer as sympathetic to a major aid program as it had long seemed to be. The

Communication Unit of the Canadian Council for International Cooperation (CCIC) concluded on the evidence of three separate polls that "public concern about international affairs and aid is slowly slipping [and] support for aid among current supporters is soft."[8] An analysis done for CIDA of a 1992 survey of socio-cultural change suggested that 46 per cent of those questioned believed that Canada was spending too much on foreign aid[9] – a far higher proportion than even a few years earlier. This last analysis speculated that this decline in popular support for ODA was related to greater awareness of the problem of the fiscal deficit and to scepticism about the effectiveness of aid.[10]

There is evidence that as the public became seized of the problem of the federal fiscal deficit, its attachment to foreign aid waned. For example, a Southam poll in May 1993 posited the deficit as a central problem and asked what government spending should be cut because of it. Seventy per cent of those questioned named development assistance – a higher proportion than mentioned any other possible cut. It seems likely, however, that factors even more fundamental than public acknowledgment of the deficit crisis are causing a shift in Canadian values away from liberal internationalism and towards narrow preoccupation with immediate national self-interest. First, the emergence of a limited but growing number of less-developed countries (LDCs) able to compete successfully with Canadian industries, along with the growing importance of international trade, have greatly increased the preoccupation of many Canadians as well as their federal government with immediate economic advantage.[11]

Second, a profound shift is occurring within the Canadian political culture concerning domestic social values. The national commitment to an effective "social net" to ensure a minimum level of welfare whatever one's income is clearly no longer as universal as it once was, nor is it identified as frequently as a valued and distinctive feature of Canadian society. As Canadian society becomes less caring towards its own poor, it is likely that it is also becoming less concerned about those beyond its borders.

Third, another factor of similar breadth and generality is identified in chapter 12 of this volume by Thérien, who suggests that erosion of Canada's sense of national identity and the apparent inability of Canadians to resolve their constitutional crisis may well lessen the nation's capacity and inclination to play a prominent role as a liberal, internationalist middle power. It is a persuasive observation, which further explains the recent marked diminution in the vigour and influence of the humane internationalist component within the Canadian political culture.

Nevertheless, however dramatic the changes perhaps taking place in political culture, the evidence is substantial that until quite recently popular sentiment largely accepted a major aid program. Moreover, the motivation for this support was always intrinsically altruistic; only a very small portion of those polled gave either commercial gain for Canada or foreign policy advantages as a main reason for supporting the aid program. The 1989 version of *Report to CIDA: Public Attitudes towards International Development Assistance* that CIDA commissioned annually from 1985 to 1992 indicated that a high percentage of people continued to believe "that one of the best things about Canadians is that we are generous and ready to help people in need," and the report in 1991 found a similarly large proportion believing that Canada should have an aid program because "people are suffering and we have a responsibility to help."[12]

One of the companies that had done some of this polling, Decima Research Ltd, in 1985 came to a conclusion similar to that of the Western Middle Powers Project: "[the image of] Canada as a moral, humane, peaceable, caring society is a very deeply embedded image, and is a very important aspect of the Canadian identity."[13]

This humane internationalism found expression in two unanimous parliamentary reports, one in 1980 and the second in 1987.[14] Each recommended in uncompromising terms that the primary purpose of the aid program must be to help the poorest. In response to the persistent evidence that public support for CIDA was motivated primarily by humanitarian considerations, from the mid-1960s on, the rhetoric used by CIDA about ODA has been cast principally in humanitarian and internationalist terms. This was true, for example, of the statement of objectives that accompanied the estimates when they were presented to Parliament each year. It was also true of the three most important official policy statements on ODA issued by the government – in 1970, 1975, and 1988.[15]

We thus arrive at a central paradox about Canadian ODA at least until 1992. This assistance was presented by the government to the Canadian public primarily as a humanitarian undertaking and has been supported by this public and by Parliament with that understanding. Most commentators on Canadian aid, however, see these policies as having been shaped by quite different considerations. No consensus has emerged on what have been the most important of these considerations. The long-term interests of capitalism in Canada, the importance attached by senior decision makers to Canada's major alliances, changing views on foreign aid within the OECD, the dominant ideology among senior decision makers, immediate commercial gains, and bureaucratic self-interest have each been emphasized by different au-

thors. However, almost all have agreed that humanitarian considerations have not been a major determinant of Canadian aid policies.

Canadian aid policies have in fact been shaped largely by senior decision makers rather than driven by public opinion or dominated by
partisan political calculations. This statist view of decision making on
ODA is common in the literature and is substantially reflected in this
volume. There have been decisions imposed on the bureaucracy by its
political masters, and these have increased in number in recent
years.[16] However, they have not been so persistent as to undermine the
validity of an overall statist view of decision making on aid. Even less
has that view been challenged by examples of the importance of public
opinion. Few if any major policies have been a direct consequence of
an insistent tide of popular pressure. Even the very large increases in
aid expenditures between 1965 and 1975 are seen best as facilitated
by, rather than caused by, the public's increasing responsiveness to the
humane internationalism of that era. Similarly, the rapid series of cuts
to CIDA's budget in the years 1989–93 were generated by the shifting
judgment of senior decision makers about what was in Canada's interest. These reductions paralleled weakening of Canadian internationalism but hardly seem to have been summoned forth by it.

Thus we must seek the main explanation for the evolution of Canadian aid policies in the factors and influences to which senior decision
makers have been responsive, rather than in the dynamics of domestic
politics or in any gradual value shifts within the political culture as a
whole. The section that follows examines the main considerations that
have influenced senior decision makers as they shaped Canadian ODA
policies. Because the content of these considerations and their comparative importance have shifted over the years, we shall look in turn
at changes in these policies in six periods – 1950–64, 1964–76, 1977–
85, 1985–88, and 1989–92, and 1992–95.

THE SHAPING OF CANADA'S AID POLICIES

1950–64 ⪦ FOREIGN-POLICY -DRIVEN

It is possible to write with confidence about the early years of Canadian
ODA because of the quality and comprehensiveness of three major
studies – Keith Spicer's 1965 book, Patricia Appavoo's 1989 doctoral
dissertation, and David Morrison's nearly completed history of CIDA
and Canadian aid policy.[17] They establish that foreign policy provided
the primary motivation for Canadian ODA in that period.

Canada, in consort with the United States, extended substantial assistance to Britain and to western Europe in the immediate post-war

era. US aid was motivated by two concerns – to check the expansion of Communist influence and to ensure the reintegration of the economies of western Europe into an open international economic system.[18] Ottawa, needless to say, shared these objectives. However, a few years later, when the possibility was broached of similar international assistance to the newly independent states of Southeast Asia, Canada was cautious, and it remained so until the mid-1960s. One official later recalled: "most ministers ... felt on familiar grounds when dealing with Europeans, but hundreds of millions of Asians, diseased or starving or both, raised questions of a quite different order."[19]

Ottawa thought that it could not stand apart from the American-led effort to draw the newly independent states into the anti-Soviet camp. It shared the US preoccupation with the Cold War.[20] As well, Canada's active interest in the United Nations and the Commonwealth, and its close alliance with the United States and Britain meant that it was bound to some extent to follow the American and British lead in regard to foreign aid. Canada therefore participated in the Colombo Plan, the capital assistance program to the Commonwealth states of Southeast Asia, from its beginning in 1950. Canada soon initiated aid programs in a number of newly independent African and Caribbean countries. Canada also contributed to UN and other multilateral relief and development programs.

Canada did these things cautiously and timidly.[21] Aid allocations grew only very slowly from 1950 to 1964. Indeed, net disbursements were significantly lower for 1961–63 than they had been in 1960. By 1964, Canadian ODA had fallen from an already low 0.19 per cent of Canadian GNP to 0.16 per cent.[22] In 1961, Canada's aid as a proportion of GNP ranked 11th of the 12 states then members of the Development Assistance Committee (DAC) of the OECD.[23] Lester Pearson, in his memoirs written years later, conceded that, as regards foreign aid, his government had "wished to stay out of the vanguard."[24] His government and that of John Diefenbaker had clearly realized this wish.

Foreign policy concerns thus determined both the emergence of a Canadian aid program and the choice of the countries to benefit from it, while fiscal caution limited its dimensions. The detailed content of the program, in turn, revealed Ottawa's responsiveness to corporate and commercial interests. Until 1960, the program was administered by the Department of Industry, Trade and Commerce (ITC). From the start, aid was tied entirely to domestic goods and services. No effort was made to come to a considered judgment about the long-term place of aid in foreign policy or about the development needs of recipient countries.[25] Instead, decisions about content were influenced heavily by ITC's judgment of what would be of value to Canadian exporters. In the first year of the Colombo Plan, for example, Ottawa insisted that its contribution would in significant part be made in Canadian grain, as it did again from 1957 to 1962.[26]

The External Aid Office (EAO), which had been created in 1960 and was within the Department of External Affairs, grew in size but remained without any real expertise in development economics or much knowledge of the countries that it was hoping to assist. External Affairs had blocked both creation of a career service of aid specialists and the posting overseas of EAO staff. EAO was an implementing agency located in Ottawa and staffed by administrators, engineers, and ex-military officers.

1964–76 = COLD WAR EFFORT TO ULL SHOWING INDEPENDENCE FROM US

A major change in Ottawa's attitude to ODA came in the mid-1960s. The initial reason for this was US pressure. Washington had long seen foreign aid as an important part of its Cold War effort to contain the influence of the Soviet Union. It had therefore begun to press other Western governments to expand aid. Canada was weakly placed to resist this pressure. It endorsed the twin US objectives of containing Soviet influence and integrating newly independent nations into an open international economic system. It was, moreover, one of the richest of OECD members. Wishing not to jeopardize its position as an active and influential member of the Western alliance, Canada began rapidly to increase its foreign aid. By 1970, Canadian ODA had risen to 0.41 per cent of GNP – a significant increase over the 1964 figure of 0.16 per cent. By 1975, it had reached 0.50 per cent. Total aid allocations in 1964–65 had been $149.48 million. They were $903 million in 1975.[27]

The substantial growth in ODA in the second half of the 1960s thus had its origins in a foreign policy concern to maintain Canada's standing within the US-led anti-communist alliance.[28] However, other factors must quickly have become more important, for ODA as a proportion of GNP was soon substantially higher than the equivalent American and British figures. In 1975–76, for example, when Canada's proportion was 0.50 per cent, the US and British figures were 0.26 per cent and 0.39 per cent, respectively.[29] In Lester Pearson's last years as prime minister and in Pierre Trudeau's early years in that office, new considerations had intervened. Ottawa had come to the view that a major aid program was a particularly apt way for Canada to demonstrate its independence in foreign policy and show that it was not merely a submissive US ally. Moreover, the late 1960s saw insurgent nationalism not only generally in Canada but in particular in the Liberal party. Expanded and improved ODA seemed, as indeed it was, an appropriate component of a more independent foreign policy.[30] The decision to make ODA a significant element in foreign policy coincided with the emergence in Canadian political culture of a much stronger humane internationalism (see chapter 4, above). As a result, expansion of Canada's development assistance program was facilitated by its wide popularity.[31]

Canadian foreign policy since 1945 had long been recognized as particularly internationalist in its commitments. Canada had won this reputation largely by its efforts to promote international peace and to strengthen the United Nations, NATO, GATT, and the new post-war international financial institutions (IFIs). In the late 1960s, Ottawa's internationalism expanded to include support for international development. The government had not suddenly been seized of ethical imperatives.[32] Instead, it had become convinced that a major and genuine commitment to sustained development in the Third World would serve three central objectives of Canadian foreign policy – containment of Communism, expansion of overseas markets potentially open to Canadian exports, and promotion of international security in ways suitable for a liberal, internationally responsible middle power. Expansion of ODA and the government's greater concern that it help the poorest peoples and countries took place after decision makers had concluded that such a policy would be shrewdly anti-Communist and appropriate for Canada both as a member of the Western alliance and as a middle power anxious to conduct an independent foreign policy.

We can make similar point about the claims that CIDA made at the time that development would increase opportunities for Canadian exports. The commitment to promote development is not denegrated by this claim that development of the South will expand Canadian trade any more than it is by the argument that it will make for greater international stability. Rather, as long as we see these results as consequences of an aid policy that seeks primarily to augment the productivity of the poorest, this argument provides decision makers with a basis for a generous and imaginative aid policy that they may find more persuasive than ethical considerations, however forceful.

The move within government to expand ODA affected more than just the level of resources devoted to it. The newer foreign policy purposes of the aid program would be served better if it were seen to meet the development needs of the poorest in the Third World. To that end, the political leadership moved to ensure that the aid program would be less susceptible to pressures that it serve other interests unrelated to international development. In 1966, Pearson appointed Maurice Strong, a prominent and independent-minded outsider to head the aid agency and gave the position deputy ministerial status. In 1968, the EAO became the Canadian International Development Agency (CIDA) and its head became its president. These several changes signalled that Strong had the prime minister's support for his sustained efforts to increase the autonomy of CIDA from ITC and External Affairs and to widen its policy influence. In 1970, at the end of Strong's term of office, Prime Minister Trudeau appointed another vigorous outsider, Paul Gérin-Lajoie, to head the agency.

As CIDA expanded, it recruited extensively from outside the public service, particularly from the NGO community. Gradually, it became a community of officials who were committed primarily to international development and who were strong advocates within government of aid policies that would seek to reach the poorest peoples and to assist them to meet their basic needs. This important shift in the attitudes and values of those administering the aid program was reflected in many policy developments discussed above – for example, substantial increases in total aid allocations (pp. 340–1), blocking of an effort to shift more Canadian aid to the richer less-developed countries (LDCs) (p. 128), increased emphasis on development needs and poverty alleviation in the formal criteria for country selection (p. 129), the significant drop in the proportion of aid going to the richer LDCs (p. 130), creation and rapid growth of the NGO Division and the harmonious relations between CIDA and the NGOs (pp. 91–2), greater support for the multilateral agencies (pp. 28–9), and efforts to improve the quality of Canadian food aid (p. 57).

From 1973 to 1975, CIDA fought an intense battle within the government to win cabinet acceptance of a strategy paper that would reflect a humane internationalist approach to ODA. When the strategy paper for 1975–80 finally appeared,[33] it was widely and legitimately read as just such a policy statement. It was not without deliberate vagueness and significant concessions to commercial interests and foreign policy objectives, but its analysis of the problems of the LDCs, its central goals, and many of its specific policy decisions affirmed a humanitarian commitment.

These events did not happen within an international vacuum. Thérien, in chapter 12, discusses the degree to which the major donors acted in concert as each shaped its own aid policies. This phenomenon is well illustrated in this period. The world's major aid agencies at this time rethought how best to assist development in poor countries. Led in particular by Robert McNamara, president of the World Bank, many professionals in the aid agencies began to advocate far greater emphasis on helping the poorest in the developing countries to meet their own basic needs. Changes within CIDA were thus in harmony with dominant trends in the international aid regime and were without doubt aided by them.

By 1975, it seemed reasonable at least to outsiders to conclude that humane internationalism had become a central determinant of Canadian aid policies. CIDA had substantially embraced these values. The strategy paper had promised that "assistance would be concentrated in those countries that are at the lower end of the development scale" and that CIDA would "give the highest priority to development projects and programs aimed at improving the living and working conditions of the least privileged sections of the populace of the recipient countries and at enabling these people to achieve a reasonable degree of self-reliance."[34] In presenting the strategy, the secretary of state had declared that this paper was intended to provide the "basic principles and approaches on which to build detailed policies."[35]

1977-85 = BACK TO COMMERCIAL + FOREIGN POLICY CONCERNS

This victory, if victory it was, was short-lived. Bureaucratic forces with their own designs on the aid expenditures, and the corporate lobbies that wanted to ensure that CIDA served domestic economic interests much more forthrightly,[36] quickly regrouped and triumphed.

A new president of CIDA, Michel Dupuy, was appointed in 1977 from the senior ranks of External Affairs. He was instructed to work cooperatively with other departments in shaping CIDA policies. A powerful interdepartmental committee was created to be responsible to the cabinet for CIDA's policies. The president of CIDA chaired this committee, but he now shared power on it with the deputy ministers of such influential departments as External Affairs, Finance, and ITC. Shortly after his appointment, Dupuy issued an internal policy memorandum in which he stressed that CIDA must emphasize projects that would bring economic benefits to Canada while not neglecting the essential development needs of the recipients.[37] This ordering of priorities contrasted rather sharply with that in the 1970 foreign policy review and in the 1975 strategy paper. Each document had identified the economic and social development of the developing countries as the primary objective of the aid program, while noting that it must also be relevant and sensitive to other national objectives.[38]

A major shift towards ensuring that CIDA's activities advanced domestic economic and foreign policy objectives was clearly in train. This shift, as Rawkins observes (see p. 158), was largely self-imposed, as

CIDA sought to safeguard its autonomy by anticipating what other departments were likely to want of it. CIDA, as Rawkins writes, became "a policy taker, not a policy giver."

This did not signal a total rout of humane internationalism in the aid program. Many within CIDA still defined their work principally in humanitarian terms.[39] They continued to influence policy, as can be seen in supportive and responsible policies towards the multilateral aid agencies, in efforts to improve food aid, and in the continued vitality of the responsive program of the NGO Division – subjects analysed in chapters 3, 4, and 5, respectively. Moreover, humane internationalism still had its appeal; it was at this time, for example, that Pierre Trudeau engaged in his major diplomatic effort to salvage the North-South negotiations.[40]

Nevertheless, something decisive was happening. CIDA was being brought to heel. There is abundant evidence in the chapters above that from 1977 on CIDA became much more responsive to Canadian foreign policy interests, to the long-term interests of the national economy, and to immediate commercial interests. Humane internationalism was in substantial retreat. Morrison, in chapter 5, demonstrates the rapidity with which Dupuy reasserted the importance of advancing domestic commercial interests. This led to the initiatives, discussed there, to give more aid to those richer Third World countries whose markets were potentially useful to Canadian exporters. For example, External Affairs rather than CIDA chaired the powerful committee that in 1978 redefined eligibility for Canadian aid in ways that favoured nations of greater commercial interest to Canada (p. 135). Morrison reports a major increase in the percentage of aid going to middle-income LDCs in this period (p. 140), as well as, by 1983, an increase in bilateral over multilateral aid, so as to increase the commercial benefits for Canadian businesses (p. 140). He shows also that the long-standing interest of External Affairs, for putative reasons of diplomatic advantage, in having an aid program in a large number of countries, proved more powerful than the development advantages of concentrating on fewer countries.

Charlton, in chapter 3, provides further, reinforcing evidence. He gives many examples of the greater impact in this period of commercial considerations in food aid policies – emphasis on processed commodities, persistent blocking of the "sourcing" of food aid from third World countries, the requirement that 25 per cent of food aid be commodities other than wheat, and – revealing that it had itself thoroughly internalized the new preoccupations – CIDA's failure to use even the limited scope permitted to it for untying food aid.

Gillies, in chapter 7, notes the government's failure to implement the decision in the 1975 strategy paper to permit Third World tendering for CIDA contracts. He makes it clear that although this failure to untie Canadian aid damaged the quality of that aid, pressures from business and from Finance and ITC against any relaxation of aid tying were irresistible, or at least were not resisted. Chapters 9 and 10 demonstrate forcefully how easily foreign policy or commercial concerns could overwhelm any consideration of human rights and social justice.

An important new dimension to CIDA's responsiveness to the interests of Canadian business emerged in these years. The main expression of this responsiveness until the late 1970s had been the tying of Canadian aid to the purchase of Canadian goods and services. By the late 1970s, the Liberal government had been forced by the global economic crisis to become preoccupied with the long-term prospects of the Canadian economy. It sought to assist industries that it believed had the potential to become major exporters, and it reorganized itself to facilitate more effective trade promotion and more comprehensive economic and industrial policy making.

The Department of External Affairs, responding to this shift, accepted that it must attach high priority to promoting Canadian trading interests abroad. This was the era first of the "third option," Canada's bid to lessen its dependence on the US market, and then of the short-lived policy of "bilateralism," an effort to cultivate relations with a wide range of states whose economies were rapidly expanding and should therefore be of special interest to Canadian exporters and investors.[41] It was also at this time that External Affairs assumed responsibility for promoting Canadian trade interests abroad and became the Department of External Affairs and International Trade.

Gillies notes that CIDA became quickly involved in this "broader strategy to bolster Canada's international competitiveness" (p. 204). It was no longer enough merely to assist uncompetitive domestic exporters. Imaginative ways had to be found to help Canadian firms to penetrate new and rapidly growing markets. The focus changed from helping firms that were hard pressed and often dependent on CIDA contracts to assisting those that at least might become competitive internationally. At this time, there was, for example, greater emphasis on projects involving industrial sectors in which Canada is competitive; a shift of aid to middle-income Third World countries and to large though still very poor countries that nevertheless have a substantial modern sector (p. 135); and the reservation of up to 20 per cent of bilateral aid for richer Third World nations of special interest to Canadian business (p. 18). Above all, this new preoccupation explains the major efforts to associate CIDA funding much more closely with the trade-promoting activities of the Export Development Corp. (EDC), an innovation analysed by Gillies in chapter 7 (pp. 197–9).

How then is one to explain the rapid shift from the humane internationalism of the 1975 strategy paper to this increasing emphasis on Canadian economic interests? Dupuy's answer at the time was that it was made necessary by changing economic circumstances (p. 135). This no doubt was an important factor, but the rapidity and comparative ease of this retreat suggest that much more was involved.

Perhaps what really needs explanation is the short period, at most from 1968 to 1977, of greater focus by CIDA and the government on Canada's long-term interest in generous and humanitarian development assistance. The humane internationalism of these few years was, as has just been argued, the result of an exceptional conjunction of factors and influences – a conviction that international communism could not be checked by military containment alone; a prosperous economy and rising government revenues; a government wanting an initiative that would demonstrate its capacity to reflect Canadian values in its foreign policy; a prime minister sensitive to global poverty; a shift within the international aid community towards basic needs; a strong team of officials at CIDA committed to poverty-oriented ODA; and an upsurge of community involvement with Third World issues.

This conjunction was short-lived. The older, middle-power internationalism soon yielded to preoccupation with Canada's relations with the United States and with Canada's role as a member of the Economic Summit. The global economic crisis and serious long-term structural problems in the Canadian economy crowded out any concern for international equity. After the failure of his effort to salvage the North-South dialogue in 1981, the prime minister lost interest in Third World poverty. Objectives such as seeking security through the promotion of greater international equity and giving effective expression abroad to humanitarian values that were central to the Canadian political culture suddenly sounded naive.

There was a further factor working in the same direction. The ideas emanating from the World Bank and the DAC no longer emphasized basic needs. The major national and international aid agencies were, so to speak, between paradigms – the focus on basic needs was in fast retreat, and neo-conservative belief in an unrestrained market economy was swiftly replacing it.

We can see how fast and complete the retreat was in two discussion papers: a two-part document prepared by External Affairs in 1979[42] and a paper on foreign policy that it published in 1985[43] at the instigation of the new secretary of state, Joe Clark. Each document dwelt on economic gain and military security and treated the claims of the Third World as a problem in global strategy.[44] There was no suggestion in the 1979 paper that there were any ethical grounds for any concessions to the Third World or that a generous aid program would be in Canada's long-run interest. The 1985 paper, *Competitiveness and Security*,[45] was also little interested in development. As its title suggests, those shaping Canadian foreign policy were by then looking chiefly at trade competitiveness and military security. The paper accepted without query that aid funds were used for trade promotion and for political advantage.

In this period, senior decision makers' obsession with Canada's long-term economic interests and with Canada's status and influence within the Economic Summit had a great and determining impact on Canadian aid policies.

Humane internationalist values relating to the aid program were not totally overwhelmed. They were widely accepted within the Canadian public and were the basis of its support for CIDA. As well, they continued to be championed by the NGO community and were still held strongly by many within CIDA, so that they still influenced detailed determination of aid policy. Moreover, there were political leaders such as Joe Clark for whom a major aid program was integral to their perception of Canada's international role. Thus the Winegard Committee could in 1987 legitimately judge that CIDA was "beset by a confusion of purpose."[46]

1985–88

There was no reason in 1985 to expect any humane internationalist upsurge or any reversal of CIDA's increasing concern with commercial objectives. The main factors that had led to the retreat since 1977 had neither disappeared nor lost influence. Nevertheless, for several years an impetus from the political arena generated an expectation of an infusion of humanitarian commitment into the Canadian aid program.

The Winegard Report (1987)

In 1985, Joe Clark, the new secretary of state for exernal affairs, encouraged appointment of a joint Senate–House of Commons committee to study Canadian foreign policy, and soon thereafter he welcomed the decision of the House of Commons' Standing Committee on External Affairs and International Trade (SCEAIT) to review Canadian aid policies. The joint committee reported in 1986.[47] As it knew that SCEAIT was working single-mindedly on the aid program, it did not address development issues at any length. Its limited references to Third World issues, though, were cast substantially but moderately in humane internationalist terms.

SCEAIT took its responsibility seriously. Its report, *For Whose Benefit?* (often referred to as the Winegard Report, after its chair William Winegard),[48] strongly reaffirmed a humane international approach to development assistance. "The aid program," it wrote, "is not for the benefit of Canadian business. It is not an instrument for the promotion of Canadian trade objectives."[49] It urged instead that Canadian ODA should be a response primarily to the ethical obligation to help meet "the needs of the poorest countries and people."[50] The committee made this statement in full awareness that CIDA was responsive more to geopolitical and economic considerations than to humanitarian ones. About a meeting with senior Canadian officials it observed: "When asked how they would rank the national interest in ODA one of them replied with great assurance: first political, second commercial and third development. That is one version of development assistance. It is not our version. It is not the version of the Canadian people."[51]

Humane internationalism shaped the report's principal recommendations. It stressed in turn human resource development with a focus on the poor; much greater use of aid to protect and promote human rights; a sizeable reduction in the tying of Canadian aid and great caution in any linking of aid to trade promotion; criteria for country eligibility that "would be clearly developmental and not subordinate to commercial or diplomatic considerations";[52] a legislated mandate embodying a development charter; an international development advisory council to advise on long-range policy issues; decentralization of CIDA in order to increase efficiency and improve program and project design; and a legislative commitment that the level of aid not fall below 0.5 per cent of GNP.

These two reports show that humanitarian considerations continued to ground parliamentary and public support for ODA, however diluted such ideas had become within the senior bureaucracy shaping Canadian aid.

The Government's Response and Its New Aid Strategy, 1987–88

A few months after the appearance of the Winegard Report, the government published a detailed official response, *To Benefit a Better World*, in which it claimed that it accepted in full 98 of the 115 recommendations of the report and a further 13 in part.[53] Early in 1988, CIDA issued a new strategy paper, *Sharing Our Future*, intended to "guide Canada's Official Development Assistance (ODA) policies into the next century."[54] This too was presented as being in substantial accord with the report. As one well-informed analyst commented, it represented for the Conservative government "a triumphant and even exemplary achievement in its vaunted consultative approach to policy formation."[55]

Much suggests, however, that CIDA, in preparing the response and the strategy paper, was engaged in an exercise more complex than that of consolidating and reaffirming a broad and popular consensus around a humane internationalist aid policy.[56] It was instead limiting damage. Because of SCEAIT's prestige and the importance attached by the government to its own consultative process, CIDA felt that it had no political option but to welcome the report. But it was very careful to safeguard those elements of the aid program that it and the other departments directly interested wished to retain but that the report explicitly or implicitly contradicted.

The evidence for this judgment is extensive. *To Benefit a Better World* and *Sharing Our Future* made significant retreats from *For Whose Benefit?*

- They did not accept a legislated minimum of 0.5 per cent of GNP for ODA, a legislated development charter, or creation of an advisory council.
- There would be no abandonment of parallel financing with EDC, and concessional credits financed through EDC would, with only nominal safeguards, be reported as ODA.
- Although against the whole thrust of the report and certainly not recommended by it, the proportion of bilateral assistance to be allocated to the richer LDCs of special interest to Canadian business was increased from 20 per cent to 25 per cent.
- Most of the recommendations to ensure greater emphasis on human rights were rejected or implemented minimally.
- The later documents placed greater emphasis on securing policy leverage with recipient governments, with much less sensitivity to their autonomy and with little acknowledgment that they might know more than CIDA about their development needs.
- Much more prominence was given to ensuring that recipient governments adopt economic policies acceptable to the IMF.
- Human resource development shifted from protecting and developing the productive capabilities of the poor to high-level manpower training.
- Bilateral aid was partially untied but to a lesser extent than recom-

mended and without seriously affecting the tying of aid to non-African countries whose markets were potentially important to Canadian exporters.

- Non-emergency food aid would not be limited to 10 per cent of the aid budget, and food aid would not be substantially untied "to permit third country purchases in situations where a neighbouring developing country has an exportable surplus of food."[57]

CIDA and the government had thus kept intact those major initiatives of the previous few years that ensured that CIDA's policies served Canadian foreign policy and trade promotion objectives. However, *Sharing Our Future* also included some reassertion of the humanitarian purposes of the aid program. For example, the development charter, though not embodied in legislation, had as its first principle that "the primary purpose of Canadian official development assistance is to help the poorest countries and peoples of the world."[58] As well, the new strategy added to CIDA's support for structural adjustment the need to be sensitive to the social and economic effects of that adjustment. Finally, it urged that CIDA decentralize administration of the bilateral program, an innovation that was expected to improve the quality of project aid by giving more authority to officers living close to those whom the aid is intended to help.

Those within CIDA and the government who remained committed to poverty-oriented ODA were thus still a force. *Sharing Our Future* represented a shrewd tactical compromise between humanitarian and development considerations and the very strong pressures to bend aid policies to more self-serving objectives. It was indeed given just such a sympathetic reading by some well-informed commentators,[59] and a similar view of its initial potential is taken by Rawkins in this volume (see p. 173). Had the strategy paper in fact become the authoritative, operationally effective guide to CIDA policy, thus at least entrenching its humane internationalist components, it might very well have been accepted widely by at least the more worldly segments of the NGO and development community as the best for which they could hope.

In fact, *Sharing Our Future* became substantially irrelevant even more rapidly than had the strategy paper for 1975–80. Rawkins tells us (p. 173) that the Winegard Report and *Sharing Our Future* have been seldom referred to in CIDA since they appeared. Even public references to them have been few and perfunctory. Little in the chapters above suggests that any effort was made after 1988 to bring policies into line with them. Much suggests instead that *Sharing Our Future* did not represent a stable equilibrium between contending pressures. CIDA's policy continued to alter as forces within CIDA and outside it successfully demanded major policy changes that continued to move ODA decisively away from the humane internationalism of the Winegard Report and the compromise position of *Sharing Our Future.*

1989–92

Four major developments relating to Canadian aid policies took place in the years 1989 to 1992 – severe and recurring cuts to CIDA's budget; endorsement by CIDA of the major economic policy changes that the IMF and the World Bank were requiring of countries seeking their help; CIDA's pursuit of ideological and programmatic coherence; and the increasing importance attached by CIDA to foreign policy objectives.

Recurrent Cuts to CIDA's Budget

Several contributors to this volume note that the government's sustained determination to reduce its total expenditures on ODA to the Third World emerged in this final period as a determinant of Canadian aid policies (see pp. 187 and 204). The Conservative government had promised to reach the 0.7 per cent target by 1990. However, this commitment quickly eroded. Fiscal restraining measures in 1989, 1990, 1991, and 1993 hit the aid program much harder than many other government expenditures. For example, the 1989 cuts to the ODA allocation constituted 23 per cent of the total reductions effected by the 1989 budget, even though spending on ODA was an approximate 2 per cent of Ottawa's total expenditures. Restraint measures between 1989 and 1991 dropped $3.9 billion from previously expected aid funding.[60] In December 1992, the finance minister announced that in each of the next two years there would be a further reduction of 10 per cent to previously offered projections for ODA. As in 1989, these cuts were disproportionately more severe than those proposed to other expenditure projections.

These cutbacks of course reflected the government's desire for fiscal restraint. However, many other factors had also been at work. The conjunction of motives in the 1970s that had generated a major aid program had long since substantially dispersed. In particular, neither international trade nor foreign policy any longer suggested a sizeable aid program. The end of the Cold War and the desperate economic plight of almost all of the poorer developing countries had for the government thoroughly marginalized these nations. Canada's older, middle-power ambition to be a humane internationalist in international politics was vastly weaker, replaced by concern to ensure

Canada's place and advance its interests in the Economic Summit (G-7), to consolidate its US markets, and to expand its links with major potential trading partners. A substantial aid program began to be seen as a hangover from an earlier era. That it continued was often attributed to Joe Clark's influence.

Leverage for Changes in Third World
Structural Adjustment Policy

By the early 1980s, the World Bank and the IMF had come firmly to the view that developing countries seeking their assistance should receive it only if they undertook major reforms in structural adjustment policy. Marcia Burdette, in chapter 8, provides an extended and persuasive critique of the adequacy and fairness of these policy changes, many of which were no doubt essential. Third World governments were often overextended, their currencies overvalued, and their peasant cultivators underpaid, and these features were typically targets of the reforms insisted upon. But the IMF programs often imposed high costs, especially on the urban poor. The changes being insisted on became all the more unavoidable because the Western governments and the IFIs were unwilling to consider such additional initiatives as massive debt abrogation and international action to raise and stabilize either commodity prices or foreign exchange earnings.

Two further complications confused and clouded early discussions of IMF/World Bank structural adjustment. First, powerful ideological considerations often helped shape structural adjustments insisted upon. Such programs typically went beyond reforms that were clearly called for by the circumstances of the country involved. Their emphasis on a minimal-state, outward-oriented, market-dominated strategy was seen, and reasonably so, as reflecting the neo-conservative ideology dominant in the United States.

Second, insistence that countries be fully open to foreign investment and to foreign trade, and the absence of any adequate international effort to lift their oppressive international debt burden, suggested to many that the interests of international capitalism rather than the pressing needs of the developing world were their dominant concern. This assessment was reinforced by the obvious fact that the programs themselves were unlikely to occasion sustained recovery in many of the poorest countries.

Equally important for purposes of this volume is Burdette's detailed study in chapter 8, above, of the increased and successful effort by CIDA, since Marcel Massé was reappointed its president in 1989, to deploy its bilateral program in ways that would induce and assist structural adjustment in countries receiving Canadian aid. Neither CIDA nor External Affairs had attempted in earlier years to exert any serious leverage on the domestic macro-economic policies of recipient governments. Canada had supported IMF and World Bank structural adjustment programs since the early 1980s but had done little to involve its bilateral aid in their promotion. This began to change by 1986, as Cately-Carlson, then president of CIDA, made clear to the Senate Committee on Foreign Affairs on 6 May 1986.

By 1989 there was a surfeit of influences, many accumulating for a number of years, which caused the rise to prominence of a commitment to structural adjustment. Burdette points out that within the bureaucracy, the Department of Finance had long advocated full support of such IMF/World Bank initiatives. Massé's efforts to that end were therefore well received by that powerful department. As well, his neo-conservative development ideas brought CIDA's policy into full harmony with the dominant economic ideas within the government. Thérien suggests above, in chapter 12, that forceful foreign policy reasons helped bring Canada into line with the international aid regime. Rawkins, making a similar point in chapter 6, suggests that for Massé and other senior CIDA officials the key reference group was the international donor community, where neo-conservatism had become the new conventional wisdom.

This worldview affected ODA. Massé explained in 1990: "There is clearly a change in the way we have to look at development policy ... The influence of the domestic economic policies swamps away the influence of all the aid flows ... and therefore conditionality on macro-economic policies ... is essential for us ... You have to go from the project level and the sectoral level to the macro-economic level."[61]

Rawkins shows (chapter 6) that this development was far from universally welcomed in CIDA, and Brodhead and Pratt explain (chapter 4) that it generated much unease within the NGO community. Nevertheless, the commitment to deploy bilateral aid in ways that would encourage and indeed require policy changes in the recipient countries altered policy. It added a forceful new reason for CIDA to wish to increase its influence over the NGOs that it was supporting. It reinforced the tendency to focus CIDA's interest on the richer and more rapidly developing aid recipients. It influenced food aid policy. It shifted the emphasis in CIDA from the directly developmental contribution of its bilateral program to preoccupation with policy leverage. It increased the importance of program aid and lines of credit, which in turn lessened what CIDA was doing directly to assist the poorest people.[62]

Pursuing Greater Policy Coherence within CIDA

In 1990, Marcel Massé, with the support of Monique Landry, the minister for external relations and international development, appointed a consultancy firm, Groupe Secor, to evaluate CIDA's administrative structures and managerial practices and to recommend how they could be made more effective. The report that Groupe Secor produced was made public in October 1991.[63]

The top leadership of CIDA had worked closely with the Secor team so that it is reasonable to assume that the report reflected its judgment of what should be done.[64] Massé's conviction that all CIDA-supported activities must serve the same policy objectives led to two clusters of recommendations. The first called for creation of a high-powered corporate office around the president, to be staffed by people highly trained in policy research and strategic analysis. This office would have final responsibility for allocation of mandates and resources, determination of aid strategies, and relations with recipient governments. The second was designed to give CIDA much greater policy control over the NGIs and NGOs that execute CIDA-financed projects and programs. It proposed that CIDA "build a pool of prequalified, trained and certified partners, from which it would purchase adequate design, execution and support capabilities for the aid program."[65] This recommendation, if implemented, would further transform the NGOs and NGIs into subordinate executing agencies for CIDA, thus destroying the defining characteristic of the responsive program – its respect for the organizational and policy autonomy of the NGOs.

The Secor Report also reflected Massé's concern that the auditor-general, Parliament, and the media hold CIDA responsible for any inefficiencies or failings in the implementation of aid. As a result, CIDA had developed elaborate and costly procedures to keep its projects and programs under close scrutiny. The report was anxious to free CIDA from much of this. It proposed several alternative arrangements to ensure that CIDA would retain control of the broad determination of policy objectives while delegating to businesses, NGOs, and NGIs the task of proposing, administering, and accounting for programs that would operate within objectives defined by CIDA.

Massé and his senior vice-president, Douglas Lindores, on Landry's instruction, closely controlled the development of policy recommendations arising from the Secor Report. After a consultative process involving few CIDA officials, other than its vice-presidents, and hardly at all other departments and the NGO/NGI community, their proposals were embodied in an aide-mémoire[66] to members of the Cabinet Committee on Foreign and Defense Policy dated 2 December 1992.

Great care was taken to present the proposed changes in ways that would make them attractive to this committee. The aide-mémoire accepted that CIDA was overextended and overregulated. It anticipated further cuts to CIDA's budget. It claimed that the development community had "applauded the consultative process," that "foreign policy objectives will continue to be served," and that "CIDA IS STREAMLINING TO HAVE MORE IMPACT IN A RAPIDLY CHANGING WORLD THROUGH A BETTER USE OF CANADIAN PRIVATE SECTOR CAPACITY." It expected that "CIDA's important partners will respond positively to the transformation of CIDA." The only criticism that it anticipated was from "some smaller NGOs who had in the past easy access to some CIDA funds."

CIDA would establish overall strategic objectives of the aid program, as well as program themes for each country/region. Within that framework, CIDA's partners would be invited to propose appropriate programs. CIDA would "devise the frameworks for development activities (the 'WHAT' to do) while letting agents (business, NGOs and institutions) determine the 'HOW' to do it." There would thus be increased delegation of responsibility for proposing, managing, and being accountable for CIDA-financed activities to the private sector and to "large development NGOs, universities and cooperatives," with CIDA determining the strategy, the objectives, and the framework within which they would have to operate.[67] The proposals would require appointment of a much stronger team of development strategists at the centre of CIDA, a fact that the proposals did not specify but clearly implied.

The proposals reflect as well a strong ambition to protect and advance CIDA's role within the government bureaucracy. As is noted above (p. 345), CIDA had since 1977 increasingly accepted that it must be careful to promote Canadian commercial and foreign policy objectives. Rawkins, indeed, quotes Catley-Carlson to the effect that CIDA was "a policy-taker not a policy-maker" (p. 162). Massé had determined that CIDA should be much more proactive. CIDA did not dispute that it should serve Canadian foreign policy goals, but under Massé it resisted any suggestion that External Affairs should exercise detailed supervisory oversight. Much that CIDA did, however, was bound to have foreign policy consequences. Indeed, in many Third World countries, foreign aid was Canada's most significant activity. Moreover, CIDA was making policy in a number of new areas, such as the environment and human rights, and was anxious to work with Finance and External Affairs and International Trade in shaping policies within the whole range of North-South economic issues. The managerial restructuring that CIDA proposed would have greatly increased its capacity to accomplish these ambitions.

Greater CIDA Sensitivity to Foreign Policy Objectives

With this assertion of a more substantial policy role for CIDA came greater sensitivity within CIDA to promotion of Canadian foreign policy and trade objectives. Rawkins traces this back to a desire from at least the late 1970s to lessen the likelihood that External Affairs would assert its authority over it (p. 159). Martin Rudner (p. 292) stresses that CIDA policies in Asia in recent years have been designed within a foreign policy framework. Ottawa had come to recognize the great asymmetry between the growing economic and political clout of Southeast Asia and of China and the weakness of Canadian links with their economies, governments, and people. Canadian foreign policy sought to lessen this imbalance.

Canadian ODA in these countries was one of the government's few instruments for accomplishing this objective. CIDA responded to this challenge. It rapidly expanded its program in China, Indonesia, Philippines, and Thailand. In close collaboration with External Affairs, CIDA came to see its task in these countries primarily in terms of creating mutually valuable relationships with business, governmental, educational, scientific, and social organizations in these nations. Canadian relations with them would outlast the aid program and would facilitate long-term pursuit of Canadian economic and foreign policy objectives. Massé, in his foreword to CIDA's 1989–90 annual report, presented this close integration of aid and foreign policy as a new goal, calling on CIDA in the more advanced developing countries to "build mutually beneficial linkages that will survive once our aid relationship has wound down."[68]

There are in this volume other major illustrations of CIDA showing increasing concern to reflect major foreign policy and commercial interests. Two of the most obvious are the continuing importance that CIDA has attached to richer rather than poorer countries in distributing its bilateral aid and its continuing efforts to assist Canadian investors and exporters to penetrate Third World markets (chapter 7). However, the most blatant illustration is the most recent. In February 1993, CIDA announced that as part of its implementation of the 10 per cent budget cut that it was required to make, six African countries would be dropped from the bilateral program. That decision taken, the first objective of the ODA Charter might have been expected to dictate that the richer aid recipients would be dropped, with a preference perhaps for those of the least developed that were implementing structural adjustment. As Morrison indicates (pp. 149–50), CIDA instead ceased bilateral aid to such very poor nations as Ethiopia, Tanzania, and Uganda, while continuing it in countries and areas such as Gabon,

Morocco, and southern Africa, where there is greater Canadian commercial and political interest.

These choices were not dictated to CIDA by External Affairs and International Trade, CIDA had internalized these foreign policy objectives and made them its own. At a meeting with CIDA staff in April 1993, the new president of CIDA, Jocelyne Bourgon, distributed a statement of the principles applied during budget reduction. The first was "to take into account the objectives of our foreign policy."[69] No mention was made of reaching and helping the poorest countries and peoples. It was as if CIDA wanted to prove to External Affairs and to cabinet that it could be trusted with decisions that had important commercial and foreign policy dimensions.

DECEMBER 1992 – FEBRUARY 1995*

The Winegard committee had observed in 1987 that CIDA was "beset with confusion of purpose."[70] By the end of 1992 CIDA a degree of policy coherence and unity of purpose that had long evaded it seemed to be within its grasp. Although there were many CIDA officials, particularly within its middle ranks, who still saw its role primarily in humanitarian and developmental terms, the unity and coherance Massé was determinedly pursuing centred around a neo-conservative view of development and an acceptance that CIDA should promote the interests of Canadian exporters and investors and pursue the objectives of Canadian foreign policy.

Mark Charlton suggests that public support for Canadian food aid may erode as Canadians learn more about and question the non-development purposes to which that aid is used (see p. 81). By 1992 his point could be generalized beyond food aid. There was by then a wide gap between the extraneous foreign policy and commercial purposes which the government sought to pursue through the manipulation of its aid program and the humane internationalist expectations of the NGOs, church groups, Third World solidarity organizations, and internationally minded citizens that are CIDA's natural constituency. As a result, many in this constituency became increasingly ambivalent in their support of CIDA, a development discussed in some detail by Brodhead and Pratt (pp. 96–115).

---

* As there have been important developments in Canadian aid policies in the twenty month period since October 1993, when the first edition went to press, this sub-section and the final section of this chapter replace the final pages, 357–63, of that earlier edition. I am indebted to McGill-Queen's University Press for this opportunity to add these pages.

Nevertheless in 1992 CIDA seemed well placed to successfully implement the "Massé project" – to attach a label to the sustained effort that he made to reorganize CIDA and redefine its objectives. CIDA had increasingly sought to placate External Affairs and Finance by taking initiatives that these powerful departments might otherwise have insisted on. It had also been sensitive to the interests of Canadian investors and exporters, so it faced no serious threats from that quarter. While it could not expect totally to win over critics of the new approach who were within CIDA itself or within the NGO community, its leadership was confident that it could contain its internal critics and that many of the larger NGOs and most of the NGIs were by now so dependent on CIDA funding that CIDA would be able easily to isolate its NGO critics.[71]

There were, however, warning signs that all was not proceeding smoothly. In 1991 Policy Branch of CIDA, as part of the "Massé project," produced a draft of a new mission statement for CIDA.[72] This statement re-affirmed a neo-conservative approach to economic development and embedded it within a wider policy framework that addressed what it called the five pillars of development, namely economic, environmental, political, social, and cultural sustainability. These areas were so broadly defined that almost any policy or program which CIDA might wish to pursue could be justified as falling within their orbit. Had the mission statement been officially sanctioned by cabinet, or at least by the minister, CIDA could have claimed a very wide *de facto* degree of autonomy from External Affairs.

When first issued, this mission statement carried a note from the minister saying that there would be "an extensive discussion process about it both within the agency and with our various partners, foreign as well as Canadian,"[73] which would be followed by the drafting of a revised statement. There was, in fact, little discussion and no authoritative revised edition was ever issued. Policy Branch continued to use the discussion paper as if it were an accepted and important statement of policy. However, neither the minister nor senior officials of External Affairs regarded it as an authoritative and adequate policy guideline.[74]

In December 1992, the public suddenly became aware that there was a serious crisis in relations between CIDA and External Affairs. At its heart was a severe dilemma that had long been in the making. CIDA's efforts since 1977 to promote foreign policy goals and international trade objectives, along with the substantial compatibility between CIDA's neo-conservatism and the dominant ideology in the corporate world and in much of government, had sapped NGO support for CIDA of much of its spontaneity and vigour. However, these efforts by CIDA had not converted either the business community or senior decision makers in other departments into advocates of a vigorous and more autonomous CIDA. As long there was no substantial challenge that to the existence of a major aid program, criticisms from the business community and such government departments as External Affairs and Finance had been held in check by CIDA's sensitivities to their interests. Once that program was challenged, however, there were precious few political or economic arguments likely to convince these critics that aid to the developing countries, especially to the poorest of them, should be a high priority.

With the imposition of financial restraint throughout government, CIDA found itself particularly exposed. Its normal allies in Canadian society had become far more critical of it and were not as easily rallied to its defence. Nor was their place taken by those whom CIDA had assiduously cultivated. Instead the business community focused more and more on the need to reduce government spending, while decision makers in such government departments as External Affairs and Finance were more concerned than ever to ensure that CIDA's policies advanced Canadian foreign policy and international trade objectives.

The 1991–92 budget provided an early indication of serious challenges to CIDA's comparative autonomy from more powerful government departments. That budget placed funding for ODA and assistance to Eastern Europe and the former Soviet Union within a single expenditure grouping, the International Assistance Envelope (IAE,) which was controlled by External Affairs. This did not necessarily entail any major change, for CIDA was already under the overall jurisdiction of the secretary of state. Nevertheless many felt that the creation of the IAE blurred the distinction between development assistance and other economic transfers. They feared that this was the prelude to a diversion of funds from ODA to other international assistance that would serve a wide range of other foreign policy objectives. Indeed, in the next year a 3 per cent increase in the IAE was divided equally between ODA and assistance to Eastern Europe and the former Soviet Union.

Early in 1993, dramatic evidence came to light that External Affairs, under its new minister Barbara McDougall, was extremely hostile to the Massé project for CIDA. It was implicit in that project that CIDA would strengthen its strategic planning capabilities and pursue its development mandate through long term contracts with its Canadian stakeholders. McDougall wanted Canada to play a more significant role in Eastern Europe and the former Soviet Union. Whatever the logic of the argument that funds for that purpose should come from economies in the defence budget, it was the IAE, not the defence envelope, that was under her immediate control. The CIDA proposals would lessen the flexibility External Affairs had in the disposition of the IAE and thus rob it of the one straightforward way it had to finance this major new foreign policy objective. This issue also reminded External Affairs how unsatisfactory it was that it had so little policy control over CIDA. At the last minute, therefore, the Cabinet refused to support the CIDA proposals and instead asked External Affairs for an international assistance policy update paper that would provide a policy framework for allocations from the IAE.

A close reading of this policy update paper, which was leaked to the press and to the NGO community, makes it possible to identify authoritatively why External Affairs wished to assert far more control over CIDA and how little influenced it was by humane internationalist considerations.[75] The paper proposes "an over-arching policy framework to provide coherence in objectives, strategies, and funding in accordance with foreign policy priorities." From its first paragraph, development assistance is bracketed with other forms of international assistance and its allocation is to be decided "on the basis of foreign policy priorities, including development objectives." The paper thus totally abandons not only any talk of first priority being given to the poorest countries and peoples but even the assumption that development is the aid program's first purpose.

It is clear from the policy update paper that many of CIDA's own policies had correctly anticipated the direction in which External Affairs wished policy to go. This is true, for example, of the policy paper's emphasis on using aid "to position the private sector for long term market penetration," on concentrating aid in fewer countries in order to increase Canadian influence, on focusing on themes that reflect foreign policy interests such as the environment, good governance and open markets, and on food aid and emergency assistance. However External Affairs clearly wanted CIDA to be much more direct than it had been in its pursuit of Canadian interests.

This is most dramatically illustrated in what it proposed for CIDA's geographic program.[76] It was to be divided into four different activities – traditional development assistance, which would go to "some 8–10 countries/units"; economic cooperation programs for some 6–8 countries "to position itself for long term market penetration into priority markets"; "foreign policy thematic funds ... [that] ... would permit us to remain in countries of significant importance to Canada"; and "a responsive priority reserve." As an illustration of what was intended, the more radical (and preferred[77]) option in one of the leaked versions allocated $200m for Eastern Europe and the former Soviet Union; $170m for the countries that were still to receive traditional development assistance; $246m for the economic cooperation countries; $548m for foreign policy thematic funds, of which $328m would be for a fund for economic cooperation and $110m each would be for two additional funds, one for human rights, democratic development, and good governance and the other for the environment; and $75m for a reserve fund. There could hardly be more dramatic evidence that commercial and foreign policy concerns had substantially replaced any commitment to reaching and helping the poorest countries and peoples.[78]

At least as important was the precedent that the policy paper sought to establish – that External Affairs rather than CIDA would now set the main heads of expenditure in Canada's aid budget. This applied to more than the important heads just itemized. The same option would have cut the voluntary program from $260m to $160m, reduced Canada's contributions to the international financial institutions by 20 per cent, concentrated environmental aid on activities of specific interest to Canada, and entirely dropped the $7m allocated in 1992–93 for development education and information.

Whether the policy update paper should be read as intending to shift significant funds away from genuine development assistance or as a statement largely reflecting current actual practice is open to debate.[79] However, what seems undeniable is that the department did not intend any return to the humanitarian priorities of *Sharing Our Future* and was eager to convert CIDA into a subordinate agency responsible for implementing policies determined by External Affairs.

The policy update paper was not an ill-conceived aberration that was quickly withdrawn once it had become public. For several weeks the secretary of state insisted that it should be implemented. It was neither abandoned nor put on hold until after it had been leaked to the press. There was then a major campaign against it, orchestrated by the NGO community (see p. 112). This campaign had as its most effective argument that major policy changes should not be made without public discussion, particularly just months before a federal election.

Before the crisis finally subsided, it became clear that CIDA had seriously over-reached itself. Massé was moved from CIDA and soon thereafter resigned from the public service in order to run as a Liberal Party candidate in the forthcoming election. Douglas Lindores, the senior vice-president of CIDA most closely associated with Massé, also resigned. The recommendations of CIDA's December 1992 submission were put on hold, except for those that were purely administrative. With an election pending, the prime minister decided that External Affairs should abandon its effort to secure rapid cabinet approval of the policy update paper and there was wide acceptance that after the federal election there would be a major review of aid policy, either on its own or as part of a wider foreign policy review.

Early in December 1993, some six weeks after the election of the new Liberal government, André Ouellet, the new Canadian minister of foreign affairs, announced that there would be a parliamentary review of foreign policy early in the new year and that development assistance policies would be integral to it. It was clear that Ouellet did not intend the Special Joint Parliamentary Committee (SJPC) to undertake an aid review that would be as thorough and as independent as that undertaken by the Standing Committee on External Affairs and International Trade in 1986–87. This time the aid review was to be part of a foreign policy review, thus ensuring that issues other than aid and development would predominate. The co-chairs of the SJPC were Allan MacEachen and Jean-Robert Gauthier, two senior Liberals who would be very unlikely to champion any major new ideas that upset the new Liberal government. And, finally, the committee was given very few months to produce its report, a further constraint on its originality and its thoroughness.

Nevertheless the scene was finally set for a resolution of the crisis in relations between External Affairs and CIDA and for an authoritative restatement of the objectives of Canada's development assistance program. The foreign policy review and the government's response to it would answer these two central questions:

Would the Special Joint Parliamentary Committee and, following its report, the Liberal government, endorse or challenge the substantial diversion of Canadian aid to serve commercial and foreign policy objectives that had been such a marked feature of CIDA policy for a number of years?

Would the committee and the government finally concede to the Department of Foreign Affairs and International Trade (as External Affairs had now become) the closer operational policy control over development assistance that it so clearly desired?

As the analysis in this chapter suggests, the continuing lack of clarity on these questions had plagued the operation of CIDA at least since the appearance of the Winegard Report in 1988 and had discouraged a great many Canadians who had long been its strongest proponents. Although the predominant trend of public policy since 1988 suggested that both questions would finally be answered in the affirmative, such affirmative answers would run counter to a long series of earlier official pronouncements on aid policy. At least since 1975, parliamentary reviews of Canadian development assistance and official policy statements had agreed that the primary purpose of Canadian aid should be humanitarian. CIDA's 1975–80 strategy had said that highest priority was to be given to "projects and programs aimed at improving the living and working conditions of the least privileged."[80]

In 1988 the Standing Committee of External Affairs and International Trade (SCEAIT), after the most thorough review ever of Canadian development assistance, stated that "[t]he primary purpose of Canadian official development assistance is to help the poorest countries and people."[81] Ten months later the government strategy paper *Sharing Our Future* embodied this statement of primary purpose in CIDA's Development Charter.[82] Moreover, references to development assistance in the major policy paper produced by the Liberal Party before the election[83] were much closer in spirit to these humane internationalist policy affirmations than to the policy proposals that External Affairs had embodied in its policy update paper of January 1993. It was therefore conceivable that although budgetary constraints were sure to require cuts to the funds allocated to CIDA, the new government would seek to ensure that these lesser funds would be used without concession to meet the Liberal Party policy paper's wish that CIDA express "the humanitarian and compassionate side of Canadian society."[84]

How then did the SJPC in the first instance, and the government on receipt of its report, respond to these two questions?[85]

THE DEVELOPMENT ASSISTANCE RECOMMENDATIONS OF THE SPECIAL JOINT PARLIAMENTARY COMMITTEE, NOVEMBER 1994.

Although the SJPC concentrated on how Canada's international economic position could be improved and on how best to promote Canada's security, the primary emphasis of its chapter on international assistance was on the need to clarify and sharpen the humanitarian focus of Canada's development assistance. On that, the committee could hardly have been more emphatic:

Help for those most in need expresses the basic moral vision of aid and corresponds closely to what the vast majority of Canadians think development assistance is all about.

Accordingly, ... the primary purpose of Canadian Official Development Assistance is to reduce poverty by providing effective assistance to the poorest people, in those countries that most need and can use our help.[86]

The report drew out the implications of this, its central recommendation on development assistance, in a series of further recommendations:

The aid program must be designed to help people help themselves and must be undertaken as a true partnership based on a local consensus.

The Committee is persuaded that one of the strongest factors muddling the aid program is the blurring of the distinction between aid and trade promotion ... and that any functions of CIDA found to be essentially Canadian trade promotion activities be transferred to the Department of Foreign Affairs and International Trade or to the Export Development Corporation.

The Committee also recommends additional untying of Canadian aid, in concert with other donors.

Human rights, good governance, and democratic development are universal values that should find central expression in Canadian foreign policy.

The Committee recommends that the government commit itself to stabilizing ODA at the present GNP ratio.[87]

The committee recognized that "there is now an unprecedented degree of consensus on what makes good development policy." It identified "two of the main lessons of development: first that it must concentrate on human endowments and well-being; and, second, that it must be self-sustaining."[88] This provided the committee with the basic policy framework for the proposed aid program – "sustainable development ... with a primary focus on the development of the human potential."[89] It then spelled out the six priorities that would be most appropriate within this policy framework: basic human needs; human rights, good governance and democratic development; the participation of women; environmental sustainability; private sector development; and public participation.

The SJPC recognized, as had the SCEAIT before it, that it would be no easy task for the government, even if it so wished, to ensure that CIDA was able to stand against the inevitable pressures to promote immediate commercial and foreign policy objectives. It therefore saw the need to protect CIDA, to use its endearing phrase, "from random and wayward pressures."[90] To that important end, in addition to its recommendation that those CIDA activities which were primarily related to commercial objectives be moved from CIDA, it recommended that CIDA's basic principles and program priorities receive legislative enactment and that an appropriate House of Commons Committee regularly review Canadian ODA, with as many Canadians as possible engaged in these reviews.

The aid chapter of the report of the SJPC lacks the intellectual authority of the Winegard report. Given that the government had determined that aid should be reviewed as part of an overall review of the whole of foreign policy and that the committee must complete its work in very few months, this was inevitable. Nevertheless what the committee proposed for CIDA's primary purpose, its basic policy framework, and its six program priorities, along with the various safeguards which it recommended to help ensure that its mandate would be diligently pursued, reflect a determination to reject the self-serving commercial and narrow foreign policy objectives that had relentlessly intruded upon the putative primacy of CIDA's humane internationalist purpose.

How then did the government deal with these recommendations in its official response to them and in the *Statement* which it issued in February 1995 to conclude the foreign policy review?

THE PLACE OF DEVELOPMENT ASSISTANCE IN THE *GOVERNMENT RESPONSE* TO THE *SPECIAL JOINT PARLIAMENTARY COMMITTEE* AND IN *CANADA IN THE WORLD: GOVERNMENT STATEMENT, FEB. 1995*[91]

Canada in the World builds Canadian foreign policy around the pursuit of three objectives: jobs and prosperity, common security, and Canadian values and culture. It then immediately gives this innocuous statement of objectives an unnecessary and ominous twist by stating that the aid program, as one of the instruments of foreign policy, should directly contribute to the promotion of each of these three objectives. Logically, and indeed reasonably, all that was necessary was that the instruments of foreign policy, taken together, contribute to an integrated and balanced strategy which would promote all three objectives. The government could therefore have decided that development assistance was to be primarily a mechanism through which Canada would pursue part of the third objective, that is, the international expression of Canadian values. Similarly, other mechanisms could have concentrated on one or both of the other objectives. Had the government constructed its argument along such lines, it would have preserved the centrality of the humane internationalist objective of the aid program without in any way breaking with the foreign policy framework to which the government was now committed. However, this was not how the government chose to present the aid program. Instead it required the aid program itself to promote all three foreign policy objectives, with the expression of Canadian values and culture internationally taking third place.[92]

That this signals a major new orientation towards Canadian aid is confirmed in the first instance by the tone and preoccupations of *Canada in the World* and the *Response*. Their overwhelming emphasis is on strengthening Canada's international economic position and securing Canada from the threats to security that will flow from increasing social unrest, economic decline, and governmental breakdown beyond our borders. These preoccupations have been allowed to squeeze out of *Canada in the World* and the *Response* any adequate policy expression of compassion for the world's poorest, recognition that the vast disparities in the distribution of the world's wealth are ethically indefensible, concern that the international order operates to the comparative disadvantage of the poorest countries, and pride in the liberal internationalist activities through which Canadians once significantly defined themselves as a people.

The most persuasive evidence that the government has in large part rejected the dominant thrust of the JSPC's chapter on development assistance is provided by its detailed handling of the committee's central and primary recommendations concerning development assistance. What follows is a restatement and consolidation of JSPC's recommendations into three, each accompanied by discussion of how the government has in fact received them.

JSPC RECOMMENDATION 1   The central purpose of CIDA should be to reduce poverty by providing effective assistance to the poorest people, in those countries that most need and can use our help.

This recommendation has been thoroughly subverted. The *Response* declares instead that CIDA's purpose "is to support sustainable development in developing countries in order to reduce poverty and to contribute to a more secure, equitable, and prosperous world."[93] Every phrase and missing phrase counts here. The reference to countries most in need has been dropped, thus legitimating aid to those richer Third World countries that are politically or commercially of more interest to Canada. The final clause of the *Response*'s statement of CIDA's purpose, "and to contribute to a more secure, equitable, and prosperous world," is not offered as a consequence of the first purpose – that would have required the use of "thereby" rather than "and" to link the last two clauses. Rather, this clause states a second, distinct objective for CIDA that is of such wide generality that it could cover almost any aid program desired by Foreign Affairs.

More conclusive still is the expanded clarification of CIDA's purpose given in *Canada in the World*.[94] In that version, trade and foreign policy objectives are presented before any mention is made of any humanitarian purpose:

International Assistance is a vital instrument for the achievement of the three key objectives being pursued by the Government. It is an investment in prosperity and employment.[95] It connects the Canadian economy to some of the world's fastest growing markets. ... [It] contributes to global security ... [and] is one of the clearest international expressions of Canadian values ...[96]

JSPC RECOMMENDATION 2   Sustainable development with a primary focus on the development of human potential should be the aid program's basic policy framework. Within that framework the Committee recommended six program priorities: basic human needs; human rights good governance and democratic development; the participation of women; environmental sustainability; private sector development, and public participation.

There were still many officials within CIDA, as well as some in Foreign Affairs, who favoured an aid program that primarily expressed humane internationalist values. Evidence of their continuing influence is found in particular in the fact that all but the last of the six program priorities recommended by the JSPC have been reaffirmed in the *Response* and only one, infrastructural services, has been added. As well, a number of other recommendations in the official position papers suggest some continuing responsiveness to humane internationalism. The main examples of these are the reaffirmation of reduction of poverty as part of the purpose of CIDA; allocation of 25 per cent of Canadian aid for support for basic human needs; specification of guidelines that emphasize local participation and ownership at all stages of programs, and thorough knowledge of local conditions; the requirement of a detailed annual report from CIDA on the implementation of these priorities, which will be debated by SCFAIT; and the promise that the government will promote human rights and democratic development through a wide range of instruments.

All this means that the proponents of a liberal and humane aid program, by picking and choosing their way through *Canada in the World* and the *Response*, can find support for their advocacy on a number of specific points, some of which could be of major significance. For example, despite the much stronger rhetoric of *Sharing Our Future*, expenditures on basic human needs did not exceed 17–18 per cent of CIDA's budget by 1992–93. The specific 25 per cent requirement should thus ensure an important improvement over previous practice. Equally important are the official acceptance of five of the recommended six program priorities and the requirement that CIDA report annually on their implementation. If it can be quickly established that this reporting should be detailed and complete, these features of *Canada in the World* should inhibit the minister and his department from insisting that CIDA engage in activities that go too blatantly beyond these priorities.

Nevertheless these elements moderate but do not offset the predominant impression that the *Response* and *Canada in the World* significantly dilute the humanitarian focus which the SJPC had recommended. They drop any suggestion that sustainable human development is the basic policy framework for CIDA and, as just noted, they greatly widen the purposes Canadian aid is to serve. They do not repeat that Canadian aid should be concentrated in the poorest countries. The emphasis in the Asia program on building lasting relationships, though often cited by critics as evidence that the Asia Branch, in particular, had emphasized foreign policy and commercial objectives, is re-affirmed. The quite gentle suggestion that Canada support a further untying of aid is rejected. Infrastructural services, a form of aid of particular interest to Canadian business, is inserted as the third of CIDA's six program priorities. CIDA is now required to administer the assistance program in Eastern Europe and the former Soviet Union, a further blurring of the focus of its responsibilities and is also instructed to coordinate its bilateral aid programs more closely with Foreign Affairs and International Trade, and with the Export Development Corporation. There is very inadequate recognition that Canadian aid should be concentrated in a few countries so that CIDA activities can solidly reflect a real knowledge of the development needs and experience of the aid recipients.

JSPC RECOMMENDATION 3   A variety of safeguards should be employed to help protect CIDA from powerful forces within and outside of government that have diverted CIDA resources to the pursuit of trade and other objectives.

The JSPC accepted, as had *For Whose Benefit?*, that safeguards were necessary. The government has rejected every one of the proposed safeguards. CIDA's mandate, as already noted, has not been clarified and is in fact now much more loosely defined than had been recommended. CIDA's mandate is not to be embodied in legislation and its budget as a proportion of GNP is not to be frozen at its present level. The promotion of public participation, so important to public accountability, has been dropped from the list of program priorities. The recommendation that the SCFAIT should involve as many Canadians as possible in its annual review of CIDA is ignored. Nor will the funds for development assistance be administered through a separate financial envelope.

All of these omissions serve to augment the capacity of Foreign Affairs to shape CIDA policies as it wishes. This intention is solidly confirmed with the decision that the inter-departmental committee that will determine development assistance policies will be chaired by the deputy minister of Foreign Affairs not by the president of CIDA.

THE END OF AN ERA

The government of Canada has clearly decided to bring to an end an era in which it presented its aid program as an exercise in liberal internationalism, an era during which it affirmed that its primary objective was to reach and help the poorest countries and people while encouraging Canadians to take pride in the quality and integrity of its development assistance. That era began in 1966 with the appointment of Maurice Strong as the head of the aid agency that preceded CIDA. Despite pressures from within government and from business lobbies that aid policies should also benefit Canadian business, the government issued a five-year aid strategy paper in 1975 that strongly affirmed Canada's commitment to a generous poverty-focused aid program. (pp. 340–3)

I argued earlier (pp. 346–7) that this era had been made possible by a conjunction of factors and influences that for a short period, at most from 1966 to 1976, generated official recognition that Canada had a long-term interest in humanitarian development assistance. That conjunction was extraordinary and began to disintegrate almost immediately after the announcement of the 1975–80 aid strategy. The view among senior decision makers who had briefly accepted that a commitment to the alleviation of global poverty reflected an important Canadian national interest quickly shifted and the dominant worldview in Ottawa came to increasingly emphasize the importance to Canada of its relations with the US, its membership in the G-7, and the negotiation of regional and global trade agreements that would increase Canadian trade prospects.

This ideological shift within senior decision-making circles meant that the poor countries of the Third world – or at least those of no geopolitical or economic interest – were quickly regarded as of marginal interest to Canada. The Canadian retreat from humane internationalism merely reflected a general trend, as the aid policies of other industrialized countries were also being similarly curtailed and diluted. Finally, there has been a diminishing Canadian attachment to that ethical liberalism which had been a major component of Canadian political values in the first twenty-five years after 1945. Those social values had an obvious affinity with humane internationalist values. As their salience within the Canadian political culture declined in recent years, humane internationalism gradually came to fit less easily within the dominant Canadian political culture.[97]

Yet popular acceptance of a generous and humanitarian aid program continued to be suprisingly strong throughout the 1980s (see pp. 334–6). Community support for a generous and poverty-focused aid program was effectively mobilized and articulated by a strong and active network of NGOs, church organizations, development education centres, and other community organizations sensitive to Third World needs. This poverty-oriented approach to development assistance received strong parliamentary reaffirmation, not only in the Winegard report of 1987 but also, as has been seen, in the 1994 report of the Special Joint Parliamentary Committee.

This conflict between the vigorous support from both the aid community and parliamentarians for a generous poverty-focused aid program and the determined dilution of this focus in Canada's official aid policy seriously bedeviled the operation of CIDA and clearly called for resolution. The government response to the 1994 foreign policy review and the official statement, *Canada in the World*, which accompanied that response attempt to achieve this resolution. They abandon the humane internationalist rhetoric altogether. They make abundantly clear that development assistance will be deployed in pursuit of the whole range of foreign policy objectives, including trade promotion and expanded overseas investment, and that the Department of Foreign Affairs and International Trade will exercise a controlling influence in the shaping of aid policies. Foreign Affairs has thus finally won open government endorsement of the perspective on foreign aid that, as seen in the argument of this chapter, it has championed with increasing effect since at least 1977.

Humane internationalism, though markedly in retreat, is not yet overwhelmed. Its influence is discernable in the 1995 *Canada and the World*. More than that, CIDA itself, accepting its lesser role and its smaller budget, is making a valiant effort to build on the humane internationalist components of this statement. It has, for example, issued a strong policy paper on poverty reduction.[98] This paper starts with the fact that poverty reduction is the first objective specified for CIDA in the mandate for Canadian aid set out in *Canada in the World*. Thus legitimized, the paper then sets out a detailed statement of CIDA policies that address the role of Canadian development assistance in reducing poverty with a vigour, precision, and insight long absent from CIDA pronouncements.[99]

There is a further component of the new foreign policy rhetoric that, if effectively exploited, could have positive consequences for the quality and integrity of Canadian development assistance. Alongside the powerful emphasis on trade promotion, there is a new emphasis on the fact that Canada's security is closely dependent on the achievement of a shared human security.

the threats to security now are more complex than before. A whole range of issues ... transcend borders – including mass migration, crime, disease, environment, over-population and under-development ... Our well-being and our national interest are inextricably linked to global developments. As the Special Joint Committee stated: "We will have shared security, shared prosperity and a healthy environment for all or none will have any in the long-term."[100]

There are persuasive long-term Canadian interests in international stability and in the successful management of a wide range of issues that can only be dealt with on an international basis and with the cooperation of the Third World. These international issues are unlikely to be successfully managed if mass poverty in developing countries increases. It can surely be argued that an aid program that reaches and helps the poorest countries and people is an essential component of any effective pursuit of shared human security. The new government statements, while demonstrating a rather impervious unresponsiveness to ethical arguments favouring a poverty-focused aid program, open up the possibility that government might be more receptive to arguments which cast the case for such an aid program in terms of global, and therefore national, security. Some now see this as the more effective way to argue the case for development assistance.[101] Nevertheless, given Foreign Affairs' perspective on development assistance, the preoccupation of cabinet and government with the promotion of Canadian international trade interests, and the diminished responsiveness within the Canadian political culture to the welfare needs of others, it is hard to be optimistic that such arguments will reverse the major retreat from humane internationalism that has been traced in the preceding pages.

A rearguard action to preserve some measure of concentration on the needs of the poorest countries and people can be expected from CIDA itself, from some within Foreign Affairs, and from most within the aid community. Nevertheless, by the summer of 1995 when this final section was being written, much suggested that the most likely prospects are: that the aid budget will continue to be cut; expenditures from the declining budget will be concentrated increasingly on those activities and in those countries that Foreign Affairs judges to be of special interest to Canadian business; funding of activities not as likely to advance foreign policy and commercial interests will be cut, such as aid to multilateral institutions and to international NGOs; even greater efforts will be made to ensure that CIDA-funded NGO programs are well integrated into CIDA's aid strategy for the countries affected; major cuts will be made to the funding of NGO activities that the government feels augment public criticism of CIDA policies; and funds putatively intended for development purposes will be diverted to activities quite distinct from poverty reduction and development in the world's poorest countries.

The challenge we face, if aid policies are not to continue to evolve along lines such as these, is to ensure that Foreign Affairs and the government become much more responsive to the humane internationalist component of Canadian values and to Canada's real and substantial long-term interests, both of which require what the Winegard Report in 1987 and the report of the Special Joint Committee in 1994 had urged – a substantial aid program that concentrates on reaching and helping the most destitute nations and people. It is, at heart, an ethical issue and a political challenge.

NOTES

1 The most substantial of the studies of Canadian aid policies that discuss their determinants include, in chronological order, Keith Spicer, *The Samaritan State: External Aid in Canadian Foreign Policy* (Toronto: University of Toronto Press 1966); S.G. Triantis, "Canada's Interest in Foreign Aid," *World Politics* 24 (October 1971), 1–18; Clyde Sanger, "Canada and Development in the Third World," in Peyton Lyon and Tareq Ismael, eds. *Canada and the Third World* (Toronto: Macmillan 1976), 277–306; Louis Sabourin, "Analyse des politiques de coopération internationale du Canada: des projets d'aide à la stratégie de développement," in Paul Painchaud, ed., *Le Canada et le Québec sur la scène internationale* (Quebec: CQRI 1977); Leonard Dudley and Claude Monmarquette, *The Supply of Canadian Foreign Aid: Explanation and Evaluation* (Ottawa: Economic Council of Canada 1978); Robert Carty and Virginia Smith, *Perpetuating Poverty: The Political Economy of Canadian Foreign Aid* (Toronto: Between the Lines 1981); Peter Wyse, *Canadian Foreign Aid in the 1970's: An Organizational Audit* (Montreal: Centre for Developing Area Studies 1983); Monique Dupuis, *Crise mondiale et aide internationale: stratégie canadienne et développement du Tiers-Monde* (Montreal: Édition nouvelles optique 1984); Linda Freeman, "The Effect of the World Crisis on Canada's Involvement in Africa," *Studies in Political Economy* 17 (summer 1985), 794–820; Martin Rudner, "The Evolving Framework of Canadian Development Assistance Policy," in Brian Tomlin and Maureen Molot, eds., *Canada among Nations, 1984: Year of Transition* (Toronto: James Lorimer 1985), 124–45; David Gillies, "Commerce over Conscience? Canada's Foreign Aid Programme in the 1980s," MA thesis, McGill University, 1986; Cranford Pratt, "Ethics and Foreign Policy: The Case of Canada's Development Assistance," *International Journal* 43 no. 2 (spring 1988), 264–301; Kim Nossal, "Mixed Motives Revisited: Canada's Interest in Development Assistance," *Canadian Journal of Political Science* 21 no. 2 (1988), 35–56; Patricia Appavoo, "The Small State as

Donor: Canadian and Swedish Development Assistance Polic
pared, 1960–1976," PhD dissertation, University of Toronto,
P. Lavergne, "Determinants of Canadian Aid Policy," in Olav
Western Middle Powers and Global Poverty: The Determinants of the
Canada, Denmark, The Netherlands, Norway and Sweden (Uppsal:
vian Institute of African Studies 1989), 33–89; Cranford Prat
An Eroding and Limited Internationalism," in Cranford Pratt
tionalism under Strain: The North-South Policies of Canada, The Ne
way and Sweden (Toronto: University of Toronto Press 1989), 24–69; Brian
Tomlinson, "Development in the 1990's: Critical Reflections on Canada's
Economic Relations with the Third World," in Jamie Swift and Brian
Tomlinson, eds., *Conflicts of Interest: Canada and the Third World* (Toronto:
Between the Lines 1991), 25–78; Martin Rudner, "Canada's Official Devel-
opment Strategy: Process, Goals and Priorities," *Canadian Journal of Develop-
ment Studies* 12 no. 1 (1991), 1–19; and Mark W. Charlton, *The Making of
Canadian Food Aid Policy* (Montreal and Kingston: McGill-Queen's Univer-
sity Press 1992).

2 Four volumes were produced. For this study, two, both published in 1989,
are relevant – Stokke, ed., *Western Middle Powers;* and Pratt, ed., *Internationalism under Strain.*

3 The concept of public philosophy is drawn from Ronald Manzer's *Public
Philosophy and Political Development in Canada* (Toronto: University of
Toronto Press 1985). It refers to the dominant values that are at the core
of a society's political culture.

4 Réal Lavergne, "Determinants of Canadian Aid Policy," in Stokke, ed.,
Western Middle Powers, 38.

5 Calculated from *Report to CIDA: Public Attitudes towards International Development Assistance, 1991* (Hull: Communications Branch, CIDA, 1991), 14.

6 In *Public Philosophy,* Manzer identifies the Canadian public philosophy as a
liberalism that holds in tension within it both an economic strand and an
ethical strand. He illustrates the public policy expression of this liberalism
in a number of major domestic policy areas. We are concerned here with
the international component of this public philosophy and with the difficulty of translating that component into public policy.

7 *Report to CIDA: Public Attitudes, 1989,* 13 and 17; *1991,* 12 and 25.

8 CCIC, *How the Public Sees International Development and North-South Issues: A
Summary of Public Opinion 1993* (Ottawa: CCIC Communications Unit,
February 1993), 3.

9 I am grateful to Evan Browne of CIDA's Communications Branch for this
information.

10 Ibid.

11 I discuss this factor in Pratt, "Canada: An Eroding and Limited Internationalism."

12 *Public Attitudes, 1991*, 11, 33. In 1989, 89 per cent and 87 per cent of respondents agreed with these two opinions, respectively, and in 1991, 87 per cent and 85 per cent. Moreover, in this latter year, with high unemployment, 77 per cent agreed that trade barriers should be lowered for imports from developing countries; ibid., 34.

13 Quoted in Lavergne, "Determinants," 37.

14 Parliamentary Task Force on North-South Relations, *Report to the House of Commons on the Relations between Developed and Developing Countries* (Hull: Supply and Services 1980); House of Commons, Standing Committee on External Affairs and International Trade (SCEAIT) *For Whose Benefit? Report of the Standing Committee on External Affairs and International Trade on Canada's Official Development Assistance Policies and Programs* (Ottawa: Supply and Services 1987).

15 Department of External Affairs, *Foreign Policy for Canadians: International Development* (Ottawa: Information Canada 1970); CIDA, *Strategy for International Development 1975–1980* (Ottawa: CIDA 1975); CIDA, *Sharing Our Future: Canada's International Development Assistance.* (Ottawa: Supply and Services 1987).

16 This increase in politically motivated decisions has been a direct consequence of the appointment since 1985 of a minister of state to oversee the aid program. Julian Payne, a senior CIDA official, in a speech to the Canadian Association for the Study of International Development in June 1993, identified ministerial interventions as the first of five factors external to CIDA that have become important in the last few years.

17 Spicer, *Samaritan State*; and Appavoo, "The Small State as Donor." I am particularly indebted to David Morrison for letting me read an early draft of the initial chapters of his forthcoming study of CIDA and Canadian aid policies.

18 The centrality of these two preoccupations is brilliantly demonstrated in Robert Wood, *From Marshall Plan to Debt Crisis: Foreign Aid and Development Choices in the World Economy* (Berkeley: University of California Press 1986).

19 A.F.W. Plumptre, "Perspective on Our Aid to Others," *International Journal* 22 no. 3 (summer 1967), 485.

20 Robert Matthews, on the basis of extensive research, wrote in 1976 that Canada decided in 1958 to extend development assistance first to Ghana and then to other African states on the grounds that Canada was better placed than Britain or the United States to draw Ghana into the Western orbit. Matthews, "Canada and Anglophone Africa," in Lyon and Ishmael, eds., *Canada and the Third World*, 89.

21 In 1947–48, the Canadian contribution to UNICEF constituted only 1.1 per cent of total contributions by governments, according to John Holmes, *The Shaping of Peace: Canada and the Search for World Order*, Vol. I, *1943–1957* (Toronto: University of Toronto Press 1979), 86.

22 External Aid Office, *Annual Review 1967* (Ottawa: Queen's Printer 1967), 3. In contrast to the Canadian proportion of 0.19 per cent in 1961, the US, British, and Dutch figures were 0.73 per cent, 0.66 per cent, and 0.62 per cent, respectively. Spicer, *Samaritan State*, 41.

23 Calculated from official figures in Spicer, *Samaritan State*, 41.

24 *Mike: The Memoirs of the Rt. Hon. Lester B. Pearson*, Vol. II (Toronto: University of Toronto Press 1973), 112.

25 Keith Spicer sees this as "the central and decisive fault in Canada's early programme"; *Samaritan State*, 103. He provides substantial evidence of a serious indifference towards Third World development in the first decade of Canadian foreign aid.

26 Ibid., 36.

27 External Aid Office, *Annual Review 1966–67*, and Tables 1 and 2 of chapter 1, above.

28 An internal CIDA memorandum in 1969 identified as the first objective of aid policy" to establish within recipient countries those political attitudes or commitments, military alliances or military bases that would assist Canada or Canada's western allies to maintain a reasonably stable and secure international political system." Quoted in Clyde Sanger, *Half a Loaf: Canada's Semi-Role among Developing Countries* (Toronto: Ryerson Press 1969), xi.

29 *Development Cooperation, 1987 Report* (Paris: OECD 1988), 55.

30 Peyton Lyon, in writing of this sudden major increase in Canadian ODA, attributes it in part to a nationalist response to the need for "a sense not just of national identity but of purpose." Lyon, "Introduction," in Lyon and Ishmael, eds., *Canada and the Third World*, xlvi.

31 Patricia Appavoo reports that the new Liberal government in 1964 was much encouraged by the almost total support given by the press to its first important increase in Canadian aid. Appavoo, "The Small State as Donor," 70.

32 Nevertheless, the foreign policy White Paper of 1970 provided a careful, extended argument, based largely on ethical considerations and long-term global interests, for a substantial Canadian development program. *Foreign Policy for Canadians: International Development* (Ottawa: Queen's Printer 1970), 5–11.

33 CIDA, *Strategy 1975–1980*. For an insightful discussion of this paper written shortly after it was issued, see Sanger "Canada."

34 CIDA, *Strategy 1975–1980*, 23.

35 Ibid., i.

36 I say little in this chapter on the role of business lobbies, because I believe that senior decision makers had wide autonomy in the shaping of aid policies and were responsive to the interests of Canadian exporters as a result of their own assessment of what should be done. However, these lobbies did mobilize quickly when they saw their interests threatened, as they did

when CIDA's strategy for 1975–80 promised to relax the tying of Canadian aid. "Canadian businessmen have fought for tied aid in Canada and we do not intend to see the policy changed," wrote Camille Dagenais, chair of the board of the SNC Group, as quoted in John Hendra, "Only Fit to Be Tied: A Comparison of Canadian Tied Aid Policies and the Tied Aid Policies of Sweden, Norway and Denmark," *Canadian Journal of Development Studies* 8 no. 2 (1988).

37 Carty and Smith, *Perpetuating Poverty*, 70.

38 External Affairs, *Foreign Policy for Canadians*, 12–13; and CIDA, *Strategy 1975–1980*, 23.

39 An interesting indication of this is provided by an overview of Canadian aid policies produced by CIDA in 1984: *Elements of Canada's Official Development Assistance Strategy 1984* (Hull: CIDA 1984). This background paper was significantly less ambivalent in its affirmation of the central humanitarian objectives of CIDA than were the several policy papers that External Affairs produced. See notes 42 and 43, below.

40 For the argument that this 1980–81 initiative by Trudeau was a personal one, largely unsupported by External Affairs, see Pratt, "A Limited and Eroding Internationalism," 35–6.

41 These important developments and their significance for Canadian relations with the Third World are analysed in ibid., 56–9.

42 "Canada in a Changing World: Part 1, The Global Framework, and Part 2, Canadian Aid Policies," issued by the secretary of state for external affairs and published in Canada, House of Commons, Standing Committee on External Affairs and National Defence, *Minutes of Proceedings and Evidence*, Issue No. 3 (10 June 1980), 3A:28–3A:80.

43 External Affairs, *Competitiveness and Security: Directions for Canada's International Relations* (Ottawa: Supply and Services 1985).

44 The worldview implicit in these two documents is discussed and contrasted with *Foreign Policy for Canadians* (1970) and CIDA's *Strategy 1975–1980* in Pratt, An Eroding and Limited Internationalism," 59–63.

45 With the Conservative victory in 1984, this lack of interest became even more explicit. An important internal CIDA document of 1986, for example, referred to the need "to ensure improved linkages between Canadian development assistance and Canadian economic objectives, particularly export promotion." CIDA, *Briefing Notes for the Minister, 1986*, 60.

46 This judgment is offered in the very first sentence of SCEAIT, *For Whose Benefit?* (Winegard Report), 1.

47 Parliament, Special Joint Committee, *Independence and Internationalism: Report of the Special Joint Committee of the Senate and of the House of Commons on Canada's International Relations* (Ottawa: Supply and Services 1986).

48 Winegard Report.

49 Ibid., 8.

50 Ibid., 10.

51 Ibid., 7.

52 Ibid., 65.

53 Canada, *Canadian International Development Assistance: To Benefit a Better World. Response of the Government of Canada to the Report of the Standing Committee on External Affairs and International Trade* (Ottawa: Supply and Services 1987), 1.

54 From the statement of the minister for external relations and international trade when tabling the strategy paper. It is reproduced without pagination at the beginning of CIDA, *Sharing Our Future.*

55 Martin Rudner, "Canada's Official Development Assistance Strategy," 13.

56 The argument of this and the next several paragraphs is summarized from my "Ethics and Foreign Policy," especially 283–93.

57 Ibid., 58 and 39.

58 CIDA, *Sharing Our Future*, 23.

59 Substantially favourable readings of CIDA's *Sharing Our Future*, for example, appear in Rudner, "Development Assistance Strategy," and in North-South Institute, "Canadian Aid Delivery and the New Strategy," *Review '88 Outlook '89*, 8–17.

60 For a detailed analysis of these cuts, see Maureen O'Neil and Andrew Clark, "Canada and International Development: New Agendas," in Fen Osler Hampson and Maureen Appel Molot, eds., *Canada among Nations 1992–93* (Ottawa: Carleton University Press 1993); ICFID and Canadian Council of Churches, *Diminishing Our Future* (Toronto: ICFID 1991), 37–9; and Andrew Clark, "Secret Paper Steers Aid Policy Changes," *Review: A Newsletter of the North-South Institute* (spring 1993), 1.

61 This quotation is from a transcript of an address by Massé to Canadian executive directors of the IFIs meeting in Ottawa, 29–30 October 1990.

62 As an illustration, by 1989 only 10.9 per cent of Canadian bilateral aid went to assisting with basic human concerns – that is, basic education, primary health care, safe drinking water, family planning, and nutrition programs. United Nations Development Programme, *Human Development Report 1992* (New York: Oxford University Press 1992), 43.

63 Groupe Secor, Strategic Management Review: Working Document (Secor Report) (9 October 1991). The analysis that follows draws on Cranford Pratt, "Towards a Neo-conservative Transformation of CIDA: The Secor Report on CIDA," *International Journal* 47 no. 3 (summer 1992), 595–613.

64 The Secor Report referred (4/2) to "validation exercises" that the team had had with "the President and Executive Vice President" (presumably the senior vice-president).

65 Secor Report, 70/4–70/5.

66 The summary of this aide-mémoire that follows was made from a copy that came into the possession of the Canadian Council for International

Cooperation (CCIC). The quotations given in the text are also from this leaked copy.

67 Although the term "responsive" was used in the aide-mémoire, these arrangements would be such only as long as these partners "respond" with proposals that are within the "development framework" devised by CIDA. The only program suggested that would finance activities that reflect the policy judgment of the NGOs themselves, and therefore be genuinely responsive, was a limited one for "small responsive activities."

68 CIDA, *Annual Report 1989–90* (Ottawa: Supply and Services 1991), 7.

69 The other four principles and goals were "to share the reductions equitably between regions of the developing world; to continue to respect Canada's international commitments; to slow down the encashment of notes to limit the impact on developing countries and Canadian partners; and to protect the funding of priority activities." This statement was seen at both the CCIC and the North-South Institute.

70 *Winegard Report*, 5.

71 This is the clear implication of the passage quoted a few pages earlier from the leaked CIDA aide mémoire paper on its strategic management proposals. See p. 355.

72 Policy Branch, *Sustainable Development Discussion Paper*, (Hull: CIDA, 15 July 1991).

73 Ibid., note from the Minister, no pagination.

74 It was, for example ignored in the policy update paper prepared by External Affairs in the crisis that developed between it and CIDA from December 1992 to March 1993. This crisis and the policy update paper are discussed immediately below.

75 I am grateful to CCIC and to the North-South Institute for making available to me copies of the External Affairs paper "International Assistance Policy Update" which had come into their possession. It was often suggested at the time that Massé himself had instructed that the paper be leaked. There is no way to establish whether this is actually the case but the fact that it circulated as a credible rumour is itself a measure of the intensity of the dispute.

76 The figures and the quotation in the next several paragraphs are taken from annex 2 and section 9.1 of the North-South Institute's version of the policy update paper. As the paper went through several drafts and several versions of it were leaked, the details were not always the same.

77 It is fair to say "preferred," for the paper says this option "would be the biggest step towards the updated policy framework."

78 This did not inhibit the author of the paper from advising that the government "must repeat that the "poorest of the poor" continue to be a priority." Ibid., section 10.2.

79 This second view was put to me by a senior official of External Affairs. He reminded me of CIDA's efforts to dampen External Affairs' criticisms by

anticipating what the department might wish it to do and suggested that the gap between actual practice and the options outlined in the update paper was slight.

80 CIDA *Strategy 1975–80*, 23.

81 Winegard Report, 12.

82 CIDA, *Sharing Our Future*, 23. This paper, although carrying 1987 as its publication date, was not released until March 1988.

83 *Creating Opportunity: The Liberal Plan for Canada* and its annex, *Liberal Foreign Policy Handbook* (Ottawa, The Liberal Party 1993).

84 Ibid., 13.

85 An earlier version of the analysis that follows appears in Cranford Pratt, "Development Assistance and Canadian Foreign Policy: Where We Now Are," *Canadian Foreign Policy* 2 no. 3 (Winter 1994), 77–85.

86 House of Commons, Special Joint Committee Reviewing Canadian Foreign Policy, *Canada's Foreign Policy: Principles and Priorities for the Future.* (Ottawa: Parliamentary Publications Directorate 1994), 48.

87 Ibid. 49, 51, 52, 54, 58.

88 Ibid., 48–9.

89 Ibid., 48.

90 Ibid., 51.

91 Canada, *Government Response to the Recommendations of the Special Joint Parliamentary Committee Reviewing Canadian Foreign Policy* (Ottawa: Department of Foreign Affairs and International Trade 1995) and Canada, *Canada in the World: Government Statement* (Ottawa: Department of Foreign Affairs and International Trade 1995)

92 *Canada in the World*, 40.

93 *Government Response to the Recommendations*, 58.

94 *Canada in the World*, 40.

95 In the fuller presentation of this first key objective the statement makes it clear that the reference is to Canadian prosperity and employment. *Canada in the World*, 10.

96 This contrasts rather dismally with the firm, proud rejection by the Winegard Committee in 1987 of an approach to Canadian aid that was put to it in 1986–87 and closely parallels that of the new statement – "When asked how they [senior Canadian officials] would rank the national interest in ODA, one of them replied with great assurance: First political, second commercial, and third development. This is one version of development assistance. It is not our version. It is not the version of the Canadian people." *For Whose Benefit?*, 7.

97 For a fuller exposition of this view of the relationship between domestic political values and Canadian international policies see my chapter in Pratt, *Internationalism Under Strain*, esp. 49–56.

98 CIDA, *CIDA's Policy on Poverty Reduction* (Hull: CIDA June 1995).

99 The paper, however, also illustrates the narrow constraints that CIDA has accepted as it engaged in this exercize, staying within narrowly defined parameters in its discussion of the role CIDA will play. In particular, it does not mention the need for major debt forgiveness for at least the poorest LDCs, nor is there any discussion of international commodity pricing, non-tariff barriers to greater LDC exports to Canadian markets; or the need for increased resource transfers to the LDCs. All that it permits itself is the inclusion, in a list of "activities which affect the policy environment," of the single clause, "working in the international policy area to reduce global poverty." *CIDA's Policy on Poverty Reduction*, 4.

100 *Canada in the World*, 10–11.

101 An important effort to introduce the concept of common security to the discussion of Canadian foreign policy was made by Canada 21 Council, a newly mobilized group of prominent Canadians, many of them internationalists from earlier decades. (See *Canada 21. Canada and Common Security in the Twenty-First Century* [Toronto: Centre for International Studies 1994].) For an interesting discussion of this effort to influence the way in which security issues are considered in Canada, see Janice Gross Stein, "Ideas, even good ideas, are not enough: changing Canadian foreign and defence policies," *International Journal* 50 no. 1 (Winter 1994–95), 40–70. For those concerned with Canadian development assistance it is a depressing omen that the section on aid in *Canada 21* is the weakest in that volume, while development assistance policies are not discussed at all in the Stein article.

Contributors

TIM BRODHEAD is vice-president and chief operating officer of the J.W. McConnell Family Foundation and was executive director of the Canadian Council of International Cooperation (1987–92) and of Inter Pares (1977–84). He is co-author of *Bridges of Hope?: Canadian Voluntary Agencies and the Third World* (1988) and has written several articles on Canadian NGOs.

MARCIA M. BURDETTE has been an analyst of African political economy for over fifteen years. Her particular interest in structural adjustment began while in Zambia and Zimbabwe, 1982–88. As a university teacher and researcher there, she published *Zambia: Between Two Worlds* (1988) and several articles on Zimbabwean industry and SADC. From 1989 to 1991, she was director of the North-South Institute's program on aid effectiveness and development cooperation, supervising six studies on structural adjustment in Africa. From 1991 to 1993 she combined teaching at the University of Ottawa and Carleton University with consultancy for UNIFEM, Partnership Africa Canada, and CIDA. From 1992 to 1993, she was senior consultant to the Canadian parliamentary subcommittee on international financial institutions. She was OXFAM-Canada's Southern African program development officer and recently became policy adviser to the secretary of state for Latin America and Africa.

MARK W. CHARLTON is associate professor of political science at Trinity Western University. His PhD dissertation for Université Laval was on Canadian food aid policies. His publications include "The Management of Canada's Bilateral Food Aid," *Canadian Journal of Development Studies* 7 no. 1 (1986), and "The Food Aid Conundrum and Canadian Aid Policy," *International Journal* (Summer 1987). He is the author of *The Making of Canadian Food Aid Policy* (1992) and co-editor of *Crosscurrents: Contemporary Political Issues* (1991) and *Crosscurrents: International Relations in the Post–Cold War Era* (1993).

TIMOTHY DRAIMIN is director, Development Policy, Canadian Council for International Cooperation (CCIC). He was for some years a fellow of the Centre for Research in Latin America and the Caribbean at York University, Toronto. He is co-author of "The Decay of the Security Regime in Central America," *International Journal* (spring 1990), and a contributor to *Between War and Peace in Central America: Choices for Canada* (1991).

DAVID GILLIES is policy coordinator with the International Centre for Human Rights and Democratic Development in Montreal. He recently completed a doctorate in political science at McGill University, with a dissertation on the place of human rights in Canadian, Dutch, and Norwegian North-South policies. He has published numerous scholarly articles on Canadian aid and human rights and democratic development. He is co-author with Gerry Schmitz of *The Challenge of Democratic Development: Sustaining Democracy in Developing Societies* (1992). He prepared his chapter in this volume in a personal capacity.

T.A. KEENLEYSIDE has been professor of political science, University of Windsor, since 1971. Previous to that, he was a foreign service officer with the Department of External Affairs. His principal research focus has been on Canadian foreign policy, with particular interest in human rights and Third World development. He has written several chapters in books relating to his interest and a number of articles on Canadian foreign policy in such academic periodicals as the *Canadian Journal of African Studies, Canadian Public Administration, International Journal, Journal of Canadian Studies, and Pacific Affairs.*

DAVID R. MORRISON is professor of political studies, provost, and dean of arts and science, Trent University, in Peterborough, Ontario. He is currently completing a major history of CIDA and Canadian aid policies for the North-South Institute in Ottawa. He was editor of and a contributor to a special issue on Canada and the Third World of the *Journal of Canadian Studies* in 1985 and author of "Canada and North-South Conflict" in Maureen Molot and Brian Tomlin, eds., *Canada among Nations 1987* (1988).

KATHARINE PEARSON is Americas program officer in the Development Policy Unit of the Canadian Council for International Development (CCIC). Formerly with CUSO briefly and with Oxfam Canada for 10 years, she served as project officer (1985–90) in Central America.

CRANFORD PRATT is professor emeritus of political science at the University of Toronto. He has worked in Tanzania and Uganda and is author or co-author of several books and numerous articles on African themes, including *The Critical Phase in Tanzania, 1945–1968* (1976). More recently he has concentrated on Canada's relations with the Third World. With Robert O. Matthews, he edited *Human Rights in Canadian Foreign Policy* (1988). He edited and contributed to *Internationalism under Strain: The North-South Policies of Canada, The Netherlands, Norway and Sweden* (1989) and *Middle Power Internationalism: The North-South Dimension* (1990).

DAVID R. PROTHEROE is a private consultant. He worked for several years at CIDA and at the North-South Institute in Ottawa. He is the author of *Imports and Politics* (1980); *The United Nations and Its Finances* (1988); and *Canada and Multilateral Aid: Working Paper* (1989).

PHILLIP RAWKINS is a professor of political science and public administration at Ryerson Polytechnic University in Toronto. From 1980 to 1992, he was director of the Ryerson International Development Centre; in that capacity he designed and directed a range of projects in Asia and the Middle East. He has published extensively in comparative and international politics, as well as the development field. He is author of *Human Resource Development in Aid Process* (1992), and was principal researcher for UNFPA's *State of the World Population Report* (1993). He is also a consultant for CIDA, the ILO, JICA, and UNICEF.

MARTIN RUDNER is professor of international affairs and associate director of the Norman Paterson School of International Affairs at Carleton University, Ottawa. He has served as consultant to CIDA and has published extensively on Southeast Asia, development studies, and international assistance, including monographs and articles on Canadian aid programs and policies. Recent publications include "ASEAN, Asia Pacific Economic Cooperation and Hemispheric Free Trade for the Americas," *World Competition* (1992), and "European Community Development Assistance to Asia: Policies, Programs and Performance," *Modern Asian Studies* (1992).

JEAN-PHILIPPE THÉRIEN has since 1992 been associate professor of political science at the Université de Montréal. He was editor of *La quête du développement: horizons canadien et africain* (1988) and author of a number of articles relating to development assistance, including "Aide et commerce dans les relations Canada–Tiers Monde," *Revue canadienne d'études du développement* 11 no. 1 (1990), "Le Canada et le régime international de l'aide," *Études internationales* 20 no. 2 (1989), and "Non-governmental Organizations and International Development Assistance," *Canadian Journal of Development Studies* 12 no. 2 (1991).

Index